Pascal Programs for Data Base Management

Tom Swan

HAYDEN BOOK COMPANY
a division of Hayden Publishing Company, Inc.
Hasbrouck Heights, New Jersey

To Barb

Acquisitions Editor: DOUGLAS McCORMICK
Production Editor: RONNIE GROFF
Design: JIM BERNARD
Cover illustration: GEORGE BAQUERO
Technical Illustrations: JOHN McCAUSLAND
Composition: PUBLISHERS PHOTOTYPE INTERNATIONAL, INC.

Library of Congress Cataloging in Publication Data

Swan, Tom.
    Pascal programs for data base management.

    Includes index.
    1. Data base management—Computer programs.   2. PASCAL (Computer
program language)   3. Apple II (Computer)—Programming.   I. Title.
QA76.9.D3S943 1984   001.64'25   84-8997   ISBN 0-8104-6272-9

Printed in the United States of America

2	3	4	5	6	7	8	9	PRINTING
84	85	86	87	88	89	90	91	92	YEAR

Pascal Programs for Data Base Management

PREFACE

The thirty-one programs and four library units in this book make up the Pascal Data Base System (PDBS), a relational data base manager written in UCSD Pascal. Four additional programs make up the PDBS Payroll System, an example of an application program written in PDBS format. Versions of PDBS are also available on diskette for the Apple II (Apple Pascal 1.1) and the IBM Personal Computer (UCSD Pascal IV.1). Both versions are fully documented in the book, with all source code included.

By entering the programs in Part One, and following the many examples, you'll learn about relational data base methods while building a set of programs to create and maintain your own personal information system. If you are planning to type in the software, please refer to the section "How to Enter and Use the Programs," under System Notes.

For those of you who want to write custom data base software, Part Two explains in detail the finer points of the PDBS data file structure, and describes the workings of the Virtual Memory Operating System (VMOS), the foundation on which PDBS is built.

By separating the operation of a data base manager from its programming, I have tried to write this book with two users in mind: the business person who needs an inexpensive, but fully capable, data base manager and wants to learn more about how to use one effectively, and the programmer or hobbyist who wants to learn about data base management, but also wants to examine and modify the source code, take it apart, and see what makes it tick.

I'd like to thank especially my wife Anne for her help in preparing this manuscript, editor Doug McCormick for his good advice, and friends Joe Duckworth,

Bill Parnes, David Hendel, and Carl Helmers for their contributions, more important than they may realize, to the success of this project. Any bugs that remain are all mine. Shoo fly!

Tom Swan

SYSTEM NOTES

Equipment Needed

To use the programs in this book on an Apple computer, you will need the following equipment.

1—Apple II or IIe with 65K RAM and display monitor
1—Apple Pascal Language system
1—Apple Disk Drive (2 recommended)
1—Printer (optional)

If you are not using Apple equipment, you need to purchase a version of UCSD Pascal as supplied by Softech Microsystems, San Diego, CA. The operating system is available either in a system-dependent, preconfigured version for many computers or in an adaptable form for a particular micro or mini processor.

Because the programs in this book were prepared on an Apple II computer, they are likely to run unmodified only on the same equipment. If you own a different system, you should be able to make use of the programs, but you may have to make changes to the listings here before they can be compiled and run on your computer.

At the time of this writing, UCSD Pascal has been implemented on all of the following processors (source: Softech Microsystems).

6502	68000	9900
PDP-11	LSI-11	6809
Z80	8080	8085
8086	8088	

If your computer uses one of the above processors, chances are there is a preconfigured version of UCSD Pascal available.

How to Enter and Use the Programs

Programs are printed with line numbers along the left borders. These numbers are for reference only, are not part of the programs, and should not be entered.

Comments, surrounded by the opening and closing braces, { and }, or by the alternate symbols (* and *) or a mixture of both, may be left out.

The book is organized as a reference guide to the use and programming of the Pascal Data Base System. To install PDBS on your computer, you may enter and compile the programs in any order you find convenient. However, because the programs in Part One depend on many of the routines in Part Two, a compiling order different from the order of chapters in the book will make installation easier.

I suggest the following steps to bringing up PDBS on your computer. Places for checking off each step as you go are provided.

Steps for Installing PDBS

——1. Compile *pdbsunit* in Part Two, Chapter Eight. Install the code in SYSTEM.LIBRARY using the *library* program.

——2. Compile and execute *crtsetup* to configure the software for your terminal as explained in Part Two, Chapter Eight.

——3. Compile and execute *testunit* in Part Two, Chapter Eight to verify that *pdbsunit* is operating correctly. Do not proceed until *testunit* passes all tests.

——4. Compile *evalunit* in Part Two, Chapter Nine. Install the code in SYSTEM.LIBRARY.

——5. Compile programs *create, status,* and *editor*, trying out the examples in Part One, Chapter One.

——6. Create and enter the optional ERRORS.PDBF file as explained in Appendix A. Use the *create* and *editor* programs to do this.

——7. Compile the rest of the units in Part Two, *calcunit*, and *indexunit*. Install their code files in SYSTEM.LIBRARY.

——8. Compile the rest of the PDBS programs in Part One, Chapters Two through Seven.

——9. Try the sample payroll application program in Part Two, Chapter Ten.

The Keypress Function

One of the library units used by many of the programs is called Applestuff and is supplied by Apple Computer, Inc., along with Apple Pascal 1.1. The only routine used from those in Applestuff is the *keypress* function, which returns the value *true* if a character is waiting to be read from the keyboard.

On the Apple II and IIe, you may want to link in your own external assembly language *keypress* routine that does the same thing as the one in Applestuff. In that case, you may remove all references to the Applestuff unit. This will give a little extra room in memory for those programs.

On other computers, you will have to provide a *keypress* function that works for your system. The following routine may be used temporarily until you can devise your own *keypress* function, which for best results should be encoded in machine language. Insert this routine into every program (or better, into *pdbsunit*), and remove all references to Applestuff.

```
FUNCTION keypress : boolean;
{ True if key was pressed since last checking. }
VAR
   k : integer;
BEGIN
   write( chr(0) );          { Possibly not required. }
                             { Forces keyboard scan in }
                             { Apple Pascal. }
   unitstatus( 1, k, 1 );
   keypress := ( k > 0 )
END; { keypress }
```

CONTENTS

7

OTHER DATA BASE OPERATIONS 155

P A R T T W O

THE COMPUTER'S POINT OF VIEW 171

8

PASCAL DATA BASE SYSTEM LIBRARY UNIT 175

9

MISCELLANEOUS LIBRARY UNITS 223

10

WRITING A PDBS APPLICATION 245

APPENDIX A

ERROR MESSAGES 269

APPENDIX B

MANAGING FREE DISK SPACE 271

APPENDIX C

PDBS ON THE IBM PC 273

INDEX 283

Pascal Programs for Data Base Management

ONE

The User's Point of View

The user of a data base management system does not need to be concerned with the bits and bytes that make up a data file, or the intricacies of the programming needed to access the information stored there, make it readable, and give it sense.

Part One of *Pascal Programs for Data Base Management* presents twenty-eight programs that can be used, among other things, to enter, edit, list, sort, join, and project data stored in disk files. Very little computer programming experience is required to run the programs.

As far as the user is concerned, the data in the files are stored in exactly the way they appear—as simple lists or row-and-column tables, the "logical view" of the data. For all practical purposes, the data really are what they appear to be from the user's point of view.

In Part Two we will see the opposite side of the coin when we examine The Computer's Point of View, where the physical form of data files, and the way programs access that data, are of primary importance.

THE COMPANY

Throughout Part One, an example data base is developed for The Company, Inc., a manufacturer of . . . (On second thought, books of this nature have a rather thin plot line, so I'll let you discover on your own what The Company does.)

Many listings and examples of The Company's data base are given, and you can follow along or try to make up your own sample files. In either case, do not be concerned with entering everything too precisely. None of the examples depends on the exact records as printed, and you may as well enter your own name and those of your friends, and make up your own figures. In fact, you will undoubtedly learn more about the programs that way.

THE PROGRAMS

Each program listed here demonstrates one data base process. After wrestling with the various means available for presenting the information, I decided that individual programs would be the easiest format to understand and, more important, the simplest to improve and modify. Also, you can skip those programs you have no need for without affecting the others. Although the programs may be used together in certain sequences, there are no functional dependencies among them.

Eventually, you may want to combine the programs into a menu or command-driven data base program, using UCSD Pascal segments and separately compiled units. You could also use chaining and a paddle or "mouse" input device to point to the program you want, and have the menu software run that program as an alternative to typing in the name of the program every time you need it.

These possibilities, while certainly attractive, would only add bulk to an already lengthy amount of programming, and are more in the realm of "user interface" techniques anyway than they are of "data base programming" methods. But if you do decide to combine the programs, you will appreciate their independence from one another. It shouldn't be a terribly difficult job to accomplish.

1

Putting Data into the Computer

CREATE / STATUS / EDITOR

CREATE

Before data can be stored in a computer, a place for it must be created. This place is called a "data file," and like a file drawer in an office filing cabinet, a computer data file can hold many related and unrelated pieces of information. Together, the numerous files likely to be stored in a computer make up a "data base."

There are many ways to organize data base files in a computer. In a relational data base, by far the simplest method for most people to understand, a data file is organized as a table containing rows and columns. (Fig. 1-1).

In common data base terminology, each row of a table is called a "record"; each column a "field." Some programmers use the more technically correct terms "tuples" for records and "attributes" for fields. We will stay with the simpler and more familiar words, records and fields, throughout this book.

To create a data file, you tell the computer about the file's structure and organization. In a name and address file, for example, you would need to reserve positions for the name, address, city, state, zip code, and telephone number fields. In an accounts receivable file you might have an account number in one field and the current balance in another. An inventory file may need many fields to describe the materials in stock.

Before typing all this information into the computer, you should probably spend some time planning and thinking about what you want the computer to accomplish with your data. Don't spend too much time, however. Experience has led me to believe, with some surprise, that too much advance planning spoils the experience of working with a data base. A good data base management program will

```
Rows        |  Columns
------------------------------------------------------------------
Record 1 - |  Field 1  |  Field 2  |  Field 3  |  Field 4
Record 2 - |  Field 1  |  Field 2  |  Field 3  |  Field 4
Record 3 - |  Field 1  |  Field 2  |  Field 3  |  Field 4
Record 4 - |  Field 1  |  Field 2  |  Field 3  |  Field 4
```

Fig. 1-1. *In a relational data base, files are organized as simple tables where the rows are equivalent to records, and the columns to fields. Each table is stored in a data file with all the tables together making up the data base.*

allow you to change the structure of your files later. Of course, PDBS allows you to do exactly that.

Using Create

Our first program is *create*, which is used to create new data files. After creating a data file, you are ready to begin entering information.

```
PARTS.PDBF
Record size ............. 42
Number of fields ........ 5
Maximum record number ... 24
Records in use .......... 6
Records not used ........ 18
Date created ............ 30-Jun-83
Date last updated ....... 15-Jul-83
```

#	NAME	TYPE	LEN	DEC	POS
1	P.NUM	Char	5	0	1
2	P.NAME	Char	20	0	6
3	P.COLOR	Char	8	0	26
4	P.REO	Number	4	0	34
5	P.STOCK	Number	4	0	38

```
SOURCES.PDBF
Record size ............. 19
Number of fields ........ 3
Maximum record number ... 53
Records in use .......... 5
Records not used ........ 48
Date created ............ 30-Jun-83
Date last updated ....... 01-Jul-83
```

#	NAME	TYPE	LEN	DEC	POS
1	P.NUM	Char	5	0	1
2	V.KEY	Char	5	0	6
3	COST	Number	8	2	11

```
VENDORS.PDBF
Record size ............. 135
Number of fields ........ 8
Maximum record number ... 7
Records in use .......... 3
Records not used ........ 4
Date created ............ 30-Jun-83
Date last updated ....... 30-Jun-83
```

#	NAME	TYPE	LEN	DEC	POS
1	V.KEY	Char	5	0	1
2	V.NAME	Char	30	0	6
3	V.ADDRESS	Char	30	0	36
4	V.CITY	Char	20	0	66
5	V.STATE	Char	2	0	86
6	V.ZIP	Char	5	0	88
7	V.CONTACT	Char	30	0	93
8	V.PHONE	Char	12	0	123

```
CUSTOMERS.PDBF
Record size ............. 121
Number of fields ........ 9
Maximum record number ... 8
Records in use .......... 7
Records not used ........ 1
Date created ............ 04-Jul-83
Date last updated ....... 04-Jul-83
```

#	NAME	TYPE	LEN	DEC	POS
1	C.KEY	Char	5	0	1
2	C.NAME	Char	30	0	6
3	C.ADDRESS	Char	30	0	36
4	C.CITY	Char	20	0	66
5	C.STATE	Char	2	0	86
6	C.ZIP	Char	5	0	88
7	C.PHONE	Char	12	0	93
8	C.LIMIT	Number	8	2	105
9	C.BALANCE	Number	8	2	113

Fig. 1-2. *The four main data files of The Company's relational data base. These listings were produced by the status program.*

Figure 1-2 shows a group of data file definitions that make up a sample data base to be used throughout Part One of this book. Some of these data files will change as we go along. We will probably need to add some forgotten items, or delete an unused field or two, but they will serve in their present forms for now. If you want to follow along with all the examples in the sections to come, create each data file as shown in Fig. 1-2.

Each table, or data file, described in Fig. 1-2 is a printout from the next program to be presented, *status*. The name of the data file is in capital letters at the top of each status report. When the *create* program asks

Create what file?

this is the name you should enter. You do not have to type the file name extension ''.PDBF'', which will be automatically supplied by the software. For now, you may ignore most of the information in the status report. To create each file, refer to the four columns, NAME, TYPE, LEN (length), and DEC (decimals).

To make this easier, the step-by-step dialogue you will have with the computer to create the PARTS.PDBF file is shown in Fig. 1-3. Compile and execute the *create* program, then follow the dialogue in Fig. 1-3. Type in the parts that are underlined in the dialogue. You will not see these underlines on your screen; they are used here and in subsequent dialogues to distinguish the items you enter into the computer from the computer's own responses.

Notice that in each status report of Fig. 1-2 the data types are spelled out in

```
Create what file ? PARTS

PARTS.PDBF

Enter 1 to 35 fields.
Specify name, type, length, decimals.
Press <return> when done.
NAME      : 1 to 10 characters
TYPE      : C(har, N(umber, L(ogical
LENGTH    : 1 to 255
DECIMALS  : 1 to 13 (Number only)

Examples. [1023] 1 : cost, n, 8, 2
          [1015] 2 : phone, c, 12
          [1003] 3 : <cr>

[1023]    1 : P.NUM, C, 5
[1018]    2 : P.NAME, C, 20
[ 998]    3 : P.COLOR, C, 8
[ 990]    4 : P.REO, N, 4
[ 986]    5 : P.STOCK, N, 4
[ 982]    6 : <cr>
```

Fig. 1-3. *To create the Parts data file, follow this dialogue while using the create program. The items that you are to enter are underlined in this printout of the computer's display. The symbol <cr> shows where you should press the return key without entering anything else on the line.*

full. When you create a data file, however, specify only the first letter of the type. For example, instead of "Char," enter "C."

After following the dialogue in Fig. 1-3, you should end up with a file named PARTS.PDBF on your data diskette. If you are having trouble, reread the dialogue carefully, review the System Notes, and then try again. After creating PARTS.PDBF, create the other three files from the information in Fig. 1-2.

PDBS Data Types

When designing your own data files, you will need to know more about the limits of the three data types available in PDBS. These limitations are described next.

Each field in the description of a record must have a unique name. A field name may not contain any spaces, and may be from one to ten characters long. Field names may be entered in lower case, but will be converted to all upper-case letters by the software.

Figure 1-4 lists the three data types recognized in PDBS along with the restrictions that exist for entering information into fields of these types. You may change the type, as well as the length and name, of a field later (see program *modify*).

Numeric fields may or may not have decimal positions. If you define a number field with a length of eight plus two decimals, you will have a field with *five* digits to the left of the decimal point, and *two* digits to the right—a total of eight characters altogether including the decimal point. (See fields 8 and 9 in the CUSTOMERS.PDBF file in Fig. 1-2.) This is a common setup for a dollar-amount field, and can be entered as shown here.

[1023] 1: *amount, n, 8, 2*

The values −9999.99 through 99999.99 may now be stored in the AMOUNT field. The largest value that PDBS can handle is 9,999,999,999,999 (one less than ten trillion). The lowest integer value is −999,999,999,999 (one greater than negative one trillion). The smallest fraction is .000,000,000,001 or −.000,000,000,01.

Logical fields may be no more than one character long. The characters [T, t] stand for true, and [F, f] for false. Only those fields that are explicitly false will be

Data Type	Maximum Length	Use in create	Restrictions
Character	255	C	None
Logical	1	L	[T, t, F, f] only
Number	13	N	[0..9, ., −] only

Fig. 1-4. *The three data types allowed in PDBS. The restrictions show what characters may be entered into fields declared to be one of the three types.*

found on a search for all fields equal to false. In other words, if you leave a logical field blank, it will be *neither* true nor false. (Blank logical fields are, therefore, "not true," and at the same time "not false." Careful thought will verify that these definitions are correct, and that a search for all "not true" fields will find the blanks as well as the explicitly false fields, while a search for "false" will find only those fields equal to "F" or "f.")

Character fields are the most general type. A character field may contain anything you can type on your keyboard, except for control characters with ASCII values less than decimal 32, and may be from 1 to 255 characters long. Upper- and lower-case letters may be used freely. Searches will ignore upper and lower case so that "robby," "Robby," and "RoBby" will all be considered to be the same name. Software that is designed to ignore the difference in alphabetic case is said to be "case insensitive."

It is possible to turn on case sensitivity. Any PDBS program may be compiled with the following line as the first line in its main body:

case_switch := false;

The program will now consider "Robby" and "robby" to be different. To find "Robby," you would have to enter the exact upper- and lower-case spelling, or the search will fail. Also, unless everything is already in upper case, sorting may not work correctly when the *case_switch* is set to false.

```
001: {$S+,I-}       { Compiler swapping on; I/O error checking off }
002:
003: PROGRAM create; uses pdbsunit;
004:
005: {----------------------------------------------------------------------}
006: {                                                                      }
007: {     PROGRAM          :  Create new data base file                    }
008: {     LANGUAGE         :  UCSD Pascal / Apple Pascal 1.1                }
009: {                                                                      }
010: {     Copyright (C) 1983 by Tom Swan. All commercial rights reserved.  }
011: {                                                                      }
012: {----------------------------------------------------------------------}
013:
014: VAR
015:     file_name    : pdbs_fname;      { PDBS data file name }
016:     msc_rec      : msc_descriptor;  { Record descriptor }
017:
018:
019: PROCEDURE instruct;
020: { Display some helpful instructions }
021: BEGIN
022:     writeln;
023:     writeln( 'Enter 1 to ', max_fld, ' fields.' );
024:     writeln( 'Specify name, type, length, decimals.' );
025:     writeln( 'Press <return> when done.' );
026:     writeln( '  NAME     : 1 to ', alpha_size + 1, ' characters' );
027:     writeln( '  TYPE     : C(har, N(umber, L(ogical' );
028:     writeln( '  LENGTH   : 1 to ', string_size );
029:     writeln( '  DECIMALS : 1 to ', max_digits, ' (Number only)' );
030:     writeln;
031:     writeln( 'Examples. [1023] 1 : cost, n, 8, 2' );
```

```
032:    writeln( '              [1015] 2 : phone, c, 12' );
033:    writeln( '              [1003] 3 : <cr>' );
034:    writeln
035: END; { instruct }
036:
037:
038: FUNCTION name_ok( VAR response : string;
039:                   VAR msc_rec  : msc_descriptor;
040:                   VAR fld_rec  : fld_descriptor ) : boolean;
041: { Assign field name from response to fld_rec.fld_name }
042: VAR
043:    name : alpha;
044:    token : string;
045: BEGIN
046:    next_token( response, token );
047:    name_ok := false;
048:    WITH fld_rec DO
049:        IF length( token ) > alpha_size + 1
050:            THEN writeln( 'Name too long' ) ELSE
051:        IF length( token ) = 0
052:            THEN writeln( 'No field name' )
053:            ELSE BEGIN
054:                    str2alpha( token, name );
055:                    IF fld_number( msc_rec, name ) <> 0
056:                        THEN writeln( 'Field name duplicated' )
057:                        ELSE BEGIN
058:                            name_ok := true;
059:                            fld_name := name
060:                        END { else }
061:                END { else }
062: END; { name_ok }
063:
064:
065: FUNCTION type_ok( VAR response : string;
066:                   VAR  fld_rec : fld_descriptor ) : boolean;
067: { Assign field type to field record }
068: VAR
069:    token : string;
070: BEGIN
071:    next_token( response, token );
072:    type_ok := true;
073:    WITH fld_rec DO
074:        IF token = 'C' THEN fld_type := dat_char     ELSE
075:        IF token = 'N' THEN fld_type := dat_number   ELSE
076:        IF token = 'L' THEN fld_type := dat_logical
077:            ELSE BEGIN
078:                    writeln( 'Bad field type' );
079:                    type_ok := false
080:                END
081: END; { type_ok }
082:
083:
084: FUNCTION len_ok(  VAR    response : string;
085:                   VAR    fld_rec : fld_descriptor;
086:                       bytes_left : integer        ) : boolean;
087: { Assign field storage and display / entry lengths }
088: VAR
089:    ti : integer;
090:    token : string;
091: BEGIN
092:    next_token( response, token );
093:    ti := value( token );               { Entry length requested }
094:    len_ok := false;
095:    IF ti <= 0
096:        THEN
097:        writeln( 'Error in length' )  { Probably a typo or forgotten }
```

```
098:        ELSE
099:          WITH fld_rec DO
100:            BEGIN
101:
102:              { Assign field entry-display length. }
103:
104:                CASE fld_type OF
105:                    dat_char    : fld_len := min( ti, string_size );
106:                    dat_logical : fld_len := min( ti, 1 );
107:                    dat_number  : fld_len := min( ti, max_digits )
108:                END; { case }
109:
110:                IF fld_len > bytes_left
111:                    THEN writeln( 'Too large.  Bytes left = ', bytes_left )
112:                    ELSE
113:                IF fld_len < ti
114:                    THEN writeln( 'Maximum length for type = ', fld_len )
115:                    ELSE len_ok := true
116:            END { else / with }
117: END; { len_ok }
118:
119:
120: FUNCTION dec_ok( VAR response : string;
121:                  VAR  fld_rec : fld_descriptor ) : boolean;
122: { Assign number decimals }
123: VAR
124:    ti : integer;
125:    token : string;
126: BEGIN
127:    next_token( response, token );
128:    ti := value( token );
129:    dec_ok := false;
130:    WITH fld_rec DO
131:        IF fld_type = dat_number
132:            THEN
133:              IF ( ti < 0 ) OR ( ti > fld_len - 1 )
134:                  THEN
135:                    writeln( 'Maximum decimals = ', fld_len - 1 )
136:                  ELSE
137:                    BEGIN
138:                        fld_decimals := ti;
139:                        dec_ok := true
140:                    END { else }
141:            ELSE
142:              IF ( ti <> 0 )
143:                  THEN writeln( 'Decimals not allowed' )
144:                  ELSE dec_ok := true
145: END; { dec_ok }
146:
147:
148: FUNCTION fields_assigned(     response    : string;
149:                              bytes_left : integer;
150:                        VAR msc_rec    : msc_descriptor;
151:                        VAR fld_rec    : fld_descriptor ) : boolean;
152: { Assign response to field descriptor record.  True if no errors. }
153: BEGIN
154:    WITH fld_rec DO
155:
156:        fields_assigned :=
157:
158:            name_ok( response,                 { Assign field name }
159:                     msc_rec,
160:                     fld_rec  ) AND
161:
162:            type_ok( response,                 { Assign field type }
163:                     fld_rec  ) AND
```

```
164:
165:            len_ok( response,                  { Assign field length }
166:                    fld_rec,
167:                    bytes_left ) AND
168:
169:            dec_ok( response,                  { Assign number decimals }
170:                    fld_rec )
171:
172: END; { fields_assigned }
173:
174:
175: FUNCTION fields_entered( VAR msc_rec : msc_descriptor ) : boolean;
176: { Input field names, and other parameters }
177: { Returns true if at least one legal field is entered }
178: VAR
179:     bytes_left : integer;
180:     response : string;
181: BEGIN
182:     instruct;
183:     WITH msc_rec DO
184:     BEGIN
185:      REPEAT
186:        IF msc_nflds < max_fld THEN
187:            BEGIN { Add another field to record design }
188:                bytes_left := page_size - msc_recsize + 1;
189:                write( '[', bytes_left:4, ']', ( msc_nflds + 1 ) : 4, ' : ' );
190:                readln( response );
191:                IF length( response ) > 0 THEN
192:                    IF fields_assigned( response, bytes_left, msc_rec,
193:                                                msc_flds[ msc_nflds + 1 ] )
194:                        THEN
195:                            BEGIN   { Entry accepted }
196:                                msc_nflds := msc_nflds + 1;
197:                                { Assign last known recsize as relative position }
198:                                msc_flds[ msc_nflds ].fld_pos := msc_recsize;
199:                                { Keep track of total record length }
200:                                msc_recsize :=
201:                                    msc_recsize + msc_flds[ msc_nflds ].fld_len
202:                            END { if }
203:             END { if }
204:      UNTIL ( length( response ) = 0     )    { User pressed RETURN }
205:        OR ( msc_nflds = max_fld        )    { Max fields reached }
206:        OR ( msc_recsize = page_size + 1 );   { Max length reached }
207:      fields_entered := ( msc_nflds > 0 )    { True if at least one }
208:     END { with }
209: END; { fields_entered }
210:
211:
212: BEGIN { create }
213:     clrscrn;
214:     WHILE get_file_name( 'Create what file ? ', file_name ) DO
215:     BEGIN
216:        IF file_not_in_use( file_name ) THEN
217:        BEGIN
218:            clreosc;
219:            writeln( file_name );
220:            init_msc( msc_rec );
221:            IF fields_entered( msc_rec ) THEN
222:            IF executed( make_file( file_name, msc_rec ) )
223:                THEN write( file_name, ' --> created' )
224:        END; { if }
225:        gotoxy( 0, 0 )
226:     END { while }
227: END.
```

STATUS

You will often need a way to view or print out the structure of a data file that you created. In a complex data base there can be dozens, even hundreds, of different files, each with its own set of fields. It's not hard to become lost and confused when you can't remember just where it was you stored that special phone list of preferred customers. I like to keep a binder handy with the status reports of all my data files. As soon as I create a new file, I print out a report and place it in the book.

Status lists many facts about a data file and shows the structure of each field. The Company's data files in Fig. 1-2 were printed by *status*.

Using *status* to produce one of these reports is very simple. First, you are asked to supply a data file name. If you do not enter the extension ''.PDBF'', it will be added for you automatically by the software. These initials, by the way, stand for ''Pascal Data Base File,'' and indicate that this file is the most general of the various kinds of files recognized by PDBS. We will see other kinds of special-purpose files, with different file name endings, as we go along.

Next you are asked a question that will be seen at various times during the execution of other PDBS programs.

Output report to ?

This prompt allows you to direct the output of the *status* program to the printer (enter PRINTER:), or to a text file (enter <file name>.TEXT). Whenever you see this kind of prompt, you may simply press the return key. In that case, the output will be sent to the screen.

If you are following along with The Company, Inc. examples, try printing status reports for each of the files you created in the last section. Except for some of the details in the first part of the status report, your printouts should closely match those shown in Fig. 1-2.

The Parts of a Status Report

File Name   The first line of a status report is always the file name. File names may be changed using the UCSD Filer program's C(hange command. This will not affect the contents or the use of the PDBS data file.

Record Size   The size of a record is shown in bytes. This figure will always be one greater than the number of characters declared for all fields combined in the record. The extra byte is used to mark records that are to be deleted (see programs *mark* and *delete*).

Number of Fields   The number of fields declared in the record. This number should match the last number in the left column of the status report, verifying that the list of fields is complete.

Maximum Record Number   In UCSD Pascal, a file expands in physical sequence disk block for disk block until the end of the available space on the disk is reached. This could be one less than the starting block of the next file in physical sequence, or the last block of the last track available on the disk.

PDBS files expand automatically as needed, provided there is free space available at the end of the file. The maximum record number in a status report indicates how many records can be stored in the amount of space *currently* occupied by the file without requiring an expansion. The number will automatically be adjusted after an expansion takes place. (See Appendix B for more information about managing free disk space.)

Records in Use   This number represents the number of records currently stored in the data file. It may be less, but is never greater, than the maximum record number. The number of records in use includes records that are marked for deletion as well as those that are not marked.

Records Not Used   The number of unused records is equal to the maximum record number minus the number of records in use. This figure is the number of records that can be entered before PDBS will attempt to expand the size of the file.

Date Created/Date Last Updated   These dates are copied from the boot (also called "root") volume. When you first switch on the computer, you can use the UCSD filer program to set the current date. If you have a clock, you may have a software package that automatically sets the date for you. In any case, the created and last updated dates will be stored and maintained by PDBS for each data file. The "Date created" never changes. The "Date last updated" changes only when a file is opened, written to, and closed, but not if the file is opened purely for reading. For example, printing a status report—a read-only operation on the data file—never affects the "Date last updated."

Field Structure List   Each field in the file is listed at the end of a status report. The field number is followed by the field name, type, and length in characters. Numeric fields may also have a number of decimal positions listed. "POS" is the relative position of the field in the record. The first field always begins at position number one. After that, the position of a field depends upon the length of the previous field. This number is of use only to programmers who want to access individual fields without using the PDBS software.

```
001: {$S+,I-}        { Compiler swapping on; I/O error checking off }
002:
003: PROGRAM status; uses pdbsunit;
004:
005: {-------------------------------------------------------------------}
006: {                                                                   }
007: {    PROGRAM          : Report status of a data base file           }
008: {    LANGUAGE         : UCSD Pascal / Apple Pascal 1.1              }
009: {                                                                   }
010: {    Copyright (C) 1983 by Tom Swan. All commercial rights reserved. }
011: {                                                                   }
012: {-------------------------------------------------------------------}
013:
014: CONST
015:    indent       = ' ';                  { As many spaces as you want }
016:
017: VAR
018:    file_name    : pdbs_fname;           { PDBS data file name }
019:    file_number  : integer;              { Fil_recs file number }
020:
021:
022: PROCEDURE show_type( VAR pf : text; dat_type : dat_descriptor );
023: { Display this data type name to the print file pf }
024: BEGIN
025:    CASE dat_type OF
026:       dat_char    : write( pf, 'Char    ' );  { 8 characters each }
027:       dat_logical : write( pf, 'Logical ' );  {   including blanks }
028:       dat_number  : write( pf, 'Number  ' )
029:    END { case }
030: END; { show_type }
031:
032:
033: PROCEDURE report_status( fn : integer );
034: { Report on the status of this file number }
035: VAR
036:    field    : integer;        { Field number }
037:    out_name : pdbs_fname;     { Output file name }
038:    pf       : text;           { Output "Print File" }
039:    s        : string;         { For printing dates }
040: BEGIN
041:    REPEAT
042:       IF NOT get_file_name( 'Output report to ? ', out_name )
043:          THEN out_name := 'CONSOLE:';       { Default to console }
044:       remove_ext( out_name );         { PDBS file name not allowed }
045:       rewrite( pf, out_name )
046:    UNTIL executed( ioresult );       { i.e. until no error }
047:
048:    clrscrn;
049:    WITH fil_recs[ fn ] DO WITH fil_msc DO
050:       BEGIN
051:          writeln( pf, chr(ret), indent, fil_name );
052:          writeln( pf, indent, 'Record size ............. ', msc_recsize );
053:          writeln( pf, indent, 'Number of fields ........ ', msc_nflds );
054:          writeln( pf, indent, 'Maximum record number ... ', msc_maxrec );
055:          writeln( pf, indent, 'Records in use .......... ', msc_lastrec );
056:          writeln( pf, indent, 'Records not used ........ ',
057:          msc_maxrec - msc_lastrec );
058:          write(   pf, indent, 'Date created ............ ' );
059:          date2string( msc_created, s );
060:          writeln( pf, s );
061:          write(   pf, indent, 'Date last updated ....... ' );
062:          date2string( msc_updated, s );
063:          writeln( pf, s, chr(ret) );
064:
065:          writeln( pf, indent, '#':2,
066:                   'NAME':6, 'TYPE':12, 'LEN':8, 'DEC':4, 'POS':4 );
```

```
067:          writeln( pf );
068:
069:          FOR field := 1 TO msc_nflds DO
070:            WITH msc_flds[ field ] DO
071:              BEGIN
072:                write( pf, indent, field:2,
073:                  chr(blank):2, fld_name, chr(blank):2 );
074:                show_type( pf, fld_type );
075:                writeln( pf, fld_len:4, fld_decimals:4, fld_pos:4 )
076:              END { for / with }
077:
078:        END; { with }
079:      close( pf, lock )    { In case output file is a disk text file }
080: END; { report_status }
081:
082:
083: BEGIN { status }
084:    clrscrn;
085:    WHILE get_file_name( 'Status for what file ? ', file_name ) DO
086:    BEGIN
087:      IF executed( open_file( file_number, file_name ) ) THEN
088:      BEGIN
089:        report_status( file_number );
090:        IF NOT executed( close_file( file_number, no_update ) )
091:          THEN exit( status )  { Extremely unlikely }
092:      END; { if }
093:      gotoxy( 0, 0 )
094:    END { while }
095: END.
```

EDITOR

Most of your time with a computer data base will be spent entering, changing, and searching information. The general-purpose data editor here allows new entries to be made and old entries to be searched and changed.

Figure 1-5 is a copy of the screen format you will usually see when using the *editor* program. In this example, the first record of The Company's parts data file is on display. (There is more room on the computer screen than shown here. I've removed some of the blank lines to save space.)

Reversed or enhanced video, if you have inserted the proper commands for your terminal using the *crtsetup* program in Part Two, Chapter Eight, will be used for the field names along the left edge of the screen. This feature, of course, is not shown in Fig. 1-5.

When you first start the *editor*, you are asked "Edit what file?" and should enter the name of the PDBS data file you want to edit. By this time, you should be used to entering a file name as the first operation of a program. Most of the programs in this book need to be given a file name in the same way.

After that, the first record, if the file is not empty, will be shown on the display. The top line shows the current and last-used record numbers, the status (active or deleted) of the record on display, the file name, the date the file was last updated, and the current typing mode (insert or replace). The typing mode will be

```
00001 of 00006 -Active-  PARTS.PDBF              Updated 15-Jul-83    Replace
Editor: A(ppnd C(hng D(bug I(nsrt L(st N(xt O(pt R(ec S(rch U(ndo V(fy Q(uit

P.NUM     : P1
P.NAME    : Photometric eye
P.COLOR   : Blue
P.REO     :    50
P.STOCK   :    61


^R-Copy     ^X-Reset    ^Z-Erase    ^D-Del char   ^E-Del rec    ^C-Etx
^I-Insert   ^K-Up       ^J-Down     ^H-Left       ^U-Right
```

Fig. 1-5. *The editor in action showing the first of six records in The Company's parts data file.*

shown only during and just after entering something, and may at times be invisible. (See the top right corner of Fig. 1-5.)

Each operation of the editor is selected by typing the first letter of the command you want. The available commands, most of which have been abbreviated to fit in an 80-column line, are shown on the second line of the display. To append new records, for example, press key A. You do not have to press the return key after selecting an operation.

The editor is designed to automatically format the display for you, placing all fields along the left column. This is acceptable for records with up to nineteen fields, such as those in The Company's data base. For more complex records, there is a way to redesign a screen format, putting each field of a record anywhere you want on the screen. If your records have more than nineteen fields, the number that will comfortably fit along the left border, you *must* set up your own screen format. We will see how to do this after examining each operation of the editor.

A(PPND—Append New Records

Press A to begin appending, or adding, new records. The cursor will jump to the first field of the record being edited. All of the control keys listed at the bottom of the screen are then active. After entering something into a field, press the return key, signaling that you are finished with that line or field. When you press return after entering the last line, the screen will clear to prepare for the next append. This makes entering many records at a time very fast. You may also enter a control C (depicted as ^C) by pressing the key marked CTRL along with the C key. This saves the record you are typing and advances to a new append.

To stop appending, press the escape key. The last record you entered will be redisplayed, and the command line will reappear.

After appending, remember to press Q to Quit editing this file. Until you quit by pressing Q, your data is stored in memory, not on disk. Quitting writes your appended records to disk, where they will be available the next time you use the editor and other PDBS programs.

C(HNG—Change Old Records

Press C to change or edit the record shown on the screen. At that time, all the control keys available when appending are active. Press return on the last line, or enter 'C, to stop editing this record. The command line will then reappear.

D(BUG—Debug Virtual Memory

Until you study Part Two of this book, you may not appreciate what you are seeing during the debugging operation. The Virtual Memory Operating System (VMOS), described in more detail along with the PDBS library unit (see Part Two, Chapter Eight), keeps as much as possible of a data file in memory where it can be searched and listed at high speed. Debugging displays the data file, usually only a

```
Debug to what file? <cr>

Memory=7144
File  Status      Fil-    Vir-    Vir-    Vir-    Vir-     Vir-
                  Page    Last    Next    Count   Blknum   Changed
   0  Disposed
   1  Open
                  2898    2898    2898      0        1     F
   2  Closed
   3  Closed
   4  Closed
   5  Closed
   6  Closed

Dump file? (0=list; RET=quit) 1

File 1=PARTS.PDBF  Rec=1  Rel=0  Bpp=2  Rpp=24  Eof=F  Opn=T
Siz=42  Max=24  Flds=5  Last=6  Created=30-Jun-83  Updated=15-Jul-83
** Virtual Page Address=2898  Count=0  Blknum=1  Changed=F
.P1   Photometric eye     Blue      50  61.P2   Arm assembly          Silver    5
0  59.P3  Body                Red       3  18.P4   Leg                   Black
   50  76.P5  Foot wheel         Black    100 110.P6   Hand                    S
ilver    25  20.........................................................................
..............................................................................
..............................................................................
..............................................................................
..............................................................................
..............................................................................
..............................................................................
..............................................................................
..............................................................................
..............................................................................

Dump file? (0=list; RET=quit) <cr>
```

Fig. 1-6. *The Company's parts data file as seen by the computer. This is a printout of the debugging operation of the editor program. The first part shows the status of PDBS files and the amount of free memory available in the computer. The second part shows one page of the parts data file as it is stored on disk. In a large file, there may be many pages of data held in memory.*

portion of the whole file, as it appears in the computer's memory. Figure 1-6 shows what The Company's parts data base looks like during debugging.

The purpose of the debugging operation is to help you to understand how virtual memory pages are manipulated by the computer. You may also want to use this command to examine, with the hope of finding a way to repair, a data file damaged by a bad disk sector.

I(NSRT—Insert a Record

Sometimes you will care about the location of certain records. You may, for instance, want record number five to be a certain record. This is more important when designing a report or screen format where the order of the records is critical. (Also see Appendix A, where PDBS error codes are equated to record numbers in the ERRORS.PDBF file.) In most data files, the order of record storage is not important, and will change anyway when sorting or deleting records. In those cases, the insert operation will probably not be used.

Before inserting a record, you are asked a question something like this.

6 records must be moved. Ok? (y/n)

The number will probably be different. Press Y to begin the insertion; press N if you do not want to insert a record after all. If the number of records to be moved is very large, inserting can be a time-consuming way to add new records to a data file. After the records are moved, the screen will clear and you can enter your information using the same commands that work for appending and changing.

Records are inserted *before* the current record on display. If the current record is number four, then the inserted record will become the new record number four. The old number four is then number five, the old five is now six, and so on.

L(ST N(XT—Last and Next Records

Press L to go back one record in numerical sequence. Press N to advance to the next record. These keys give you a quick way to browse through your data.

Trying to view the last record before number one or the next record past the last active record will produce an end of file error message.

O(PT—Options Selection

There are two options that you may select from within the editor. First press key O. The screen will be replaced as shown in Fig. 1-7.

To change an option from "On" to "Off," enter its number and press return. Do the same to switch an option from "Off" back to "On." To return to editing your file, press the return key.

There are currently two options. The first sets the case switch. If the case switch is on, then upper- and lower-case letters may be used in the data file. If the

```
Options: [1..2|ret]

1) Case switch is ................. On
2) Keys help legend is ............ On
```

Fig. 1-7. *The editor's O(pt command screen.*

case switch is off, only upper-case letters will be allowed. To search on mixed up-per- and lower-case fields, the case switch should be on; otherwise turn it off.

The second option controls the last two lines of the display. If this switch is off, then the control keys listed at the bottom of the screen will not be shown. You may want to use this option to edit large records with many fields. Turning the legend off allows up to twenty-one fields to be displayed without having to design a custom screen format.

R(EC—Record Number Search

Press key R, then enter the record number of the record you want to see. You might think of the R(ec command as a "random access" operation. It allows you to select records instantly by number. This number is the same as that shown in the upper left corner while the record is on display.

Of course you have to know the record number of the record you want. This might be taken from a list of your data (see program *list*), or a report (see program *report*). You can also use the R(ec command to jump to the approximate middle of your file. If you know that the record you are searching for is not in the first half, jumping to the middle before searching will save a little time.

S(RCH—Search Contents of File

Searching is covered in detail in the next chapter in the instructions to the programs *list* and *report*. Briefly, a search for various combinations of data may be performed. Each search requires a field name, an operator, and an argument. This combination of elements is called an expression, abbreviated in the prompt as <expr>. For example, to find all the parts in The Company's parts data file that are black, press S then:

Search for [N(ext|<expr>|<ret>]? <u>P.COLOR=BLACK</u>

In a moment, you will see the first record that has the word BLACK in the P.COLOR field. To find the next record with that same value (in other words, to continue a search using the same argument), press key S followed by key N (for next record) and hit the return key. While the computer is searching, you will see a message such as this.

Searching for P.COLOR=BLACK

If such a record can't be found, you will see:

Searching for P.COLOR = BLACK failed

A failed search usually ends with the last record of the data file on the screen. This is not an error but a concession to the editor, which requires at least one record, except when the file is empty, to be displayed at all times on the main screen.

You may interrupt a long search by pressing any key while the "Searching for . . ." message is displayed. This forces a search failure, and results in a record at random to be displayed on the screen.

U(NDO—Undo Changes Made

Press the U key to throw away changes made to a data file since you began editing. In many cases, you can totally undo all appends and changes made. In very long editing sessions, however, some of the changes you made may have been written to disk to make room for new data to be read into memory. Those changes cannot be undone. Appends can always be undone, however, even if some of them were written to disk.

Use this command with care. If you have made any changes to a file, you will be asked to confirm your intentions to throw everything away. After answering Y to the prompt "Throw away (most) changes (y/n)?" you cannot go back to the way things were.

V(FY—Verify Screen

In the event that the display becomes garbled because of a (Murphy forbid) programming error or a data transmission fault, press V to redisplay the screen. If this does not repair the difficulty, your record is probably too large to fit along the left edge and you will have to design a screen format file as described a little later.

Q(UIT—Quit and Save

Quitting writes all changes made to the data file to disk. If no changes were made, no appends, inserts, or edits, then no update will be performed. Otherwise, the current date will also be stored in the file indicating the date the file was last edited.

I suggest you quit and reedit a file every fifteen minutes to guard against power failures. Until you quit, the data held in memory is subject to loss. Because there are no invisible link or pointer fields in PDBS data files, however, the most you are likely ever to lose is the current work. Data already stored in a file is as safe as it possibly can be.

CONTROL KEYS

The set of control keys shown at the bottom of the editor's display can be used while the cursor is positioned in any field of a record. The controls are selected by pressing the key marked CTRL, holding it down, then pressing and releasing the appropriate letter key. CTRL is often abbreviated, as it is here, with a caret (∧). Each control option is listed here. Different computer terminals may use different keys to select these options. See the program listing for more details.

COPY—^R

This control key copies into the current field the data field of the previous record entered. You can use this operation to repeat identical city, state, and zip codes, for example, when entering a list of persons who all live in the same area.

One time, by the way, when working with a computer operator who had just typed "Baltimore, MD" about ten thousand times, I was asked if there wasn't a better way. Indeed there is, and I believe this is it. I wish I had thought of it ten thousand Baltimores ago.

RESET—^X

Resets the current field to whatever it was before you began typing. This works only if you have not yet pressed the return key for that field.

ERASE—^Z

Clears the current field to all spaces. Use RESET to recover if you accidentally erase.

DEL CHAR—^D

Deletes one character at the cursor position. All subsequent characters are moved up one position.

DEL REC—^E

Marks the record for deletion. Changes the status of the record from active to deleted, or back again from deleted to active. Marked records may be searched and edited along with active records. The program *delete* must be used to actually remove marked records from a file.

ETX—^C

Saves changes and ends editing the current record. If appending, ETX advances to a new append.

INSERT—ˆI

Toggles the replace/insert setting for character entry. The current setting is shown at the top right corner of the display. Inserting is always *before* the character at the current cursor position. Because inserting is slightly slower, you will want to leave the editor in replace mode most of the time.

UP DOWN LEFT RIGHT—ˆK ˆJ ˆH ˆU

Move from field to field (up and down), or from character to character in a field (left and right). In a custom screen design, where fields can be anywhere on the display and in any order, you may want to think of ''up'' as moving forward and ''down'' as moving backward through the fields of a record.

ESCAPE—ESC Key

While changing or appending, press escape to reset the entire record to the way it was before you began. The escape key also ends the append operation.

CUSTOM SCREEN FORMATS

Normally, fields are listed along the left edge of the editor's display. A more professional look can be achieved by setting up a custom screen format.

First, *create* a new data file using the format shown in Fig. 1-8. Use the same file name as the data file for which you want to design a custom screen format, but

```
CUSTOMERS.SCRN
Record size ............. 13
Number of fields ........ 6
Maximum record number ... 78
Records in use .......... 0
Records not used ........ 78
Date created ............ 19-Jul-83
Date last updated ....... 19-Jul-83
```

#	NAME	TYPE	LEN	DEC	POS
1	FIELD	Number	2	0	1
2	XHEADER	Number	2	0	3
3	YHEADER	Number	2	0	5
4	XENTRY	Number	2	0	7
5	YENTRY	Number	2	0	9
6	WIDTH	Number	2	0	11

Fig. 1-8. *Use the create program to prepare a screen format file as described by this status report. Notice that the file name ends in the extension .SCRN. This tells the editor to use the information stored in CUSTOMERS.SCRN as a screen format design for the CUSTOMERS.PDBF data file.*

add the extension .SCRN to the name. To create a custom screen for The Company's customer data file, use the file name CUSTOMERS.SCRN in the *create* program.

A custom screen format file is a PDBS data file, as are all files in this system. Therefore, after creating the screen format file (CUSTOMERS.SCRN if you are following the example), use the *editor* to enter the information for reformatting the screen.

It may seem strange at first to use the *editor* to design screens for the *editor*. The advantage of using what you might call a "homogeneous data base system" such as PDBS is that you have only one editor to learn. Many data base managers use one editor for data, one editor for screen formats, one editor for reports, all with different formats and key arrangements, an unnecessary confusion. You can also sort, list, and print reports on .SCRN files in the same way you do with your other data files.

After creating the CUSTOMERS.SCRN file, use the *editor* to enter the information listed in Fig. 1-9. This list, by the way, was prepared by the *report* program in Chapter Two.

After everything is entered, edit The Company's customer data file again. The new screen format will be automatically loaded and used in place of the standard left-edge display. This new screen is shown in Fig. 1-10.

When you are creating your own custom screen formats, it helps to have a status report (see program *status*) handy. For each field, enter the field number from the field list of the status report, the x and y screen coordinates for displaying the field name (xheader, yheader), the x and y screen coordinates where you want to enter data (xentry, yentry), and the width.

The width of a field in a screen format does not have to be the same as the length of the field. A shorter width will cause a field to be displayed and edited in a sort of window on the screen. You should not set the width to a value greater than the field length, however.

You do not have to include every field from a record in a screen format design. Also, fields may be edited in an order that is different from the order in which

	Field	Xheader	Yheader	Xentry	Yentry	Width
	==	==	==	==	==	==
00001	1	4	4	17	4	5
00002	8	48	4	61	4	8
00003	9	48	5	61	5	8
00004	2	4	7	17	7	30
00005	3	4	9	17	9	30
00006	4	4	10	17	10	20
00007	5	39	10	52	10	2
00008	6	56	10	69	10	5
00009	7	4	12	17	12	12

Fig. 1-9. *A report (prepared by the* report *program) of the values to be entered into the CUSTOMERS.SCRN custom screen format file. The record numbers are along the left edge of the report, and are not entered.*

```
00003 of 00007 -Active- CUSTOMERS.PDBF          Updated 19-Jul-83    Replace
Editor: A(ppnd C(hng D(bug I(nsrt L(st N(xt O(pt R(ec S(rch U(ndo V(fy Q(uit


      C.KEY      : C4                      C.LIMIT    : 5000.00
                                           C.BALANCE  : 2500.00

      C.NAME     : Franklin, Benjamin

      C.ADDRESS  : South Print Street
      C.CITY     : Philadelphia           C.STATE    : PA   C.ZIP     : 17662

      C.PHONE    : 900-555-1212


^R-Copy       ^X-Reset      ^Z-Erase      ^D-Del char   ^E-Del rec    ^C-Etx
^I-Insert     ^K-Up         ^J-Down       ^H-Left       ^U-Right
```

Fig. 1-10. *The Company's customer file shown with a custom screen format gives a more professional look to data entry.*

they are stored in the record. In this way, you can easily produce different ''views'' of a record without actually changing its structure. In an office, different people might have different views of a record's contents depending on what sort of information they need to see or enter. You may want to hide sensitive information—an account balance, for example, at the reception area—but have this information available to the accounting department. Unless it appears on the screen, a field cannot be entered, viewed, or edited.

THE EDITOR PROGRAM LISTING

The *editor* is one of the larger programs in this book, and is stored in four separate text files. The first file, EDITOR.TEXT, is the one to compile. The other three files, EDITOR1.TEXT, EDITOR2.TEXT, and EDITOR3.TEXT, will be automatically included at the proper positions by the compiler.

When you are running the program, the code file (EDITOR.CODE) must be on line—that is, on a disk in a drive—at all times. Because of the size of this program, it has been partitioned into segments which are read as needed from disk. Most of the operations are individual segments. When you select the append operation, for example, the operating system attempts to read that segment from the EDITOR.CODE file. You may lose data if you do not observe this restriction.

To change what keys do what in the editor, alter the constants listed in lines 15 through 28 of EDITOR.TEXT. If you have a set of function keys, for example, you may want to use them in place of the current assignments.

You can switch off the typing barrier, ([), by setting the character variable *barrier* to a space. This is best done in the main body of the program between lines 76 and 77 in EDITOR.TEXT.

EDITOR3.TEXT contains a large function *edit_string* from line 26 through line 314. You can extract this function for use in other PDBS programs if you want to write custom data base software. This editor is superior to the *get_response* procedure listed in the *Xtrastuff* unit in *Pascal Programs for Business* and *Pascal Programs for Games and Graphics*. The *edit_string* function has the ability to edit multiple line strings; *get_response* does not.

You may also use the *edit_rec* function in conjunction with *edit_string* to design your own editor. This function begins at line 317 in EDITOR3.TEXT. It calls *edit_string* repeatedly for each field of the record being edited according to the current screen format plan. The details of a screen format can be seen by examining the type declarations *scrn_rec* and *scrn_plan* at line 31 in EDITOR.TEXT. In a custom program, you can set up a screen format manually by assigning the values directly, or by reading a <name>.SCRN file. The method for reading a data file is shown in the *load_scrn* procedure at line 388 in EDITOR1.TEXT. Studying this procedure carefully will reveal much about the way records can be accessed using the PDBS operating system.

```
001: {$S++}        { Compiler swapping on double }
002: {$I-}         { I/O error check off }
003:
004: PROGRAM editor; uses applestuff, pdbsunit, evalunit;
005:
006: {-----------------------------------------------------------------}
007: {                                                                 }
008: {     PROGRAM          :  Edit, Delete, Append records in a PDBS file. }
009: {     LANGUAGE         :  UCSD Pascal / Apple Pascal 1.1          }
010: {                                                                 }
011: {     Copyright (C) 1983 by Tom Swan. All commercial rights reserved. }
012: {                                                                 }
013: {-----------------------------------------------------------------}
014:
015: CONST
016:     keycopy      = 18;          { (^R) Key to copy or repeat }
017:     keydel       = 4;           { (^D) Key to delete character }
018:     keydown      = 10;          { (^J) Key to move cursor down }
019:     keyenter     = 13;          { (^M) Key to enter (RETURN) }
020:     keyesc       = 27;          { (--) Key to escape (ESC) }
021:     keyetx       = 3;           { (^C) Key to accept entry }
022:     keyinsert    = 9;           { (^I) Key to toggle insertion mode }
023:     keykill      = 05;          { (^E) Key to mark / unmark for deletion }
024:     keyleft      = 8;           { (^H) Key to move cursor left }
025:     keyreset     = 24;          { (^X) Key to reset }
026:     keyright     = 21;          { (^U) Key to move cursor right }
027:     keyup        = 11;          { (^O) Key to move cursor up }
028:     keyzero      = 26;          { (^Z) Key to zero }
029:
030: TYPE
031:     scrn_rec =                  { Describes a screen display plan }
032:         RECORD
033:             field,                      { Data file field number }
034:             xheader,                    { X,Y for field name (header) }
035:             yheader,
036:             xentry,                     { X,Y for display / entry }
037:             yentry,
038:             width    : integer          { Column width ( <= len usually ) }
039:         END;
040:
041:     scrn_plan =                 { Screen format plan records }
042:         ARRAY[ 1 .. max_fld ] OF scrn_rec;
043:
```

```
044: VAR
045:     arg                 : string;        { Search arguments }
046:     barrier             : char;          { End of typing area mark }
047:     exitset             : SET OF char;   { Editing exit characters }
048:     file_number         : integer;       { Data file number }
049:     inserting           : boolean;       { Edit insert / replace switch }
050:     legend              : boolean;       { Display help legend switch }
051:     plan_max            : integer;       { Entries in screen plan }
052:     plan                : scrn_plan;     { The screen format plan }
053:     screen_ok           : boolean;       { Edit display switch }
054:     user_quits          : boolean;       { End program flag }
055:
056:
057: { ----- Forward Declarations ----- }
058:
059: PROCEDURE show_rec(      fn, scmax : integer;
060:                     VAR scplan    : scrn_plan );
061:     forward;
062: FUNCTION edit_rec(       fn, scmax : integer;
063:                     VAR scplan    : scrn_plan;
064:                     VAR old_rec   : binary_page ) : boolean;
065:     forward;
066:
067: { ----- End Forward Declarations ----- }
068:
069:
070: (*$I EDITOR1.TEXT *)          { Include segment procedures }
071: (*$I EDITOR2.TEXT *)          { Include common routines }
072: (*$I EDITOR3.TEXT *)          { Include forward declared routines }
073:
074:
075: BEGIN
076:     clrscrn;
077:     REPEAT
078:         initialize( file_number, plan_max, plan, user_quits, arg );
079:         IF NOT user_quits
080:             THEN edit_file( file_number, plan_max, plan )
081:     UNTIL user_quits
082: END.

001: {------------------------------------------------------------------------}
002: {                                                                        }
003: {    EDITOR1.TEXT -- Segment procedures                                  }
004: {                                                                        }
005: {------------------------------------------------------------------------}
006:
007:
008: segment PROCEDURE append(      fn, scmax : integer;
009:                           VAR scplan    : scrn_plan;
010:                           VAR old_rec   : binary_page );
011: { Add new records to end of file (fn), using scrn_plan }
012: VAR
013:     done      : boolean;      { True when file full or user done appending }
014:     work_area : binary_page;
015: BEGIN
016:     REPEAT
017:
018:         { The idea here is to append a blank record onto the end }
019:         { of the file, and then edit that record as usual.  The }
020:         { only special handling required is if the user presses }
021:         { escape in which case the blank append must be deleted. }
022:
023:         promptat( 0, 1,
024:           '>Append: {edit keys} [<etx> accepts, <esc> escapes]' );
025:         gotoxy( 0, 2 );    { Position cursor on error message line }
026:         zero_rec( fn, work_area );
```

```
027:                done := NOT executed( append_rec( fn, work_area ) );
028:                IF NOT done
029:                  THEN
030:                    BEGIN
031:                      show_rec( fn, scmax, scplan );   { Clears all fields }
032:                      IF edit_rec( fn, scmax, scplan, old_rec )
033:                        THEN
034:                          BEGIN   { Save contents of new record in old_rec }
035:                            gotoxy( 0, 2 );
036:                            IF executed( get_rec( fn, old_rec ) )
037:                              THEN prompt( 'Record accepted' )
038:                          END
039:                        ELSE
040:                          BEGIN      { Cancel append if escape key pressed }
041:                            gotoxy( 0, 2 );
042:                            WITH fil_recs[fn].fil_msc DO        { Delete blank }
043:                              msc_lastrec := msc_lastrec - 1;
044:                            IF NOT file_empty( fn ) THEN
045:                              IF executed( last_rec( fn ) )      { Reset to eof }
046:                                THEN show_rec( fn, scmax, scplan );
047:                            done := true           { Prepare to exit repeat loop }
048:                          END { else }
049:                    END { if }
050:      UNTIL done
051: END; { append }
052:
053:
054: segment PROCEDURE change(      fn, scmax : integer;
055:                            VAR scplan      : scrn_plan;
056:                            VAR old_rec     : binary_page );
057: { Edit contents of the current record in file (fn), using scrn_plan }
058: BEGIN
059:    IF file_empty( fn )
060:       THEN writeln( 'File empty' )
061:       ELSE
062:       BEGIN
063:          promptat( 0, 1,
064:           '>Change: {edit keys} [<etx> accepts, <esc> escapes]' );
065:          IF edit_rec( fn, scmax, scplan, old_rec ) THEN
066:          BEGIN
067:             gotoxy( 0, 2 );    { Position cursor on error message line }
068:             IF executed( get_rec( fn, old_rec ) ) { Load defaults }
069:                THEN prompt( 'Changes accepted' )
070:          END { if }
071:       END { else }
072: END; { change }
073:
074:
075: segment PROCEDURE insrt(      fn, scmax   : integer;
076:                           VAR scplan      : scrn_plan;
077:                           VAR old_rec     : binary_page );
078: { Insert a blank record at current position and edit }
079: { Note : Insert is purposely misspelled "insrt" to avoid }
080: {        a conflict with the UCSD string procedure, "insert." }
081: VAR
082:    work_area : binary_page;       { For inserting a blank }
083: BEGIN
084:    IF file_empty( fn )
085:       THEN writeln( 'File empty' )
086:       ELSE
087:       WITH fil_recs[fn] DO
088:       BEGIN
089:          write( fil_msc.msc_lastrec - fil_recptr + 1 );   { Recs to move }
090:          IF verified( ' records must be moved.  Ok' ) THEN
091:             BEGIN
092:                promptat( 0, 2, 'Moving records...' );
093:                zero_rec( fn, work_area ):
```

```
094:                    IF executed( insert_rec( fn, work_area ) ) THEN
095:                    BEGIN
096:                       show_rec( fn, scmax, scplan );
097:                       promptat( 0, 1,
098:                       '>Insert: {edit keys} [<etx> accepts, <esc> escapes]' );
099:                       IF edit_rec( fn, scmax, scplan, old_rec ) THEN
100:                       BEGIN
101:                          gotoxy( 0, 2 );    { Position cursor on error line }
102:                          IF executed( get_rec( fn, old_rec ) )
103:                             THEN prompt( 'Insert accepted' )
104:                       END { if }
105:                    END { if }
106:                 END; { if }
107:       END { else }
108: END; { insrt }
109:
110:
111: segment PROCEDURE options;
112: { Select among various editor options }
113: { Screen must be reset following return }
114: CONST
115:    nopts      = 2;                { Number of options to select }
116: VAR
117:    s          : string;       { Input / display string }
118:
119:    PROCEDURE show_bool( b : boolean );
120:    { Display boolean true false value }
121:    BEGIN
122:       IF b THEN
123:          BEGIN
124:             evon;
125:             write( ' On ' );
126:             evoff
127:          END ELSE
128:             write( 'Off ' )
129:    END; { show_bool }
130:
131:    PROCEDURE show_line( n : integer );
132:    { Display this individual setting }
133:    BEGIN
134:       gotoxy( 0, n + 2 );
135:       clreoln; write( n:2, ') ' );
136:       CASE n OF
137:          1 : BEGIN
138:                 write( 'Case switch is .................. ' );
139:                 show_bool( case_switch )
140:              END;
141:          2 : BEGIN
142:                 write( 'Keys help legend is ............. ' );
143:                 show_bool( legend )
144:              END;
145:
146:          { You may add other settings here }
147:
148:       END { case }
149:    END; { show_line }
150:
151:    PROCEDURE show_settings;
152:    { Display current options settings }
153:    VAR
154:       line : 1 .. nopts;
155:    BEGIN
156:       gotoxy( 0, 2 );
157:       clreosc;
158:       FOR line := 1 TO nopts DO
159:          show_line( line )
160:    END; { show_settings }
```

```
161:
162: BEGIN
163:     show_settings;
164:     REPEAT
165:         str( nopts, s );
166:         promptat( 0, 1, concat( 'Options: [1..', s, '|ret] ' ) );
167:         readln( s );
168:         CASE value( s ) OF
169:             1 : BEGIN
170:                     case_switch := NOT case_switch;
171:                     show_line( 1 )
172:                 END;
173:             2 : BEGIN
174:                     legend := NOT legend;
175:                     show_line( 2 )
176:                 END;
177:
178:         { You may add other option selections here }
179:
180:         END { case }
181:     UNTIL length( s ) = 0
182: END; { options }
183:
184:
185: segment PROCEDURE search(       fn, scmax  : integer;
186:                             VAR scplan     : scrn_plan;
187:                             VAR arg        : string       );
188: { Search for first or next occurrence of a record by content. }
189: VAR
190:     err      : boolean;         { Error flag }
191:     found    : boolean;         { True on match found }
192:     last_rn  : integer;         { Last known record number }
193:     rn       : integer;         { Record number }
194:     s        : string;          { Temporary input string }
195: BEGIN
196:     promptat( 0, 1, 'Search for [N(ext|<expr>|<ret>]? ' );
197:     readln( s );
198:     IF length( s ) > 0 THEN
199:     BEGIN
200:         last_rn := fil_recs[fn].fil_recptr;              { Save current rec num }
201:         bumpstrup( s );                                  { Convert to upper case }
202:         IF s <> 'N'
203:             THEN
204:                 BEGIN                                    { Start a new search }
205:                     rn := 0;
206:                     arg := s;
207:                     gotoxy( 0, 1 );          { In case of an error while parsing }
208:                     err := NOT parse_eval( fn, arg )
209:                 END
210:             ELSE
211:                 BEGIN                                    { Proceed with search }
212:                     rn := last_rn;
213:                     err := false
214:                 END; { else }
215:
216:         IF NOT err THEN
217:         BEGIN
218:             promptat( 0, 2, concat( 'Searching : ', arg, ' ' ) );
219:             found := false;
220:             WHILE ( rn < fil_recs[fn].fil_msc.msc_lastrec ) AND
221:                   ( NOT found ) AND
222:                   ( NOT err   ) AND
223:                   ( NOT keypress ) DO
224:             BEGIN
225:                 rn := rn + 1;
226:                 IF executed( seek_rec( fn, rn ) )
227:                     THEN found := match( fn )
```

```
228:                    ELSE err := true
229:            END; { while }
230:            IF ( NOT found ) AND ( NOT err )
231:               THEN write( 'failed' );
232:            IF ( found ) OR ( last_rn <> rn )
233:               THEN show_rec( fn, scmax, scplan )
234:         END { if }
235:      END { if }
236: END; { search }
237:
238:
239: segment PROCEDURE debug;
240: { Dump virtual page lists showing links and status for all files. }
241: CONST
242:    print_width       = 79;    { Maximum print columns less one }
243: VAR
244:    fn                : integer;       { PDBS file number }
245:    pfname            : pdbs_fname;    { Print file name }
246:    pf                : text;          { Output file }
247:    s                 : string;        { Miscellaneous string }
248:
249:    PROCEDURE dump;
250:    { Dump virtual pages for file fn }
251:    { Rewrite pf to output file to use, e.g. 'printer:'; 'console:', etc. }
252:    VAR
253:       i, k : integer;
254:       tp : vir_ptr;    { Temporary pointer }
255:    BEGIN
256:       writeln( pf );
257:       evon;
258:       WITH fil_recs[ fn ] DO
259:          BEGIN
260:             writeln( pf, 'File ', fn, '=', fil_name,
261:                          ' Rec=', fil_recptr,
262:                          ' Rel=', fil_relptr,
263:                          ' Bpp=', fil_bpp,
264:                          ' Rpp=', fil_rpp,
265:                          ' Eof=', tf( fil_eof ),
266:                          ' Opn=', tf( fil_open )        );
267:             WITH fil_msc DO
268:                BEGIN
269:                   date2string( msc_created, s );
270:                   write( pf, 'Siz=', msc_recsize,
271:                              ' Max=', msc_maxrec,
272:                              ' Flds=', msc_nflds,
273:                              ' Last=', msc_lastrec,
274:                              ' Created=', s            );
275:                   date2string( msc_updated, s );
276:                   writeln( pf, ' Updated=', s )
277:                END; { with }
278:             evoff;
279:             tp := fil_page;
280:             IF tp <> NIL THEN
281:                REPEAT
282:                   evon;
283:                   write( pf, '** Virtual Page Address=', ord( tp ),
284:                              ' Count=', tp^.vir_count,
285:                              ' Blknum=', tp^.vir_blknum,
286:                              ' Changed=', tf( tp^.vir_changed ) );
287:                   evoff;
288:                   FOR i := 0 TO page_size DO
289:                      BEGIN
290:                         IF i MOD print_width = 0
291:                            THEN writeln( pf );
292:                         k := tp^.vir_page[ i ];
293:                         IF ( NOT inrange( k, 32, 127 ) )
294:                            THEN write( pf, '.' )
295:                            ELSE write( pf, chr(k) )
```

```
296:                          END; { for }
297:                          tp := tp^.vir_next;
298:                          writeln( pf, chr( ret ) )
299:                    UNTIL ( tp = fil_page ) OR ( keypress )
300:              END { with }
301:       END; { dump }
302:
303:       PROCEDURE list_vir( vp : vir_ptr );
304:       { List virtual page list starting with page vp }
305:       VAR
306:          tp : vir_ptr;
307:       BEGIN
308:          tp := vp;      { Remember starting point }
309:          IF vp <> NIL THEN
310:          REPEAT
311:             writeln( pf, chr( blank ) : 16,
312:                         ord( vp ) : 6,
313:                         ord( vp^.vir_last ) : 8,
314:                         ord( vp^.vir_next ) : 8,
315:                         vp^.vir_count : 8,
316:                         vp^.vir_blknum : 8,
317:                         chr( blank ) : 2,
318:                         tf( vp^.vir_changed ) );
319:             vp := vp^.vir_next
320:          UNTIL ( vp = tp ) OR ( vp = NIL )
321:       END; { list_vir }
322:
323: BEGIN { debug }
324:     clreoln;
325:     write( 'Debug to what file ? ' );
326:     readln( pfname );
327:     IF length( pfname ) = 0
328:        THEN pfname := 'CONSOLE:';
329:     rewrite( pf, pfname );
330:     fn := 0;
331:     IF executed( ioresult ) THEN
332:     REPEAT
333:        clreosc;
334:        writeln( pf );
335:        IF fn = 0 THEN
336:        BEGIN { List virtual pages and file status }
337:        writeln( pf, 'Memory=', memavail );
338:           evon;
339:        writeln( pf,
340:        'File Status     Fil-    Vir-    Vir-    Vir-    Vir-    Vir-' );
341:        {.....................................................................}
342:        writeln( pf,
343:        '                Page    Last    Next   Count  Blknum  Changed');
344:        {.....................................................................}
345:           evoff;
346:           writeln( pf, ' 0   Disposed' );
347:           list_vir( page_pool );      { Show disposed pages }
348:           FOR fn := 1 TO max_files DO
349:              BEGIN
350:                 write( pf, fn : 3, chr( blank ) : 3 );
351:                 IF fil_recs[ fn ].fil_open THEN
352:                    BEGIN
353:                       writeln( pf, 'Open' );
354:                       list_vir( fil_recs[ fn ].fil_page )
355:                    END ELSE
356:                       writeln( pf, 'Closed' )
357:              END; { for }
358:           writeln( pf )
359:        END; { if }
360:        write( 'Dump file ? (0=list; RET=quit) ' );
361:        readln( s );
362:        fn := value( s );
```

```
363:         IF ( fn >= 1 ) AND ( fn <= max_files )
364:              THEN dump
365:      UNTIL length( s ) = 0;
366:      close( pf, lock )        { In case output is to a text file }
367: END; { segment debug }
368:
369:
370: segment PROCEDURE initialize( VAR fn, plan_max : integer;
371:                               VAR plan         : scrn_plan;
372:                               VAR quit         : boolean;
373:                               VAR arg          : string     );
374: { Initialize editor returning file number fn and screen format plan }
375: { Return quit = true if no file entered }
376: VAR
377:      file_name,                        { Data file name }
378:      scrn_name      : pdbs_fname;      { Screen format file name }
379:      sn             : integer;         { Screen file number }
380:
381:      FUNCTION check_ext( ext, s : pdbs_fname ) : boolean;
382:      { True if ext found as an extension to s }
383:      BEGIN
384:         check_ext := ( pos( ext, s ) = ( length( s ) - length( ext ) + 1 ) )
385:      END; { check_ext }
386:
387:
388:      PROCEDURE load_scrn(      sn     : integer;
389:                           VAR scmax  : integer;
390:                           VAR scplan : scrn_plan );
391:      { Load scplan, and scmax from PDBS data file sn }
392:      VAR
393:         fld_num,
394:         n,                             { Numeric value of string field }
395:         rec_num     : integer;
396:         s           : string;          { For reading fields }
397:      BEGIN
398:         promptat( 0, 1, 'Loading screen format...' );
399:         scmax := fil_recs[sn].fil_msc.msc_lastrec;
400:         FOR rec_num := 1 TO scmax DO
401:           IF executed( seek_rec( sn, rec_num ) ) THEN
402:             WITH scplan[ rec_num ] DO
403:               FOR fld_num := 1 TO 6 DO
404:                 BEGIN
405:                    get_field( sn, fld_num, s );
406:                    n := value( s );
407:                    CASE fld_num OF
408:                      1 : field   := n;
409:                      2 : xheader := n;
410:                      3 : yheader := n;
411:                      4 : xentry  := n;
412:                      5 : yentry  := n;
413:                      6 : width   :=            { "Field len or n, whichever is less, }
414:                          max( 1,               {    but not less than 1" }
415:                          min( n, fil_recs[fn].fil_msc.msc_flds[field].fld_len ) ) )
416:                    END { case }
417:                 END; { for / if / with / for }
418:         promptat( 0, 2, '' )  { Erase "Loading" message }
419:      END; { load_scrn }
420:
421:
422:      PROCEDURE make_scrn(      fn     : integer;
423:                           VAR scmax  : integer;
424:                           VAR scplan : scrn_plan );
425:      { Make up a default screen format for file fn }
426:      VAR
427:         i, line_count    : integer;
428:      BEGIN
429:         line_count := 3;              { Reserve top 3 lines }
```

```
430:          WITH fil_recs[fn].fil_msc DO
431:            BEGIN
432:              scmax := msc_nflds;
433:              FOR i := 1 TO msc_nflds DO
434:                WITH scplan[ i ] DO WITH msc_flds[ i ] DO
435:                  BEGIN
436:                    field := i;
437:                    xheader := 0;
438:                    yheader := line_count;
439:                    xentry := alpha_size + 3;
440:                    yentry := yheader;
441:                    width := min( fld_len, (screen_width - xentry) );
442:                    line_count := line_count + ( fld_len DIV width );
443:                    IF fld_len > width
444:                        THEN line_count := line_count + 1
445:                  END { for / with / with }
446:            END { with }
447:      END; { make_scrn }
448:
449:
450: BEGIN { initialize }
451:
452: { Initialize global variables }
453:
454:      barrier := '[';              { End of typing area marker }
455:      inserting := false;          { Start out in replace mode }
456:      legend := true;              { Display help legend at bottom }
457:      screen_ok := true;           { False to redisplay in edit_string }
458:      exitset := [ chr( keycopy  ),   { Keys to end edit_string }
459:                   chr( keydown  ),
460:                   chr( keyenter ),
461:                   chr( keyesc   ),
462:                   chr( keyetx   ),
463:                   chr( keyup    ),
464:                   chr( keykill  )  ];
465:
466: { Open data file }
467:
468:      REPEAT
469:        gotoxy( 0, 0 );
470:        quit := NOT get_file_name( 'Edit what file? ', file_name );
471:        IF quit
472:            THEN exit( initialize )
473:      UNTIL executed( open_file( fn, file_name ) );
474:
475:      arg := '';        { Must be a null string, NOT a space }
476:
477: { Parsing a null string reinitializes the evaluation unit. }
478: { If an error occurs, then EVALUNIT is not working, and }
479: { the editor should not be used.  This error will probably }
480: { never be seen, but ... }
481:
482:      IF NOT parse_eval( fn, arg ) THEN     { Initialize EVALUNIT globals }
483:        BEGIN
484:            promptln( 'Error in EVALUNIT' );
485:            halt
486:        END; { if }
487:
488: { Form <name>.SCRN name out of <name>.PDBF or other file name }
489: { unless the file is one of the special format files. }
490:
491:      IF ( check_ext( ext_rprt, file_name ) ) OR
492:         ( check_ext( ext_scrn, file_name ) ) OR
493:         ( check_ext( ext_spec, file_name ) ) OR
494:         ( check_ext( ext_strc, file_name ) )
495:      THEN
496:        scrn_name := ''    { Force default format for special files }
497:      ELSE
498:        BEGIN
```

```
499:              remove_ext( file_name );               { <name>.xxxx --> <name> }
500:           scrn_name :=
501:              concat( file_name, ext_scrn )          { <name> --> <name>.SCRN }
502:        END; { else }
503:
504: { Open screen format file or use default values }
505:
506:     plan_max := 0;
507:     IF open_file( sn, scrn_name ) = 0              { Avoid extraneous error msg }
508:       THEN
509:         BEGIN
510:            load_scrn( sn, plan_max, plan );                     { User format }
511:            IF NOT executed( close_file( sn, no_update ) )
512:                THEN halt      { Extremely unlikely }
513:         END;
514:     IF plan_max = 0          { Because .SCRN file empty or not there }
515:        THEN make_scrn( fn, plan_max, plan )                  { Use default }
516: END; { initialize }
517:
518:
519: segment PROCEDURE deinitialize( fn : integer; mode : close_option );
520: { Close data file and prepare to exit program }
521: { Set mode = no_update to "undo" as many changes as possible }
522: BEGIN
523:     promptat( 0, 1, 'Closing file with' );
524:     IF mode = no_update
525:        THEN write( 'out' );
526:     writeln( ' update' );
527:     clreoln;
528:     WHILE ( NOT executed( close_file( fn, mode ) ) ) DO
529:         IF NOT verified( 'Try again' )
530:             THEN exit( deinitialize );          { File not updated }
531:     clreoln;
532:     write( 'File ' );
533:     IF mode = update
534:        THEN write( 'updated' )
535:        ELSE write( 'closed' )
536: END; { deinitialize }
537:
538:
539: segment FUNCTION seek_record( fn : integer ) : boolean;
540: { Search for a record by record number }
541: VAR
542:     rn       : integer;     { Record number }
543:     s        : string;      { Input string }
544: BEGIN
545:     REPEAT
546:         promptat( 0, 1, 'Record number ? ' );
547:         readln( s );
548:         IF length( s ) = 0
549:             THEN exit( seek_record );
550:         rn := value( s )
551:     UNTIL inrange( rn, 1, fil_recs[fn].fil_msc.msc_lastrec );
552:     clreoln;           { Message / error line }
553:     seek_record := executed( seek_rec( fn, rn ) )
554: END; { seek_record }
555:
556:
557: segment FUNCTION browse( fn : integer; ch : char ) : boolean;
558: { Browse forward or back, depending on ch selector character }
559: { True if executed properly }
560: BEGIN
561:     clreoln;           { Message / error line }
562:     IF ch = 'L'
563:        THEN
564:           browse := executed( last_rec( fn ) )
565:        ELSE
566:           browse := executed( next_rec( fn ) )
567: END; { browse }
```

```
001: {---------------------------------------------------------------------}
002: {                                                                     }
003: {   EDITOR2.TEXT -- Editor procedures continued                       }
004: {                                                                     }
005: {---------------------------------------------------------------------}
006:
007:
008: PROCEDURE show_scrn(       fn, scmax : integer;
009:                       VAR scplan     : scrn_plan );
010: { Display blank screen format using scplan }
011: VAR
012:    i : integer;
013: BEGIN
014:    FOR i := 1 TO scmax DO WITH scplan[i] DO
015:       BEGIN
016:          gotoxy( xheader, yheader );
017:          evon;
018:          write( fil_recs[fn].fil_msc.msc_flds[field].fld_name, ':' );
019:          evoff
020:       END { for / with }
021: END; { show_scrn }
022:
023:
024: PROCEDURE show_keys;
025: { Display editing keys legend (optional) }
026: CONST
027:    y        = 22;               { Y coordinate to begin.  2 lines needed. }
028: TYPE
029:    short_string = PACKED ARRAY[ 1 .. 8 ] OF char;
030:
031:    PROCEDURE show_one( ctrl : integer; s : short_string );
032:    { Display one control key value }
033:    CONST
034:       offset = 64;              { ord( 'A' ) - 1 }
035:    BEGIN
036:       write( '^', chr( ctrl + offset ), '-', s, chr(blank):2 )
037:    END; { show_one }
038:
039: BEGIN
040:    IF legend THEN
041:    BEGIN
042:       gotoxy( 0, y );
043:       clreoln;
044:
045:       show_one( keycopy,   'Copy    ' );
046:       show_one( keyreset,  'Reset   ' );
047:       show_one( keyzero,   'Erase   ' );
048:       show_one( keydel,    'Del char' );
049:       show_one( keykill,   'Del rec ' );
050:       show_one( keyetx,    'Etx     ' );
051:
052:       writeln;
053:       clreoln;
054:       show_one( keyinsert, 'Insert  ' );
055:       show_one( keyup,     'Up      ' );
056:       show_one( keydown,   'Down    ' );
057:       show_one( keyleft,   'Left    ' );
058:          show_one( keyright,  'Right   ' )
059:    END
060: END; { show_keys }
061:
062:
063: PROCEDURE show_file( fn : integer );
064: { Show main file info on top line }
065: CONST
066:    y = 0;   { Line to display information }
067: VAR
068:    s : string;
```

```
069: BEGIN
070:     WITH fil_recs[fn] DO
071:         BEGIN
072:             num2string( fil_recptr, 5, '0', s );
073:             promptat( 0, y, s );
074:             num2string( fil_msc.msc_lastrec, 5, '0', s );
075:             write( ' of ', s );
076:             gotoxy( 25, y );
077:             write( fil_name );
078:             gotoxy( 50, y );
079:             date2string( fil_msc.msc_updated, s );
080:             write( 'Updated ', s );
081:         END { with }
082: END; { show_file }
083:
084:
085: PROCEDURE show_status( fn : integer );
086: { Display deleted/undeleted status of current record }
087: CONST
088:     y          = 0;                  { Same as in "show_file" }
089: BEGIN
090:     gotoxy( 15, y );
091:     IF rec_status( fn ) = active
092:         THEN
093:             write( '-Active- ' )          { Length string = 9 }
094:         ELSE
095:             BEGIN
096:                 evon;
097:                 write( '-Deleted-' );        { Length string = 9 }
098:                 evoff
099:             END
100: END; { show_status }
101:
102:
103: FUNCTION command( s : string; VAR ch : char ) : char;
104: { Prompt for a command. }
105: { Character typed is returned in ch and as the function value. }
106: CONST
107:     y          = 1;              { Y coordinate for prompt }
108: BEGIN
109:     promptat( 0, y, s );
110:     IF getch( ch ) > chr( 31 )          { If not a CTRL char }
111:         THEN writeln( ch )              {    then show the char }
112:         ELSE writeln;                   {    else drop down a line }
113:     clreoln;                            { Clear error message line }
114:     ch := cap( ch );                    { Convert command to capital }
115:     command := ch                       { Return as function value }
116: END; { command }
117:
118:
119: PROCEDURE edit_file( fn, plan_max : integer; VAR plan : scrn_plan );
120: { Main command loop for editing this file. }
121: CONST
122:     id_prompt          = 'Editor: ';
123:     cmd_prompt         =
124: 'A(ppnd C(hng D(bug I(nsrt L(st N(xt O(pt R(ec S(rch U(ndo V(fy Q(uit ';
125: VAR
126:     ch                 : char;          { Keyboard input character }
127:     change_made        : boolean;       { Update file only if true }
128:     edit_change_set,                    { Commands that set change_made true }
129:     edit_exit_set      : SET OF char;   { Commands that end edit session }
130:     old_rec            : binary_page;   { Holds default record fields }
131:
132:     PROCEDURE redisplay;
133:     { Reset screen after certain operations that may destroy display }
134:     BEGIN
135:         clrscrn;
136:         show_scrn( fn, plan_max, plan );
```

```
137:        show_keys;
138:        show_rec( fn, plan_max, plan )
139:     END; { redisplay }
140:
141: BEGIN
142:     edit_change_set := [ 'A', 'C', 'I' ];     { Append, Change, Insert }
143:     edit_exit_set   := [ 'Q', 'U' ];          { Quit, Undo }
144:     change_made := false;
145:     clrscrn;
146:     zero_rec( fn, old_rec );         { Init default fields }
147:     show_scrn( fn, plan_max, plan );
148:     show_keys;
149:     IF NOT file_empty( fn )
150:        THEN show_rec( fn, plan_max, plan );
151:     REPEAT
152:        CASE command( concat( id_prompt, cmd_prompt ), ch ) OF
153:           'A' : append( fn, plan_max, plan, old_rec );
154:           'C' : change( fn, plan_max, plan, old_rec );
155:           'D' : BEGIN
156:                    debug;
157:                    redisplay
158:                 END;
159:           'I' : insrt( fn, plan_max, plan, old_rec );
160:           'L','N'
161:               : IF browse( fn, ch )
162:                    THEN show_rec( fn, plan_max, plan );
163:           'O' : BEGIN
164:                    options;
165:                    redisplay
166:                 END;
167:           'R' : IF seek_record( fn )
168:                    THEN show_rec( fn, plan_max, plan );
169:           'S' : search( fn, plan_max, plan, arg );
170:           'U' : IF change_made THEN
171:                    IF NOT verified( 'Throw away (most) changes' )
172:                       THEN ch := chr(0)   { So "until" will not end }
173:                       ELSE change_made := false; { So no update is made }
174:           'V' : redisplay
175:        END; { case }
176:        IF ch IN edit_change_set   { Don't use "change_made := ch in..." }
177:           THEN change_made := true
178:     UNTIL ch IN edit_exit_set;
179:     IF change_made
180:        THEN deinitialize( fn, update )
181:        ELSE deinitialize( fn, no_update )
182: END; { edit_file }


001: {------------------------------------------------------------------------}
002: {                                                                        }
003: {    EDITOR3.TEXT -- Forward declared and other routines                 }
004: {                                                                        }
005: {------------------------------------------------------------------------}
006:
007:
008: PROCEDURE show_rec{     fn, scmax : integer;
009:                        VAR scplan    : scrn_plan };
010: { Show current record in scplan screen format }
011: { Declared forward }
012: VAR
013:     s : string;
014:     i : integer;
015: BEGIN
016:     show_file( fn );            { Miscellaneous file info }
017:     show_status( fn );          { Active or Deleted }
018:     FOR i := 1 TO scmax DO WITH scplan[i] DO
019:        BEGIN
020:           get_field( fn, field, s );
```

```
021:                show_string( s, xentry, yentry, width )
022:          END { for / with }
023: END; { show_rec }
024:
025:
026: FUNCTION edit_string( VAR s          : string;           { String to edit }
027:                           dat_type : dat_descriptor;  { Data type }
028:                           x, y,                        { X, y position }
029:                           width,                       { Display width }
030:                           max_len,                     { Maximum chars }
031:                           decimals : integer ) : char; { Number decimals }
032: { Edit character buffer at these coordinates, parameters. }
033: { Return last character entered as function value. }
034: VAR
035:     ch                  : char;                    { Input character }
036:     chset               : SET OF char;             { Allowed characters }
037:     si                  : integer;                 { String index }
038:     s1                  : ucsd_string[1];          { Single char string }
039:     userquits           : boolean;                 { True to exit edit }
040:     original            : string;                  { For resetting string }
041:
042:
043:     FUNCTION scx( i : integer ) : integer;
044:     { Return relative x coordinate per index i }
045:     BEGIN
046:         scx := ( ( i - 1 ) MOD width ) + x
047:     END; { scx }
048:
049:
050:     FUNCTION scy( i : integer ) : integer;
051:     { Return relative y coordinate per index i }
052:     BEGIN
053:         scy := ( ( i - 1 ) DIV width ) + y
054:     END; { scy }
055:
056:
057:     PROCEDURE replace_char( ch : char );
058:     { Replace and display ch at si }
059:     BEGIN
060:         s[ si ] := ch;
061:         write( ch );
062:         si := si + 1
063:     END; { replace_char }
064:
065:
066:     PROCEDURE insert_char( ch : char );
067:     { Insert and display ch at si }
068:     BEGIN
069:         IF length( s ) < max_len THEN
070:         BEGIN
071:             s1[1] := ch;
072:             insert( s1, s, si );
073:             write( ch );
074:             si := si + 1;
075:             screen_ok := false          { Force redisplay }
076:         END { if }
077:     END; { insert_char }
078:
079:
080:     PROCEDURE delete_char;
081:     { Delete character at si }
082:     BEGIN
083:         IF si <= length( s ) THEN
084:         BEGIN
085:             gotoxy( scx( length( s ) ), scy( length( s ) ) );
086:             write( chr( blank ) );
087:             delete( s, si, 1 );
```

```
088:              screen_ok := false           { Force redisplay }
089:           END { if }
090:       END; { delete_char }
091:
092:
093:       PROCEDURE set_barrier( ch : char );
094:       { Mark / unmark end of typing area with ch }
095:       BEGIN
096:          IF ch <> chr( blank )
097:             THEN evon;             { Enhanced video except for blanks }
098:          gotoxy( scx( max_len ), scy( max_len ) );
099:          goright;                 { Cursor at last position + 1, same line }
100:          write( ch );
101:          evoff
102:       END; { set_barrier }
103:
104:
105:       PROCEDURE redisplay( new_s : string );
106:       { Reset and display new string }
107:       BEGIN
108:          clear_col( x, y, width, max_len );
109:          set_barrier( barrier );                    { Redisplay marker }
110:          s := new_s;                                { Assign new string }
111:          show_string( s, x, y, width );
112:          screen_ok := true;
113:          si := 1                                    { Send cursor to top }
114:       END; { redisplay }
115:
116:
117:       PROCEDURE left_justify;
118:       { Left justify and display string }
119:       BEGIN
120:          IF length( s ) > 0 THEN
121:          BEGIN
122:             strip( s );           { Remove leading and trailing blanks }
123:             redisplay( s )
124:          END { if }
125:       END; { left_justify }
126:
127:
128:       PROCEDURE right_justify;
129:       { Right justify and display string }
130:       BEGIN
131:          IF length( s ) > 0 THEN
132:          BEGIN
133:             strip( s );           { Remove leading and trailing blanks }
134:             WHILE length( s ) < max_len DO
135:                insert( ' ', s, 1 );
136:             redisplay( s )
137:          END { if }
138:       END; { right_justify }
139:
140:
141:       PROCEDURE show_mode;
142:       { Display insert / replace mode setting }
143:       BEGIN
144:          gotoxy( screen_width - 8, 0 );
145:          IF inserting
146:            THEN
147:              BEGIN
148:                 evon;
149:                 write( ' Insert ' );     { Length string = 8 }
150:                 evoff
151:              END
152:            ELSE
153:              write( ' Replace' )          { Length string = 8 }
154:       END; { show_mode }
```

```
155:
156:
157:     PROCEDURE crlf( VAR i : integer );
158:     { Return index position of head of next line from i }
159:     BEGIN
160:         i := ( ( scy(i) - y ) * width ) + width + 1
161:     END; { crlf }
162:
163:
164:     PROCEDURE show_from( si : integer );
165:     { Display string contents starting at si. }
166:     { Simulate keyboard interrupt using keypress function. }
167:     VAR
168:         sj              : integer;        { Alternate char index }
169:     BEGIN
170:         sj := si;                { Preserve current string index, si }
171:         WHILE sj <= length( s ) DO
172:         BEGIN
173:             IF keypress                          { Simulate }
174:               THEN exit( show_from );            {   keyboard interrupt }
175:
176:            { Display whichever is less, characters left in string from }
177:            { current cursor position, or columns left on the line. }
178:
179:             gotoxy( scx( sj ), scy( sj ) );     { Position cursor }
180:             unitwrite( 1, s[sj],                { Write to console from s[sj] }
181:               min( ( length(s) - sj + 1 ),             { Chars left or }
182:                    ( width - ( ( sj - 1 ) MOD width ) ) ) );  { Columns left }
183:
184:             crlf( sj )                          { Advance to next line }
185:         END; { while }
186:         screen_ok := true      { Operation complete / no interruption }
187:     END; { show_from }
188:
189:
190:     PROCEDURE do_command( ch : char; VAR done : boolean );
191:     { Perform this command.  Return done=true if an exit key pressed. }
192:     BEGIN
193:         CASE ord( ch ) OF
194:             keydel    : delete_char;
195:             keydown   : BEGIN
196:                             si := si + width;        { Line feed }
197:                             IF si < length( s ) + width
198:                               THEN ch := chr( blank )   { To avoid exit }
199:                         END;
200:             keyenter  : BEGIN
201:                             crlf( si );
202:                             IF si <= length( s )
203:                               THEN ch := chr( blank )    { To avoid exit }
204:                         END;
205:             keyinsert : BEGIN
206:                             inserting := NOT inserting;
207:                             show_mode
208:                         END;
209:             keyleft   : si := si - 1;
210:             keyreset  : redisplay( original );
211:             keyright  : si := si + 1;
212:             keyup     : BEGIN
213:                             si := si - width;        { Reverse lf }
214:                             IF si >= 1
215:                               THEN ch := chr( blank )   { To avoid exit }
216:                         END;
217:             keyzero   : redisplay( '' )              { Null string }
218:         END; { case }
219:         done := ( ch IN exitset )
220:     END; { do_command }
```

```
221:
222:
223:     PROCEDURE edit_init;
224:     { Initialize for procedure edit }
225:     BEGIN
226:         userquits := false;
227:         set_barrier( barrier );
228:         si := 1;
229:         s1 := ' ';     { Single blank space between the quotes }
230:         show_mode;
231:
232:      { Select appropriate character entry set for this }
233:      { field's data type.  }
234:
235:         CASE dat_type OF
236:            dat_char :
237:               BEGIN
238:                  chset := [ chr(32) .. chr(126) ];  { [' ' .. '~'] }
239:
240:                  { Remove trailing blanks.  Borrowed from }
241:                  { procedure strip(s) in PDBS7.TEXT. }
242:
243:                  IF length(s) > 0 THEN
244:            {$r-}                { Range checking off }
245:                     s[0] := chr( length( s ) + scan( -length( s ),
246:                                              <>chr( blank ),
247:                                              s[ length( s ) ] ) )
248:            {$r+}                { Range checking on }
249:               END;
250:            dat_number :
251:               BEGIN
252:                  chset := [ '0' .. '9', '-', '.' ];
253:                  left_justify
254:               END;
255:            dat_logical :
256:               chset := [ 'T', chr(116), 'F', chr(102) ] {['T','t','F','f']}
257:         END;  { case }
258:
259:         original := s                        { Save copy of original string }
260:
261:     END; { edit_init }
262:
263:
264: BEGIN { edit_string }
265:     edit_init;
266:     REPEAT
267:        IF si < 1
268:           THEN si := 1
269:           ELSE
270:        IF si > length( s )
271:           THEN si := min( max_len, length( s ) + 1 ); { Whichever is less }
272:
273:        IF NOT screen_ok
274:           THEN show_from( si );
275:
276:        gotoxy( scx( si ), scy( si ) );
277:
278:        IF getch( ch ) < chr( 32 )
279:          THEN
280:            do_command( ch, userquits )
281:          ELSE
282:            IF ( ch IN chset )
283:              THEN
284:                IF ( inserting ) OR ( si > length( s ) )
285:                   THEN
286:                     insert_char( ch )
287:                   ELSE
```

```
288:                       replace_char( ch )
289:             ELSE
290:                beep                       { Char not legal - sound alarm }
291:
292:     UNTIL userquits;
293:
294:     IF dat_type = dat_number THEN
295:     BEGIN
296:        normalize( s, decimals );       { Limit / expand decimal positions }
297:        IF length( s ) > max_len        { Limit length of string to maximum }
298:           THEN s := copy( s, 1, max_len );
299:        right_justify
300:     END; { if }
301:
302:     { Before leaving, insure screen correctly matches characters in buffer.}
303:     { Also, clear any leftover keypresses. }
304:
305:     WHILE NOT screen_ok DO
306:     BEGIN
307:        show_from( si );
308:        IF keypress
309:           THEN read( keyboard, ch )
310:     END;
311:
312:     edit_string := ch;                   { Return last character typed }
313:     set_barrier( chr( blank ) )          { Remove barrier mark (optional) }
314: END; { edit_string }
315:
316:
317: FUNCTION edit_rec{      fn, scmax : integer;
318:                     VAR scplan    : scrn_plan;
319:                     VAR old_rec   : binary_page ) : boolean };
320: { Return true if changes made to current record }
321: {  using scplan display format. }
322: { Old_rec contains default information or the previous }
323: {  record edited, and must be initialized by the caller. }
324: { Declared forward }
325: VAR
326:     last_char        : char;           { Last character typed in edit }
327:     s                : string;         { Holds fields in character form }
328:     sci              : integer;        { Screen plan index }
329:     stat_byte        : stat;           { New record status byte }
330:     copy_rec         : binary_page;    { Holds copy of record pre changes }
331: BEGIN
332:     sci := 1;
333:     edit_rec := false;
334:     IF NOT executed( get_rec( fn, copy_rec ) ) { Retain copy of record }
335:        THEN exit( edit_rec )    { Error reading record }
336:        ELSE
337:        REPEAT
338:        WITH scplan[sci] DO
339:         WITH fil_recs[fn] DO WITH fil_msc DO WITH msc_flds[field] DO
340:           BEGIN
341:             get_field( fn, field, s );                    { Read field }
342:             last_char :=                                  { Edit field }
343:               edit_string( s, fld_type, xentry, yentry,
344:                         width, fld_len, fld_decimals );
345:             put_field( fn, field, s );                    { Write field }
346:
347:             IF last_char = chr( keyup )
348:               THEN
349:                 IF sci > 1                    { If above first field, go to last }
350:                   THEN sci := sci - 1
351:                   ELSE sci := scmax
352:               ELSE
353:
354:             IF last_char IN [ chr( keydown ), chr( keyenter ) ]
```

```
355:          THEN
356:            IF sci < scmax              { If beyond last field, exit }
357:              THEN sci := sci + 1
358:              ELSE last_char := chr( keyetx )  { Force exit }
359:            ELSE
360:
361:          IF last_char = chr( keycopy )
362:            THEN
363:              BEGIN
364:              { Move default field into current record field }
365:              moveleft(
366:                old_rec[ fld_pos ],                      { Source }
367:                fil_page^.vir_page[ fil_relptr + fld_pos ], { Destination }
368:                fld_len );                               { Count }
369:              IF fld_type <> dat_number THEN
370:              BEGIN  { Numbers are automatically displayed in edit }
371:                 get_field( fn, field, s );              { Load string }
372:                 show_string( s, xentry, yentry, width )  { Display }
373:              END { if }
374:              END
375:            ELSE
376:
377:          IF last_char = chr( keykill )
378:            THEN
379:              BEGIN
380:                IF rec_status( fn ) = active
381:                  THEN stat_byte := deleted     { Toggle record status byte }
382:                  ELSE stat_byte := active;
383:                IF executed( mark_rec( fn, stat_byte ) )
384:                  THEN show_status( fn )
385:                  ELSE exit( edit_rec )          { Error marking record }
386:              END  { if }
387:            ELSE
388:
389:          IF last_char = chr( keyesc )
390:            THEN        { "Undo" changes on escape key }
391:              IF executed( put_rec( fn, copy_rec ) )
392:                THEN show_rec( fn, scmax, scplan )
393:                ELSE exit( edit_rec )            { Error writing record }
394:
395:        END { withs }
396:      UNTIL ( last_char IN [ chr( keyesc ), chr( keyetx ), chr( keykill ) ] );
397:      edit_rec := ( last_char <> chr( keyesc ) )
398: END; { edit_rec }
```

2

Getting Data out of the Computer

LIST / REPORT

LIST

In Chapter One, the idea of a relational data base composed of nothing more than tables with rows and columns was presented (see Fig. 1-1). *List* is a program that can be used to print or view your data in this familiar tabular form. It is the quickest and easiest program for finding a lot of data without much of a fuss.

Figure 2-1 contains the printouts of The Company's four main data files, customers, vendors, parts, and sources. If you want to follow along with the example, you should use the *editor* to enter the information from Fig. 2-1 into your sample data files now.

When you first execute *list*, you are asked to supply a data file name. After that, you are given a series of options. For now, just press the return key for each one. A list of all the records in the file will then appear on your screen.

There are a few problems with *list* that need to be explained. First, the column headers, as you can see in Fig. 2-1, do not always line up perfectly. This happens only when the column name, which is the same as the field name, is longer than the field width. If this bothers you, there are two things you can do. One, use the more intelligent, but slower, *report* program instead. Two, never use a field name that is more than one or two characters longer than the field width.

Another problem with *list* may become apparent depending on the kind of computer terminal or printer you are using. If the terminal's cursor, or printer's print head, automatically does a carriage return and line feed at the extreme right border, your records will "wrap around," with each record taking up several lines in most cases. If your cursor or printer does not have this wrap-around feature, then

CUSTOMERS.PDBF :

C.KEY	C.NAME	C.ADDRESS	C.CITY	C.STATE	C.ZIP	C.PHONE	C.LIMIT	C.BALANCE
00001 C3	Danzig, Irving	9 Nightmare Hollow	Transylvania	PA	18605	800-555-1212	250.00	325.00
00002 C1	Diffenforker, Cecil	400 W. Parkway Terrace	Los Angeles	CA	90786	801-555-1234	1000.00	.00
00003 C4	Franklin, Benjamin	South Print Street	Philadelphia	PA	17666	900-555-1212	5000.00	2500.00
00004 C7	Pascal, Blaise	75 Programmers Hwy	Computer City	WA	97777	901-555-4321	1250.00	1375.78
00005 C6	Slumgullion, Stewart	800 Potage Way	Cincinnati	OH	77612	800-555-1212	500.00	500.00
00006 C5	Stallion, Horace	45 Barnyard Place	Corral City	TX	54671	900-555-1212	750.00	825.50
00007 C2	West, Martin Quincy	82 Phast Lane Apt 2B	Baltimore	MD	21531	801-555-1111	750.00	125.00

VENDORS.PDBF :

V.KEY	V.NAME	V.ADDRESS	V.CITY	V.STATE	V.ZIP	V.CONTACT	V.PHONE
00001 V1	Robotics Manufacturers, Inc.	45 West Setting Sun Hwy	Baltimore	MD	22098	Ms. Paula Taylor	301-555-1212
00002 V2	Mechanical Assemblies Corp.	800 Lincoln East	San Diego	CA	90666	Jonathan Rapport	912-888-5098
00003 V3	Lord's Electroscopics	Android Industrial Park	Boston	MA	08712	Mr. James McCarthy	101-901-4231

PARTS.PDBF :

P.NUM	P.NAME	P.COLOR	P.RED	P.STOCK
00001 P1	Photometric eye	Blue	50	61
00002 P2	Arm assembly	Silver	50	59
00003 P3	Body	Red	3	18
00004 P4	Leg	Black	50	76
00005 P5	Foot wheel	Black	100	110
00006 P6	Hand	Silver	25	20

SOURCES.PDBF :

P.NUM	V.KEY	COST
00001 P3	V2	545.00
00002 P1	V3	129.00
00003 P6	V2	50.00
00004 P4	V3	45.00
00005 P3	V1	100.00

Fig. 2-1. The contents of The Company's four main data files. Use the editor to enter the information, printed here by the list program, into the computer.

44

```
List what file ? CUSTOMERS
Search for? [<expr>|ret|?]
<cr>
List fields? [<field>,<field>,..,|ret|?]
C.NAME, C.PHONE
Output report to ? <cr>


DATA:CUSTOMERS.PDBF :
            C.NAME----------------------- C.PHONE-----
    00001  Danzig, Irving                 800-555-1212
    00002  Diffenforker, Cecil            801-555-1234
    00003  Franklin, Benjamin             900-555-1212
    00004  Pascal, Blaise                 901-555-4321
    00005  Slumgullion, Stewart           800-555-1212
    00006  Stallion, Horace               900-555-1212
    00007  West, Martin Quincy            801-555-1111
```

Fig. 2-2. *Follow the dialogue above using the* list *program to produce a simple phone list, a subset of The Company's customer data file.*

a portion of the record will either be cut off at the right edge or, in the case of the printer, will overprint on the same line, producing more garbage on the page than information. Again, you can use the *report* program, which is not affected by these differences in the hardware. A better way, however, is simply to limit the number of columns to those that will fit on your screen or page.

To demonstrate one possibility for producing better-looking lists unaffected by these problems, *list* The Company's customer file. Follow the dialogue in Fig. 2-2 to produce the phone listing also shown in Fig. 2-2. Remember, you should enter the things that are underlined. Where you see the symbol <cr>, just press the return key.

Whenever you are asked to supply a list of field names, you can enter a question mark for a list of the possibilities. Pressing the return key tells *list* to send all fields to the output. You can enter field names separated by commas or spaces in any order to produce a variety of different tables all from the same file.

Pressing the return key to the prompt ''Output report to?'' sends the listing to the console. To print out a copy, enter PRINTER: and press return. The colon indicates to the UCSD operating system that the output is going to a device rather than to a file named ''printer.''

You can send the output to a named text file if you want. This is helpful when writing documents, such as books about data base programming, where reports are to be included in other text files. If you intend to edit the results using the UCSD editor, be sure to enter the .TEXT extension to your file name when *list* asks for the output file name.

Searching for Information

Often, you will not want to list all of the data in a file but, instead, only those records that satisfy some argument. You may want to find the associated data for someone by name, or you may want to list all the balances greater than zero.

```
<operator> ::=   =  |  <>  |  <  |  >  |  <=  |  >=  |  @

<simple expr> ::= <field name> <operator> <literal or field name>

<complex expr> ::= <simple expr> { AND | OR <simple expr>, }
```

Fig. 2-3. *The syntax for PDBS search arguments described in Backus-Naur Form (BNF). An expression can be either simple or complex. The @ symbol is pronounced "contains." See text for examples of search arguments.*

To search for records, you have to enter an expression or argument in a form the computer understands. The syntax of a search argument is given in Fig. 2-3.

The elements of a search argument can be literal (actual values that you enter) or variable. An example of a literal search is:

Search for?
P.STOCK >= 50

This would find all the stock levels in The Company's parts file that are greater than or equal to fifty units. Another kind of search compares the values among the fields in each record to determine if a matching condition exists. For example, you might enter:

Search for?
P.STOCK <= P.REO

Instead of a literal value (50), another field name is entered as a variable in the expression. The above search finds all the records for which the stocking levels are less than or equal to the reorder point (P.REO), a very useful determination in an inventory file. The printout could then be given to the purchasing agent for ordering those items that have been depleted.

Using AND & OR

You can combine arguments using the logical names "AND" and "OR." To find all the customers in Pennsylvania with account limits less than $500, you could enter the following search argument.

Search for?
C.STATE=PA AND C.LIMIT<500

Changing "AND" to "OR" produces a different result.

Search for?
C.STATE=OH OR C.BALANCE=0

A search argument may be up to 255 characters long, which would be a very complex search. The more complicated the argument, the longer the search will take. If you get tired of waiting, or if you make a mistake, you can always interrupt a search by pressing any key while the search is in progress.

To find words with spaces or commas in them, enclose the search argument in quotes. For example, *list* the parts data file, and try to enter this search argument.

Search for?
P.NAME = ARM ASSEMBLY

You should receive an error message. To find the arm assembly record, the following search argument must be used.

Search for?
P.NAME = "ARM ASSEMBLY"

Often, you won't know the exact spelling of the thing you are trying to find. This frequently occurs when searching for a person's name when you may know only the first initial and last name. For this kind of search, you can use the embedded word operator. In PDBS this is the "at" symbol (@). Try the following search on The Company's customer file. You can pronounce the @ symbol as "contains."

Search for?
C.NAME @ BEN

That successfully finds Franklin, Benjamin. It would also find Jack Benny and Barney Benito, if those names were in the same file. False matches such as these are called "drop outs" and are common when searching for short embedded words. Sometimes the results are surprising, even comical.

Searching can be used in the *editor* and *report* programs as well as *list*. Other programs in PDBS also permit searching, and all use the same format as described here.

The List Program

For such a capable program, *list* is quite short, only 127 lines including blanks. It uses two library units which must be compiled and installed in SYSTEM-.LIBRARY before the program can itself be compiled and executed. These units, *pdbsunit* and *evalunit,* are detailed in Part Two.

Procedure *new_list* at line 22 prints the column headers. If you are ambitious, you may want to solve the problem of long field names not lining up properly with short columns.

To accomplish this, you have to understand the purpose of the *fld_order* array named *order*. This is simply a list, or map, of the field numbers in the order they are to be processed. The first value in an order array, indexed at *order[0]*, is the number of field numbers contained in the array. For example, if you were to print out an order array, it might look like this.

ORDER[0] = 3
ORDER[1] = 2
ORDER[2] = 1
ORDER[3] = 5

The first number indicates how many numbers are stored in the array. Here, *order[0]* equals three, and we would expect to find field numbers at indexed positions one, two, and three. In those positions are the field numbers two, one, and five. These are the fields to be listed. Fields three and four, and any higher than five, are not to be processed at all.

Going back to *new_list,* look at line 47. You will see this kind of statement often in PDBS programs. To fully understand what is being done here, you need to study the PDBS library unit in Part Two. However, for the purpose of rewriting *list,* you can access the field length with a line such as this.

fil_recs[fn].fil_msc.msc_flds[order[i]].fld_len;

Variable *fn* is the internal file number, and *i* is an index into the *order* array. You can use a *with* statement (see line 40) to save typing.

```
001: {$S+,I-}              { Compiler swapping on; I/O error checking off }
002:
003: PROGRAM list; uses applestuff, pdbsunit, evalunit;
004:
005: {-----------------------------------------------------------------}
006: {                                                                 }
007: {    PROGRAM       :  List contents of a data base file           }
008: {    LANGUAGE      :  UCSD Pascal / Apple Pascal 1.1              }
009: {                                                                 }
010: {    Copyright (C) 1983 by Tom Swan. All commercial rights reserved. }
011: {                                                                 }
012: {-----------------------------------------------------------------}
013:
014: CONST
015:    esc             = 27;                     { ASCII escape char }
016:
017: VAR
018:    file_name       : pdbs_fname;             { PDBS data file name }
019:    file_number     : integer;                { Fil_recs file number }
020:
021:
022: PROCEDURE new_list( VAR pf        : text;         { Output file }
023:                         fn        : integer;      { File number }
024:                     VAR arg       : string;       { Arguments string }
025:                         order     : fld_order );  { Field order }
026: { Print file and field names at the beginning of a new listing }
027: { Attempt to display field names above the columns where data }
028: { will appear.  May not work perfectly if there are many short }
```

```
029: {  fields with long names, but ok for most uses.  If this is a }
030: {  problem, use the slower but more flexible  REPORT program instead. }
031: VAR
032:     column_len,
033:     cursor_pos,
034:     field,
035:     i                   : integer;
036: BEGIN
037:     clrscrn;
038:     gotoxy( 0, 1 );
039:     evon;
040:     WITH fil_recs[fn] DO
041:     BEGIN
042:         writeln( pf, chr( blank ), fil_name, ' : ', arg );
043:         column_len := 6;                  { Indent past record number }
044:         cursor_pos := column_len;
045:         write( pf, chr( blank ) : cursor_pos );        { Step to cursor pos }
046:         FOR field := 1 TO order[0] DO
047:           WITH fil_msc.msc_flds[ order[field] ] DO      { Fld_descriptor }
048:           BEGIN
049:             write( pf, chr( blank ) : 2 );
050:             cursor_pos := cursor_pos + 2;             { Space between names }
051:             FOR i := 0 TO alpha_size DO
052:                 IF fld_name[i] <> chr( blank ) THEN    { Print up to first }
053:                    BEGIN                               {  blank char in name.}
054:                        write( pf, fld_name[i] );       { Print one char. }
055:                        cursor_pos := cursor_pos + 1
056:                    END;
057:             column_len := column_len + fld_len + 2;
058:             WHILE cursor_pos < column_len DO           { Tab to column end }
059:             BEGIN
060:                 write( pf, '-' );                      { Show boundaries of }
061:                 cursor_pos := cursor_pos + 1           {  longer columns. }
062:             END { while }
063:           END { for / with }
064:     END;
065:     evoff;
066:     writeln( pf )
067: END; { new_list }
068:
069:
070: PROCEDURE list_file( fn : integer );
071: { List selected contents of data base file fn }
072: { Assume file is not empty }
073: VAR
074:     flds_to_list    : fld_order;   { Field numbers }
075:     out_name        : string;      { Output file name }
076:     pf              : text;        { Output "Print File" }
077:     rn              : integer;     { Record number }
078:     arg             : string;      { Search arguments }
079: BEGIN
080:     REPEAT
081:         load_arg( 'Search for?', fn, arg );   { Load search arguments }
082:         IF load_order( 'List fields?', fn, flds_to_list ) THEN
083:         BEGIN
084:             REPEAT
085:                 IF NOT get_file_name( 'Output report to ? ', out_name )
086:                     THEN out_name := 'CONSOLE:'; { Default to console }
087:                 remove_ext( out_name ); { Disallow PDBS file name }
088:                 rewrite( pf, out_name )
089:             UNTIL executed( ioresult );        { i.e. until no error }
090:
091:             new_list( pf, fn, arg, flds_to_list ); { File name, headers }
092:
093:             rn := 0;
094:             WHILE ( rn < fil_recs[fn].fil_msc.msc_lastrec ) AND
095:                   ( NOT keypress ) DO
```

```
096:              BEGIN
097:                rn := rn + 1;
098:                IF NOT executed( seek_rec( fn, rn ) )
099:                  THEN
100:                    exit( list_file )     { Closes pf file normally }
101:                  ELSE
102:                    IF match( fn )
103:                        THEN display_record( pf, fn, flds_to_list )
104:              END;
105:
106:              close( pf, lock )            { Lock in case it's a disk text file }
107:           END { if }
108:      UNTIL NOT verified( 'Another list' )
109: END; { list_file }
110:
111:
112: BEGIN { list }
113:    clrscrn;
114:    WHILE get_file_name( 'List what file ? ', file_name ) DO
115:    BEGIN
116:       IF executed( open_file( file_number, file_name ) ) THEN
117:       BEGIN
118:          clreosc;
119:          IF file_empty( file_number )
120:             THEN writeln( 'No records in file' )
121:             ELSE list_file( file_number );
122:          IF NOT executed( close_file( file_number, no_update ) )
123:             THEN exit( PROGRAM )     { Extremely unlikely }
124:       END; { if }
125:    gotoxy( 0, 0 )
126:    END { while }
127: END.
```

REPORT

Lists are adequate for viewing data and for informal reports. For more professional results, use the *report* program.

The disadvantage of using *report* to get data out of the computer is the time it takes to set up a report format. However, *report* is more versatile than *list*. It can print and total data fields in a variety of ways. It understands how to break long lines between words, and will number and title each page for publishable results.

The first step in designing a report is to *create* a report format file. A report format file is a PDBS data file, and can itself be edited, listed, sorted, and processed by any PDBS program. Report format files are distinguished by their file name extensions, .RPRT. All report format files must end in .RPRT and must be defined as shown in Fig. 2-4.

To create a report format for The Company's customer file, use the *create* program to design the report format file described in Fig. 2-4. You may call the file anything you like as long as it ends in .RPRT. For this example, the file name R1.RPRT is used.

After creating the report format file, use the *editor* to enter the format for this

```
DATA:R1.RPRT
Record size ............ 42
Number of fields ........ 8
Maximum record number ... 24
Records in use .......... 0
Records not used ........ 24
Date created ............ 19-Jul-83
Date last updated ....... 19-Jul-83

#   NAME        TYPE     LEN DEC POS

1   FIELD       Number     2   0   1
2   COLUMN      Number     3   0   3
3   WIDTH       Number     3   0   6
4   TRUNC       Logical    1   0   9
5   EOLN        Logical    1   0  10
6   TOTAL       Logical    1   0  11
7   HEADER.1    Char      15   0  12
8   HEADER.2    Char      15   0  27
```

Fig. 2-4. *Report format files are created with this structure. The report file may have any file name, but must end in the file name extension, .RPRT.*

report into the R1.RPRT file. The information for The Company's customer report is listed in Fig. 2-5. First execute the *editor*, then type R1.RPRT when asked which file you want to edit. Because a report format file is a special-purpose file and doesn't end in .PDBF, you must type the file name extension. Use the *editor's* append command to enter all the information from Fig. 2-5 into the R1.RPRT file.

You are now ready to print out the report according to the design you just entered. Execute the *report* program, and follow this dialogue.

Report on what file? <u>CUSTOMERS</u>
Using .RPRT format file? <u>R1</u>
Loading report format
Search for? [<expr>¦ret¦?]
<u><cr></u>
What .SPEC file (ret=default)? <u><cr></u>

After you press the return key, the screen is replaced with a long list of options shown in more detail in Fig. 2-6. To change any of these options, enter the number of the line you want to change. If you are following along with this example, change "Lines between recs" from 0 to 1 before printing the customer report. This makes the results easier to read.

Press return when you are ready to begin printing. You will see this prompt at the top of the screen.

Prepare PRINTER: Ready ? (y/n) <u>Y</u>

Field	Column	Width	TRN	EOL	TOT	Header.1	Header.2
==	===	===	=	=	=	================	================
00001	2	0	15	F	F	F	Customer	Name
00002	3	17	15	F	F	F	Street	Address
00003	4	34	15	F	F	F		City
00004	5	50	2	F	F	F		St
00005	6	53	5	F	F	F	Zip	Code
00006	8	60	8	F	F	F	Account	Limit
00007	9	70	8	F	F	T	Account	Balance

Fig. 2-5. *Enter the values here into the report format file R1.RPRT using the editor append command. These values produce the report shown in Fig. 2-7. The record numbers on the extreme left edge are not entered.*

Enter Y and press return to begin printing. While printing is in progress, you can pause the report by pressing the space bar. Follow the messages at the top of the screen to resume printing or to quit and start over. Your report should be similar to the one shown in Fig. 2-7.

Designing Your Own Reports

When designing a report format for your own data files, it is helpful to use graph paper numbered across the top starting with zero. You should also have a status report (see program *status*) for referring to the format of your records.

Each .RPRT format file (see Fig. 2-4) has one entry for each field in the record you want to print. Each of these items has a different function described in more detail in Fig. 2-8.

```
#  Output specification   Default      Purpose

1) Top margin .........      3         Blank lines at top of page
2) Bottom margin .......      5         Blank lines at bottom of page
3) Lines per page ......     66         Total length of page in lines
4) Chars per line ......     80         Total width of page in characters
5) Line spacing ........      0         Blank lines between every line
6) Lines between recs ..      0         Blank lines between every record
7) Spaces to indent ....      0         Left margin setting
8) First page number ...      1         0=no page numbers or report titles
9) Print headers .......    true        True to print column titles
10) Use form feeds ......   false        True if printer uses form feeds
11) Pause each page .....   false        True to wait at top of new page
12) Output file name ....  PRINTER:      Send output to this file or device
13) Printer init ........  <null>        Printer initialization (see text)
14) Title 1 ............  <file name>    Report title top line
15) Title 2 ............   <null>        Optional report title second line
```

Fig. 2-6. *The report program's output specifications can be selected while using the program, or can be loaded from a special .SPEC data file. These options control general output settings while the .RPRT file controls the format of the data in the report.*

```
Date : 19-Jul-83                CUSTOMERS.PDBF                    Page-1

========================================================================
    Customer           Street                      Zip    Account   Account
      Name            Address          City     St Code    Limit    Balance
================   ================ ================ == ===== ======== ========

Danzig, Irving     9 Nightmare      Transylvania  PA 18605   250.00   325.00
                   Hollow

Diffenforker,      400 W. Parkway   Los Angeles   CA 90786  1000.00      .00
Cecil              Terrace

Franklin,          South Print      Philadelphia  PA 17666  5000.00  2500.00
Benjamin           Street

Pascal, Blaise     75 Programmers   Computer City WA 97777  1250.00  1375.78
                   Hwy

Slumgullion,       800 Potage Way   Cincinnati    OH 77612   500.00   500.00
Stewart

Stallion,          45 Barnyard      Corral City   TX 54671   750.00   825.50
Horace             Place

West, Martin       82 Phast Lane    Baltimore     MD 21531   750.00   125.00
Quincy             Apt 2B

                                                          ========
Total                                                      5651.28
Minimum                                                          0
Maximum                                                    2500.00
Average                                                     807.32

7 records processed
```

Fig. 2-7. *The Company's customer file as printed by the report program using the re-*
port format R1.RPRT described in Figs. 2-4 and 2-5. Notice how long fields
have been broken between words into double lines.

```
#  NAME        DESCRIPTION

1  FIELD       Field number of field to print in this column
2  COLUMN      Starting column number (#0 is at left border)
3  WIDTH       Column width.  Auto paragraph if less than length
4  TRUNC       False for word break.  True to cut off long fields
5  EOLN        Insert carriage return after printing field
6  TOTAL       Maintain and print total, min, max, and avg for field
7  HEADER.1    First line of column title header (optional)
8  HEADER.2    Second line of column title header (optional)
```

Fig. 2-8. *A format file, ending in .RPRT, is composed of the above information for*
each field of the record to be printed.

You may choose to have record numbers print along the left edge of the report. If you want record numbers, leave the first five columns (at least) blank. In other words, have no column settings less than six in the report format.

If you do not want record numbers to appear in the report, you must cover up the first five columns with one of the fields from your own data. Another way to delete record numbers is to remove the programming lines from 497 through 502 in file REPORT1.TEXT. You may also want to consider a modification that would allow optional selection of record numbers.

Using a Custom Output Specification

When you see the prompt

What .SPEC file (ret = default)?

you have the option of pressing return or entering the name of another special-purpose data file, one that ends in the file name extension .SPEC. Rather than entering the output specifications described in Fig. 2-6 every time you run the *report* program, you can store your custom settings in a PDBS .SPEC data file. The *report* program will then use those settings in place of the default values listed in Fig. 2-6.

The format for a specifications file ending in .SPEC is listed in Fig. 2-9. Cre-

```
CONSOLE.SPEC
Record size ............. 188
Number of fields ........ 15
Maximum record number ... 5
Records in use .......... 0
Records not used ........ 5
Date created ............ 01-Jul-83
Date last updated ....... 01-Jul-83
```

#	NAME	TYPE	LEN	DEC	POS
1	TOP	Number	3	0	1
2	BOT	Number	3	0	4
3	LPP	Number	3	0	7
4	CPL	Number	3	0	10
5	SPACING	Number	3	0	13
6	REC.SPACE	Number	3	0	16
7	INDENT	Number	3	0	19
8	PAGE.NUM	Number	3	0	22
9	HEADERS	Logical	1	0	25
10	FORM.FEEDS	Logical	1	0	26
11	PAUSE	Logical	1	0	27
12	OUT.FILE	Char	40	0	28
13	PRINT.INIT	Char	40	0	68
14	TITLE.1	Char	40	0	108
15	TITLE.2	Char	40	0	148

Fig. 2-9. Create a data file using this format, and a file name ending in .SPEC.

```
Top Bot Lpp Cpl Lsp Rsp Ind Pgn Hd FF Ps  Out File
=== === === === === === === === =  =  =   ==========

 1   0  20  79   0   1   0   0 T  F  T   CONSOLE:
```

Fig. 2-10. *Use the editor to enter these values into a file named CONSOLE.SPEC cre-*
ated with the format shown in Fig. 2-9. For brevity, the printer initialization
and two title strings are missing from the values here. You may leave these
blank. These output specifications may be used with the report program to
produce a readable, paged screen display.

ate this file in the same way you created all other data files using the *create* program. Use the *editor* program to enter the values you want. When the *report*
program asks for what .SPEC file to use, supply your file name (you do not have to
enter the .SPEC), and your own values will be loaded.

You can set up a very nice paged screen report using the values listed in Fig.
2-10. When I want to have a display better than the *list* program is capable of producing, I use the CONSOLE.SPEC settings in Fig. 2-10.

Selecting Printer Options

Item number 13 of the output specifications (see Figs. 2-6 and 2-9) accepts a
printer initialization sequence that can be used to select compressed, 132-column
output on most modern dot matrix printers.

A printer initialization sequence is a list of numbers separated by commas.
You will have to consult your printer's manual for the values needed by your hardware. On my system, using a rather well-worn Centronics 737 printer for rough
draft work, the following sequence causes a switch to 132-column output.

13) Printer init **27,20**

The two values, 27 and 20, are the ASCII control characters in decimal that
my printer understands as a command to switch to compressed printing. These two
characters are sent to the printer at the start of each report. Also see procedure
init_printer starting at line 107 in REPORT1.TEXT.

Searching and Reporting

When using the *report* program, you are also given an opportunity to enter a
search argument to select a subset of a data file for the report. The argument is
entered exactly as described in the instructions for the *list* program using the syntax
shown in Fig. 2-3.

```
R2.RPRT

                Field  Column  Width  TRN EOL TOT
                ==     ===     ===    =   =   =

        00001   2       0      30     F   T   F
        00002   3       0      30     F   T   F
        00003   4       0      20     F   F   F
        00004   5      22       2     F   F   F
        00005   6      25       5     F   T   F
```

Fig. 2-11. *A set of mailing labels (see Fig. 2-13) can be printed from The Company's customer file using the above report format. Enter these values into a file named R2.RPRT. The structure for a .RPRT file is shown in Fig. 2-4. Only non-blank items are listed above.*

```
LABELS.SPEC

        Top Bot Lpp Cpl Lsp Rsp Ind Pgn Hd FF Ps  Out File
        === === === === === === === === =  =  =   ==========

00001    0   0   6  30   0   2   2   0  F  F  F   PRINTER:
```

Fig. 2-12. *Enter these output specifications into a file named LABELS. SPEC. The structure for a .SPEC file is shown in Fig. 2-9. Only the non-blank items are listed above.*

```
            Danzig, Irving
            9 Nightmare Hollow
            Transylvania        PA 18605

            Diffenforker, Cecil
            400 W. Parkway Terrace
            Los Angeles         CA 90786

            Franklin, Benjamin
            South Print Street
            Philadelphia        PA 17666

            Pascal, Blaise
            75 Programmers Hwy
            Computer City       WA 97777
```

Fig. 2-13. *Mailing labels from The Company's customer file. These labels were printed with the report program using the report format in Fig. 2-11 along with the output specifications in Fig. 2-12.*

PRODUCING MAILING LABELS IN PDBS

The *report* program is also able to print mailing labels from a data file containing names and addresses. The example here is from The Company's customer file, but the format should operate with a few adjustments on your own data files.

First *create* a report format file named R2.RPRT using the same structure that you used for R1.RPRT shown in Fig. 2-4. Enter the values from Fig. 2-11 into this new file. This tells *report* which fields to include in each label and in what order. Obviously, we don't want to print the account balances on the mailing labels. To delete that field, its field number is simply left out of the report format.

Next, *create* an output specifications file named LABELS.SPEC using the same structure shown in Fig. 2-9. Enter the values shown in Fig. 2-12 into this file. This information tells *report* about the size and spacing of the labels, and could be adjusted to print on a variety of formats. The values here are about right for single-column labels spaced one to an inch at six printer lines per inch, a commonly available format. To print pages of labels with three or more across, you could use the *columns* program in *Pascal Programs for Business* to further process the output of *report*.

Finally, execute *report* and supply R2.RPRT and LABELS.SPEC when you are prompted. Of course, the main data file is CUSTOMERS. A sample of the result is shown in Fig. 2-13.

```
001: {$S++}        { Compiler swapping on double }
002: {$I-}         { I/O error checking off }
003:
004: PROGRAM report; uses applestuff, pdbsunit, evalunit;
005:
006: {-------------------------------------------------------------------}
007: {                                                                   }
008: {      PROGRAM        :  Write a formatted report                   }
009: {      LANGUAGE       :  UCSD Pascal / Apple Pascal 1.1             }
010: {                                                                   }
011: {      Copyright (C) 1983 by Tom Swan. All commercial rights reserved. }
012: {                                                                   }
013: {-------------------------------------------------------------------}
014:
015: CONST
016:    default_width    = 80;        { Default printer width }
017:    esc              = 27;        { ASCII escape character }
018:    header_len       = 15;        { Max chars in column headers }
019:    max_spec         = 15;        { Number of things in a print_spec }
020:
021: TYPE
022:    print_spec =                  { Printer specifications }
023:
024:    { Note: if you add or subtract from print_spec, change the  }
025:    {       constant max_spec to equal the number of items in   }
026:    {       the new record. Then, modify procedures init_spec,  }
027:    {       show_spec, and get_spec. }
028:
029:       RECORD
030:          top,                    { Top margin }
031:          bot,                    { Bottom margin }
```

```
032:          lpp,                        { Lines per page }
033:          cpl,                        { Chars per line }
034:          lsp,                        { Line spacing }
035:          lbr,                        { Blank lines between records }
036:          indent,                     { Spaces to indent each line }
037:          pn  : integer;              { Starting page number }
038:          headers,                    { Print column headers switch }
039:          ff,                         { Use form feeds switch }
040:          pause : boolean;            { Sheet-feed pause switch }
041:          outfile,                    { Output file name }
042:          init,                       { Printer initialization string }
043:          title1,                     { First line of title }
044:          title2 : string             { Second line of title }
045:       END;
046:
047:    rprt_rec =                  { Report format record }
048:       RECORD
049:          field,                      { Field number }
050:          column,                     { Column number }
051:          width      : integer;       { Column width }
052:          trunc,                      { Truncation switch }
053:          eoln,                       { End line with c/r switch }
054:          total      : boolean;       { Field statistics switch }
055:          header1,
056:          header2    : ucsd_string[ header_len ]    { Column headers }
057:       END; { rprt_rec }
058:
059:    rprt_plan =                 { Array containing one rprt_rec per field }
060:       ARRAY[ 1 .. max_fld ] OF rprt_rec;
061:
062: VAR
063:    arg                : string;          { Search arguments }
064:    file_name          : pdbs_fname;      { Data file name }
065:    file_num           : integer;         { Data file number }
066:    pr_spec            : print_spec;      { Output specifications }
067:    rp_plan            : rprt_plan;       { Report format plan }
068:    rp_max             : 0 .. max_fld;    { Number of rp_plan entries }
069:    specs_initialized  : boolean;         { True if output initialized }
070:
071: (*$I REPORT1.TEXT*)          { Include part one; print report procedures }
072: (*$I REPORT2.TEXT*)          { Include part two; initializing procedures }
073:
074: BEGIN
075:    clrscrn;
076:    specs_initialized := false;        { So that init happens only once }
077:    WHILE get_file_name( 'Report on what file? ', file_name ) DO
078:    BEGIN
079:       IF executed( open_file( file_num, file_name ) ) THEN
080:       BEGIN
081:          clreosc;
082:          IF executed( load_rprt( rp_plan, rp_max ) ) THEN
083:          BEGIN
084:             load_arg( 'Search for?', file_num, arg );
085:             get_spec( file_num, pr_spec, specs_initialized, arg );
086:             print_report( file_num, rp_plan, rp_max, pr_spec )
087:          END; { if }
088:          IF NOT executed( close_file( file_num, no_update ) )
089:             THEN exit( PROGRAM )    { Extremely unlikely }
090:       END; { if }
091:       gotoxy( 0, 0 )
092:    END { while }
093: END.

001: {-----------------------------------------------------------------------}
002: {                                                                       }
003: {    REPORT1.TEXT  --  Part one of the REPORT program                   }
004: {                                                                       }
005: {-----------------------------------------------------------------------}
```

```
006:
007:
008: segment PROCEDURE print_report(       fn  : integer;          { File num }
009:                               VAR rp  : rprt_plan;        { .RPRT fmt }
010:                               VAR rpn : integer;          { # fields }
011:                               VAR pr  : print_spec  );    { .SPEC fmt }
012: { Print out the data file report }
013:
014: CONST
015:     maxcpl          = 255;            { Maximum chars per output line }
016:     uch             = '=';            { Underscore character }
017:
018: TYPE
019:     col_rec =                         { Column status record }
020:         RECORD
021:             count : integer;              { Chars printed so far }
022:             sum,                          { Numeric item total }
023:             maxnum,                       { Numeric maximum }
024:             minnum    : long_integer;     { Numeric minimum }
025:         END; { col_rec }
026:
027: VAR
028:     col :                             { Column statistics }
029:      ARRAY[ 1 .. max_fld ] OF col_rec;
030:     line :                            { Output line }
031:      PACKED ARRAY[ 0 .. maxcpl ] OF char;
032:     lines_done      : integer;        { Lines per page printed }
033:     pf              : text;           { Output text file }
034:     rec_num         : integer;        { File record number }
035:     recs_done       : long_integer;   { Number records processed }
036:
037:
038:     PROCEDURE new_line;
039:         forward;
040:
041:
042:     PROCEDURE quit_early;
043:     { Perform orderly early exit from procedure }
044:     BEGIN
045:         prompt( 'Report stopped' );
046:         close( pf );
047:         exit( print_report )
048:     END; { quit_early }
049:
050:
051:     PROCEDURE perform( n : pdbs_err );
052:     { Check result of some function, exiting on any error }
053:     BEGIN
054:         IF NOT executed( n )
055:             THEN quit_early
056:     END; { perform }
057:
058:
059:     PROCEDURE new_screen;
060:     { Reset display before printing or after a pause }
061:     BEGIN
062:         clrscrn;
063:         writeln( 'Press ESC to quit; SPACE to pause...' )
064:     END; { new_screen }
065:
066:
067:     PROCEDURE checkkey;
068:     { After keypress is sensed, read char and check for a command }
069:     VAR
070:         ch : char;
071:     BEGIN
072:         read( keyboard, ch );
073:         IF ch = chr( esc )
```

```
074:            THEN
075:              BEGIN
076:                 gotoxy( 0, 0 );
077:                 IF verified( 'Escaping: do you want to quit' )
078:                      THEN quit_early
079:              END
080:            ELSE
081:            IF ch = chr( blank )
082:              THEN
083:                BEGIN
084:                   promptat( 0, 0, 'Paused: any key resumes...' );
085:                   read( keyboard, ch )
086:                END;
087:          new_screen
088:      END; { checkkey }
089:
090:
091:      PROCEDURE init_columns;
092:      { Initialize nc entries in column statistics array }
093:      VAR
094:         i : integer;
095:      BEGIN
096:         FOR i := 1 TO rpn DO
097:            WITH col[i] DO
098:               BEGIN
099:                  count := 0;
100:                  sum := 0;
101:                  maxnum := -maxlong;      { Init max with smallest value }
102:                  minnum := maxlong        { Init min with largest value }
103:               END { for / with }
104:      END; { init_columns }
105:
106:
107:      PROCEDURE init_printer;
108:      { Initialize printer special features }
109:      VAR
110:         token          : string;
111:      BEGIN
112:
113:      { Initialization string is a series of ASCII codes such as:   }
114:      {                   27, 20, 25                                 }
115:      { which would send the three ASCI characters with these       }
116:      { values to the printer before printing begins.  This method  }
117:      { can be used to select various print options, select a custom }
118:      { character set, set forms lengths, etc. }
119:
120:         WITH pr DO
121:            WHILE length( init ) > 0 DO
122:               BEGIN
123:                  next_token( init, token );
124:                  write( pf, chr( value( token ) ) )
125:               END;
126:      END; { init_printer }
127:
128:
129:      PROCEDURE new_col;
130:      { Reinitialize nc entries in column statistics array }
131:      VAR
132:         i : integer;
133:      BEGIN
134:         FOR i := 1 TO rpn DO
135:            WITH col[i] DO
136:               count := 0
137:      END; { new_col }
138:
139:
140:      PROCEDURE form_feed;
```

```
141:    { Advance to top of form.  Set lines_done = 0 }
142:    BEGIN
143:       WITH pr DO
144:       IF pn > 0 THEN          { Prevent form feeds for labels, etc. }
145:          BEGIN
146:             writeln( pf );  { To flush some kinds of printer buffers }
147:             lines_done := lines_done + 1;
148:             IF ff
149:                THEN page( pf )                    { Use form feeds }
150:                ELSE WHILE lines_done < lpp DO
151:                     BEGIN
152:                        writeln( pf );        { Use slower line feeds }
153:                        lines_done := lines_done + 1
154:                     END { else / while }
155:          END; { if }
156:       lines_done := 0
157:    END; { form_feed }
158:
159:
160:    PROCEDURE zero_line;
161:    { Clear output line to all blanks }
162:    BEGIN
163:       fillchar( line, pr.cpl, chr( blank ) )
164:    END; { zero_line }
165:
166:
167:    PROCEDURE indent_line;
168:    { Indent a new line }
169:    BEGIN
170:       WITH pr DO
171:         IF indent > 0
172:            THEN write( pf, chr( blank ) : indent )
173:    END; { indent_line }
174:
175:
176:    FUNCTION line_len : integer;
177:    { Return current length of output line, ignoring trailing blanks }
178:    BEGIN
179:       WITH pr DO
180:          line_len := cpl + scan( -cpl, <>chr( blank ), line[ cpl - 1 ] )
181:    END; { line_len }
182:
183:
184:    PROCEDURE print_line;
185:    { Send line, if not blank, to output file pf }
186:    VAR
187:       len : integer;
188:    BEGIN
189:       len := line_len;
190:       IF len > 0 THEN
191:          BEGIN
192:             indent_line;
193:             write( pf, line : len );
194:             new_line
195:          END { if }
196:    END; { print_line }
197:
198:
199:    PROCEDURE underscore;
200:    { Write underscores under totaled columns }
201:    VAR
202:       i    : integer;
203:    BEGIN
204:       zero_line;
205:       FOR i := 1 TO rpn DO WITH rp[i] DO
206:          IF total
207:             THEN fillchar( line[ column ], width, uch );
```

```
208:        print_line
209:    END; { underscore }
210:
211:
212:    PROCEDURE center_line( s : string );
213:    { Insert the string in the center of the output line }
214:    VAR
215:       j : integer;
216:    BEGIN
217:       IF length( s ) > 0 THEN
218:          WITH pr DO
219:             BEGIN
220:                j := ( cpl DIV 2 ) - ( length(s) DIV 2 );
221:                moveleft( s[1],                  { Source }
222:                          line[ j ],             { Destination }
223:                          length( s ) )          { Count }
224:          END { if / with }
225:    END; { center_line }
226:
227:
228:    PROCEDURE new_page;
229:    { Advance to a new page }
230:    VAR
231:       i : integer;
232:
233:       PROCEDURE print_title;
234:       { Print title at top of a new page }
235:       VAR
236:          j : integer;
237:          s : string;
238:       BEGIN
239:          WITH pr DO
240:          BEGIN
241:             zero_line;
242:             date2string( today, s );
243:             s := concat( 'Date : ', s );
244:             moveleft( s[1],                  { Source }
245:                       line[0],               { Destination }
246:                       length(s) );           { Count }
247:
248:             str( pn, s );
249:             s := concat( 'Page-', s );
250:             j := cpl - length(s) - 2;
251:             moveleft( s[1],                  { Source }
252:                       line[ j ],             { Destination }
253:                       length(s) );           { Count }
254:
255:             center_line( title1 );
256:             print_line;
257:             IF length( title2 ) > 0 THEN
258:                BEGIN
259:                   zero_line;
260:                   center_line( title2 );
261:                   print_line
262:                END;
263:
264:             new_line;
265:             zero_line;
266:             fillchar( line, cpl - indent, uch );
267:             print_line
268:          END { with }
269:       END; { print_title }
270:
271:       PROCEDURE print_headers;
272:       { Print column headers using field names }
273:       VAR
274:          i, j : integer;
```

```
275:
276:              PROCEDURE insert_header( s  : string;
277:                                       c,
278:                                       w  : integer );
279:              { Center string "s" in output line at these coordinates }
280:              VAR
281:                 k : integer;
282:              BEGIN
283:                 IF length( s ) > 0 THEN
284:                    BEGIN
285:                       k := ( c + ( w DIV 2 ) ) - ( length( s ) DIV 2 );
286:                       IF k < c
287:                          THEN k := c;
288:                       moveleft( s[ 1 ],              { Source }
289:                                 line[ k ],           { Destination }
290:                                 length( s ) )        { Count }
291:                    END { if }
292:              END; { insert_header }
293:
294:           BEGIN
295:              FOR j := 1 TO 3 DO              { Three lines, second line optional }
296:              BEGIN
297:                 zero_line;
298:                 FOR i := 1 TO rpn DO
299:                 WITH rp[i] DO
300:                    CASE j OF
301:                       1 : insert_header( header1, column, width );
302:                       2 : insert_header( header2, column, width );
303:                       3 : fillchar( line[ column ], width, uch )
304:                    END; { case }
305:                 print_line
306:              END { for }
307:           END; { print_headers }
308:
309:     BEGIN { new_page }
310:
311:     { Pause for a new page if pause switch is on }
312:
313:        IF pr.pause THEN
314:           BEGIN
315:              gotoxy( 0, 0 );
316:              WHILE NOT verified( 'Paused: is the next page ready' ) DO
317:                 IF verified( 'Do you want to quit' )
318:                    THEN
319:                       quit_early
320:                    ELSE
321:                       gotoxy( 0, 0 );    { Repeat pause message }
322:              new_screen
323:           END; { if }
324:
325:        IF lines_done > 0               { Advance to top of next page }
326:           THEN form_feed;
327:
328:     { Print titles and headers, unless page number <= 0 (not paging) }
329:
330:        IF pr.top > 0 THEN
331:           BEGIN                         { Advance to top margin }
332:              FOR i := 1 TO pr.top DO
333:                 writeln( pf );
334:              lines_done := lines_done + pr.top
335:           END; { if }
336:
337:        IF pr.pn > 0 THEN
338:           BEGIN
339:              print_title;
340:              pr.pn := pr.pn + 1         { Advance page number }
341:           END; { if }
```

```
342:
343:          IF pr.headers
344:             THEN print_headers;
345:
346:          writeln( pf );
347:          lines_done := lines_done + 1
348:      END; { new_page }
349:
350:
351:      PROCEDURE new_line;
352:      { Advance to a new line }
353:      VAR
354:         i : integer;
355:      BEGIN
356:         FOR i := 0 TO pr.lsp DO
357:            BEGIN                          { Add carriage return(s) }
358:               writeln( pf );
359:               lines_done := lines_done + 1
360:            END;
361:         IF lines_done >= pr.lpp - pr.bot      { Check if new page needed }
362:            THEN new_page
363:      END; { new_line }
364:
365:
366:      PROCEDURE col_stat;
367:      { Update statistics with the current record }
368:      VAR
369:         i         : integer;
370:         new_value : long_integer;      { Temporary field value }
371:         s         : string;            { Fields as strings }
372:      BEGIN
373:         FOR i := 1 TO rpn DO
374:            WITH rp[i] DO
375:               IF ( total ) AND ( field > 0 ) THEN
376:               BEGIN
377:                  get_field( fn, field, s );
378:                  WITH fil_recs[fn].fil_msc.msc_flds[field] DO
379:                     lvalue( s, fld_decimals, new_value );  { String to value }
380:                  WITH col[i] DO
381:                  BEGIN
382:                     sum := sum + new_value;
383:                     IF new_value > maxnum THEN maxnum := new_value;
384:                     IF new_value < minnum THEN minnum := new_value
385:                  END { with }
386:               END { if }
387:      END; { col_stat }
388:
389:
390:      FUNCTION col_done( cn : integer ) : boolean;
391:      { True if the possibly multiple-line columns are finished }
392:      VAR
393:         i : integer;
394:      BEGIN
395:         IF cn <> 0                        { Column number }
396:            THEN
397:            col_done := false
398:            ELSE
399:            BEGIN
400:               FOR i := 1 TO rpn DO
401:                  WITH col[i] DO
402:                  WITH rp[i] DO
403:                  WITH fil_recs[fn].fil_msc.msc_flds[field] DO
404:                     IF ( count < fld_len ) AND ( NOT trunc ) THEN
405:                        BEGIN
406:                           col_done := false;
407:                           exit( col_done )
408:                        END; { if }
```

```
409:                    col_done := true
410:                END; { else }
411:        END; { col_done }
412:
413:
414:        PROCEDURE assemble( VAR cn : integer );
415:        { Assemble fields from current record into a new output line }
416:        { "cn" = starting column number }
417:        VAR
418:            last_blank    : integer;        { Last blank in character string }
419:            offset        : integer;        { Column right just. offset }
420:            s             : string;         { Fields as strings }
421:        BEGIN
422:            REPEAT
423:                cn := cn + 1;                       { Do next column, 1 .. rpn }
424:                WITH rp[cn] DO
425:                 WITH col[cn] DO
426:                  WITH fil_recs[fn].fil_msc DO
427:                   WITH msc_flds[ field ] DO
428:                BEGIN
429:                  get_field( fn, field, s );                   { Read field }
430:
431:                { Delete characters already printed if any }
432:
433:                  delete( s, 1, count );
434:                  IF length( s ) > 0 THEN
435:                  BEGIN
436:
437:                { Force break between words for character fields }
438:                { unless truncating (trunc=true) or if entire }
439:                { field can fit in the column width remaining. }
440:
441:                    IF ( length(s) > width ) THEN
442:                      BEGIN
443:                        s := copy( s, 1, width );
444:                        IF ( NOT trunc ) AND ( fld_type = dat_char ) THEN
445:                        BEGIN
446:                          last_blank := length(s) +
447:                            scan( -length(s),
448:                                  =chr( blank ),
449:                                  s[ length(s) ] );
450:                          IF ( last_blank > 0 ) AND ( last_blank < length(s) )
451:                              THEN s := copy( s, 1, last_blank )
452:                        END
453:                      END; { if }
454:
455:                { Set column offset so that numeric fields are right }
456:                { justified even if the column width is greater than }
457:                { the field length. }
458:
459:                    IF fld_type = dat_number
460:                        THEN offset := max( 0, width - length(s) )
461:                        ELSE offset := 0;
462:
463:                { Insert characters from string into the output line }
464:
465:                    fillchar( line[ column ], width, chr(blank) );
466:                    moveleft( s[ 1 ],                      { Source }
467:                              line[ column + offset ],     { Destination }
468:                              length( s ) );               { Count }
469:
470:                { Keep track of how many characters have been printed }
471:
472:                    count := count + length( s )
473:
474:                  END { if }
475:                END { withs }
476:            UNTIL ( rp[cn].eoln ) OR ( cn >= rpn ): { Forced eoln or last column}
```

```
477:        IF cn >= rpn
478:            THEN cn := 0         { Cn is a "circular" index. }
479:    END; { assemble }
480:
481:
482:    PROCEDURE print_rec;
483:    { Print current record }
484:    VAR
485:        cn,                          { Column number }
486:        i     : integer;
487:        num_done : boolean;
488:        s : string;
489:    BEGIN
490:        new_col;                     { Start new column stats }
491:        cn := 0;
492:        col_stat;                    { Adjust sum, min, max. }
493:        num_done := false;
494:        WHILE NOT col_done( cn ) DO  { While not finished with record }
495:            BEGIN
496:                zero_line;           { Start a new output line }
497:                IF NOT num_done THEN
498:                    BEGIN            { Insert record number }
499:                        num2string( fil_recs[fn].fil_recptr, 5, '0', s );
500:                        moveleft( s[1], line[0], 5 );
501:                        num_done := true  { Don't repeat until next record }
502:                    END;
503:                assemble( cn );      { Assemble an output line }
504:                print_line           { Print the line }
505:            END; { while }
506:        FOR i := 1 TO pr.lbr DO      { Blank lines between records }
507:            new_line
508:    END; { print_rec }
509:
510:
511:    PROCEDURE stat_line( stat_num : integer; stat_name : alpha );
512:    { Print a line of statistics }
513:    VAR
514:        i            : integer;
515:        name_done   : boolean;
516:        s           : string;
517:    BEGIN
518:        zero_line;
519:        name_done := false;
520:        FOR i := 1 TO rpn DO
521:         WITH rp[i] DO
522:          WITH fil_recs[fn].fil_msc.msc_flds[ field ] DO
523:           WITH col[i] DO
524:        IF total THEN
525:        BEGIN
526:            IF NOT name_done THEN
527:                BEGIN
528:                    moveleft( stat_name,            { Source }
529:                              line[0],              { Destination }
530:                              alpha_size + 1 );     { Count }
531:                    name_done := true
532:                END; { if }
533:            CASE stat_num OF
534:                1 : str( sum, s );
535:                2 : str( minnum, s );
536:                3 : str( maxnum, s );
537:                4 : str( ( sum DIV recs_done ), s )      { Average }
538:            END; { case }
539:            IF length( s ) > 0 THEN
540:                BEGIN
541:                    IF fld_decimals > 0
542:                        THEN insert( '.', s,
543:                                     ( length( s ) - fld_decimals + 1 ) );
544:                    moveleft( s[1],
```

```
545:                                line[ column + width - length( s ) ],
546:                                length( s ) )
547:                 END { if }
548:             END; { if }
549:             print_line
550:         END; { stat_line }
551:
552:
553:     PROCEDURE print_statistics;
554:     { Print totals, etc for this run }
555:     CONST
556:         lines_needed = 7; { Lines needed for the statistics report }
557:     BEGIN
558:         IF lines_done >= pr.lpp - pr.bot - lines_needed
559:             THEN new_page;
560:
561:         underscore;
562:         { .............1234567890. }              { <--- Typing aid }
563:         stat_line( 1, 'Total      ' );            { Note : these assume }
564:         stat_line( 2, 'Minimum    ' );            {  alpha_size = 9      }
565:         stat_line( 3, 'Maximum    ' );            {  in PDBSUNIT.        }
566:         stat_line( 4, 'Average    ' );
567:
568:         new_line;
569:         indent_line;
570:         writeln( pf, recs_done, ' records processed' );
571:         lines_done := lines_done + 1;
572:         form_feed
573:     END; { print_statistics }
574:
575:
576: BEGIN { print_report }
577:     clrscrn;
578:     IF verified( concat( 'Prepare ', pr.outfile, '  Ready' ) ) THEN
579:     BEGIN
580:         close( pf );
581:         rewrite( pf, pr.outfile );
582:         perform( ioresult );
583:         zero_line;
584:         init_printer;
585:         init_columns;
586:         lines_done := 0;
587:         recs_done := 0;
588:
589:         new_screen;
590:         new_page;
591:         FOR rec_num := 1 TO fil_recs[fn].fil_msc.msc_lastrec DO
592:             BEGIN
593:                 IF keypress
594:                     THEN checkkey;
595:                 perform( seek_rec( fn, rec_num ) );
596:                 IF match( fn ) THEN
597:                     BEGIN
598:                         print_rec;          { Print current record }
599:                         recs_done := recs_done + 1
600:                     END
601:             END; { for }
602:         print_statistics;
603:
604:         close( pf, lock )      { Lock in case its a disk file }
605:     END { if }
606: END; { segment print_report }
001: {-----------------------------------------------------------------------}
002: {                                                                       }
003: {    REPORT2.TEXT  --  Part two of the REPORT program                    }
004: {                                                                       }
005: {-----------------------------------------------------------------------}
006:
```

```
007:
008: segment FUNCTION load_rprt( VAR rp        : rprt_plan;
009:                             VAR rpmax      : integer    ) : pdbs_err;
010: { Load report format file }
011: VAR
012:    err_code            : pdbs_err;
013:    i                   : integer;       { Miscellaneous index }
014:    rprt_name           : pdbs_fname;    { Report data file name }
015:    rprt_num            : integer;       { Report data file number }
016:
017:    PROCEDURE perform( n : pdbs_err );
018:    { Perform function returning n.  Exit on any errors. }
019:    BEGIN
020:       IF n <> 0 THEN
021:          BEGIN
022:             load_rprt := n;
023:             exit( load_rprt )
024:          END { if }
025:    END; { perform }
026:
027:    FUNCTION report_loaded : pdbs_err;
028:    { Load report using load_rprt globals }
029:    VAR
030:       err_code        : pdbs_err;
031:       fld_num         : integer;       { Field number }
032:       i               : integer;       { Miscellaneous index }
033:       s               : string;        { Holds fields as strings }
034:    BEGIN
035:       promptln( 'Loading report format' );
036:       report_loaded := 0;   { Unless something goes wrong }
037:       WITH fil_recs[ rprt_num ] DO
038:       BEGIN
039:          rpmax := fil_msc.msc_lastrec;
040:          FOR i := 1 TO rpmax DO
041:          BEGIN
042:             err_code := seek_rec( rprt_num, i );
043:             IF err_code <> 0 THEN
044:                BEGIN
045:                   report_loaded := err_code;
046:                   exit( report_loaded )
047:                END;
048:             WITH rp[i] DO
049:             FOR fld_num := 1 TO 8 DO
050:             BEGIN
051:                get_field( rprt_num, fld_num, s );
052:                strip( s );
053:                IF fld_num IN [ 4, 5, 6 ]
054:                   THEN bumpstrup( s );       { Upper case conversion }
055:                CASE fld_num OF
056:                   1 : field  := value( s );
057:                   2 : column := value( s );
058:                   3 : width  := value( s );
059:                   4 : trunc  := ( s = 'T' );
060:                   5 : eoln   := ( s = 'T' );
061:                   6 : total  := ( s = 'T' );
062:                   7 : header1 := s;
063:                   8 : header2 := s
064:                END { case }
065:             END { with / for / with }
066:          END { for }
067:       END { with }
068:    END; { report_loaded }
069:
070: BEGIN { load_rprt }
071:    rpmax := 0;
072:    IF get_file_name( 'Using .RPRT format file ? ', rprt_name ) THEN
073:    BEGIN
```

```
074:         remove_ext( rprt_name );                        { name.PDBF -> name }
075:         rprt_name := concat( rprt_name, ext_rprt );     { name -> name.RPRT }
076:         perform( open_file( rprt_num, rprt_name ) );    { Open report file }
077:         err_code := report_loaded;                      { Delay err check }
078:         perform( close_file( rprt_num, no_update ) );   {  until file closed }
079:         perform( err_code );                            {  then check load. }
080:         IF rpmax <= 0
081:           THEN
082:             load_rprt := 23        { File empty error }
083:       END ELSE
084:         load_rprt := 25            { Interrupted by user error }
085: END; { segment load_rprt }
086:
087:
088: segment PROCEDURE get_spec(      file_num              : integer;
089:                            VAR pr                     : print_spec;
090:                            VAR specs_initialized : boolean;
091:                                 arg                   : string        );
092: { Load output specifications }
093: CONST
094:    xspec               = 27;            { X coordinate for spec entry }
095:    yspec               = 2;             { Y coordinate for first spec line }
096:
097: VAR
098:    bool_set : SET OF 1 .. max_spec;
099:    command,
100:    item                : string;
101:    spec_name           : pdbs_fname;
102:    spec_num,
103:    num                 : integer;
104:    ok                  : boolean;
105:
106:    PROCEDURE init_spec;
107:    { Initialize default settings for printer specifications }
108:    BEGIN
109:       IF NOT specs_initialized THEN
110:         WITH pr DO
111:           BEGIN
112:             top           := 3;              { Top margin }
113:             bot           := 5;              { Bottom margin }
114:             lpp           := 66;             { Lines per page }
115:             lsp           := 0;              { Line spacing }
116:             lbr           := 0;              { Blank lines between records }
117:             indent        := 0;              { Spaces to indent each line }
118:             cpl           := default_width;       { Chars per line }
119:             pn            := 1;              { Starting page number }
120:             headers       := true;           { Print column headers switch }
121:             ff            := false;          { Use form feeds switch }
122:             pause         := false;          { Sheet-feed pause switch }
123:             outfile       := 'PRINTER:';     { Output file name }
124:             init          := '';             { Printer initialization }
125:             title1        := fil_recs[ file_num ].fil_name;
126:             title2        := arg            { Search arguments }
127:           END { with }
128:       END; { init_spec }
129:
130:
131:    PROCEDURE show_bool( b : boolean );
132:    { Display "True" or "False" }
133:    BEGIN
134:       IF b
135:         THEN writeln( 'True' )
136:         ELSE writeln( 'False' )
137:    END; { show_bool }
138:
139:
140:    PROCEDURE get_bool( VAR b : boolean );
```

```
141:    { Read true / false value from keyboard }
142:    VAR
143:       ch : char;
144:    BEGIN
145:       ch := cap( getch( ch ) );
146:       b := ( ch = 'T' );
147:       show_bool( b )
148:    END; { get_bool }
149:
150:
151:    PROCEDURE show_spec( VAR pr : print_spec   );
152:    { Display current setting in the print rec plan }
153:    BEGIN
154:       gotoxy( 0, yspec );
155:       WITH pr DO
156:          BEGIN
157:             writeln( '  1) Top margin .......... ', top );
158:             writeln( '  2) Bottom margin ....... ', bot );
159:             writeln( '  3) Lines per page ...... ', lpp );
160:             writeln( '  4) Chars per line ...... ', cpl );
161:             writeln( '  5) Line spacing ........ ', lsp );
162:             writeln( '  6) Lines between recs .. ', lbr );
163:             writeln( '  7) Spaces to indent .... ', indent );
164:             writeln( '  8) First page number ... ', pn );
165:             write(   '  9) Print headers ....... ' ); show_bool( headers );
166:             write(   ' 10) Use form feeds ...... ' ); show_bool( ff );
167:             write(   ' 11) Pause each page ..... ' ); show_bool( pause );
168:             writeln( ' 12) Output file name .... ', outfile );
169:             writeln( ' 13) Printer init ........ ', init );
170:             writeln( ' 14) Title 1 ............. ', title1 );
171:             writeln( ' 15) Title 2 ............. ', title2 );
172:             writeln;
173:             writeln( '  >> Press RETURN to begin report <<' )
174:          END { with }
175:    END; { show_spec }
176:
177:
178:    FUNCTION load_spec( file_name : string ) : pdbs_err;
179:    { Load global pr output specifications from .SPEC file }
180:    CONST
181:       s_len        = 40;   { Maximum string length in spec file }
182:    VAR
183:       prn, i       : integer;
184:       err_code     : pdbs_err;
185:       s            : string;
186:
187:       PROCEDURE perform( n : pdbs_err );
188:       { Perform function returning n.  Exit on any errors. }
189:       BEGIN
190:          IF n <> 0 THEN
191:             BEGIN
192:                load_spec := n;
193:                exit( load_spec )
194:             END { if }
195:       END; { perform }
196:
197:    BEGIN { load_spec }
198:       remove_ext( file_name );
199:       file_name := concat( file_name, ext_spec );
200:       perform( open_file( prn, file_name ) );
201:       err_code := seek_rec( prn, 1 );
202:       IF err_code = 0 THEN
203:          WITH pr DO
204:             FOR i := 1 TO max_spec DO
205:                BEGIN
206:                   get_field( prn, i, s );
207:                   strip( s );        { Remove leading & trailing blanks }
```

```
208:                        IF i IN bool_set
209:                           THEN bumpstrup( s );    { Upper case conversion}
210:                        CASE i OF
211:                           1 : top        := value(s);
212:                           2 : bot        := value(s);
213:                           3 : lpp        := value(s);
214:                           4 : cpl        := value(s);
215:                           5 : lsp        := value(s);
216:                           6 : lbr        := value(s);
217:                           7 : indent     := value(s);
218:                           8 : pn         := value(s);
219:                           9 : headers    := ( s = 'T' );
220:                          10 : ff         := ( s = 'T' );
221:                          11 : pause      := ( s = 'T' );
222:                          12 : BEGIN
223:                                   IF length( s ) > 0
224:                                      THEN outfile := s
225:                                      ELSE outfile := 'CONSOLE:'
226:                               END;
227:                          13 : init       := s;
228:                          14 : BEGIN
229:                                   IF length( s ) > 0
230:                                      THEN title1 := s
231:                                      ELSE title1 := fil_recs[ file_num ].fil_name
232:                               END;
233:                          15 : BEGIN
234:                                   IF length( s ) > 0
235:                                      THEN title2 := s
236:                                      ELSE title2 := arg
237:                               END
238:                        END   { case }
239:                   END; { for }
240:         perform( close_file( prn, no_update ) );
241:         perform( err_code );              { Check seek errors after file closed }
242:         load_spec := 0                    { No errors detected }
243:      END; { load_spec }
244:
245: BEGIN { get_spec }
246:    bool_set := [ 9, 10, 11 ];            { Boolean items in print_spec }
247:    REPEAT
248:       ok := true;
249:       IF get_file_name( 'What .SPEC file (ret=default)? ', spec_name )
250:          THEN ok := executed( load_spec( spec_name ) )
251:          ELSE init_spec      { Use default formats }
252:    UNTIL ok;
253:    clrscrn;
254:    show_spec( pr );
255:    REPEAT
256:       promptat( 0, 0, 'Enter number to change ' );
257:       readln( command );
258:       num := value( command );
259:       IF inrange( num, 1, max_spec ) THEN
260:          BEGIN
261:             gotoxy( xspec, yspec + num - 1 );
262:             clreoln;
263:             IF NOT ( num IN bool_set )
264:                THEN readln( item );
265:             WITH pr DO CASE num OF
266:                1 : top        := value( item );
267:                2 : bot        := value( item );
268:                3 : lpp        := value( item );
269:                4 : cpl        := value( item );
270:                5 : lsp        := value( item );
271:                6 : lbr        := value( item );
272:                7 : indent     := value( item );
273:                8 : pn         := value( item );
274:                9 : get_bool( headers );
275:               10 : get_bool( ff );
```

```
276:                   11 : get_bool( pause );
277:                   12 : outfile  := item;
278:                   13 : init     := item;
279:                   14 : title1   := item;
280:                   15 : title2   := item
281:             END { with / case }
282:          END { if }
283:    UNTIL length( command ) = 0;
284:    remove_ext( pr.outfile );          { Output cannot be PDBS data file }
285:    specs_initialized := true          { Prevent reinitialization next time }
286: END; { segment get_spec }
```

3

Transfers and Transformations

COPY / APPEND / MERGE / MODIFY /
READTEXT / WRITETEXT

COPY

By the time you have created the same report format file two or three times, you'll realize the value of being able to make copies of your data files.

Copy creates a new data file with the same structure as another file. It creates an exact duplicate of the original or source file structure. It does *not* copy data that may be stored in the file.

One good use for *copy* is to create a series of report formats (.RPRT files), output specifications (.SPEC files) for the *report* program, and custom screen designs (.SCRN files) for the *editor*. You might want to *create* a set of template files and then make copies of their structures for preparing special-purpose files. I like to keep REPORTS.PDBF, SPECS.PDBF, and SCREENS.PDBF templates on disk for this reason. To design a new report format, I *copy* REPORTS.PDBF to R1.RPRT or to some other file name.

Safe Data Entry Using Copy

You may also want to use copies of your data files for new record entry instead of appending new records directly onto the end of the main files. This is a good way to guard against accidents and gives an extra degree of control over new entries into the data base.

It would be possible, for example, to create copies of the structure of a main data file stored on a hard disk drive. These copies could be placed on inexpensive floppy disks and given to operators for keying in data on their own personal com-

73

puters, perhaps at home. After the information is verified, using *list* or *report*, the data stored on the ''floppy copies'' are inserted into the main data base using the next program in this chapter, *append*.

We will see other uses for *copy* as we develop other PDBS programs.

Using Copy

When you execute *copy*, you are asked:

Copy structure of?

Supply the name of any PDBS data file. If the file ends in .PDBF, you do not have to type the file name extension. To copy .SCRN, .RPRT, and other special-purpose data files, you must enter both the file name and the extension.

Next, you are asked:

Copy to what file?

Enter the name of the file to which you want to copy. The same file name rules apply. *Copy* will refuse to erase a file if it finds one with the same name. To reuse a name, the old file must first be removed with the UCSD filer's R(emove command.

```
001: {$S+,I-}              { Compiler swapping on; I/O error checking off }
002:
003: PROGRAM copy; uses pdbsunit;
004:
005: {-----------------------------------------------------------------------}
006: {                                                                       }
007: {    PROGRAM        :  Copy data file structure to a new file.          }
008: {    LANGUAGE       :  UCSD Pascal / Apple Pascal 1.1                    }
009: {                                                                       }
010: {    Copyright (C) 1983 by Tom Swan. All commercial rights reserved.    }
011: {                                                                       }
012: {-----------------------------------------------------------------------}
013:
014: VAR
015:    from_name, to_name      : pdbs_fname;    { File names }
016:    from_number             : integer;       { File numbers }
017:
018:
019: BEGIN
020:    clrscrn;
021:    WHILE get_file_name( 'Copy structure of? ', from_name ) DO
022:    BEGIN
023:       clreosc;
024:       IF executed( open_file( from_number, from_name ) ) THEN
025:       BEGIN
026:          IF get_file_name( 'Copy to what file? ', to_name ) THEN
027:          IF file_not_in_use( to_name ) THEN
028:          IF executed(
029:           make_file( to_name, fil_recs[ from_number ].fil_msc ) )
030:             THEN writeln( fil_recs[ from_number ].fil_name,
031:                          ' --> ', to_name );
```

```
032:            IF NOT executed( close_file( from_number, no_update ) )
033:               THEN exit( PROGRAM )      { Extremely unlikely }
034:         END; { if }
035:         gotoxy( 0, 0 )
036:      END { while }
037: END.
```

APPEND

When you want a quick way to attach records from one file onto the end of another, use *append*. As mentioned in the instructions for *copy*, one use for *append* is to add records from data entry files into a main data base.

Append requires that the two files to be appended have identical structures. If you are not sure, use *status* to check the file structure of both files before appending. If the structures are not equal, *append* will refuse to operate. To attach records from a file with a different structure, use the slower *merge* program, presented next.

It is possible to append in the wrong direction. You would not, for example, want to append from the main data file into the data entry copy. To prevent such an error, you would be wise to write-protect the data entry file—in other words, write-protect the file *from* which you are copying. If you enter the file names in the wrong order, no changes will be made to either file, and you can repeat the *append* operation.

It is also possible to append a file to itself. The file will grow to exactly twice as long as it was before appending and will contain a duplicate record for each record in the file. To be honest, I haven't found a practical use for this "feature," but no doubt someone somewhere will.

The best way to prevent errors when appending is to make backup copies of all files before beginning. This should go without saying, but I am continually surprised to find people ignoring this most basic computer rule.

As a real-life example, I installed a program two years ago to manage a large film library in a school system. Every day for two years, with unfailing repetition, people in the library copied all their data onto floppy disks. A couple of days ago, after something like a billion rotations,* the motor on their hard disk drive burned out.

After purchasing a new hard disk, it took about 45 minutes to recover all their data and restore their programming. Altogether, they lost about a day's worth of work, which was easily reentered. Without the backup copy, an entire year's worth of film reservations would have been irretrievably lost. Although they were very pleased with my successful efforts to restore their computer system, the truth is they are their own heroes in this story.

---

*At 3,600 RPM, that's 1.7 million rotations in an eight-hour day. Given a conservative 250 working days a year, that disk drive went around about 900 million times before giving up.

```
001: {$S+,I-}                { Compiler swapping on; I/O error checking off }
002:
003: PROGRAM append; uses pdbsunit;
004:
005: {-----------------------------------------------------------------------}
006: {                                                                       }
007: {    PROGRAM        :  Append records from one file onto another        }
008: {    LANGUAGE       :  UCSD Pascal / Apple Pascal 1.1                    }
009: {                                                                       }
010: {    Copyright (C) 1983 by Tom Swan. All commercial rights reserved.    }
011: {                                                                       }
012: {-----------------------------------------------------------------------}
013:
014: VAR
015:     from_name, to_name       : pdbs_fname;    { PDBS file names }
016:     from_number, to_number   : integer;       { PDBS file numbers }
017:     mode                     : close_option;
018:
019:
020: FUNCTION append_files( sn, dn : integer ) : pdbs_err;
021: { Append file sn (source) records to file dn (destination) }
022: VAR
023:     recs_appended,                            { Number of records appended }
024:     rn                   : integer;           { Record number }
025:     work_area            : binary_page;       { Holds records }
026:
027:     PROCEDURE perform( n : pdbs_err );
028:     { Execute functions that return error codes.  Exit on any error. }
029:     BEGIN
030:        IF n <> 0 THEN
031:           BEGIN
032:              append_files := n;       { Pass error back to caller }
033:              exit( append_files )
034:           END
035:     END; { perform }
036:
037: BEGIN
038:     clreosc;
039:     recs_appended := 0;
040:     writeln( 'Appending' );
041:     FOR rn := 1 TO fil_recs[sn].fil_msc.msc_lastrec DO
042:     BEGIN
043:        perform( read_rec( sn, rn, work_area ) );
044:        perform( append_rec( dn, work_area ) );
045:        recs_appended := recs_appended + 1;
046:        write( '.' )  { Feedback }
047:     END; { for }
048:     writeln( chr( ret ), recs_appended, ' record(s) appended ' );
049:     append_files := 0
050: END; { append_files }
051:
052:
053: FUNCTION formats_equal( fn1, fn2 : integer ) : boolean;
054: { Test data format (structure) of both files }
055: { Return true if equal; false if not equal }
056: VAR
057:     i : integer;
058: BEGIN
059:     formats_equal := false; { Unless passing all tests }
060:     WITH fil_recs[fn1].fil_msc DO
061:     BEGIN
062:      IF ( msc_recsize = fil_recs[fn2].fil_msc.msc_recsize ) AND
063:         ( msc_nflds   = fil_recs[fn2].fil_msc.msc_nflds   ) THEN
064:      BEGIN
065:       FOR i := 1 TO msc_nflds DO
066:        WITH msc_flds[i] DO
067:         IF ( fld_type <> fil_recs[fn2].fil_msc.msc_flds[i].fld_type ) OR
```

```
068:              ( fld_len   <> fil_recs[fn2].fil_msc.msc_flds[i].fld_len   ) OR
069:              ( fld_pos   <> fil_recs[fn2].fil_msc.msc_flds[i].fld_pos   )
070:            THEN exit( formats_equal ); { Failed }
071:      formats_equal := true
072:    END { if }
073:   END { with }
074: END; { formats_equal }
075:
076:
077: BEGIN
078:   clrscrn;
079:   WHILE get_file_name( 'Append from what file? ', from_name ) DO
080:   BEGIN
081:     mode := no_update;
082:     IF executed( open_file( from_number, from_name ) ) THEN
083:     BEGIN
084:        IF get_file_name( 'Append onto what file? ', to_name ) THEN
085:        IF executed( open_file( to_number, to_name ) ) THEN
086:        BEGIN
087:          IF NOT formats_equal( from_number, to_number )
088:             THEN writeln( 'Data formats not equal' )
089:             ELSE
090:          IF executed( append_files( from_number, to_number ) )
091:             THEN mode := update;
092:          IF ( executed( close_file( to_number, mode        ) ) ) AND
093:             ( mode = update )
094:             THEN write( from_name, ' appended to ', to_name )
095:        END; { if }
096:        IF NOT executed( close_file( from_number, no_update ) )
097:           THEN exit( PROGRAM )      { Extremely unlikely }
098:     END; { if }
099:     gotoxy( 0, 0 )
100:   END { while }
101: END.
```

MERGE

The previous program, *append*, can only be used to attach records from one file onto another file with an identical structure. *Merge* does the same job as *append*, except that the two files are allowed to have different structures.

There are many reasons why you would want to do this. The primary use for *merge* is to reorganize your data into new formats. When used in conjunction with the *modify* program, *merge* allows fields to be deleted, added, and changed to new data types or lengths.

Another use for merge is to insert data from one file into a main data file, much in the way *copy* and *append* were used to maintain floppy disk data entry files. You might have a file containing only names and phone numbers. These can be merged into a data file that contains those fields as well as places for addresses, states, and zip codes.

How to Use Merge

For a successful merge, the field names to be combined must be equal. The two fields may be defined to be different data types and may be of different lengths. Only their names must be the same.

The best way to learn how to use merge is with an example. Using The Company's data base, first *create* the phone list data file, named PHONE.PDBF, with a structure as shown in Fig. 3-1. In this case, the field definitions are similar to the fields of the same names in the CUSTOMERS.PDBF data file (see Fig. 1-2). I decided, however, to allow only 15 characters for the name and increased the length of a phone number from 12 to 14.

Execute *merge* and follow the dialogue in Fig. 3-2. Provided no errors were received, you should be able to *list* the data in PHONE.PDBF. This new list should be similar to the list in Fig. 3-3.

```
PHONE.PDBF
Record size ............. 30
Number of fields ........ 2
Maximum record number ... 34
Records in use .......... 0
Records not used ........ 34
Date created ............ 20-Jul-83
Date last updated ....... 20-Jul-83

#  NAME          TYPE      LEN DEC POS

1  C.NAME        Char       15   0   1
2  C.PHONE       Char       14   0  16
```

Fig. 3-1. *The structure of a file to be merged with The Company's customer file. The length of field C.NAME has been shortened from 30 to 15 characters.*

```
Merge from what file? CUSTOMERS
Merge into what file? PHONE
Merge fields? [<field>,<field>,|ret|?]
C.NAME, C.PHONE
Merging
.......
7 record(s) --> PHONE.PDBF
```

Fig. 3-2. *Execute the merge program and follow this dialogue to merge the names and phone numbers from The Company's customer data file into the new phone list file.*

```
PHONE.PDBF :
        C.NAME---------  C.PHONE-------
00001  Danzig, Irving    800-555-1212
00002  Diffenforker, C   801-555-1234
00003  Franklin, Benja   900-555-1212
00004  Pascal, Blaise    901-555-4321
00005  Slumgullion, St   800-555-1212
00006  Stallion, Horac   900-555-1212
00007  West, Martin Qu   801-555-1111
```

Fig. 3-3. *A listing of the new phone list file after merging from The Company's customer file. The short name field caused many of the names to be truncated, or chopped off at the end.*

Notice what happened to the names. The ones that were longer than 15 characters had their tail ends chopped. This is always a danger when decreasing the size of a field and merging.

Changing Data Types

When merging to different data types (merging a character field into a number field, for example), other peculiarities may become evident. Any alphabetic characters in the original data will be ignored, as these characters are not allowed in the number data type. (See Fig. 1-4).

Usually you will have more of a need to change the lengths of fields rather than the data types. You are not restricted to this kind of merge but should probably perform a few tests before doing major surgery on your data.

The Merge Program

The function *match_fields* at line 21 is similar to the function *common_fields* in the PDBS library unit. (See Chapter Eight.) *Match_fields* returns a boolean "true" or "false" value. If "true," then at least one field name was found to be the same in both the source (*sn*) and destination (*dn*) files. If *match_fields* returns "true," then the two *fld_order* arrays, *source* and *dest*, are set to the field numbers in the two files that match.

Function *merge_files* uses the two arrays, or maps, to find out which fields to transfer where. The action of the transfer can be seen in lines 92 through 101. *Get-_field* reads a source field into the string variable *s*. If the destination field is a number, then lines 97–99 make sure that number is in the proper format (line 97) and is right-justified (lines 98 and 99), as all numbers must be in PDBS files. Finally, line 101 writes the converted field to the destination file with a call to procedure *put-_field*.

```
001: {$S+,I-}              { Compiler swapping on; I/O error checking off }
002:
003: PROGRAM merge; uses pdbsunit;
004:
005: {------------------------------------------------------------------}
006: {                                                                  }
007: {     PROGRAM        :  Merge (selected fields) from PDBS files     }
008: {     LANGUAGE       :  UCSD Pascal / Apple Pascal 1.1              }
009: {                                                                  }
010: {     Copyright (C) 1983 by Tom Swan. All commercial rights reserved. }
011: {                                                                  }
012: {------------------------------------------------------------------}
013:
014: VAR
015:     from_name, to_name      : pdbs_fname;    { PDBS file names }
016:     from_number, to_number  : integer;       { PDBS file numbers }
017:     mode                    : close_option;
018:     recs_merged             : integer;       { Number of records merged }
019:
020:
021: FUNCTION match_fields(    sn, dn      : integer;
022:                       VAR source, dest : fld_order ) : boolean;
```

```
023: { True if fields in source array can be matched with fields of }
024: {  identical names in destination file.  If so, a mapping of each }
025: {  field number is returned in dest array.  i.e. source[i]==>dest[i] }
026: { This routine differs from the PDBSUNIT common_fields function }
027: {  which requires exact matches of fields in two files.  Match_fields }
028: {  only requires the field names to be the same. }
029: VAR
030:     field, k       : integer;      { Field number, misc integer }
031:     name           : alpha;        { Field names }
032: BEGIN
033:     match_fields := false;   { Unless all operations completed }
034:     FOR field := 1 TO source[0] DO WITH fil_recs[sn].fil_msc DO
035:        BEGIN
036:           name := msc_flds[ source[ field ] ].fld_name;
037:           k := fld_number( fil_recs[dn].fil_msc, name );
038:           IF k <= 0 THEN
039:              BEGIN
040:                 writeln( 'No field ', name );
041:                 exit( match_fields )      { No match on fld_name }
042:              END; { if }
043:           dest[field] := k
044:        END; { for }
045:     dest[0] := source[0];    { Number of field numbers in array }
046:     match_fields := true
047: END; { match_fields }
048:
049:
050: FUNCTION merge_files(    sn, dn       : integer;
051:                     VAR recs_merged : integer ) : pdbs_err;
052: { Merge selected fields from file sn to file dn.  Report num recs merged. }
053: VAR
054:     field,                         { Field number }
055:     rn                : integer;   { Record number }
056:     dest,                          { Destination field numbers }
057:     source            : fld_order; { Source field numbers }
058:     s                 : string;    { Fields as strings }
059:     blank_rec         : binary_page; { For appending blank records }
060:
061:     PROCEDURE perform( n : pdbs_err );
062:     { Execute a function that returns an error code }
063:     BEGIN
064:        IF n <> 0 THEN
065:           BEGIN
066:              merge_files := n;      { Pass error code back to caller }
067:              exit( merge_files )    { Cancel the merge }
068:           END { if }
069:     END; { perform }
070:
071: BEGIN
072:     recs_merged := 0;
073:     IF load_order( 'Merge fields?', sn, source ) THEN
074:     IF match_fields( sn, dn, source, dest ) THEN
075:     BEGIN
076:        writeln( 'Merging' );
077:        zero_rec( dn, blank_rec );          { Prepare a blank record }
078:        FOR rn := 1 TO fil_recs[sn].fil_msc.msc_lastrec DO
079:        BEGIN
080:          { Advance source file to record number rn }
081:             perform( seek_rec( sn, rn ) );
082:
083:          { Append a blank record onto the destination file }
084:             perform( append_rec( dn, blank_rec ) );
085:
086:          { Copy status byte of source record to destination }
087:             perform( mark_rec( dn, rec_status( sn ) ) );
088:
089:          { Convert and transfer each field specified by user }
```

```
090:                 FOR field := 1 TO source[0] DO   { Source[0]=number of fields }
091:                 BEGIN
092:                    get_field( sn, source[ field ], s );
093:                    strip( s );    { Remove leading, trailing spaces }
094:                    WITH fil_recs[dn].fil_msc.msc_flds[ dest[ field ] ] DO
095:                      IF ( fld_type = dat_number ) AND ( length(s) > 0 ) THEN
096:                       BEGIN { normalize and right justify s if numeric }
097:                          normalize( s, fld_decimals );
098:                          WHILE length( s ) < fld_len DO
099:                             insert( ' ', s, 1 )
100:                       END; { with / if }
101:                       put_field( dn, dest[ field ], s )
102:                    END; { for }
103:
104:                    recs_merged := recs_merged + 1;
105:                    write( '.' )       { Feedback }
106:
107:          END { for }
108:      END; { if }
109:      writeln;
110:      merge_files := 0            { No errors }
111: END; { merge_files }
112:
113:
114: BEGIN
115:    clrscrn;
116:    WHILE get_file_name( 'Merge from what file? ', from_name ) DO
117:     BEGIN
118:       clreosc;
119:       mode := no_update;
120:       IF executed( open_file( from_number, from_name ) ) THEN
121:       BEGIN
122:          IF get_file_name( 'Merge into what file? ', to_name ) THEN
123:          IF executed( open_file( to_number, to_name ) ) THEN
124:          BEGIN
125:             IF executed(
126:               merge_files( from_number, to_number, recs_merged ) )
127:                  THEN mode := update;
128:             IF ( executed( close_file( to_number, mode        ) ) ) AND
129:                  ( mode = update )
130:                  THEN writeln( recs_merged, ' record(s) --> ', to_name )
131:          END; { if }
132:          IF NOT executed( close_file( from_number, no_update ) )
133:             THEN exit( PROGRAM )    { Extremely unlikely }
134:       END; { if }
135:       gotoxy( 0, 0 )
136:     END { while }
137: END.
```

MODIFY

The ability to modify the structure of a data file is essential to good data base management but is not always provided by the software. PDBS allows any file to be retailored as many times as needed. Fields can be added or subtracted and changed in any way with little or no effect on the data already entered.

Some modifications require the old records to be merged into the new format; some do not require a merge. If you are following along with The Company's example data base, you already know how to merge one file into another with a different structure. (See program *merge* and Figs. 3-1, 3-2, and 3-3.) *Modify* will tell you if you need to follow up a modification with a *merge*.

The steps for performing a successful modification may at first be confusing, but after you have done the operation once or twice, you should be able to modify your own files without any trouble. Because of the potential here for making mistakes, always modify a *copy* of the original file, never the original itself. Each step is numbered below to make the process easier to follow.

Steps to a Successful Modification

To demonstrate how to modify a data file's structure, we will add two new fields to The Company's parts data file. A decree has been received from the president that henceforth (a good word to use if you are in the habit of decreeing your intentions) all parts in the inventory will have their weights and warehouse locations stored in the PARTS.PDBF file. (Experienced data base users will notice that I have introduced an error here in storing the location along with the parts themselves. We will attempt to right this wrong in Chapter Four.)

1. *Copy* the structure of The Company's PARTS file to a new file called NEW. Use *status* to verify that the structures of NEW.PDBF and PARTS.PDBF are the same.
2. Execute the *modify* program. *Modify* operates a little differently from most PDBS programs. You should see this prompt line at the top of your screen. To see some additional instructions, press "H".

    >Modify: H(elp, R(ead, W(rite, Q(uit

3. Press "W" to select the write command. Follow the dialogue in Fig. 3-4 to write the structure of NEW.PDBF to a file called NEW.STRC. A "structure file" (.STRC) is created automatically by *modify*. This file contains the structure of the file being modified and is itself a PDBS data file that can be operated on by any of the PDBS programs.

```
Copy structure of what file? NEW
Opening NEW.STRC
Writing .STRC record 1
Writing .STRC record 2
Writing .STRC record 3
Writing .STRC record 4
Writing .STRC record 5
Structure copied
```

Fig. 3-4. *Select the W(rite operation of the modify program to create a file named NEW.STRC containing the structure of the data file NEW.PDBF.*

```
NAME       : P.LOC          NAME       : P.WGT
TYPE       : C              TYPE       : N
LENGTH     : 5              LENGTH     : 5
DECIMALS   : 0              DECIMALS   : 0
```

Fig. 3-5. *Using the insert command in editor, add these new field definitions to the NEW.STRC file. You will have to make two insertions, one for P.LOC (part location) and one for P.WGT (part weight).*

4. Quit the *modify* program. Use *editor* to edit the NEW.STRC file. Remember to enter the .STRC file name extension when you are asked what file you want to edit.
5. Use keys ''N'' and ''L'' repeatedly until you have record number 4, NAME = P.REO, on the screen. Press ''I'' to insert a blank record and answer ''Y'' when you are asked to verify moving two records to make room. Enter the new field definitions shown in Fig. 3-5. You will have to use the insert command a total of two times.
6. Quit the editor, going back to the main UCSD command line. Execute *modify* again and select the read command by pressing key ''R''. Follow the dialogue in Fig. 3-6. This operation reads the edited NEW.STRC file back into the structure of the NEW.PDBF file. Because you are operating on a copy of the PARTS file, you can safely answer ''Y'' when asked if all records should be deleted.

```
Modify what data file? NEW
Opening NEW.STRC
                         Name      Type     Len  Dec  Pos   Total
Reading .STRC record  1 - P.NUM    Char      5    0    1      6
Reading .STRC record  2 - P.NAME   Char     20    0    6     26
Reading .STRC record  3 - P.COLOR  Char      8    0   26     34
Reading .STRC record  4 - P.WGT    Number    5    0   34     39
Reading .STRC record  5 - P.LOC    Char      5    0   38     44
Reading .STRC record  6 - P.REO    Number    4    0   43     48
Reading .STRC record  7 - P.STOCK  Number    4    0   47     52
Maximum records = 19

WARNING: This structural change requires all records
         to be deleted if you answer "Yes" to the
         next question.

Delete all records ? (y/n) Y

NEW.PDBF structure modified.
```

Fig. 3-6. *After inserting the new field definitions into NEW.STRC, use the modify R(ead command and follow the dialogue as shown here to complete the structural modification of NEW.PDBF. Because NEW.PDBF is a copy of the PARTS.PDBF file, it is safe to delete all records from the file.*

```
PARTS.PDBF :
        P.NUM  P.NAME-------------- P.COLOR- P.WGT P.LOC P.REQ P.STOCK
00001   P1     Photometric eye       Blue      175  L4      50      61
00002   P2     Arm assembly          Silver   5500  L1      50      59
00003   P3     Body                  Red      8000  L3       3      18
00004   P4     Leg                   Black    2500  L3      50      76
00005   P5     Foot wheel            Black     375  L2     100     110
00006   P6     Hand                  Silver    425  L2      25      20
```

Fig. 3-7. *A listing of the modified parts file now containing places for the weight and location of each part. You can use the editor to enter this new information into the P.WGT and P.LOC fields for each record.*

7. Quit the *modify* program. *Merge* the PARTS file into the NEW data file. When you are asked what fields to merge, just press the return key to merge all fields from PARTS to NEW. This is always the correct response when adding or changing fields. When subtracting fields from the structure of a file, you will have to manually enter at this point a list of the fields to be merged.

8. That completes the modification. Use *list* to verify the results of the NEW.PDBF file. (See Fig. 3-7.) If everything appears to be correct, use the UCSD filer C(hange command to change the file name NEW.PDBF to PARTS.PDBF, removing the old parts file. It is a good idea to retain a copy of the old PARTS.PDBF file until you are sure everything has been completed successfully. When you are finished modifying a file, you can remove the .STRC file using the UCSD filer R(emove command. It will not be used again.

Although the process of modifying a file's structure may seem overly complex when described step by step, it is really easy to do once you understand the sequence. It would have been possible to design a special editor strictly for modifying the structure of a data file. Somehow, even though that approach would probably be easier to learn, it seems less capable. I like the idea of being able to sort, delete, list, and edit the structures of data files as well as the data themselves, using all of the same programs. It would be possible, for instance, to construct a data base of data file structures, a sort of grand directory to the formats of everything in the computer. Individual .STRC files could be appended to a MASTER.STRC information file for further processing.

Some kinds of modifications do not require the deletion of all records followed by a merge. You can, for example, change the name of any field directly on the data file. Generally, if any changes are made to field length or type definitions, though, a merge must follow a modification. It is always best to modify a copy of a data file anyway until the results can be studied and verified.

```
001: {$S+,I-}              { Compiler swapping on; I/O error checking off }
002:
003: PROGRAM modify; uses pdbsunit;
004:
005: {----------------------------------------------------------------}
006: {                                                                }
007: {    PROGRAM        :  Modify a PDBF data file structure         }
008: {    LANGUAGE       :  UCSD Pascal / Apple Pascal 1.1            }
009: {                                                                }
010: {    Copyright (C) 1983 by Tom Swan. All commercial rights reserved. }
011: {                                                                }
012: {----------------------------------------------------------------}
013:
014: VAR
015:    ch                 : char;           { Command character }
016:    userquits          : boolean;
017:
018:
019: PROCEDURE show_type( dat_type : dat_descriptor );
020: { Display this data type name }
021: { Similar to procedure of same name in program STATUS }
022: BEGIN
023:    CASE dat_type OF
024:        dat_char    : write( 'Char   ' );  { 7 characters each }
025:        dat_logical : write( 'Logical' );  {   including blanks }
026:        dat_number  : write( 'Number ' )
027:    END { case }
028: END; { show_type }
029:
030:
031: PROCEDURE help1;
032: { R(ead operation instructions }
033: BEGIN
034:    writeln( chr( ret ), chr( ret ), 'R(ead' );
035:    writeln( '  Use this procedure to copy an edited ', ext_strc,' file' );
036:    writeln( 'into a .PDBF (or other) data file.  This data' );
037:    writeln( 'file will then be modified according to the contents' );
038:    writeln( 'of the ', ext_strc, ' file.' );
039: END; { help1 }
040:
041:
042: PROCEDURE help2;
043: { W(rite operation instructions }
044: BEGIN
045:    writeln( chr( ret ), chr( ret ), 'W(rite' );
046:    writeln( '  Use this procedure to create a new ', ext_strc, ' file' );
047:    writeln( 'containing a copy of a .PDBF (or other) data file''s' );
048:    writeln( 'structure.  The newly created ', ext_strc, ' file can then' );
049:    writeln( 'be edited as any other PDBS file.  Use the "R(ead"' );
050:    writeln( 'option to copy the edited ', ext_strc, ' file back to the' );
051:    writeln( '.PDBF (or other) data file, and complete the' );
052:    writeln( 'modification.' )
053: END; { help2 }
054:
055:
056: PROCEDURE help;
057: { Display instructions }
058: BEGIN
059:    clrscrn;
060:    help1;
061:    help2
062: END; { help }
063:
064:
065: FUNCTION string2name( VAR s       : string;
066:                       VAR fld_rec : fld_descriptor ) : boolean;
067: { True if string converted to name in field descriptor }
```

```
068: BEGIN
069:    strip( s );        { Remove leading, trailing blanks }
070:    bumpstrup( s );    { Convert to all upper case }
071:    IF length( s ) = 0
072:      THEN
073:        BEGIN
074:           writeln( chr(ret), 'No field name' );
075:           string2name := false
076:        END
077:      ELSE
078:        BEGIN
079:           str2alpha( s, fld_rec.fld_name );
080:           string2name := true
081:        END { else }
082: END; { string2name }
083:
084:
085: FUNCTION string2TYPE( VAR s     : string;
086:                      VAR fld_rec : fld_descriptor ) : boolean;
087: { True if string converted to type in field descriptor }
088: VAR
089:    ch : char;
090: BEGIN
091:    string2TYPE := false;    { Unless successful. }
092:    strip( s );              { Remove leading, trailing blanks }
093:    IF length( s ) = 0
094:      THEN
095:        writeln( chr(ret), 'No field type' )
096:      ELSE
097:      BEGIN
098:        ch := cap( s[1] );    { Only use first letter of field }
099:        IF NOT ( ch IN [ 'C', 'L', 'N' ] )
100:          THEN
101:            writeln( chr(ret), 'No field type = ', ch )
102:          ELSE WITH fld_rec DO
103:            BEGIN
104:              CASE ch OF
105:                'C' : fld_type := dat_char;
106:                'L' : fld_type := dat_logical;
107:                'N' : fld_type := dat_number
108:              END; { case }
109:              string2TYPE := true
110:            END { else }
111:      END { else }
112: END; { string2type }
113:
114:
115: FUNCTION string2len( VAR s      : string;
116:                     VAR fld_rec : fld_descriptor ) : boolean;
117: { True if string converted to length in field descriptor }
118: VAR
119:    max, n : integer;
120: BEGIN
121:    WITH fld_rec DO
122:    BEGIN
123:
124:    { Set max = maximum length for field type }
125:
126:      CASE fld_type OF
127:        dat_char    : max := string_size;
128:        dat_logical : max := 1;
129:        dat_number  : max := max_digits
130:      END; { case }
131:
132:    n := value( s );        { Convert string to integer value }
133:
134:    IF NOT inrange( n, 1, max )
```

```
135:       THEN
136:         BEGIN
137:           writeln( chr(ret), 'Length (', n, ') out of range' );
138:           string2len := false
139:         END
140:       ELSE
141:         BEGIN
142:           fld_len := n;       { Assign checked value to field }
143:           string2len := true
144:         END { else }
145:     END { with }
146: END; { string2len }
147:
148:
149: FUNCTION string2dec( VAR s     : string;
150:                      VAR fld_rec : fld_descriptor ) : boolean;
151: { True if string converted to decimals in field descriptor }
152: VAR
153:     n : integer;
154: BEGIN
155:     string2dec := false;     { Unless successful }
156:     n := value( s );         { Convert string to number }
157:     WITH fld_rec DO
158:     IF ( n > 0 ) AND ( fld_type <> dat_number )
159:       THEN
160:         writeln( chr(ret), 'Decimals not allowed' )
161:       ELSE
162:       IF ( n > fld_len ) OR ( n > max_digits )
163:         THEN
164:           writeln( chr(ret), 'Decimals (', n, ') out of range' )
165:         ELSE
166:           BEGIN
167:             fld_decimals := n;              { Assign checked value to field }
168:             string2dec := true
169:           END
170: END; { string2dec }
171:
172:
173: PROCEDURE name2string( VAR fld_rec : fld_descriptor;
174:                        VAR s       : string );
175: { Convert name in field descriptor to string }
176: BEGIN
177: {$r-}        { Range checking off }
178:     s[0] := chr( alpha_size + 1 );     { Set string length = name length }
179: {$r+}        { Range checking on }
180:     moveleft( fld_rec.fld_name,     { Source }
181:               s[1],                 { Destination }
182:               alpha_size + 1 )      { Count }
183: END; { name2string }
184:
185:
186: PROCEDURE TYPE2string( VAR fld_rec : fld_descriptor;
187:                        VAR s       : string );
188: { Convert type in field descriptor to string }
189: BEGIN
190:     CASE fld_rec.fld_type OF
191:       dat_char    : s := 'C';
192:       dat_logical : s := 'L';
193:       dat_number  : s := 'N'
194:     END { case }
195: END; { type2string }
196:
197:
198: PROCEDURE len2string( VAR fld_rec : fld_descriptor;
199:                       VAR s       : string );
200: { Convert length in field descriptor string }
201: BEGIN
```

```
202:    str( fld_rec.fld_len, s )          { Use standard procedure }
203: END; { len2string }
204:
205:
206: PROCEDURE dec2string( VAR fld_rec : fld_descriptor;
207:                       VAR s       : string );
208: { Convert decimals in field descriptor to string }
209: BEGIN
210:    str( fld_rec.fld_decimals, s )   { Use standard procedure }
211: END; { dec2string }
212:
213:
214: FUNCTION copy_from_strc( sn, dn : integer ) : boolean;
215: { Copy structure from file sn (contents) to file dn (structure) }
216: { Return true if no errors. }
217: VAR
218:    field,
219:     old_recsize,
220:     old_nflds,
221:     npages            : integer;
222:    fld_rec           : fld_descriptor;
223:    s                 : string;
224:    must_zero         : boolean;
225: BEGIN
226:    copy_from_strc := false;          { Unless all operations are completed }
227:    must_zero := false;               { True for some structural changes }
228:    WITH fil_recs[dn] DO WITH fil_msc DO
229:    BEGIN
230:       writeln( 'Name':30, 'Type':12, 'Len':8, 'Dec':5,
231:                'Pos':5, 'Total':8 );
232:       old_recsize := msc_recsize;
233:       old_nflds := msc_nflds;
234:       msc_recsize := 1;               { Skips status byte of record }
235:       msc_nflds := fil_recs[sn].fil_msc.msc_lastrec;  { From strc file }
236:       FOR field := 1 TO msc_nflds DO
237:        WITH fld_rec DO
238:          BEGIN
239:            write( 'Reading ', ext_strc, ' record', field:3, ' - ' );
240:
241:            IF NOT executed( seek_rec( sn, field ) )  {Get next .STRC rec}
242:               THEN exit( copy_from_strc );
243:
244:            { Assemble a single field descriptor taking each }
245:            { element from the .STRC record, and exiting the }
246:            { procedure if any errors occur. }
247:
248:            get_field( sn, 1, s );                    { Field name }
249:            IF NOT string2name( s, fld_rec )
250:               THEN exit( copy_from_strc );
251:            write( fld_name, chr( blank ) : 2 );
252:
253:            get_field( sn, 2, s );                    { Field type }
254:            IF NOT string2TYPE( s, fld_rec )
255:               THEN exit( copy_from_strc );
256:            show_type( fld_rec.fld_type );
257:
258:            get_field( sn, 3, s );                    { Field length }
259:            IF NOT string2len( s, fld_rec )
260:               THEN exit( copy_from_strc );
261:            write( fld_len:5 );
262:
263:            get_field( sn, 4, s );                    { Field decimals }
264:            IF NOT string2dec( s, fld_rec )
265:               THEN exit( copy_from_strc );
266:            write( fld_decimals : 5 );
267:
268:            { Compute the remaining items, which cannot be }
```

```
269:              { directly edited... }
270:
271:              { First, the field's byte position in the record. }
272:
273:                   fld_pos := msc_recsize; { Field position = recsize so far }
274:                   write( fld_pos : 6 );
275:
276:              { Then, the total record length assembled so far. }
277:
278:                   msc_recsize := msc_recsize + fld_len;  { Compute new recsize }
279:                   writeln( msc_recsize : 6 );
280:                   IF msc_recsize > page_size THEN
281:                      BEGIN
282:                         writeln( 'Total length exceeds ', page_size );
283:                         exit( copy_from_strc )
284:                      END; { if }
285:
286:              { Check if changes require deleting records, and assign }
287:              { the new field descriptor to the file.  This allows }
288:              { changing field names without having to delete and merge }
289:              { the records. }
290:
291:                   IF ( msc_flds[field].fld_type <> fld_type ) OR
292:                      ( msc_flds[field].fld_len  <> fld_len  ) OR
293:                      ( msc_flds[field].fld_pos  <> fld_pos  )
294:                   THEN must_zero := true;
295:
296:                   msc_flds[field] := fld_rec
297:
298:           END; { for / with }
299:
300:      { Last, calculate the new file maximums and delete all records }
301:      { if the size, position, or type of any field was changed. }
302:
303:        npages := msc_maxrec DIV fil_rpp;             { Old num pages }
304:        fil_rpp := ( page_size + 1 ) DIV msc_recsize; { New recs per page }
305:        msc_maxrec := npages * fil_rpp;               { New maxrec }
306:        writeln( 'Maximum records = ', msc_maxrec );
307:        IF ( must_zero                    ) OR
308:           ( msc_recsize <> old_recsize   ) OR
309:           ( msc_nflds <> old_nflds       ) THEN
310:          BEGIN
311:            beep;
312:            writeln;
313:            writeln( 'WARNING: This structural change requires all records' );
314:            writeln( '         to be deleted if you answer "Yes" to the' );
315:            writeln( '         next question.' );
316:            writeln;
317:            IF NOT verified( 'Delete all records' )
318:               THEN exit( copy_from_strc );          { For no update }
319:            IF NOT executed( zero_file( dn ) )        { Error zeroing }
320:               THEN exit( copy_from_strc )
321:          END { if }
322:      END; { with }
323:      copy_from_strc := true
324: END; { copy_from_strc }
325:
326:
327: FUNCTION copy_to_strc( dn, sn : integer ) : boolean;
328: { Copy structure from file dn (structure) to file sn (contents) }
329: { Return true if no errors. }
330: VAR
331:    field                : integer;
332:    s                    : string;
333:    blank_rec            : binary_page;
334: BEGIN
335:    copy_to_strc := false;              { Unless all operations are completed }
```

```
336:     zero_rec( sn, blank_rec );          { Prepare a blank record }
337: { Remove any previous structure recs }
338:     IF NOT executed( zero_file( sn ) )
339:       THEN
340:         exit( copy_to_strc )
341:       ELSE
342:     WITH fil_recs[dn].fil_msc DO
343:         FOR field := 1 TO msc_nflds DO
344:             BEGIN
345:                 writeln( 'Writing ', ext_strc, ' record ', field );
346:
347:                 { Append a blank record onto the .STRC file }
348:
349:                 IF NOT executed( append_rec( sn, blank_rec ) )
350:                     THEN exit( copy_to_strc );
351:
352:                 { Insert each field descriptor element into the }
353:                 {  appended blank record for editing. }
354:
355:                 name2string( msc_flds[field], s );
356:                 put_field( sn, 1, s );
357:                 TYPE2string( msc_flds[field], s );
358:                 put_field( sn, 2, s );
359:                 len2string( msc_flds[field], s );
360:                 put_field( sn, 3, s );
361:                 dec2string( msc_flds[field], s );
362:                 put_field( sn, 4, s )
363:
364:             END; { for }
365:     copy_to_strc := true
366: END; { copy_to_strc }
367:
368:
369: PROCEDURE make_name( VAR dname, sname : pdbs_fname );
370: { Create structure file name (sname) out of data file name (dname ) }
371: BEGIN
372:     sname := dname;          { Preserve original data file name }
373:     remove_ext( sname );     { Remove any extensions (e.g. .PDBF) }
374:     sname := concat( sname, ext_strc )       { Add .STRC extension }
375: END; { make_name }
376:
377:
378: FUNCTION add_field( VAR msc_rec  : msc_descriptor;
379:                         name     : string;
380:                         dat_type : dat_descriptor;
381:                         len      : integer;
382:                         decimals : integer  ) : boolean;
383: { True if new field added successfully to msc_rec record descriptor }
384: VAR
385:     n : integer;
386: BEGIN
387:     add_field := false;      { Unless completed successfully }
388:     WITH msc_rec DO  { Check number of fields and if a name is entered }
389:     IF ( msc_nflds < max_fld ) AND ( length( name ) > 0 ) THEN
390:     BEGIN
391:         n := msc_recsize + len;
392:         IF n <= page_size THEN          { Check total record length }
393:         BEGIN
394:             msc_nflds := msc_nflds + 1;
395:             WITH msc_flds[ msc_nflds ] DO
396:                 BEGIN                   { Add new field descriptors }
397:                     bumpstrup( name );
398:                     str2alpha( name, fld_name );
399:                     fld_type := dat_type;
400:                     fld_len := len;
401:                     IF dat_type = dat_number
402:                         THEN fld_decimals := decimals
```

```
403:                       ELSE fld_decimals := 0;
404:                  fld_pos := msc_recsize        { End of last field entered }
405:              END; { with }
406:          msc_recsize := n;
407:          add_field := true              { No errors }
408:        END { if }
409:    END { with / if }
410: END; { add_field }
411:
412:
413: FUNCTION make_strc( fname : pdbs_fname ) : pdbs_err;
414: { Create structure file of this file name }
415: VAR
416:    msc_rec : msc_descriptor;             { Describes record structure }
417: BEGIN
418:    init_msc( msc_rec );
419:    make_strc := 14;              { Bad format error if next commands fail }
420:    IF add_field( msc_rec, 'NAME', dat_char, 10, 0 ) THEN
421:    IF add_field( msc_rec, 'TYPE', dat_char,  1, 0 ) THEN
422:    IF add_field( msc_rec, 'LENGTH', dat_number, 3, 0 ) THEN
423:    IF add_field( msc_rec, 'DECIMALS', dat_number, 1, 0 )
424:        THEN make_strc := make_file( fname, msc_rec )
425: END; { make_strc }
426:
427:
428: PROCEDURE read_strc;
429: { Read a .STRC file into a .PDBF file to modify its structure. }
430: VAR
431:    mode              : close_option; { Data file update / no_update }
432:    sn, dn            : integer;      { Structure / Data file numbers }
433:    strc_name,
434:    data_name         : pdbs_fname;   { File names }
435: BEGIN
436:    clrscrn;
437:    help1;
438:    writeln;
439:    mode := no_update;        { Unless all operations are completed. }
440:    IF get_file_name( 'Modify what data file? ', data_name ) THEN
441:    IF executed( open_file( dn, data_name ) ) THEN
442:        BEGIN
443:          make_name( data_name, strc_name );
444:          writeln( 'Opening ', strc_name );
445:          IF executed( open_file( sn, strc_name ) ) THEN
446:          IF file_empty( sn )
447:              THEN writeln( 'Structure file empty' )
448:              ELSE
449:              IF copy_from_strc( sn, dn )
450:                  THEN mode := update
451:        END; { if }
452:    IF ( executed( close_file( sn, no_update ) ) ) AND
453:       ( executed( close_file( dn, mode      ) ) ) AND
454:       ( mode = update )
455:       THEN write( data_name, ' structure modified.' )
456:       ELSE write( 'Structure not modified.' )
457: END; { read_strc }
458:
459:
460: PROCEDURE write_strc;
461: { Write a new .STRC file from a .PDBF file for editing its structure. }
462: VAR
463:    mode              : close_option; { Data file update / no_update }
464:    sn, dn            : integer;      { Structure / Data file numbers }
465:    strc_name,
466:    data_name         : pdbs_fname;   { File names }
467: BEGIN
468:    clrscrn;
469:    help2;
470:    writeln;
```

```
471:     mode := no_update;          { Unless all operations are completed. }
472:     IF get_file_name( 'Copy structure of what file? ', data_name ) THEN
473:     IF executed( open_file( dn, data_name ) ) THEN
474:     BEGIN
475:        make_name( data_name, strc_name );
476:        writeln( 'Opening ', strc_name );
477:        IF file_not_in_use( strc_name ) THEN
478:        IF executed( make_strc( strc_name ) ) THEN
479:        IF executed( open_file( sn, strc_name ) ) THEN
480:        BEGIN
481:           IF copy_to_strc( dn, sn )
482:              THEN mode := update;
483:           IF ( executed( close_file( sn, mode      ) ) ) AND
484:              ( mode = update )
485:              THEN write( 'Structure copied' )
486:              ELSE write( 'Structure not copied' )
487:        END; { if }
488:        IF NOT executed( close_file( dn, no_update ) )
489:           THEN exit( PROGRAM )      { Extremely unlikely }
490:     END { if }
491: END; { write_strc }
492:
493:
494: BEGIN
495:     clrscrn;
496:     userquits := false;
497:     REPEAT
498:        promptat( 0, 0, '>Modify: H(elp, R(ead, W(rite, Q(uit ' );
499:        CASE cap( get_ch( ch ) ) OF
500:           'H' : help;
501:           'R' : read_strc;          { Read .STRC --> .PDBF }
502:           'W' : write_strc;         { Write .PDBF --> .STRC }
503:           'Q' : userquits := true
504:        END { case }
505:     UNTIL userquits
506: END.
```

READTEXT

Readtext reads lines of text from a standard UCSD text file ending with the file name extension .TEXT. There are several uses for this program.

At times, it may be useful to enter data using a text editor instead of the PDBS data *editor* program. Also, you may already have some data in this form, perhaps a list of names and addresses, that you would like to be able to process using PDBS programs.

Readtext considers each line in the text file to be one field for inserting into the PDBS data file. If the data file has two fields per record, then line one of the text file would be read into the first field of the first record, line two into the second field, line three into the first field of the second record, and so on until the end of the text file is reached. *Readtext* appends new records to whatever is already in the data file. If you already have nine records in the data file, the first new record will start at number ten.

Figure 3-8 shows a portion of The Company's vendor data file as it might be entered in a text file. If you are going to enter data this way, you are responsible for

```
V1
Robotics Manufacturers, Inc.
45 West Setting Sun Hwy
Baltimore
MD
22098
Ms. Paula Taylor
301-555-1212
V2
Mechanical Assemblies Corp.
800 Lincoln East
San Diego
CA
90666
Jonathan Rapport
912-888-5098
```

Fig. 3-8. *A portion of The Company's vendor file written using* writetext *to a text file. Each field of the original record (see Fig. 2-1) becomes one line of text with no separations between records. The* readtext *program could be used to read a text file in this format into a PDBS data file.*

making sure that every line is in the exact, correct position. If there is no information to be entered into a field, there must be a corresponding blank line in the text file.

Converting from Other Data Formats

Readtext is also very useful for translating data stored in other formats to the PDBS format. If you can write your data into a line-by-line text file, and I can't think of any situation where this would not be possible, then *readtext* can read your data into a PDBS data file where you can process the information using all the other programs in the system.

As an example of such a transformation, for about four years I have been maintaining a magazine index using a well-done, although a bit outdated, program written in Apple Integer BASIC and assembly language by the respected Paul Lutus. I was able to transfer the data to a Pascal text file using a conversion program from a magazine and load them into a PDBS data file using *readtext* with no trouble at all. (I added an intermediate step of breaking up the data into several lines, but this would not have been necessary.) In the process, I discovered several errors and omissions in the original file and saved myself the chore of retyping all that information—a job I was not looking forward to.

Using Readtext

First, *create* the data file into which you want to insert text. You should have both the data file in PDBS format and your text file available before running *readtext*.

Execute the program. Supply the name of the text file followed by the name of your PDBS data file. The rest is automatic.

One problem you may have when reading text into data fields declared as numbers occurs because of the PDBS requirement that all numbers be right-justified. If this is not done, searching and sorting on those fields will not operate correctly.

The problem can be fixed by using the *calc* program in Chapter Five to right-justify all numbers in a field. Setting a numerical field equal to itself has the added effect of rejustifying the number within that field. This is accomplished with a simple assignment. Replace ''<field>'' with the same field name.

<field> = <field>

Another fix, which may take a little longer, is to *merge* the data file into a copy of itself. This will right-justify all number fields in one operation and could be used if you have a lot of fields with this problem.

```
001: {$S+,I-}              { Compiler swapping on; I/O error checking off }
002:
003: PROGRAM readtext; uses pdbsunit;
004:
005: {-----------------------------------------------------------------------}
006: {                                                                       }
007: {    PROGRAM        :  Read text file into PDBS data file format        }
008: {    LANGUAGE       :  UCSD Pascal / Apple Pascal 1.1                    }
009: {                                                                       }
010: {    Copyright (C) 1983 by Tom Swan. All commercial rights reserved.    }
011: {                                                                       }
012: {-----------------------------------------------------------------------}
013:
014: VAR
015:    mode              : close_option;
016:    file_name,                                  { PDBS data file name }
017:    text_name         : pdbs_fname;             { UCSD text file name }
018:    file_number       : integer;                { PDBS file number }
019:    text_file         : text;                   { UCSD text file }
020:    num_recs          : integer;                { Number of records loaded }
021:
022:
023: FUNCTION text_open( VAR text_file : text;
024:                     VAR text_name : pdbs_fname ) : pdbs_err;
025: { Open (reset) this text file for reading. }
026: VAR
027:    s : string;                    { Temporary working string }
028: BEGIN
029:    remove_ext( text_name ); { Remove any PDBS file name extensions. }
030:    s := text_name;              { Use longer string to avoid overflow errors }
031:    bumpstrup( s );                            { Convert to upper case chars }
032:    IF pos( '.TEXT', s ) = 0
033:       THEN s := concat( s, '.TEXT' );         { Add .TEXT if not there }
034:    IF length( s ) > fname_len
035:       THEN s := copy( s, 1, fname_len );      { Limit to max file name len }
036:    text_name := s;                            { Reassign string to variable }
037:    reset( text_file, text_name );             { Attempt to open the file }
038:    text_open := ioresult                      { Report success / failure }
039: END; { text_open }
040:
```

```
041:
042: FUNCTION load_text(        fn         : integer;
043:                        VAR text_file : text;
044:                        VAR num_recs  : integer  ) : pdbs_err;
045: { Read text from file text_file into PDBS data file number fn }
046: { Report number of records loaded }
047: { Note: one line per field expected from input file }
048: VAR
049:     blank_rec          : binary_page;
050:     err_code           : pdbs_err;
051:     field              : integer;       { Field number }
052:     s                  : string;        { Fields and text strings }
053: BEGIN
054:     writeln( 'Reading' );
055:     zero_rec( fn, blank_rec );          { Prepare blank record for appends }
056:     err_code := 0;
057:     num_recs := 0;
058:     WHILE ( NOT eof( text_file ) ) AND ( err_code = 0 ) DO
059:     BEGIN
060:         err_code := append_rec( fn, blank_rec );
061:         IF err_code = 0 THEN
062:             FOR field := 1 TO fil_recs[fn].fil_msc.msc_nflds DO
063:                 BEGIN
064:                     readln( text_file, s );      { Read text into s }
065:                     put_field( fn, field, s )    { Write s to PDBS record }
066:                 END;
067:         num_recs := num_recs + 1;
068:         write( '.' )           { Visual feedback }
069:     END; { while }
070:     writeln;
071:     load_text := err_code            { Report success / failure }
072: END; { load_text }
073:
074:
075: BEGIN
076:     clrscrn;
077:     WHILE get_file_name( 'Read what text file? ', text_name ) DO
078:     BEGIN
079:         IF executed( text_open( text_file, text_name ) ) THEN
080:         BEGIN
081:             IF get_file_name( 'Write to what data file? ', file_name ) THEN
082:             IF executed( open_file( file_number, file_name ) ) THEN
083:             BEGIN
084:                 clreosc;
085:                 mode := no_update;
086:                 IF executed( load_text( file_number, text_file, num_recs ) ) )
087:                     THEN mode := update;
088:                 IF ( executed( close_file( file_number, mode ) ) ) AND
089:                    ( mode = update )
090:                     THEN write( num_recs, ' records --> ', file_name )
091:             END; { if }
092:             close( text_file )
093:         END; { if }
094:         gotoxy( 0, 0 )
095:     END { while }
096: END.
```

WRITETEXT

The opposite of *readtext* is, quite naturally, *writetext*. The reasons for using the program are equally contrary.

You may have a program, such as the word processing programs in *Pascal Programs for Business*, that will only operate on data stored in text files. To use one of those programs on a PDBS data file, the data must first be written to a UCSD format text file ending in the file name extension, .TEXT.

Writetext is also useful for converting PDBS files to other data base formats. I imagine, to use the same example from the instructions to *readtext,* that with *writetext* as a first step, I could convert my magazine index back to its original format.

Data could also be translated to a severely modified version of the PDBS file format by using *writetext* followed by *readtext*. This may bypass writing a complicated conversion program. (Also see the notes to the *convert* program in Chapter Seven.)

Using Writetext

Unlike *readtext, writetext* does not append data to the destination file, which in this case is the text file. If a text file already exists for the name you supply, *writetext* will rewrite the original file. You will be given a chance to change your mind about removing the old file if this condition exists.

Execute the program and supply the name of the PDBS data file you wish to convert to text. Next, enter the name of the destination text file. The rest is automatic.

Each field of each record in the PDBS data file is written to a separate line of text in the destination file. Blank fields will be written as blank lines in the text file. Data retains its relative position in each field. In other words, numbers will be right-justified in the text if they were stored that way originally. An example of a text file created by *writetext* can be seen in Fig. 3-8.

Modifying Readtext and Writetext

These two programs are apparently slowed by the use of the standard procedures *readln* in line 64 of *readtext* and *writeln* in line 76 of *writetext*. You may want to replace these lines with calls to *get_line* and *put_line* procedures that read text as blocks of data. (You will have to supply these procedures.) A good way to do this appears in *Byte* magazine, January 1983, page 454, in the article "High Speed Pascal Text File I/O" by K. Brook Richan and James S. Rosenvall. The performance of *readtext* and *writetext* can be greatly improved by adding the methods discussed in the article.

```
001: {$S+,I-}              { Compiler swapping on; I/O error checking off }
002:
003: PROGRAM writetext; uses pdbsunit;
004:
005: {--------------------------------------------------------------------}
006: {                                                                    }
007: {    PROGRAM        :   Write from PDBS data file to a text file     }
008: {    LANGUAGE       :   UCSD Pascal / Apple Pascal 1.1               }
009: {                                                                    }
010: {    Copyright (C) 1983 by Tom Swan. All commercial rights reserved. }
011: {                                                                    }
012: {--------------------------------------------------------------------}
```

```
013:
014: VAR
015:     file_name,                              { PDBS data file name }
016:     text_name          : pdbs_fname;        { UCSD text file name }
017:     file_number        : integer;           { PDBS file number }
018:     text_file          : text;              { UCSD text file }
019:     num_lines          : long_integer;      { Number of lines written }
020:
021:
022: FUNCTION make_text( VAR text_file : text;
023:                     VAR text_name : pdbs_fname ) : pdbs_err;
024: { Create a new text file by this name }
025: VAR
026:     err_code           : pdbs_err;
027:     s                  : string;
028: BEGIN
029:     remove_ext( text_name );                { Remove any PDBS extensions }
030:     s := text_name;                         { Save in work string s }
031:     bumpstrup( s );                         { Convert to all upper case }
032:     IF pos( '.TEXT', s ) = 0
033:         THEN s := concat( s, '.TEXT' );         { Add .TEXT extension }
034:     IF length( s ) > fname_len
035:         THEN s := copy( s, 1, fname_len );      { Restrict to max length }
036:     text_name := s;                         { Recopy work string to file name }
037:     reset( text_file, text_name );          { Test if file already exists }
038:     err_code := ioresult;                   { Remember I/O error result }
039:     close( text_file );                     { Ignore possible error here }
040:     IF err_code = 0 THEN
041:         IF NOT verified( concat( 'Erase old ', text_name ) )
042:             THEN exit( PROGRAM )
043:             ELSE err_code := 10;            { Allowing erasure of existing file }
044:     IF err_code = 10 THEN
045:         BEGIN
046:             rewrite( text_file, text_name );    { Create the new file }
047:             err_code := ioresult                { and remember I/O result }
048:         END;
049:     make_text := err_code                   { Pass any errors back to caller }
050: END; { make_text }
051:
052:
053: FUNCTION send_text(     fn          : integer;
054:                         VAR text_file : text;
055:                         VAR num_lines : long_integer ) : pdbs_err;
056: { Write data file fields to output text file }
057: { Return number of lines written }
058: VAR
059:     err_code : pdbs_err;
060:     field,                      { Field number }
061:     rn         : integer;       { Record number }
062:     s          : string;        { Fields and lines of text }
063: BEGIN
064:     writeln( 'Writing' );
065:     err_code := 0;
066:     num_lines := 0;
067:     rn := 1;           { Start with first record of input file }
068:     WITH fil_recs[fn].fil_msc DO
069:     WHILE ( rn <= msc_lastrec ) AND ( err_code = 0 ) DO
070:     BEGIN
071:         err_code := seek_rec( fn, rn );         { Advance to record rn }
072:         field := 1;   { Start with first field of current record }
073:         WHILE ( field <= msc_nflds ) AND ( err_code = 0 ) DO
074:         BEGIN
075:             get_field( fn, field, s );          { Read field from data file }
076:             writeln( text_file, s );            { Write field to text file }
077:             err_code := ioresult;               { Note any resulting errors }
078:             IF err_code = 0 THEN
079:             BEGIN
080:                 field := field + 1;                 { Advance to next field }
```

```
081:               num_lines := num_lines + 1      { Count lines written }
082:             END { if }
083:           END; { while }
084:           write( '.' );              { Visual feedback }
085:           rn := rn + 1              { Advance to next record }
086:       END; { while }
087:       writeln;
088:       IF err_code = 0
089:         THEN
090:           BEGIN
091:             close( text_file, lock );   { Lock in directory }
092:             err_code := ioresult
093:           END
094:         ELSE                             { Some error has occurred; }
095:           close( text_file );            {  do not lock in directory }
096:       send_text := err_code      { Pass error code back to caller }
097: END; { send_text }
098:
099:
100: BEGIN
101:     clrscrn;
102:     WHILE get_file_name( 'Read from what file? ', file_name ) DO
103:     BEGIN
104:         IF executed( open_file( file_number, file_name ) ) THEN
105:         BEGIN
106:             clreosc;
107:             IF get_file_name( 'Write to what text file? ', text_name ) THEN
108:             IF executed( make_text( text_file, text_name ) ) THEN
109:             IF executed( send_text( file_number, text_file, num_lines ) )
110:                 THEN write( num_lines, ' lines --> ', text_name );
111:             IF NOT executed( close_file( file_number, no_update ) )
112:                 THEN exit( PROGRAM )         { Extremely unlikely }
113:         END; { if }
114:         gotoxy( 0, 0 )
115:     END { while }
116: END.
```

4

The Relational Operators

JOIN / PROJECT

JOIN

The distinguishing feature of relational data base software is the existence of the operators *join* and *project*. With the help of these two most powerful commands, presented here as separate programs, it is possible to extract and prepare any conceivable combination of information from a properly designed data base. It is also possible to use these operations to reconstruct a badly formed data base into a structure that will be more efficient to store and that will have more potential for telling us facts about the data.

Join combines the data in two files in a special way to produce a third file. We can talk about this third file as "the join of" the original source files.

A join must be made over one of the fields in the original two files. This field must have the same structure in both of the original files. The join is accomplished by comparing each record of the first file against each record in the second file. If the data in the field over which the join is being made are equal in both files, then all the fields from file number one are combined with the fields in file number two, with the resulting record written to the output file, number three.

You can see that joining two files is both a complex and potentially profuse operation. Joining two large files can take a long time, and the result may be very large.

If you try to join two files that have no fields common to both, you will not get very far. A relational join requires at least one common field in both files. You can always combine two dissimilar files using merges and appends, but the result is not a relational join.

```
Join what file? PARTS
And what file? SOURCES
To what file? J1
Join over what field? P.NUM
Joining
    6 of 6
5 record(s) --> J1.PDBF
```

Fig. 4-1. *Follow this dialogue to join The Company's parts and sources files over the part number to a new file named J1.PDBF.*

```
Join what file? VENDORS
And what file? J1
To what file? J2
Join over what field? V.KEY
Joining
    3 of 3
5 record(s) --> J2.PDBF
```

Fig. 4-2. *A second join of the vendor file plus the result of the join from Fig. 4-1 creates a new file, J2.PDBF. This time, the join is done over the vendor key, V.KEY, common to both files.*

```
J2.PDBF
Record size .............. 194
Number of fields ........ 16
Maximum record number ... 5
Records in use .......... 5
Records not used ........ 0
Date created ............ 20-Jul-83
Date last updated ....... 20-Jul-83

    #  NAME        TYPE     LEN DEC POS

    1  V.KEY       Char       5   0   1
    2  V.NAME      Char      30   0   6
    3  V.ADDRESS   Char      30   0  36
    4  V.CITY      Char      20   0  66
    5  V.STATE     Char       2   0  86
    6  V.ZIP       Char       5   0  88
    7  V.CONTACT   Char      30   0  93
    8  V.PHONE     Char      12   0 123
    9  P.NUM       Char       5   0 135
   10  P.NAME      Char      20   0 140
   11  P.COLOR     Char       8   0 160
   12  P.WGT       Number     5   0 168
   13  P.LOC       Char       5   0 173
   14  P.REO       Number     4   0 178
   15  P.STOCK     Number     4   0 182
   16  COST        Number     8   2 186
```

Fig. 4-3. *A status report of the joins from Figs. 4-1 and 4-2 shows how the join program can quickly produce a lot of information.*

Normalization

Before attempting to join and project files, you should understand the concept of normalization, an important consideration in the design of a relational data base.

A data file, or a "relation" in the form of a row-and-column table, as depicted in Fig. 1-1, is normalized by its own definition. Each intersection of a row and a column contains a single data element—a field—and is said to be "atomic." At this level of viewing the data, the elements cannot be broken down any further. Each field is an atom in the universe of the data base.

How to Use Join

Until now, we have ignored one of The Company's data files, the one named SOURCES.PDBF. (See Figs. 1-2 and 2-1.) The purpose of this file will become evident in a moment.

Looking at the data in The Company's parts and vendor files (Fig. 2-1), you may begin to wonder how it is possible to tell which vendor supplies which part. The information is not in the parts file, nor is it in the vendor file.

The sources file is a normalized relation, a data file, that contains this information apart from the vendor and parts files. To combine all of this information to show who supplies which part, a *join* of the three files is made.

Figure 4-1 is a dialogue showing the process of joining the parts and sources files into a third file called J1.PDBF. This file is created automatically by the *join* program. The join is made over the P.NUM field, which is common to both the parts and sources files. You may want to *list* the contents following the *join* to see the effect of the operation.

Figure 4-2 shows the dialogue of a second join, this time with the vendor and J1.PDBF files being combined into a new file called J2.PDBF. In this join, the common field is the V.KEY field. The structure of the result is shown in Fig. 4-3. As you can see, the number of fields in this new file has grown considerably from the original files.

Listing the second join, J2.PDBF, produces such a voluminous report that it is not shown here. At this point, you could design a report format for the resulting join, but there is more to joining two files than that, as you will see in the next program, *project*.

```
001: {$S+,I-}              { Compiler swapping on; I/O error checking off }
002:
003: PROGRAM join; uses pdbsunit;
004:
005: {-------------------------------------------------------------------}
006: {                                                                   }
007: {    PROGRAM        : Form the relational "join" of two files       }
008: {    LANGUAGE       : UCSD Pascal / Apple Pascal 1.1                 }
009: {                                                                   }
010: {    Copyright (C) 1983 by Tom Swan. All commercial rights reserved.}
011: {                                                                   }
012: {-------------------------------------------------------------------}
```

```
013:
014: VAR
015:    mode                      : close_option;
016:    name_a, name_b, name_c    : pdbs_fname;   { File names }
017:    nrecs                     : integer;      { Number records joined }
018:    num_a, num_b, num_c       : integer;      { File numbers }
019:    name                      : alpha;        { Field name }
020:
021:
022: FUNCTION make_join( fna, fnb : integer; fname : pdbs_fname ) : pdbs_err;
023: { Create new fname file combining fields from files fna and fnb }
024: VAR
025:    new_msc : msc_descriptor;
026:
027:    PROCEDURE add_fields( VAR msc1, msc2 : msc_descriptor );
028:    { Combine unique fields in msc1 into msc2 }
029:    VAR
030:       i, n : integer;
031:    BEGIN
032:      FOR i := 1 TO msc1.msc_nflds DO
033:       IF msc2.msc_nflds < max_fld THEN
034:        IF fld_number( msc2, msc1.msc_flds[i].fld_name ) = 0 THEN
035:         WITH msc2 DO
036:         BEGIN { Field name not found in msc2.  Add it if there is room }
037:             n := msc_recsize + msc1.msc_flds[i].fld_len;
038:             IF n <= page_size THEN
039:             BEGIN
040:                msc_nflds := msc_nflds + 1;
041:                msc_flds[ msc_nflds ] := msc1.msc_flds[i];
042:                msc_flds[ msc_nflds ].fld_pos :=
043:                    msc_recsize;        { i.e. end of last field + 1 }
044:                msc_recsize := n
045:             END { if }
046:           END { with }
047:    END; { add_fields }
048:
049: BEGIN
050:    IF NOT file_not_in_use( fname ) THEN
051:     IF NOT verified( concat( 'Remove old ', fname ) ) THEN
052:       BEGIN
053:          make_join := 25;   { Interrupted by user }
054:          exit( make_join )
055:       END;
056:
057:    init_msc( new_msc );
058:
059: { Add fields from fna and fnb to the new record }
060:
061:    add_fields( fil_recs[fna].fil_msc, new_msc );
062:    add_fields( fil_recs[fnb].fil_msc, new_msc );
063:
064: { Create the destination file using the new misc record }
065:
066:    make_join := make_file( fname, new_msc )
067: END; { make_join }
068:
069:
070: FUNCTION get_fld_name( s : string; VAR name : alpha ) : boolean;
071: { Prompt for and return field name.  True if anything typed. }
072: BEGIN
073:    clreoln;
074:    write( s );
075:    readln( s );
076:    bumpstrup( s );
077:    str2alpha( s, name );
078:    get_fld_name := ( length( s ) > 0 )
079: END; { get_fld_name }
```

```
080:
081:
082: FUNCTION find_name(      fn    : integer;
083:                          name  : alpha;
084:                     VAR field : integer ) : boolean;
085: { Find field name in file fn and return field set to its number }
086: { Return true if field name found, else return false and print error }
087: BEGIN
088:    WITH fil_recs[fn] DO
089:    BEGIN
090:       field := fld_number( fil_msc, name );
091:       IF field <= 0
092:          THEN
093:            BEGIN
094:              writeln( name, ' field not found in ', fil_name );
095:              find_name := false
096:            END
097:          ELSE
098:            find_name := true
099:    END { with }
100: END; { find_name }
101:
102:
103: FUNCTION join_files(     fa, fb, fc : integer;
104:                          name       : alpha;
105:                     VAR nrecs       : integer ) : boolean;
106: { Join files fa and fb to file fc over field "name" }
107: { Return nrecs = number of records written to file fc }
108: VAR
109:    fafc_order, fbfc_order    : fld_order;      { Field order arrays }
110:    fa_field, fb_field,                         { "Name" field numbers }
111:    fa_rn, fb_rn,                               { File record numbers }
112:    fa_nrecs, fb_nrecs,                         { Num recs in fa & fb }
113:    fc_nflds, i                  : integer;     { Num flds in fc & misc }
114:    fa_s, fb_s                   : string;      { Fields as strings }
115:    blank_rec                    : binary_page; { Blank binary record }
116:
117:    PROCEDURE common_error( fn1, fn2 : integer );
118:    { Print "no common fields" error for files fn1 and fn2 }
119:    BEGIN
120:       writeln( 'No fields common to ',
121:                fil_recs[ fn1 ].fil_name, ' and ',
122:                fil_recs[ fn2 ].fil_name )
123:    END; { common_error }
124:
125: BEGIN
126:    join_files := false;                { Unless all operations completed }
127:    zero_rec( fc, blank_rec);
128:    nrecs := 0;
129:
130: { Next three instructions avoid time consuming index operations later }
131:
132:    fa_nrecs := fil_recs[fa].fil_msc.msc_lastrec;
133:    fb_nrecs := fil_recs[fb].fil_msc.msc_lastrec;
134:    fc_nflds := fil_recs[fc].fil_msc.msc_nflds;
135:
136: { Find fields common to fa, fc and fb, fc }
137:
138:    IF NOT common_fields( fc, fa, fafc_order )
139:       THEN common_error( fc, fa ) ELSE
140:    IF NOT common_fields( fc, fb, fbfc_order )
141:       THEN common_error( fc, fb ) ELSE
142:
143: { Find field numbers in each file of "joining" field (name) }
144:
145:    IF find_name( fa, name, fa_field ) THEN
146:    IF find_name( fb, name, fb_field ) THEN
```

```
147:
148:   { Read each record in file fa, preparing the common field }
149:     BEGIN
150:      writeln( 'Joining' );
151:      FOR fa_rn := 1 TO fa_nrecs DO
152:        BEGIN
153:          writeln( fa_rn:5, ' of ', fa_nrecs:5 );
154:          goup;      { Keep cursor on same line }
155:          IF NOT executed( seek_rec( fa, fa_rn ) )
156:            THEN exit( join_files );              { Returning "false }
157:          get_field( fa, fa_field, fa_s );
158:          IF case_switch
159:            THEN bumpstrup( fa_s );
160:
161:        { Read each record in file fb, comparing with the common field }
162:
163:          FOR fb_rn := 1 TO fb_nrecs DO
164:          BEGIN
165:            IF NOT executed( seek_rec( fb, fb_rn ) )
166:              THEN exit( join_files );      { Returning "false" }
167:            get_field( fb, fb_field, fb_s );
168:            IF case_switch
169:              THEN bumpstrup( fb_s );
170:            IF fa_s = fb_s THEN              { If both fields equal }
171:            BEGIN
172:              { Append a blank record onto the destination file }
173:
174:              IF NOT executed( append_rec( fc, blank_rec ) )
175:                THEN exit( join_files );      { Returning "false" }
176:
177:              { Merge selected fields from fa and fb into fc }
178:              { Use fb_s string to transfer fields -- it is now free }
179:
180:              FOR i := 1 TO fc_nflds DO
181:                IF fafc_order[i] <> 0
182:                  THEN
183:                    BEGIN
184:                      get_field( fa, fafc_order[i], fb_s );
185:                      put_field( fc, i, fb_s )
186:                    END
187:                  ELSE
188:                    IF fbfc_order[i] <> 0 THEN
189:                      BEGIN
190:                        get_field( fb, fbfc_order[i], fb_s );
191:                        put_field( fc, i, fb_s )
192:                      END
193:
194:            END { if }
195:          END { for }
196:        END; { for }
197:      join_files := true;
198:      nrecs := fil_recs[fc].fil_msc.msc_lastrec  { Recs in output file }
199:    END { ifs }
200: END; { join_files }
201:
202:
203: BEGIN
204:    clrscrn;
205:    WHILE get_file_name( 'Join what file? ', name_a ) DO
206:    BEGIN
207:      clreosc;
208:      mode := no_update;          { Unless all operations completed }
209:      IF executed( open_file( num_a, name_a ) ) THEN
210:      BEGIN
211:        IF get_file_name( 'And what file? ', name_b ) THEN
212:        IF executed( open_file( num_b, name_b ) ) THEN
213:        BEGIN
```

```
214:              IF get_file_name( 'To what file? ', name_c ) THEN
215:              IF executed( make_join( num_a, num_b, name_c ) ) THEN
216:              IF executed( open_file( num_c, name_c ) ) THEN
217:              BEGIN
218:                 IF get_fld_name( 'Join over what field? ', name ) THEN
219:                 IF join_files( num_a, num_b, num_c, name, nrecs )
220:                    THEN mode := update;
221:                 IF ( executed( close_file( num_c, mode ) ) ) THEN
222:                    IF mode = update
223:                       THEN writeln( nrecs, ' records --> ', name_c )
224:              END; { if }
225:              IF NOT executed( close_file( num_b, no_update ) )
226:                 THEN exit( PROGRAM )          { Extremely unlikely }
227:           END; { if }
228:           IF NOT executed( close_file( num_a, no_update ) )
229:              THEN exit( PROGRAM )     { Also extremely unlikely }
230:        END; { if }
231:        gotoxy( 0, 0 )
232:     END { while }
233: END.
```

PROJECT

A relational projection of a data file is the exact opposite of a *join*. In other words, whenever you *join* two files together, you can always *project* the resulting file back into the original two.

At least one popular relational data base system on the market has a *join* operation but lacks a *project*. Such an unfortunate limitation is almost literally a kiss without a squeeze.

You might think that the *list* program offers the same ability to create a subset or projection of a data file. When using *list*, you can choose to send only selected fields to the printer or console.

But *project* does more than simply extract selected fields from the records in a file. In addition, a properly executed projection must also eliminate duplicated records from the result, and *list* does not have this capability.

To see why this is necessary, examine the unprojected list of The Company's customer file in Fig. 4-4. To make a better example, several more records have been added. (You wouldn't expect a growing business to have a static data base.) In this list, we are trying to prepare a report of the cities and states where The Company has customers. Unfortunately, the result has many duplications.

Figure 4-5 is the same list but was prepared by projecting the customer file onto another file, here named CITIES.PDBF. The contents of that file were then listed to produce a concise list of the cities and states where The Company has customers.

In the instructions to *join*, I left the file J2.PDBF in limbo. In most cases, a *join* will be followed by a projection. To complete what was started, follow the dialogue in Fig. 4-6 to project J2.PDBF onto a new file, P1.PDBF, listed in Fig. 4-8.

```
CUSTOMERS.PDBF :
            C.CITY-------------- C.STATE
      00001 Baltimore           MD
      00002 Baltimore           MD
      00003 Cincinnati          OH
      00004 Cincinnati          OH
      00005 Computer City       WA
      00006 Corral City         TX
      00007 Los Angeles         CA
      00008 Philadelphia        PA
      00009 Philadelphia        PA
      00010 Philadelphia        PA
      00011 San Francisco       CA
      00012 Transylvania        PA
```

Fig. 4-4. *A printout made by the list program of the cities and states from The Company's customer file. Unfortunately, there is a lot of unnecessary duplication.*

```
CITIES.PDBF :
            C.CITY-------------- C.STATE
      00001 Baltimore           MD
      00002 Cincinnati          OH
      00003 Computer City       WA
      00004 Corral City         TX
      00005 Los Angeles         CA
      00006 Philadelphia        PA
      00007 San Francisco       CA
      00008 Transylvania        PA
```

Fig. 4-5. *The duplications of Fig. 4-4 are automatically removed by projecting the customer file onto a new file called CITIES.PDBF. Listing this file gives us the report we want, a concise list of cities and states where The Company has customers.*

```
Project what file? J2
Giving fields? [<field>,<field>,..,|ret|?]
V.NAME, V.CITY, P.NUM, P.NAME, COST
To what file? P1
Projecting
.....
J2.PDBF projected onto P1.PDBF
```

Fig. 4-6. *A dialogue showing the projection of file J2.PDBF onto a new file, P1.PDBF. This new file will contain a subset of J2. (See Fig. 4-3.)*

```
P1.PDBF :
      V.NAME------------------------ V.CITY---- P.NUM P.NAME---------- COST----
00001 Robotics Manufacturers, Inc.  Baltimore  P3    Body            100.00
00002 Mechanical Assemblies Corp.    San Diego  P3    Body            545.00
00003 Mechanical Assemblies Corp.    San Diego  P6    Hand             50.00
00004 Lord's Electroscopics          Boston     P1    Photometric eye 129.00
00005 Lord's Electroscopics          Boston     P4    Leg              45.00
```

Fig. 4-7. *The resulting list after projecting file J2.PDBF onto P1.PDBF. To follow the steps leading to this list, refer to Figs. 4-1, 4-2, and 4-6 in sequence.*

Look closely at the vendor name (V.NAME) and city (V.CITY) fields of Fig. 4-7. The join has produced duplications here. This is quite correct, as Lord's Electroscopics supplies The Company with both Photometric eyes and legs. (I suppose you have gotten the idea by now that we are in the android manufacturing business.) A relational projection eliminates duplicated *records*, not just duplicated fields.

A further projection of P1.PDBF could give us a list of vendor names and cities. In that list, the duplications would be inappropriate, and *project* handles this for us nicely. (See Fig. 4-8.)

Have we lost any information in the process of joining and projecting all this information here and there? Apparently so, as the vendor key has not been included in the result. This would prevent us from recovering the original SOURCES.PDBF file, which needs the V.KEY field, and we should at this point go back to projecting J2.PDBF, being more careful to follow the rules.

In practice, however, a temporary *join* and *project* for the purpose of preparing reports and lists is acceptable, even if this process does bend the rules somewhat.

Righting the Wrongs

The new PARTS.PDBF file listed in Fig. 3-7 has the weight (P.WGT) and location fields (P.LOC) added to the original definition from Chapter One. Earlier, I indicated that there was something not quite right about this new format for the parts data file.

Storing the location of a part along with the part record itself may be satisfactory if one kind of part is always stored in one place. But what if the same kind of part, let's say number P6 for example, is stored in two warehouses? If we add a duplicate part record just for the purpose of showing that this part is stored in two places, we may miss this fact when editing or viewing the data. Also, if the part name must be changed, you will have to remember to update both records. With hundreds or thousands of parts, as there would be in a typical data base, it would not be possible to manage the information in such a sloppy way.

A solution is easily achieved by projecting the locations of each part out of

```
P2.PDBF :
        V.NAME----------------------- V.CITY-------------
 00001  Robotics Manufacturers, Inc.  Baltimore
 00002  Mechanical Assemblies Corp.   San Diego
 00003  Lord's Electroscopics         Boston
```

Fig. 4-8. *The result of projecting file J2.PDBF (Fig. 4-7) even further to a new file P2.PDBF containing vendor names and cities. Notice that the duplications of file J2.PDBF have been removed by* project.

```
Project what file? PARTS
Giving fields? [<field>,<field>,..,|ret|?]
P.NUM, P.LOC
To what file? LOC
Projecting
......
PARTS.PDBF projected onto LOC.PDBF

Project what file PARTS
Giving fields? [<field>,<field>,..,|ret|?]
P.NUM, P.NAME, P.COLOR, P.WGT, P.REO, P.STOCK
To what file? T1
Projecting
......
PARTS.PDBF projected onto T1.PDBF
```

Fig. 4-9. *Two projections, dialogued here, separate the location field (P.LOC) from the parts file. File T1.PDBF is the new parts file minus the location.*

the parts file to a new file, which you may as well call LOC.PDBF. Follow the dialogue in Fig. 4-9 to first project PARTS.PDBF to LOC.PDBF. Then continue the process by projecting PARTS.PDBF to a temporary data file called T1.PDBF. Finally, rename T1.PDBF to PARTS.PDBF after first saving a backup copy of the original parts data in case you make a mistake.

The results are shown in Fig. 4-10. A few new parts have been added, and you may want to update your own files at this time if you are following along. By projecting the locations of parts to an independent data file, meaning a file where the location of a part is not *dependent* on the part number, as it was before the

```
PARTS.PDBF :
         P.NUM  P.NAME--------------  P.COLOR-  P.WGT  P.REO  P.STOCK
 00001   P1     Photometric eye       Blue        175     50   61
 00002   P2     Arm assembly          Silver     5500     50   59
 00003   P3     Body                  Red        8000      3   18
 00004   P4     Leg                   Black      2500     50   76
 00005   P5     Foot wheel            Black       375    100   110
 00006   P6     Hand                  Silver      425     25   20

LOC.PDBF :
         P.NUM  P.LOC
 00001   P1     L4
 00002   P2     L1
 00003   P3     L3
 00004   P4     L3
 00005   P5     L2
 00006   P6     L2
 00007   P6     L4
 00008   P4     L2
```

Fig. 4-10. *The results of the projections dialogued in Fig. 4-9. By projecting the location of parts into a separate file, a "many-to-many" relationship can be easily represented. A few new parts and locations have been entered into the LOC.PDBF file using the editor.*

```
            LOC.PDBF : P.NUM=P6
                      P.NUM  P.LOC
            00006    P6     L2
            00007    P6     L4


            LOC.PDBF : P.LOC=L3
                      P.NUM  P.LOC
            00003    P3     L3
            00004    P4     L3
```

Fig. 4-11. *Searching for parts and locations in the LOC.PDBF file shows how it is now possible to have one part (P6) in multiple locations (L2, L4), while still showing all parts (P3, P4) stored at one place (L3).*

projection, you have added the ability to have at the same time many parts in one location and many locations where the same part may be found. (See Fig. 4-11.) You may want to spend some time using *join, project, list,* and *report* to verify that this "many-to-many relationship" is now easily maintained in The Company's data base.

For a more rigorous treatment of the subject of normalization and the uses of *join* and *project,* see C.J. Date's *An Introduction to Database Systems,* (Third Edition, The Systems Programming Series; Addison-Wesley Publishing Company), especially Chapter 14 for an explanation of first, second, third, and other normal forms of a relational data base.

```
001: {$S+,I-}              { Compiler swapping on; I/O error checking off }
002:
003: PROGRAM project; uses pdbsunit;
004:
005: {-----------------------------------------------------------------}
006: {                                                                 }
007: {     PROGRAM        :  Form the relational projection of a file  }
008: {     LANGUAGE       :  UCSD Pascal / Apple Pascal 1.1            }
009: {                                                                 }
010: {     Copyright (C) 1983 by Tom Swan. All commercial rights reserved. }
011: {                                                                 }
012: {-----------------------------------------------------------------}
013:
014: VAR
015:     from_name, to_name     : pdbs_fname;    { File names }
016:     from_number, to_number : integer;       { File numbers }
017:     mode                   : close_option;  { Update / no update }
018:     order                  : fld_order;     { Fields to project }
019:
020:
021: FUNCTION make_projection(     fn    : integer;
022:                          VAR order : fld_order;
023:                               fname : pdbs_fname ) : pdbs_err;
024: { Create new file using selected fields from fn }
025: { Assume there is at least one field in the order array }
026: VAR
027:     i       : integer;
028:     msc_rec : msc_descriptor;         { Describes record structure }
029:
030:     PROCEDURE add_field( VAR msc_rec : msc_descriptor;
031:                          VAR fld_rec : fld_descriptor );
032:     { Add field descriptor record to the new msc_rec descriptor }
```

```
033:    BEGIN
034:        WITH msc_rec DO
035:        BEGIN
036:            msc_nflds := msc_nflds + 1;
037:            msc_flds[ msc_nflds ] := fld_rec;
038:            msc_flds[ msc_nflds ].fld_pos := msc_recsize;
039:            msc_recsize := msc_recsize + fld_rec.fld_len
040:        END { with }
041:    END; { add_field }
042:
043: BEGIN
044:    IF NOT file_not_in_use( fname ) THEN
045:     IF NOT verified( concat( 'Remove old ', fname ) ) THEN
046:        BEGIN
047:            make_projection := 25;    { Interrupted by user }
048:            exit( make_projection )
049:        END;
050:
051:    init_msc( msc_rec );
052:    WITH fil_recs[fn].fil_msc DO
053:    FOR i := 1 TO order[0] DO
054:        add_field( msc_rec, msc_flds[ order[i] ] );
055:    make_projection := make_file( fname, msc_rec )
056: END; { make_projection }
057:
058:
059: FUNCTION equal_recs( n : integer; VAR a, b : binary_page ) : boolean;
060: { True if n bytes in a and b are equal }
061: { Status bytes a[0],b[0] are not considered }
062: { Better if encoded in machine language. }
063: VAR
064:    i : integer;
065: BEGIN
066:    FOR i := 1 TO n - 1 DO              { Note: n >= 2 for any record }
067:        IF a[i] <> b[i] THEN
068:            BEGIN
069:                equal_recs := false;
070:                exit( equal_recs )
071:            END;
072:    equal_recs := true
073: END; { equal_recs }
074:
075:
076: FUNCTION find_rec(      fn    : integer;
077:                    VAR bp    : binary_page;
078:                    VAR found : boolean ) : pdbs_err;
079: { Search for an exact match on this binary record (bp) }
080: VAR
081:    err_code : pdbs_err;
082:    rn       : integer;              { Record number }
083:    temp     : binary_page;          { Holds records for comparisons }
084: BEGIN
085:    err_code := 0;
086:    WITH fil_recs[fn].fil_msc DO
087:    FOR rn := 1 TO msc_lastrec DO
088:    BEGIN
089:        err_code := read_rec( fn, rn, temp );
090:        IF err_code <> 0 THEN
091:            BEGIN
092:                find_rec := err_code;  { Return error code to caller }
093:                exit( find_rec )       { Cancel the search }
094:            END;
095:        IF equal_recs( msc_recsize, temp, bp )        { Check for a match }
096:          THEN
097:            BEGIN
098:                found := true;         { Set flag indicating a find }
099:                find_rec := 0;         { Indicate no errors }
```

```
100:              exit( find_rec )        { No need to search further }
101:          END
102:     END; { for }
103:     found := false         { No matches, no runs, no hits, no errors }
104: END; { find_rec }
105:
106:
107: PROCEDURE assign_fields(     fn, tn      : integer;
108:                         VAR source_rec,
109:                             dest_rec    : binary_page;
110:                         VAR order       : fld_order );
111: { Assign equivalent fields from source_rec (file fn) }
112: { to same fields in dest_rec (file tn) using field order array }
113: { If source is marked for deletion, destination will be marked }
114: VAR
115:     field : integer;
116: BEGIN
117:     dest_rec[0] := source_rec[0];    { Transfer status byte }
118:     WITH fil_recs[ fn ].fil_msc DO
119:     FOR field := 1 TO order[0] DO
120:         moveleft(
121:           source_rec[ msc_flds[ order[ field ] ].fld_pos ], { Source }
122:           dest_rec[  fil_recs[ tn ].                        { Destination }
123:                      fil_msc.
124:                      msc_flds[ field ].fld_pos ],
125:           msc_flds[ order[ field ] ].fld_len )             { Count }
126: END; { assign_fields }
127:
128:
129: FUNCTION project_file(     fn, tn : integer;
130:                       VAR order   : fld_order ) : pdbs_err;
131: { Project common fields from file fn (from) onto file tn (to). }
132: { Duplicate records removed for a true relational projection. }
133: VAR
134:     frn        : integer;         { From record number }
135:     frec, trec : binary_page;     { From and To binary records }
136:     found      : boolean;         { Search result }
137:
138:     PROCEDURE perform( n : pdbs_err );
139:     { Do function returning n = error code }
140:     BEGIN
141:        IF n <> 0 THEN
142:           BEGIN
143:              project_file := n;
144:              exit( project_file )
145:           END
146:     END; { perform }
147:
148: BEGIN { project_file }
149:     writeln( 'Projecting' );
150:     FOR frn := 1 TO fil_recs[fn].fil_msc.msc_lastrec DO
151:     BEGIN
152:        perform( read_rec( fn, frn, frec ) );
153:        assign_fields( fn, tn, frec, trec, order );
154:        perform( find_rec( tn, trec, found ) );
155:        IF NOT found THEN
156:           BEGIN
157:              perform( append_rec( tn, trec ) );
158:              write( '.' )          { Feedback }
159:           END
160:     END; { for }
161:     writeln
162: END; { project_file }
163:
164:
165: BEGIN
166:     clrscrn;
```

```
167:    WHILE get_file_name( 'Project what file? ', from_name ) DO
168:    BEGIN
169:      mode := no_update;            { Unless all operations completed }
170:      clreosc;
171:      IF executed( open_file( from_number, from_name ) ) THEN
172:      BEGIN
173:        IF load_order( 'Giving fields?', from_number, order ) THEN
174:        IF get_file_name( 'To what file? ', to_name ) THEN
175:        IF executed( make_projection( from_number, order, to_name ) ) THEN
176:        IF executed( open_file( to_number, to_name ) ) THEN
177:        BEGIN
178:          IF executed( project_file( from_number, to_number, order ) )
179:            THEN mode := update;
180:          IF ( executed( close_file( to_number, mode ) ) ) AND
181:            ( mode = update )
182:            THEN write( from_name, ' projected onto ', to_name )
183:        END; { if }
184:        IF NOT executed( close_file( from_number, no_update ) )
185:          THEN exit( PROGRAM )    { Extremely unlikely }
186:      END; { if }
187:      gotoxy( 0, 0 )
188:    END { while }
189: END.
```

5

Data Base Calculations

CALC / TOTAL / SUBTOTAL / TABULATE

CALC

It is seldom enough to be able to enter, search, and list data. We also want to be able to compute new information from the facts stored in the files. The personnel department will need to calculate the check amounts for employees based on their pay rates, while the purchasing agent will need totals and subtotals on the stock levels of certain part records.

Calc accepts a numeric expression as a formula to be performed on all the records in a file or on a subset of those records. The result of this calculation is then assigned to one of the fields in the record.

To use *calc*, execute the program and supply the name of any PDBS data file. To follow The Company's data base examples here, enter SOURCES. You are then asked for the expression or formula you want to calculate.

Let's say all our suppliers have formed a cartel and have recently voted to increase our costs by 15 percent. We may decide to sue, but first let's adjust the data. Simply typing in the new fact automatically updates the data base.

COST = COST * .15 + COST

Fifteen percent is added to each cost. The before and after results are shown in Fig. 5-1. Expressions are evaluated strictly from left to right. Parentheses, nesting, and operator precedence are not recognized in this version of *calc*. (See *calc-unit* in Chapter Nine for more details and suggestions for improving the program.)

```
SOURCES.PDBF :                              SOURCES.PDBF :
       P.NUM  V.KEY  COST----                     P.NUM  V.KEY  COST----
00001  P3     V2        545.00          00001  P3     V2        626.75
00002  P1     V3        129.00          00002  P1     V3        148.35
00003  P6     V2         50.00          00003  P6     V2         57.50
00004  P4     V3         45.00          00004  P4     V3         51.75
00005  P3     V1        100.00          00005  P3     V1        115.00

       (Before)                                    (After)
```

Fig. 5-1. *Before and after increasing all costs in The Company's SOURCES.PDBF file by 15 percent. The formula used with the calc program was COST = COST * .15 + COST.*

You can also assign values directly to fields. For example, to set all customer balances to zero, you could enter the expression:

C.BALANCE = 0

Calc also asks you the question, "Select records?" At this point, you can enter a search argument, as explained in the instructions to *list*, to perform a calculation on a subset of your data. Only the records that match your search argument will be calculated. The dialogue in Fig. 5-2 shows how to set the account limit for customer C6 to zero after having received one too many bad checks from this chap. Of course, the *editor* could be used to do the same thing.

Spreadsheets

You can maintain a spreadsheet in PDBS and have row and column totals automatically calculated. An example of how to do this will be instructive.

The personnel manager for The Company keeps two files, one listing the members of the sales force and another showing each member's sales in units sold for each month of the year. Use *create* to make the new EMP.PDBF and SALES.PDBF files according to the status reports in Fig. 5-3.

After entering monthly sales figures for each employee (you can just make up amounts using the *editor* if you want to follow along), the total sales are calculated.

```
Calculate what file? CUSTOMERS
Expression? [?|<fld> = <fld,lit> <*,/,+,-> <fld,lit>,...,]
C.LIMIT=0
Select records? [<expr>|ret|?]
C.KEY=C6
Calculating

CUSTOMERS.PDBF:C.LIMIT=0 for C.KEY=C6
```

Fig. 5-2. *Follow this dialogue from the calc program to set the account limit for customer C6 to zero. This shows how a calculation can be performed on a subset of a data file, one record in the example here.*

```
SALES.PDBF                            EMP.PDBF
Record size ............. 45          Record size ............. 38
Number of fields ........ 14          Number of fields ........ 4
Maximum record number ... 22          Maximum record number ... 26
Records in use .......... 4           Records in use .......... 4
Records not used ........ 18          Records not used ........ 22
Date created ............ 07-Jul-83   Date created ............ 21-Jul-83
Date last updated ....... 21-Jul-83   Date last updated ....... 21-Jul-83

 #  NAME      TYPE     LEN DEC POS      #  NAME       TYPE     LEN DEC POS

 1  E#        Char      3   0   1       1  E#         Char      3   0   1
 2  JAN       Number    3   0   4       2  E.NAME     Char     20   0   4
 3  FEB       Number    3   0   7       3  E.SOC.SEC  Char     11   0  24
 4  MAR       Number    3   0  10       4  E%         Number    3   2  35
 5  APR       Number    3   0  13
 6  MAY       Number    3   0  16
 7  JUN       Number    3   0  19
 8  JUL       Number    3   0  22
 9  AUG       Number    3   0  25
10  SEP       Number    3   0  28
11  OCT       Number    3   0  31
12  NOV       Number    3   0  34
13  DEC       Number    3   0  37
14  TOTAL     Number    5   0  40
```

Fig. 5-3. *The Company's personnel records include these two files. Use the create program to enter the field specifications printed here by status.*

The dialogue in Fig. 5-4 shows how this is accomplished using *calc*. Figure 5-5 lists the resulting spreadsheet printed by the *report* program.

Calculations across Two or More Files

The president of The Company, who is in the habit of decreeing things, has decreed a bonus to all sales personnel. She's really not such a bad egg after all.

The bonus is to be based on the sales history and the current commission rate for each employee. The formula to be used is:

BONUS = Units Sold * Commission * 2.5

```
Calculate what file? SALES
Expression? [?|<fld> = <fld,lit> <*,/,+,-> <fld,lit>,...,]
TOTAL=JAN+FEB+MAR+APR+MAY+JUN+JUL+AUG+SEP+OCT+NOV+DEC
Select records? [<expr>|ret|?]
<cr>
Calculating
....
SALES.PDBF:TOTAL=JAN+FEB+MAR+APR+MAY+JUN+JUL+AUG+SEP+OCT+NOV
+DEC for all records
```

Fig. 5-4. *To calculate the yearly sales totals in the SALES.PDBF file, execute the calc program and follow this dialogue.*

```
Date : 21-Jul-83                   The Company, Inc.                      Page-1
                             Yearly Sales Report in Units Sold
```

	Emp	Jan	Feb	Mar	Apr	May	Jun	Jul	Aug	Sep	Oct	Nov	Dec	Total
00001	E1	10	25	125	62	45	99	0	76	38	29	37	49	595
00002	E2	87	76	47	38	277	8	0	388	38	0	38	939	1936
00003	E3	878	367	37	373	28	9	340	9	30	8	0	83	2162
00004	E4	757	374	273	37	99	0	552	18	82	83	645	27	2947
Total		1732	842	482	510	449	116	892	491	188	120	720	1098	7640
Minimum		10	25	37	37	28	0	0	9	30	0	0	27	595
Maximum		878	374	273	373	277	99	552	388	82	83	645	939	2947
Average		433	210	120	127	112	29	223	122	47	30	180	274	1910

```
4 records processed
```

Fig. 5-5. *Spreadsheets are easy to prepare in PDBS. The report program was used to print this example from the data in The Company's SALES.PDBF file.*

The number 2.5 is an arbitrary adjustment factor. First, *create* a BONUS-.PDBF data file using the structure outlined in Fig.5-6. The results will eventually be held in this file.

Next, *join* the SALES.PDBF and EMP.PDBF files over the employee number (E#) field to a temporary file TI.PDBF. *Merge* T1.PDBF into BONUS.PDBF, specifying the fields E#, TOTAL, and E%. Finally, use *calc* to compute the bonus with the BONUS = TOTAL*E%*2.5 formula for all records.

```
BONUS.PDBF
Record size ............ 40
Number of fields ........ 5
Maximum record number ... 25
Records in use .......... 0
Records not used ........ 25
Date created ............ 21-Jul-83
Date last updated ....... 21-Jul-83

#   NAME          TYPE      LEN DEC POS

1   E#            Char        3   0   1
2   E.NAME        Char       20   0   4
3   TOTAL         Number      5   0  24
4   E%            Number      3   2  29
5   BONUS         Number      8   2  32
```

Fig. 5-6. *The first step to calculating bonuses for The Company's employees is to use the create program to make a file with the structure listed here.*

The entire dialogue is shown in Fig. 5-7. A list of the bonuses for each employee is given in Fig. 5-8.

```
Execute what file? JOIN
Join what file? SALES
And what file? EMP
To what file? T1
Join over what field? E#
Joining
     4 of 4
4 records --> T1.PDBF

Execute what file? MERGE
Merge from what file? T1
Merge into what file? BONUS
Merge fields? [<field>,<field>,..,|ret|?]
E#, E.NAME, TOTAL, E%
Merging
....
4 record(s) --> BONUS.PDBF

Execute what file? CALC
Calculate what file? BONUS
Expression? [?|<fld> = <fld,lit> <*,/,+,-> <fld,lit>,...,]
BONUS = TOTAL * E% * 2.5
Select records? [<expr>|ret|?]
<cr>
Calculating
....
BONUS.PDBF:BONUS = TOTAL * E% * 2.5 for all records
```

Fig. 5-7. *The entire dialogue with the computer that will calculate bonuses for all employees. Three programs are needed, join, merge, and calc.*

```
BONUS.PDBF :
          E#-  E.NAME--------------  TOTAL  E%-  BONUS---
   00001  E1   Piper, Peter           595   .15   223.12
   00002  E2   Jones, Al Betoss      1936   .10   484.00
   00003  E3   Applebaum, Shirley    2162   .12   648.60
   00004  E4   Grimple, Marcy R.     2947   .10   736.75
```

Fig. 5-8. *The result of the steps shown in Fig. 5-7. Each employee bonus has been calculated and stored in the BONUS.PDBF file.*

```
001: {$S+,I-}              { Compiler swapping on; I/O error checking off }
002:
003: PROGRAM calc; uses applestuff, pdbsunit, evalunit, calcunit;
004:
005: {---------------------------------------------------------------}
006: {                                                               }
007: {    PROGRAM       :  Perform calculations on data file fields  }
008: {    LANGUAGE      :  UCSD Pascal / Apple Pascal 1.1             }
009: {                                                               }
010: {    Copyright (C) 1983 by Tom Swan. All commercial rights reserved. }
011: {                                                               }
012: {---------------------------------------------------------------}
```

```
013:
014: VAR
015:     arg                 : string;              { Search arguments }
016:     expression          : string;              { Expression to calculate }
017:     field               : integer;             { Result field number }
018:     file_name           : pdbs_fname;          { Data file name }
019:     file_number         : integer;             { Data file number }
020:     mode                : close_option;
021:
022:
023: FUNCTION calc_file( fn, field : integer ) : pdbs_err;
024: { Perform calculation on each record in file storing results in field }
025: VAR
026:     err_code            : pdbs_err;
027:     result              : long_integer; { Result of calculation }
028:     rn                  : integer;      { Record number }
029:     s                   : string;       { Result as a string }
030: BEGIN
031:     writeln( 'Calculating' );
032:     err_code := 0;
033:     rn := 0;
034:     WITH fil_recs[fn].fil_msc DO WITH msc_flds[ field ] DO
035:     WHILE ( rn < msc_lastrec ) AND
036:           ( err_code = 0     ) DO
037:     BEGIN
038:        rn := rn + 1;
039:        IF keypress
040:           THEN err_code := 25                        { Interrupted by user }
041:           ELSE err_code := seek_rec( fn, rn );
042:        IF err_code = 0 THEN IF match( fn ) THEN
043:        BEGIN
044:           compute( fn, fld_decimals, result );   { Computes current record }
045:           str( result, s );                        { Result --> string }
046:           IF fld_decimals > 0 THEN
047:           BEGIN
048:              WHILE length( s ) < fld_decimals DO
049:                 insert( '0', s, 1 );
050:              insert( '.', s, length( s ) - fld_decimals + 1 )
051:           END;
052:           WHILE length( s ) < fld_len DO
053:              insert( ' ', s, 1 );                   { Right justify }
054:           put_field( fn, field, s );                { Write result to file }
055:           write( '.' )                              { Console feedback }
056:        END { if }
057:     END; { with / with / while }
058:     writeln;
059:     calc_file := err_code
060: END; { calc_file }
061:
062:
063: BEGIN
064:     clrscrn;
065:     WHILE get_file_name( 'Calculate what file? ', file_name ) DO
066:     BEGIN
067:        IF executed( open_file( file_number, file_name ) ) THEN
068:        BEGIN
069:           clreosc;
070:           mode := no_update;          { Unless operations completed }
071:           IF load_expression( file_number, field, expression ) THEN
072:           BEGIN
073:              load_arg( 'Select records?', file_number, arg );
074:              IF executed( calc_file( file_number, field ) )
075:                 THEN mode := update
076:           END; { if }
077:           IF ( executed( close_file( file_number, mode ) ) ) AND
078:              ( mode = update ) THEN
```

```
079:                     BEGIN
080:                         IF length( arg ) = 0
081:                             THEN arg := 'all records';
082:                         write( file_name, ':', expression, ' for ', arg )
083:                     END { if }
084:             END;
085:             gotoxy( 0, 0 )
086:     END { while }
087: END.
```

TOTAL

One of the most common requests is "Give me a total of all the . . . " The *total* program is the quickest way to answer that request, and it's very handy, especially when you don't have the time to prepare a full report.

The dialogue in Fig. 5-9 shows the total amount of bonuses, following the example from the last section in Fig. 5-7, to be paid to all employees. Pressing the return key to the 'Select records?' prompt tells the program to select all records when computing the total.

You can also select a subset of the to-be-totaled records in the data file. For example, you can find the total weight of all the silver parts in The Company's PARTS.PDBF file. (See the dialogue in Fig. 5-10.)

```
Total what file? BONUS
Select records? [<expr>|ret|?]
<cr>
Total fields? [<field>,<field>,..,|ret|?]
Working
....
BONUS      : 2092.47
```

Fig. 5-9. *The total program is good for quickly adding up the contents of a field. Here the total amount of bonuses in the BONUS.PDBF file is calculated.*

```
Total what file? PARTS
Select records? [<expr>|ret|?]
P.COLOR = SILVER
Total fields? [<field>,<field>,..,|ret|?]
P.WGT, P.STOCK
Working
......
P.WGT      : 5925
P.STOCK    : 79
```

Fig. 5-10. *A subset of a data file can also be totaled. In this example, the total weights and stock levels of all the silver parts are computed.*

```
001: {$S+,I-}              { Compiler swapping on; I/O error checking off }
002:
003: PROGRAM total; uses applestuff, pdbsunit, evalunit;
004:
005: {-------------------------------------------------------------------------}
006: {                                                                         }
007: {    PROGRAM          : Total numeric fields                              }
008: {    LANGUAGE         : UCSD Pascal / Apple Pascal 1.1                     }
009: {                                                                         }
010: {    Copyright (C) 1983 by Tom Swan. All commercial rights reserved.      }
011: {                                                                         }
012: {-------------------------------------------------------------------------}
013:
014: TYPE
015:     total_array     =                      { One value per field }
016:         ARRAY[ 1 .. max_fld ] OF long_integer;
017:
018: VAR
019:     arg             : string;              { Search arguments }
020:     file_name       : pdbs_fname;          { Data file name }
021:     file_number     : integer;             { Data file number }
022:     order           : fld_order;           { Fields to total }
023:     totals          : total_array;         { Running totals }
024:
025:
026: PROCEDURE show_totals(     fn     : integer;
027:                            order  : fld_order;
028:                        VAR totals : total_array );
029: VAR
030:     i         : integer;       { Array index }
031:     s         : string;        { Totals as strings }
032: BEGIN
033:     WITH fil_recs[fn].fil_msc DO
034:       FOR i := 1 TO order[0] DO
035:         WITH msc_flds[ order[i] ] DO
036:         BEGIN
037:           str( totals[i], s );
038:           IF fld_decimals > 0 THEN
039:           BEGIN
040:             WHILE length( s ) < fld_decimals DO
041:                 insert( '0', s, 1 );
042:             insert( '.', s, length( s ) - fld_decimals + 1 )
043:           END;
044:           writeln( fld_name, ' : ', s )
045:         END { with / for / with }
046: END; { show_totals }
047:
048:
049: FUNCTION total_file(     fn     : integer;
050:                          order  : fld_order;
051:                      VAR totals : total_array ) : pdbs_err;
052: { Calculate totals on file fn fields in order array }
053: VAR
054:     err_code        : pdbs_err;
055:     long            : long_integer; { Intermediate values }
056:     i               : integer;      { Array index }
057:     rn              : integer;      { Record number }
058:     s               : string;       { Fields as strings }
059: BEGIN
060:
061:   { Initialize totals array }
062:
063:     FOR i := 1 TO order[0] DO
064:         totals[i] := 0;
065:
066:     writeln( 'Working' );
067:     rn := 0;
```

```
068:      err_code := 0;
069:      WITH fil_recs[fn].fil_msc DO
070:      WHILE ( rn < msc_lastrec ) AND
071:            ( err_code = 0 ) DO
072:      BEGIN
073:         rn := rn + 1;
074:         IF keypress
075:            THEN err_code := 25          { Interrupted by user }
076:            ELSE err_code := seek_rec( fn, rn );
077:         IF err_code = 0 THEN
078:          IF match( fn ) THEN
079:           FOR i := 1 TO order[0] DO
080:              BEGIN
081:                 get_field( fn, order[i], s );
082:                 lvalue( s, msc_flds[ order[i] ].fld_decimals, long );
083:                 totals[i] := totals[i] + long
084:              END; { for }
085:         write( '.' )                    { Console feedback }
086:      END; { while }
087:      writeln;
088:      total_file := err_code
089: END; { total_file }
090:
091:
092: BEGIN
093:      clrscrn;
094:      WHILE get_file_name( 'Total what file? ', file_name ) DO
095:      BEGIN
096:         IF executed( open_file( file_number, file_name ) ) THEN
097:         BEGIN
098:            clreosc;
099:            load_arg( 'Select records?', file_number, arg );
100:            IF load_order( 'Total fields?', file_number, order ) THEN
101:             IF executed( total_file( file_number, order, totals ) )
102:                THEN show_totals( file_number, order, totals );
103:             IF NOT executed( close_file( file_number, no_update ) )
104:                THEN exit( PROGRAM )
105:         END; { if }
106:         gotoxy( 0, 0 )
107:      END { while }
108: END.
```

SUBTOTAL

In Fig. 5-10, I added the weights and stock levels of the parts that have color fields equal to silver. But in a data base of a thousand parts, perhaps with dozens of colors and other attributes, you wouldn't want to use *total* to calculate the results for every single color. Instead, you can use *subtotal* to prepare a new file containing each unique color along with the total of any numeric field or group of fields also in the file.

Subtotal requires that the data be sorted on the field you are subtotaling. In this example, then, the PARTS.PDBF data file would have to be sorted on the color field. Unfortunately, we haven't presented the sorting program yet, and if you want to follow along with this example, you'll have to skip ahead to Chapter Six, sort the PARTS.PDBF file by color, and then return here.

For an example of using *subtotal,* see Fig. 5-11. This dialogue produces a new data file called COLOR.PDBF, which contains the color field and the totals of the weight (P.WGT) and stock level (P.STOCK) fields.

```
Subtotal what file? PARTS
Total what fields? [<field>,<field>,...,|ret|?]
P.WGT, P.STOCK
Select what field? [<field>,<field>,...,|ret|?]
P.COLOR
Is file sorted on P.COLOR   ? (y/n) Y
Write to what file? COLOR
Working
......
PARTS.PDBF subtotaled --> COLOR.PDBF


COLOR.PDBF :
          P.COLOR-  P.WGT--------  P.STOCK------
00001  BLACK             2875            186
00002  BLUE               175             61
00003  RED               8000             18
00004  SILVER            5925             79
```

Fig. 5-11. *A dialogue with the subtotal program and a list of the result, a new file named COLOR.PDBF. Each item's weight and stock level are totaled by color.*

The output of *subtotal* is always another data file. In a way, the operation of this program resembles a projection. The difference, of course, is that *project* does not have the ability to produce subtotals.

The Subtotal Program

If the requirement that the original data be sorted is bothersome to you, study the next program, *tabulate,* and use the methods there in place of the main body of the *subt_file* procedure in *subtotal* beginning at line 90.

The problem with trying to produce subtotals on an unsorted file is that each unique string value requires the *entire* file to be read from the beginning to end to find all equal values. In a sorted file, you can assume that when the current *key* (see lines 162–163) doesn't match the next record, then that subtotal is complete, and you can begin a new running total (line 168).

Producing subtotals and tabulations (see next section) on unsorted files tends to take a lot of time. PDBS's Virtual Memory Operating System helps speed up programs that make repeated passes over a data file.

Another possibility is to combine the indexing methods in Chapter Six with *subtotal,* reading the records in indexed order on the color field. Indexing is a little faster than sorting, usually, and a lot safer, as you will soon see.

```
001: {$S+,I-}            { Compiler swapping on; I/O error checking off }
002:
003: PROGRAM subtotal; uses pdbsunit;
004:
005: {-----------------------------------------------------------------}
006: {                                                                 }
```

```
007: {    PROGRAM         :  Write subtotals on any field to a data file  }
008: {    LANGUAGE        :  UCSD Pascal / Apple Pascal 1.1                }
009: {                                                                    }
010: {    Copyright (C) 1983 by Tom Swan. All commercial rights reserved. }
011: {                                                                    }
012: {--------------------------------------------------------------------}
013:
014: VAR
015:     from_name       : pdbs_fname;          { Source data file name }
016:     from_number     : integer;             { Source data file number }
017:     to_name         : pdbs_fname;          { Dest data file name }
018:     to_number       : integer;             { Dest data file number }
019:     mode            : close_option;        { Update / no update }
020:     sorder          : fld_order;           { Selection field order }
021:     torder          : fld_order;           { subTotal field order }
022:
023:
024: FUNCTION check_fields( fn : integer; VAR order : fld_order ) : boolean;
025: { Verfiy that all fields are numeric.  Others can't be subtotaled }
026: VAR
027:     i : integer;      { Field order index }
028: BEGIN
029:     WITH fil_recs[fn].fil_msc DO
030:         FOR i := 1 TO order[0] DO       { Order[0] = # fields selected }
031:             IF msc_flds[ order[i] ].fld_type <> dat_number THEN
032:                 BEGIN
033:                     check_fields := false;
034:                     beep;
035:                     writeln( msc_flds[ order[i] ].fld_name, ' not numeric' );
036:                     exit( check_fields )
037:                 END; { with / for / if }
038:     check_fields := true      { No errors detected }
039: END; { check_fields }
040:
041:
042: FUNCTION check_sort( fn, field : integer ) : boolean;
043: { True if operator verifies file to be sorted on this field }
044: BEGIN
045:     write( 'Is file sorted on ' );
046:     write( fil_recs[fn].fil_msc.msc_flds[ field ].fld_name );
047:     check_sort := verified( '' )     { Null string }
048: END; { check_sort }
049:
050:
051: FUNCTION make_subt( fn, tn : integer;
052:                     fname  : pdbs_fname;
053:                     field  : integer;
054:                     order  : fld_order ) : pdbs_err;
055: { Create new subtotal file (fname) out of fn field and field order }
056: VAR
057:     i        : integer;                 { Field order index }
058:     fld_rec  : fld_descriptor;          { Describes each field }
059:     msc_rec  : msc_descriptor;          { Describes data record }
060:
061:     PROCEDURE add_field( VAR msc_rec : msc_descriptor;
062:                          VAR fld_rec : fld_descriptor );
063:     { Add field descriptor record to the new msc_rec descriptor }
064:     BEGIN
065:         WITH msc_rec DO
066:         BEGIN
067:             msc_nflds := msc_nflds + 1;
068:             msc_flds[ msc_nflds ] := fld_rec;
069:             msc_flds[ msc_nflds ].fld_pos := msc_recsize;
070:             msc_recsize := msc_recsize + fld_rec.fld_len
071:         END { with }
072:     END; { add_field }
073:
```

```
074: BEGIN
075:    init_msc( msc_rec );
076:    WITH fil_recs[fn].fil_msc DO
077:    BEGIN
078:       add_field( msc_rec, msc_flds[ field ] );        { Key field }
079:       FOR i := 1 TO order[0] DO        { Order[0] = # fields selected }
080:       BEGIN
081:          fld_rec := msc_flds[ order[i] ];
082:          fld_rec.fld_len := max_digits;     { Use max len for totals }
083:          add_field( msc_rec, fld_rec )
084:       END { for }
085:    END; { with }
086:    make_subt := make_file( fname, msc_rec )
087: END; { make_subt }
088:
089:
090: FUNCTION subt_file( fn, tn : integer;
091:                     field  : integer;
092:                     order  : fld_order ) : pdbs_err;
093: { Subtotal fn fields in order array over contents of "field" to }
094: { destination file tn.  Source file must be sorted on "field" or }
095: { results will be wrong. Assumes file is not empty. }
096: VAR
097:    blank_rec        : binary_page;  { For appending to output file }
098:    compare_key      : string;       { Current value being subtotaled }
099:    err_code         : pdbs_err;     { Function error results }
100:    f                : integer;      { Field number }
101:    key              : string;       { Next key field }
102:    long             : long_integer; { Temporary field value variable }
103:    rn               : integer;      { Record number (main file) }
104:    run_tot          :               { Running totals }
105:       ARRAY[ 1 .. max_fld ] OF long_integer;
106:    s                : string;       { Numeric fields as strings }
107:
108:    PROCEDURE read_key;
109:    { Read global key field string from current record }
110:    BEGIN
111:       get_field( fn, field, key );  { Read key field }
112:       IF case_switch
113:          THEN bumpstrup( key )      { Convert to upper case }
114:    END; { read_key }
115:
116:    PROCEDURE init_output_record;
117:    { Start a new output record }
118:    VAR
119:       i : integer;             { Field order index }
120:    BEGIN
121:       FOR i := 1 TO order[0] DO                   { Clear running totals }
122:          run_tot[i] := 0;
123:       err_code := append_rec( tn, blank_rec )   { Append blank to output }
124:    END; { init_output_record }
125:
126:    PROCEDURE write_output;
127:    { Write current running totals to the output file }
128:    VAR
129:       i : integer;             { Field order index }
130:       s : string;              { Fields as strings }
131:    BEGIN
132:       put_field( tn, 1, compare_key );       { Subtotaled key }
133:       FOR i := 1 TO order[0] DO
134:        WITH fil_recs[tn].fil_msc.msc_flds[i+1] DO
135:          BEGIN
136:             str( run_tot[i], s );   { Running total --> string }
137:             IF fld_decimals > 0 THEN
138:             BEGIN
139:                WHILE length( s ) < fld_decimals DO
140:                   insert( '0', s, 1 );
```

```
141:                        insert( '.', s, length( s ) - fld_decimals + 1 )
142:                    END;
143:                    WHILE length( s ) < fld_len DO
144:                        insert( ' ', s, 1 ); { Right justify result }
145:                    put_field( tn, i+1, s )
146:                END { for / with }
147:     END; { write_output }
148:
149: BEGIN { subt_file }
150:     zero_rec( tn, blank_rec );           { Prepare blank record for appends }
151:     rn := 1;
152:     err_code := 0;
153:     compare_key := ' ';
154:     compare_key[1] := chr(0);            { Or any "unnatural" value }
155:     writeln( 'Working' );
156:     WITH fil_recs[fn] DO WITH fil_msc DO
157:     WHILE ( rn <= msc_lastrec ) AND ( err_code = 0 ) DO
158:     BEGIN
159:         err_code := seek_rec( fn, rn );
160:         IF err_code = 0 THEN
161:         BEGIN
162:             read_key;
163:             IF compare_key <> key
164:               THEN
165:                 BEGIN
166:                     IF rn > 1                        { Not first time through }
167:                         THEN write_output;           { Write running totals }
168:                     init_output_record;              { Start new output record }
169:                     compare_key := key               {  for this key }
170:                 END;
171:             FOR f := 1 TO order[0] DO
172:                 WITH msc_flds[ order[f] ] DO
173:                 BEGIN            { Add fields to running totals }
174:                     get_field( fn, order[f], s );    { Read field }
175:                     lvalue( s, fld_decimals, long ); { String --> value }
176:                     run_tot[f] := run_tot[f] + long  { Add to totals }
177:                 END; { with }
178:             rn := rn + 1;
179:             write( '.' )          { Console feedback }
180:         END { if }
181:     END; { while }
182:     IF err_code = 0
183:         THEN write_output;      { Write last running total to output }
184:     writeln;
185:     subt_file := err_code      { Return error code to caller }
186: END; { subt_file }
187:
188:
189: BEGIN
190:     clrscrn;
191:     WHILE get_file_name( 'Subtotal what file? ', from_name ) DO
192:     BEGIN
193:         IF executed( open_file( from_number, from_name ) ) THEN
194:         BEGIN
195:             clreosc;
196:             mode := no_update;            { Unless operations completed }
197:             IF file_empty( from_number )
198:                 THEN prompt( 'No records in file' )
199:                 ELSE
200:             IF load_order( 'Total what fields?', from_number, torder ) THEN
201:             IF check_fields( from_number, torder ) THEN
202:             IF load_order( 'Select what field?', from_number, sorder ) THEN
203:             IF check_sort( from_number, sorder[1] ) THEN
204:             IF get_file_name( 'Write to what file? ', to_name ) THEN
205:             IF file_not_in_use( to_name ) THEN
206:             IF executed( make_subt( from_number, to_number, to_name,
207:                                     sorder[1], torder ) ) THEN
```

```
208:               IF executed( open_file( to_number, to_name ) ) THEN
209:               BEGIN
210:                  IF executed( subt_file( from_number, to_number,
211:                                          sorder[1], torder ) )
212:                     THEN mode := update;
213:                  IF ( executed( close_file( to_number, mode ) ) ) AND
214:                     ( mode = update )
215:                     THEN write( from_name, ' subtotaled --> ', to_name )
216:               END; { if }
217:               IF NOT executed( close_file( from_number, no_update ) )
218:                  THEN exit( PROGRAM )    { Extremely unlikely }
219:            END; { else }
220:          gotoxy( 0, 0 )
221:    END { while }
222: END.
```

TABULATE

A tabulation is made by counting the equal items in a field of a data file and by producing a new file containing each unique item plus a count of how many units of that item were found among the data in the source information.

Tabulate operates similarly to *subtotal,* and in fact the two programs could be easily combined. They are presented separately here to demonstrate two methods for accomplishing similar ends.

Subtotal, as we just saw, requires the original data to be sorted on the field being collected. This makes the process go faster, but only if you don't count the time it takes to sort the data. If your data will be sorted anyway, then the method used in *subtotal* is the best choice. If the data are not sorted, you can use the algorithm in *tabulate* to count the occurrences of items in any field.

An example of a tabulation on The Company's parts file is given in Fig. 5-12. The output file TAB.PDBF contains a new field of data labeled COUNT. Each entry in the COUNT field is equal to the number of times the item being counted (in this example, each different part color) was found.

```
Tabulate what file? PARTS
Count what field? [<field>,<field>,..,|ret|?]
P.COLOR
To what file? TAB
Tabulating
......
PARTS.PDBF tabulated --> TAB.PDBF

   TAB.PDBF :
            P.COLOR-   COUNT
      00001  BLACK        2
      00002  BLUE         1
      00003  RED          1
      00004  SILVER       2
```

Fig. 5-12. *A dialogue with tabulate and a list of the new file TAB.PDBF containing a count of the different colors found in the PARTS.PDBF file.*

Using Tabulate

If you are following along with the examples in this book, you should have no trouble operating the program. You have to supply three things, the file name of a PDBS data file, the field name you want to tabulate, and the name of an output data file to hold the results.

When you are asked for the field name, you can enter more than one field, but only the first name you enter will be tabulated.

If the output file name you specify already exists, you will receive an error message. Remove that file from your disk or choose a different name for the output.

One possible problem arises if your original file has a field named COUNT on which you want to perform a tabulation. That would produce an output data file with two fields both labeled COUNT, thus breaking the rule that fields in a data file must have unique names. The results are still accurate, and you can use *modify* to change the name of one of these duplicate fields.

```
001: {$S+,I-}              { Compiler swapping on; I/O error checking off }
002:
003: PROGRAM tabulate; uses applestuff, pdbsunit;
004:
005: {----------------------------------------------------------------------}
006: {                                                                      }
007: {     PROGRAM        :  Tabulate contents in any field                 }
008: {     LANGUAGE       :  UCSD Pascal / Apple Pascal 1.1                  }
009: {                                                                      }
010: {     Copyright (C) 1983 by Tom Swan. All commercial rights reserved.  }
011: {                                                                      }
012: {----------------------------------------------------------------------}
013:
014: VAR
015:     from_name,
016:     to_name             : pdbs_fname;
017:     from_number,
018:     to_number           : integer;
019:     mode                : close_option;
020:     order               : fld_order;
021:
022:
023:
024: FUNCTION make_tab( fn    : integer;
025:                    fname : pdbs_fname;
026:                    field : integer ) : pdbs_err;
027: { Create tabulation output file (fname) using field from file fn }
028: VAR
029:     count_fld           : fld_descriptor;
030:     msc_rec             : msc_descriptor;
031:
032:     PROCEDURE add_field( VAR msc_rec : msc_descriptor;
033:                          VAR fld_rec : fld_descriptor );
034:     { Add field descriptor record to the new msc_rec descriptor }
035:     BEGIN
036:         WITH msc_rec DO
037:         BEGIN
038:             msc_nflds := msc_nflds + 1;
039:             msc_flds[ msc_nflds ] := fld_rec;
040:             msc_flds[ msc_nflds ].fld_pos := msc_recsize;
041:             msc_recsize := msc_recsize + fld_rec.fld_len
042:         END { with }
```

```
043:      END; { add_field }
044:
045:  BEGIN { make_tab }
046:      init_msc( msc_rec );
047:      add_field( msc_rec, fil_recs[fn].fil_msc.msc_flds[ field ] );
048:      WITH count_fld DO
049:          BEGIN
050:              str2alpha( 'COUNT', fld_name );
051:              fld_type := dat_number;
052:              fld_len := 5;
053:              fld_decimals := 0              { Fld_pos computed by add_field }
054:          END;
055:      add_field( msc_rec, count_fld );
056:      make_tab := make_file( fname, msc_rec )
057:  END; { make_tab }
058:
059:
060:  FUNCTION tab_file( fn, tn, field : integer ) : pdbs_err;
061:  { Tabulate file fn to tab file tn over field (from fn) }
062:  VAR
063:      blank_rec          : binary_page;
064:      count              : integer;
065:      err_code           : pdbs_err;
066:      rn1, rn2           : integer;
067:      s1, s2             : string;
068:
069:      PROCEDURE perform( n : pdbs_err );
070:      { Perform function returning an error code.  Exit on any error. }
071:      BEGIN
072:          IF n <> 0 THEN
073:              BEGIN
074:                  tab_file := n;
075:                  exit( tab_file )
076:              END { if }
077:      END; { perform }
078:
079:      FUNCTION found_in( fn : integer; s : string ) : boolean;
080:      { True if s found in field 1 of file fn }
081:      VAR
082:          rn    : integer;        { Record number }
083:          ts    : string;         { Test string }
084:      BEGIN
085:          FOR rn := 1 TO fil_recs[fn].fil_msc.msc_lastrec DO
086:          BEGIN
087:              perform( seek_rec( fn, rn ) );
088:              get_field( fn, 1, ts );
089:              IF ts = s THEN
090:                  BEGIN
091:                      found_in := true;
092:                      exit( found_in )
093:                  END { if }
094:          END; { for }
095:          •found_in := false
096:      END; { found_in }
097:
098:  BEGIN
099:      writeln( 'Tabulating' );
100:      zero_rec( tn, blank_rec );
101:      FOR rn1 := 1 TO fil_recs[fn].fil_msc.msc_lastrec DO
102:      BEGIN
103:          write( '.' );            { Feedback }
104:          IF keypress
105:              THEN perform( 25 );        { Interrupted by user error }
106:          perform( seek_rec( fn, rn1 ) );          { Read next field to count }
107:          get_field( fn, field, s1 );
108:          IF case_switch
109:              THEN bumpstrup( s1 );
```

```
110:
111:             IF NOT found_in( tn, s1 ) THEN              { If not already counted }
112:              BEGIN
113:                 count := 0;
114:                 FOR rn2 := 1 TO fil_recs[fn].fil_msc.msc_lastrec DO
115:                 BEGIN
116:                     perform( seek_rec( fn, rn2 ) );          { Count occurrences }
117:                     get_field( fn, field, s2 );
118:                     IF case_switch
119:                         THEN bumpstrup( s2 );
120:                     IF s1 = s2
121:                         THEN count := count + 1
122:                 END; { for }
123:                 num2string( count, 5, ' ', s2 );
124:                 perform( append_rec( tn, blank_rec ) );
125:                 put_field( tn, 1, s1 );              { Field contents }
126:                 put_field( tn, 2, s2 )               { Occurrences }
127:             END { if }
128:         END; { for }
129:         writeln;
130:         tab_file := 0                  { No errors detected }
131: END; { tab_file }
132:
133:
134: BEGIN
135:     clrscrn;
136:     WHILE get_file_name( 'Tabulate what file? ', from_name ) DO
137:     BEGIN
138:         IF executed( open_file( from_number, from_name ) ) THEN
139:         BEGIN
140:             clreosc;
141:             mode := no_update;            { Unless all operations completed }
142:             IF load_order( 'Count what field?', from_number, order ) THEN
143:             IF get_file_name( 'To what file? ', to_name ) THEN
144:             IF file_not_in_use( to_name ) THEN
145:             IF executed( make_tab( from_number, to_name, order[1] ) ) THEN
146:             IF executed( open_file( to_number, to_name ) ) THEN
147:             BEGIN
148:                 IF executed( tab_file( from_number, to_number, order[1] ) )
149:                     THEN mode := update;
150:                 IF ( executed( close_file( to_number, mode ) ) ) AND
151:                     ( mode = update )
152:                     THEN write( from_name, ' tabulated --> ', to_name )
153:             END; { if }
154:             IF NOT executed( close_file( from_number, no_update ) )
155:                 THEN exit( PROGRAM )    { Extremely unlikely }
156:         END; { if }
157:         gotoxy( 0, 0 )
158:     END { while }
159: END.
```

6

Sorting and Indexing

SORT / MERGESORT / INDEX / FIND / UPDATE

SORT

There are two primary ways to rearrange the data in a file. You can sort the information by physically moving the records to new positions in the file, or you can prepare another file, called an index, to access the records in the main data file in some sequence without having to actually move the records themselves.

Sort, the first program in this chapter, demonstrates how a sorting method normally used for sorting arrays in a computer's memory can be used to sort records in a PDBS data file. Usually, it is not a good idea to use such a method with data files stored on external materials such as floppy disks. But, because PDBS keeps as much as possible of a data file in memory at a time because of its underlying Virtual Memory Operating System (see Chapter Eight), array-sorting algorithms work better than expected.

This observation seems to remain true as long as most of the file can be read into memory. When the file begins to expand beyond that point, and much of the information has to be swapped to and from the disk drive, then the array sorter presented here will develop a miserable case of lethargy, and another method will have to be used.

Stable vs. Unstable Sorting

A stable sorting method preserves the original relative order of data, while an unstable method destroys that order. In other words, if a name-and-address file is first sorted by name and is then sorted by state, the result would be an alphabetic list of states with the names sorted within each state.

```
Sort what file? CUSTOMERS
Sort fields? [<field>,<field>,..,|ret|?]
C.BALANCE
Ascending or Descending sequence? D
Do any fields have upper and lower case letters? (y/n) N
Sorting on C.BALANCE
CUSTOMERS.PDBF sorted
```

Fig. 6-1. *An example of using the sort program to reorder the customer file from the largest to the smallest balance.*

Sorting a file with an unstable sorting program first by name and then by state would produce a list of the states in order, but the names would not retain their original relative positions and would therefore be jumbled within each state, not in the alphabetic order you want. There is an easy way to avoid this problem, as will be seen in the instructions to the next program, *mergesort*.

A common stable method, called an insertion sort, is used in the *sort* program here. There are two procedures, *sort_up* at line 22 and *sort_dn* at line 72. These procedures are nearly the same, except that the first sorts alphabetically in ascending order (A, B, C, D, E), while the second sorts in descending order (5, 4, 3, 2, 1).

Because this program is a stable sorter, you can sort files first on one field and then on another, with each successive "pass" maintaining the relative order of the last sort. You could, for example, have a file sorted by the cities in alphabetic ascending order within each state along with customer balances in descending order, from the highest to lowest, within each city.

To do this, the file first must be sorted by balance in descending order. Follow the dialogue in Fig. 6-1 and examine the list in 6-2. This list, prepared by the *list* program, of course, shows only the names and balances from the file. The highest balance is at the top of the list.

Next, follow the dialogue in Fig. 6-3 to complete the sort. This time, sort on two fields, C.STATE and C.CITY. Because you want the result to be mainly in state order, that field is entered first. C.STATE is called the *primary key;* C.CITY

```
CUSTOMERS.PDBF :
      C.NAME----------------------    C.BALANCE
00001 Franklin, Benjamin              2500.00
00002 Pascal, Blaise                  1375.78
00003 Stallion, Horace                 825.50
00004 Bell, Liber T.                   825.50
00005 Venus, Gypsy                     800.00
00006 Bear, Theodore Edward            622.00
00007 Slumgullion, Stewart             500.00
00008 Crockett, D. V.                  500.00
00009 Danzig, Irving                   325.00
00010 West, Martin Quincy              125.00
00011 Diffenforker, Cecil                 .00
00012 Quick, Jack B.                      .00
```

Fig. 6-2. *A list of the name and balance fields after sorting the customer file in descending order by balance.*

```
Sort what file? CUSTOMERS
Sort fields? [<field>,<field>,..,|ret|?]
C.STATE, C.CITY
Ascending or Descending sequence? A
Do any fields have upper and lower case letters? (y/n) Y
Sorting on C.CITY
Sorting on C.STATE
CUSTOMERS.PDBF sorted
```

Fig. 6-3. *After sorting the customer file by balance (see Figs. 6-1 and 6-2), the same file is sorted by city and state.*

the *secondary key*. The final list (see Fig. 6-4) shows the state, city, balance, and names from the sorted file. Now that you have a sorted list, notice how easy it is to find out who in Philadelphia owes you the most money. Perhaps you should send a letter suggesting the gentleman send *you* some of those pennies he has been saving.

Only a stable sorting method can produce both an ascending and descending ordering of records in the same file. Using an unstable method would not allow a mix of ascending and descending sequences. Unfortunately, the more versatile stable methods tend to be slower than the unstable ones.

Sorting Partially Sorted Files

The insertion sort algorithm used in *sort* works particularly well on files that are already partially sorted. Normally, this is the case with data base files when previous sorts leave the file in at least a semi-ordered state most of the time, and the insertion sort can just insert new data into their proper positions without having to re-sort everything all over again.

One way to take advantage of this action is to enter new records into a *copy* of the main data file, as suggested in Chapter Three. *Sort* the new records and then *append* them to the main data file. Finally, re-sort the main data file.


```
CUSTOMERS.PDBF :
        C.STATE  C.CITY---------  C.BALANCE  C.NAME--------------
00001   CA  Los Angeles               .00    Diffenforker, Cecil
00002   CA  San Francisco             .00    Quick, Jack B.
00003   MD  Baltimore              800.00    Venus, Gypsy
00004   MD  Baltimore              125.00    West, Martin Quincy
00005   OH  Cincinnati             622.00    Bear, Theodore Edward
00006   OH  Cincinnati             500.00    Slumgullion, Stewart
00007   PA  Philadelphia          2500.00    Franklin, Benjamin
00008   PA  Philadelphia           825.50    Bell, Liber T.
00009   PA  Philadelphia           500.00    Crockett, D. V.
00010   PA  Transylvania           325.00    Danzig, Irving
00011   TX  Corral City            825.50    Stallion, Horace
00012   WA  Computer City         1375.78    Pascal, Blaise
```

Fig. 6-4. *After three sorts, the customer file is in ascending order by state and city with the balances in descending order by city. It is now a simple matter to find the person with the largest balance in each city.*

About the Safety of Sorting

Sorting is a potentially dangerous operation. Records are moved during sorting, and if the power should go off during the sort, you could lose part or all of the data file.

Never sort your only copy of a file. Always make a copy of the file before sorting.

Because PDBS uses simple, so-called flat files in which there are no links or pointer fields to become damaged, there is very little that can go wrong even if you should experience a power failure. But it is always wise to be cautious.

```
001: {$S+,I-}              { Compiler swapping on; I/O error checking off }
002:
003: PROGRAM sort; uses pdbsunit;
004:
005: {-----------------------------------------------------------------}
006: {                                                                 }
007: {    PROGRAM         :  Sort a data file on any field(s)          }
008: {    LANGUAGE        :  UCSD Pascal / Apple Pascal 1.1            }
009: {                                                                 }
010: {    Copyright (C) 1983 by Tom Swan. All commercial rights reserved. }
011: {                                                                 }
012: {-----------------------------------------------------------------}
013:
014: VAR
015:     direction         : char;           { 'A'=ascending; 'D'=descending }
016:     file_name         : pdbs_fname;      { PDBS data file name }
017:     file_number       : integer;         { PDBS data file number }
018:     mode              : close_option;
019:     order             : fld_order;       { Fields to sort by }
020:
021:
022: FUNCTION sort_up( fn, field, num : integer ) : pdbs_err;
023: { Using a modified ascending straight insertion algorithm }
024: VAR
025:     i, j : integer;
026:     bp1, bp2 : binary_page;
027:     s1, s2 : string;
028:
029:     PROCEDURE perform( n : pdbs_err );
030:     { Similar to execute, except set global err_code and exit if error }
031:     BEGIN
032:         IF n <> 0 THEN
033:             BEGIN
034:                 sort_up := n;
035:                 exit( sort_up )
036:             END { if }
037:     END; { perform }
038:
039: BEGIN
040:     FOR i := 2 TO num DO
041:         BEGIN
042:             perform( read_rec( fn, i, bp2 ) );
043:             get_field( fn, field, s2 );
044:             IF case_switch
045:                 THEN bumpstrup( s2 );
046:             j := i - 1;
047:             perform( read_rec( fn, j, bp1 ) );
048:             get_field( fn, field, s1 );
049:             IF case_switch
050:                 THEN bumpstrup( s1 );
051:             WHILE s2 < s1 DO
```

```
052:                    BEGIN
053:                      perform( write_rec( fn, j + 1, bp1 ) );
054:                      j := j - 1;
055:                      IF j > 0
056:                        THEN
057:                          BEGIN
058:                            perform( read_rec( fn, j, bp1 ) );
059:                            get_field( fn, field, s1 );
060:                            IF case_switch
061:                              THEN bumpstrup( s1 )
062:                          END
063:                        ELSE
064:                            s1 := s2  { To halt WHILE loop }
065:                    END; { while }
066:              perform( write_rec( fn, j + 1, bp2 ) )
067:          END; { for }
068:      sort_up := 0     { No errors }
069: END; { sort_up }
070:
071:
072: FUNCTION sort_dn( fn, field, num : integer ) : pdbs_err;
073: { Using a modified descending straight insertion algorithm }
074: VAR
075:     i, j : integer;
076:     bp1, bp2 : binary_page;
077:     s1, s2 : string;
078:
079:     PROCEDURE perform( n : pdbs_err );
080:     { Similar to execute, except set global err_code and exit if error }
081:     BEGIN
082:         IF n <> 0 THEN
083:             BEGIN
084:                 sort_dn := n;
085:                 exit( sort_dn )
086:             END { if }
087:     END; { perform }
088:
089: BEGIN
090:     FOR i := num - 1 DOWNTO 1 DO
091:         BEGIN
092:             perform( read_rec( fn, i, bp2 ) );
093:             get_field( fn, field, s2 );
094:             IF case_switch
095:                 THEN bumpstrup( s2 );
096:             j := i + 1;
097:             perform( read_rec( fn, j, bp1 ) );
098:             get_field( fn, field, s1 ):
099:             IF case_switch
100:                 THEN bumpstrup( s1 );
101:             WHILE s2 < s1 DO
102:                 BEGIN
103:                     perform( write_rec( fn, j - 1, bp1 ) );
104:                     j := j + 1;
105:                     IF j <= num
106:                       THEN
107:                         BEGIN
108:                             perform( read_rec( fn, j, bp1 ) );
109:                             get_field( fn, field, s1 );
110:                             IF case_switch
111:                                 THEN bumpstrup( s1 )
112:                         END
113:                       ELSE
114:                             s1 := s2  { To halt the WHILE loop }
115:                 END; { while }
116:             perform( write_rec( fn, j - 1, bp2 ) )
117:         END; { for }
118:     sort_dn := 0     { No errors }
```

```
119: END; {sort_dn}
120:
121:
122: FUNCTION sorted( fn, field : integer; d : char ) : pdbs_err;
123: { Sort file fn by this field number.  d = 'A', 'D' direction }
124: { Function value returned is equivalent to ioresult error code. }
125: BEGIN { sorted }
126:    sorted := 0;   { Presume no errors unless something fails. }
127:    WITH fil_recs[fn].fil_msc DO
128:       BEGIN
129:          writeln( 'Sorting on ', msc_flds[field].fld_name );
130:          IF msc_lastrec >= 2 THEN
131:             IF d = 'A'
132:                THEN sorted := sort_up( fn, field, msc_lastrec )
133:                ELSE
134:             IF d = 'D'
135:                THEN sorted := sort_dn( fn, field, msc_lastrec )
136:                ELSE sorted := 3    { Illegal operation }
137:       END { with }
138: END; { sorted }
139:
140:
141: FUNCTION get_direction( VAR d : char ) : char;
142: { Prompt for and return 'A' for ascending, 'D' for descending }
143: BEGIN
144:    write( 'A(scending or D(escending sequence? ' );
145:    read( keyboard, d );
146:    IF d > chr( blank )
147:       THEN writeln( d );
148:    d := cap( d );
149:    get_direction := d
150: END; { get_direction }
151:
152:
153: BEGIN
154:    clrscrn;
155:    WHILE get_file_name( 'Sort what file? ', file_name ) DO
156:    BEGIN
157:       clreosc;
158:       IF executed( open_file( file_number, file_name ) ) THEN
159:       BEGIN
160:          IF load_order( 'Sort fields?', file_number, order ) THEN
161:          IF get_direction( direction ) IN [ 'A', 'D' ] THEN
162:          BEGIN
163:             mode := update;   { Unless something fails }
164:             case_switch :=
165:              verified( 'Do any fields have upper and lower case letters' );
166:             WHILE order[0] > 0 DO              { Order[0] = index }
167:                IF executed( sorted( file_number,
168:                                     order[ order[0] ],
169:                                     direction ) )
170:                   THEN
171:                      order[0] := order[0] - 1    { Sort next field }
172:                   ELSE
173:                      BEGIN
174:                         mode := no_update;
175:                         order[0] := 0             { Force exit on error }
176:                      END { else }
177:
178:          END; { if }
179:          IF NOT executed( close_file( file_number, mode ) )
180:             THEN exit( PROGRAM );
181:          IF mode = update
182:             THEN write( file_name, ' sorted' )
183:       END; { if }
184:       gotoxy( 0, 0 )
185:    END { while }
186: END.
```

MERGESORT

When a data file cannot be completely held in the computer's memory, array-sorting methods are no longer adequate. Instead, a method more suited to sorting records stored externally must be found.

The reason for this odd state of affairs appears to lie in the way array-sorting algorithms minimize the number of comparisons made in order to make the sort go faster. In the high-speed memory of a computer, shuffling data from one place to another is just about the fastest operation a processor can perform. You can afford to shuffle things about when everything is in memory at once and gain the most speed by limiting the time spent comparing data elements.

This same shuffling attempted with an external storage device—even a fast hard disk spinning at 3,600 RPM—can negate any advantage gained by minimizing the number of comparisons. When sorting with most of the data stored on disk, you must attempt to limit the amount of shuffling even if the number of comparisons increases.

The rule seems intuitive. Minimize the slowest element in a process to improve the speed of the whole. In the *index* and *find* programs, you will see how following this rule can have dramatic results.

Using Mergesort

Mergesort requires two extra disk files in addition to the data file being sorted. These "work files" are needed only while the sort is in progress, and can be removed after sorting. I like to call them A.PDBF and B.PDBF, but you can use any names you like.

```
Merge sort what file? LOC
"A" work file A
"B" work file B
Sort on what fields? [<field>,<field>,..,|ret|?]
P.LOC, P.NUM
Do any fields have upper and lower case letters? (y/n) N
Sorting
2 run(s) complete
1 run(s) complete
LOC.PDBF sorted

    LOC.PDBF :
            P.LOC   P.NUM
    00001   L1      P2
    00002   L2      P5
    00003   L2      P6
    00004   L3      P3
    00005   L3      P4
    00006   L4      P1
    00007   L4      P6
```

Fig. 6-5. *Merge sorting the LOC.PDBF file by location and number fields. Part numbers are now in sequence for each location.*

```
Merge sort what file? LOC
"A" work file A
"B" work file B
Sort on what fields? [<field>,<field>,..,|ret|?]
P.NUM, P.LOC
Do any fields have upper and lower case letters? (y/n) N
Sorting
2 run(s) complete
1 run(s) complete
LOC.PDBF sorted


     LOC.PDBF :
              P.NUM  P.LOC
     00001   P1     L4
     00002   P2     L1
     00003   P3     L3
     00004   P4     L3
     00005   P5     L2
     00006   P6     L2
     00007   P6     L4
```

Fig. 6-6. *The opposite sort from that shown in Fig. 6-5. By changing the order of the fields sorted, a completely different result is obtained. Here, the locations are in sorted order for each part number.*

Use *copy* to copy the structure of the data file to be sorted into the work files A.PDBF and B.PDBF. These files will start out empty but will eventually be expanded to accommodate new data written to them by the *mergesort* program. For this reason, you should leave plenty of blank space just after the end of each work file. If there is not enough room, the sort will fail with an error.

It is possible that this kind of error will damage the original data. You should keep a backup copy of your file for the reasons previously explained.

Figure 6-5 dialogues a *mergesort* of The Company's LOC.PDBF file, which was created in Chapter Four. Before following along, you should *copy* LOC.PDBF to work files A.PDBF and B.PDBF. The sorted locations file, listed in Fig. 6-5, shows the result of sorting on the two fields, P.LOC and P.NUM. In this list, you have the part locations in order with the part numbers in sequence for each location.

Figure 6-6 shows the opposite sort. Here the part number is the primary key, and the location of each part is the secondary key. The ability to produce such cross-references by sorting a file in different ways is important to data base management software.

The Mergesort Program Listing

Mergesort, like *sort,* is a stable sorting method. If a file is sorted at different times on different fields, each subsequent pass over the data does not disturb the relative order already present.

The way a multiple field sort is produced in *mergesort,* however, is quite different from the method used in the *sort* program. Instead of sorting first by one field and then by the next, *mergesort* makes use of a procedure called *make_key,* which allows a program to treat several fields as though they were one. (See, for example, lines 81, 114, and 116, among others.) By using this device, it is possible to sort on many fields with a single sorting operation.

Make_key accepts a *fld_order* array, described in Chapter Two (see the instructions to program *list*), and returns a string, *fx_key*, in line 81. The string, or key, is created by *make_key* out of the fields specified in the *order* array. When fields are strung together in this manner, the result is called a "concatenated key."

Although *mergesort* is a stable sorting method, the use of *make_key* here demonstrates how you could use an unstable algorithm to sort a data file on many fields at once. As long as a concatenated key is used as the sort key, the result of sorting with an unstable method will be the same as sorting in several passes using a stable sort. You cannot, apparently, have an ascending and descending sort on the same file at the same time using only an unstable sorting method, and you are limited by the maximum length of the concatenated key, 255 characters in this version of PDBS.

Mergesort goes faster than *sort* on large files because it minimizes the slowest element of the process, the transfer of data between memory and the disk drive. The method is simple to understand. "Runs," or sorted segments, are sent to the work files A and B. The program begins by writing data from the main file to work file A. As long as the data are in order, the output goes to this work file. (See procedure *merge* at line 135.) When an out-of-sequence item is found in the source file, setting the boolean variable *end_of_run* to "true" (see procedure *copy* at line 68), the program switches to work file B and starts a new run onto that file.

After all of the data are written to work files A and B, the runs in those files are merged back into the original data file, thus producing sorted runs in the original that are equal to the combined lengths of each pair of runs merged. By repeating this process until only a single run is produced, the entire file is sorted.

The display of *mergesort* informs you how many runs have been completed. When this number is one, the sort is complete. Partially sorted files produce fewer work runs and therefore take less time to sort.

(For more information about merge sorting, see *Algorithms + Data Structures = Programs* by Niklaus Wirth, Prentice-Hall, 1976, pp. 97-98. Also see Donald E. Knuth's *Sorting and Searching* in *The Art of Computer Programming* series, Vol. 3; Addison-Wesley, 1973, pp. 247-388.)

```
001: {$S+,I-}              { Compiler swapping on; I/O error checking off }
002:
003: PROGRAM mergesort; uses applestuff, pdbsunit;
004:
005: {--------------------------------------------------------------------}
006: {                                                                    }
007: {    PROGRAM        :  Merge sort a large data file                  }
008: {    LANGUAGE       :  UCSD Pascal / Apple Pascal 1.1                 }
009: {                                                                    }
010: {    Copyright (C) 1983 by Tom Swan. All commercial rights reserved. }
011: {                                                                    }
012: {--------------------------------------------------------------------}
013:
```

```
014: {-------------------------------------------------------------------}
015: {                                                                   }
016: {       Adapted from a program appearing in :                       }
017: {               Algorithms + Data Structures = Programs             }
018: {               by Niklaus Wirth; Prentice-Hall 1976; pp 97..98     }
019: {                                                                   }
020: {-------------------------------------------------------------------}
021:
022: VAR
023:     afn      : integer;              { Work file "A" number }
024:     afname   : pdbs_fname;           { Work file "A" name }
025:     bfn      : integer;              { Work file "B" number }
026:     bfname   : pdbs_fname;           { Work file "B" name }
027:     cfn      : integer;              { Main file "C" number }
028:     cfname   : pdbs_fname;           { Main file "C" name }
029:     mode     : close_option;         { Update / No update }
030:     order    : fld_order;            { Fields to sort by }
031:
032:
033: FUNCTION end_of_file( fn, rn : integer ) : boolean;
034: { True if record rn is > number recs in file }
035: BEGIN
036:     end_of_file := ( rn > fil_recs[fn].fil_msc.msc_lastrec ) OR
037:                    (rn < 0 )  { in case rn = 32,767 + 1 }
038: END; { end_of_file }
039:
040:
041: FUNCTION check_files( fx, fy : integer ) : pdbs_err;
042: { Verify that these two files have the same structures }
043: BEGIN
044:     IF fil_recs[fx].fil_msc.msc_flds <> fil_recs[fy].fil_msc.msc_flds
045:         THEN check_files := 3           { Illegal operation }
046:         ELSE check_files := 0           { No error }
047: END; { check_files }
048:
049:
050: FUNCTION natural_merge( afn, bfn, cfn : integer;
051:                         order         : fld_order ) : pdbs_err;
052: VAR
053:     arn, brn, crn    : integer;      { Record numbers }
054:     buf_key          : string;       { Global buffer key for copying }
055:     end_of_run       : boolean;      { End merge run flag }
056:     nruns            : integer;      { Number of runs merged }
057:
058:     PROCEDURE perform( n : pdbs_err );
059:     { Execute any function that returns an error code. }
060:     BEGIN
061:         IF n <> 0 THEN
062:             BEGIN
063:                 natural_merge := n;
064:                 exit( natural_merge )
065:             END
066:     END; { perform }
067:
068:     PROCEDURE copy( VAR fx, xrn, fy, yrn : integer );
069:     VAR
070:         buffer       : binary_page;
071:         fx_key       : string;
072:     BEGIN
073:         perform( get_rec( fx, buffer ) ); xrn := xrn + 1;
074:         perform( append_rec( fy, buffer ) ); yrn := yrn + 1;
075:         IF end_of_file( fx, xrn )
076:           THEN
077:             end_of_run := true
078:           ELSE
079:             BEGIN
080:                 perform( seek_rec( fx, xrn ) );
```

```
081:              make_key( fx, order, fx_key );
082:              end_of_run := buf_key > fx_key;
083:              buf_key := fx_key        { Save for next comparison }
084:          END { else }
085:    END; { copy }
086:
087:    PROCEDURE copy_run( VAR fx, xrn, fy, yrn : integer );
088:    { Copy one run from fx to fy }
089:    BEGIN
090:       perform( seek_rec( fx, xrn ) );
091:       make_key( fx, order, buf_key );        { Reset global key }
092:       REPEAT
093:          copy( fx, xrn, fy, yrn )
094:       UNTIL end_of_run
095:    END; { copy_run }
096:
097:    PROCEDURE distribute;
098:    { From cfn to afn and bfn }
099:    BEGIN
100:       REPEAT
101:          copy_run( cfn, crn, afn, arn );
102:          IF NOT end_of_file( cfn, crn )
103:             THEN copy_run( cfn, crn, bfn, brn )
104:       UNTIL end_of_file( cfn, crn )
105:    END; { distribute }
106:
107:    PROCEDURE merge_run;
108:    { From afn and bfn to cfn }
109:    VAR
110:       a_key, b_key  : string;
111:    BEGIN
112:       REPEAT
113:          perform( seek_rec( afn, arn ) );
114:          make_key( afn, order, a_key );
115:          perform( seek_rec( bfn, brn ) );
116:          make_key( bfn, order, b_key );
117:          IF a_key <= b_key
118:             THEN
119:                BEGIN
120:                   buf_key := a_key;                { Reset global key }
121:                   copy( afn, arn, cfn, crn );
122:                   IF end_of_run
123:                      THEN copy_run( bfn, brn, cfn, crn )
124:                END
125:             ELSE
126:                BEGIN
127:                   buf_key := b_key;                { Reset global key }
128:                   copy( bfn, brn, cfn, crn );
129:                   IF end_of_run
130:                      THEN copy_run( afn, arn, cfn, crn )
131:                END
132:       UNTIL end_of_run
133:    END; { merge_run }
134:
135:    PROCEDURE merge;
136:    { From and and bfn to cfn }
137:    BEGIN
138:       WHILE ( NOT end_of_file( afn, arn ) ) AND
139:             ( NOT end_of_file( bfn, brn ) ) DO
140:       BEGIN
141:          merge_run;
142:          nruns := nruns + 1
143:       END;
144:       WHILE NOT end_of_file( afn, arn ) DO
145:       BEGIN
146:          copy_run( afn, arn, cfn, crn );
147:          nruns := nruns + 1
```

```
148:        END;
149:        WHILE NOT end_of_file( bfn, brn ) DO
150:        BEGIN
151:           copy_run( bfn, brn, cfn, crn );
152:           nruns := nruns + 1
153:        END
154:     END; { merge }
155:
156: BEGIN { natural_merge }
157:     IF fil_recs[cfn].fil_msc.msc_lastrec < 2      { >= 2 records required }
158:        THEN perform( 20 );   { Aborts with error 20 = end of file }
159:     writeln( 'Sorting' );
160:     REPEAT
161:        perform( zero_file( afn ) );              { rewrite( a ) }
162:        arn := 1;
163:        perform( zero_file( bfn ) );              { rewrite( b ) }
164:        brn := 1;
165:        crn := 1;                                 { reset( c ) }
166:        distribute;
167:        arn := 1;                                 { reset( a ) }
168:        brn := 1;                                 { reset( b ) }
169:        perform( zero_file( cfn ) );              { rewrite( c ) }
170:        crn := 1;
171:        nruns := 0;
172:        merge;
173:        writeln( nruns, ' run(s) completed' )
174:     UNTIL nruns = 1;
175:     natural_merge := 0        { No errors detected }
176: END; { natural_merge }
177:
178:
179: BEGIN
180:     clrscrn;
181:     WHILE get_file_name( 'Merge sort what file? ', cfname ) DO
182:     BEGIN
183:        IF executed( open_file( cfn, cfname ) ) THEN
184:        BEGIN
185:           mode := no_update;        { Unless all operations completed }
186:           IF get_file_name( '"A" work file? ', afname ) THEN
187:           IF executed( open_file( afn, afname ) ) THEN
188:           BEGIN
189:              IF executed( check_files( cfn, afn ) ) THEN
190:              IF get_file_name( '"B" work file? ', bfname ) THEN
191:              IF executed( open_file( bfn, bfname ) ) THEN
192:              BEGIN
193:                 clreosc;
194:                 IF executed( check_files( cfn, bfn ) ) THEN
195:                 IF load_order( 'Sort on what fields? ', cfn, order ) THEN
196:                 BEGIN
197:                    case_switch := verified(
198:                      'Do any fields have upper and lower case letters' );
199:                    IF executed( natural_merge( afn, bfn, cfn, order ) )
200:                       THEN mode := update;
201:                    IF NOT executed( close_file( bfn, no_update ) )
202:                       THEN exit( PROGRAM )      { Extremely unlikely }
203:                 END { if }
204:              END; { if }
205:              IF NOT executed( close_file( afn, no_update ) )
206:                 THEN exit( PROGRAM )            { Also unlikely }
207:           END; { if }
208:           IF ( executed( close_file( cfn, mode ) ) ) AND
209:              ( mode = update )
210:              THEN write( cfname, ' sorted' )
211:        END; { if }
212:        gotoxy( 0, 0 )
213:     END { while}
214: END.
```

INDEX

As your files become larger and larger, you will need better ways to quickly search through your records. Preparing an index is one answer.

Of the many possible kinds of indexes, a structure known as a multiway B-tree appears to be the best. It is so good, in fact, that when first used, its speed never fails to astonish the operators and please the programmers. A search for a name in a file of 20,000 names and addresses, for example, is accomplished in the blink of an eye—never more than a couple of seconds usually.

To understand how this can be possible, remember how sorting was improved by limiting the activity of the slowest part of the system, the disk drive. A multiway tree works as well as it does because of its ability to greatly minimize disk reads. Even a very large file seldom requires more than three disk accesses to locate the first occurrence of any record. When coupled with the PDBS Virtual Memory Operating System, in which a lot of the index is kept in the computer's memory, searching is even faster, almost instantaneous in fact.

In addition to all this in its favor, the multiway B-tree is a self-reorganizing, balanced system, meaning that index files never require maintenance as they do with some other inferior schemes. The most notorious of the alternatives is ISAM, technically an acronym for "Indexed Sequential Access Method," but irreverently relabeled by many the "Incredibly Slow Access Method."

Still another advantage in using indexes over sorting is safety. Because the data file records are never changed or moved in any way, the dangers that exist when sorting a file do not have to be considered when indexing. It is possible to damage an index, of course, but there is almost no chance of harming the data file by creating or updating an index. You should still maintain backups of your files, however.

Using the Index Program

Figure 6-7 shows how the *index* program can be used to create or build an index for The Company's customer file. Any field of the customer records can be indexed, but here I have decided to index on the C.NAME field. The index is stored in another file that I choose to call CNAME. The program automatically adds .INDX to this file name to indicate that the file contains an index.

A data file can be indexed on as many fields as you want. Each .INDX file must, however, be given a different file name and must be separately created with the *index* program. If you try to specify more than one field name at a time, only the first field will be used to prepare the index.

Fields do not have to be unique to be inserted in the index. You can index as many duplicate names or other values as occur in the data file. Searching will always locate the first of the duplicated index entries, but as you will see in the *find* program, the rest of the records can be easily found as well by listing the file in indexed order.

```
Index what file? CUSTOMERS
To what file? CNAME
On what field? [<field>,<field>,..,|ret|?]
C.NAME
Opening index file
Start with record # (ret to quit)? 1
Indexing
...........
CUSTOMERS.PDBF indexed to CNAME.INDX on C.NAME
```

Fig. 6-7. *Using the* index *program to prepare an index on the names in The Company's customer file. After indexing, any name can be found in seconds, even among thousands of records.*

When selecting a candidate field for an index, it is usually a good idea to stay with fields that are not too long. Generally, the longer the values in a field, the less useful the index will be. It would hardly be of much use, for example, to index an entire paragraph of 255 characters, although you can do this if you want. A better approach would be to index on a subject key field stored along with the text. I like to keep notes in this way.

Notice in Fig. 6-7 that the *index* program asks for the record number from which you want to begin indexing. This makes it easy to add newly appended records into indexes without having to reindex the entire file. When appending new records with the *editor,* note the record number of the first new entry and supply this number to the index program. The index will then be updated with the new records.

If you change any of the fields on which a file is indexed, then you should reindex the file as soon as possible. Likewise, any deletions from a data file (see program *delete* in Chapter Seven) require indexes to be reconstructed.

Before reindexing a file, remove the old index file first. If you forget to do this, the index will contain duplications, and although searches will still work in many cases, they may produce strange results. This is not a serious error and can be easily repaired by removing the .INDX file and running the *index* program again.

How the Multiway B-Tree Index Is Organized

An index file, one that ends in the .INDX file name extension, is also a PDBS data file, as are all files in this system. However, you cannot use other PDBS programs to edit or list index files because of their special nature. If you try to do this, you will probably receive an error and may have to reset the computer. I have tried listing and editing index files repeatedly with no success, but with no damage to any data files either. I do not recommend the practice, though.

In Fig. 6-8, a *status* report of the CNAME.INDX file is shown. *Status* is one PDBS program that can be used with index files because it does not attempt to read any of the records in the file. The only field in an index is named INDEX-.PAGE, a 1,023-byte-long character field. This field is really a phony place holder for the real data in the index and is illegal anyway, as character fields cannot nor-

```
CNAME.INDX
Record size ............. 1024
Number of fields ........ 1
Maximum record number ... 2
Records in use .......... 2
Records not used ........ 0
Date created ............ 22-Jul-83
Date last updated ....... 22-Jul-83

#  NAME          TYPE      LEN DEC POS

1  INDEX.PAGE    Char     1023   0   1
```

Fig. 6-8. *Status report of the CNAME.INDX file created by the index program (see Fig. 6-7). The single field INDEX PAGE is an "illegal" character string, and because of its special nature, the index file cannot be processed by other programs in the PDBS group.*

mally exceed a maximum length of 255. That is one reason, although there are others, why PDBS programs cannot be used to edit index files.

To better understand how indexing works, you will have to study the *index-unit* routines in Chapter Nine. There are, however, a few modifications you may wish to make to the *index* program.

Modifying the Program

Entries into an index are made by the procedure *insert_index*, which can be seen in action in line 89. Variable *inx* is declared to be of type *index_rec* (lines 17 and 51) and is used by PDBS to keep track of various parameters more fully explained in Part Two.

New index files are created in line 110 with the *make_index* procedure. You may want to allow creating and updating more than one index at a time. In the current version of PDBS, you can have up to six files open at once and can therefore manipulate one data file and five indexes together without having to adjust *pdbsunit* in Part Two.

Another possibility would be to allow indexing on concatenated keys using the methods shown in *mergesort* for treating multiple fields as one. This could be of use in a file where records are arranged in a hierarchy with one field, for instance, being a category, another a code of some kind, and a third a name. Together, the three fields form a key to individual records, but you may also want to search for all the records in one category, or in one category plus a code, and so on. Indexing on all three fields concatenated together would allow these searches to be made.

Still another tempting modification would be to index a file on something other than the data in the file. You may want to take each name, convert it somehow into a different, meaningful value, and insert that value into the index instead of the name itself. Airline computer systems make heavy use of a method in this

category called "soundex," which groups names, unrelated by spelling, by their
sounds. The soundex algorithm, discovered by Margaret K. Odell and Robert C.
Russell, can be found in D. E. Knuth's *Sorting and Searching,* Vol. 3, *The Art of
Computer Programming,* Addison-Wesley, chapter 6.

```
001: {$S+,I-}              { Compiler swapping on; I/O error checking off }
002:
003: PROGRAM index; uses applestuff, pdbsunit, indexunit;
004:
005: {-------------------------------------------------------------------}
006: {                                                                   }
007: {     PROGRAM        :  Index a file on any field                   }
008: {     LANGUAGE       :  UCSD Pascal / Apple Pascal 1.1              }
009: {                                                                   }
010: {     Copyright (C) 1983 by Tom Swan. All commercial rights reserved. }
011: {                                                                   }
012: {-------------------------------------------------------------------}
013:
014: VAR
015:     file_name       : pdbs_fname;          { Data file name }
016:     file_number     : integer;             { Data file number }
017:     index_file      : index_rec;           { Index file info }
018:     index_name      : pdbs_fname;          { Index file name }
019:     mode            : close_option;        { Update / no update }
020:     order           : fld_order;           { Field to index }
021:
022:
023: FUNCTION make_index( VAR inx   : index_rec;
024:                          fn    : integer;
025:                          field : integer;
026:                      VAR fname : pdbs_fname ) : pdbs_err;
027: { Create or reopen an index file for file fn }
028: VAR
029:     err_code        : pdbs_err;
030: BEGIN
031:     write( 'Opening index file' );
032:     err_code := open_index( inx, fname );
033:     IF err_code = 10                { File not found }
034:       THEN
035:         BEGIN
036:           err_code :=
037:             create_index( inx, fn, field,
038:                           fil_recs[fn].fil_msc.msc_flds[field].fld_len,
039:                           fname );
040:           IF err_code = 0
041:             THEN err_code := open_index( inx, fname )
042:         END; { if }
043:     IF err_code = 0 THEN            { Check that field numbers match }
044:       IF inx.field <> field
045:         THEN err_code := 14;        { Bad format }
046:     make_index := err_code;
047:     writeln
048: END; { make_index }
049:
050:
051: FUNCTION update_index( VAR inx : index_rec;
052:                            fn  : integer ) : pdbs_err;
053: { Index file fn over field specified in index rec }
054: VAR
055:     err_code : pdbs_err;
056:     rn       : integer;        { Running record number }
057:     s        : string;         { Key field as a string }
058:     start    : integer;        { Starting record number }
```

```
059: BEGIN
060:     IF file_empty( fn )
061:       THEN
062:         err_code := 23                    { File empty error }
063:       ELSE
064:     WITH fil_recs[fn].fil_msc DO
065:     BEGIN
066:         write( 'Start with record # (ret to quit) ? ' );
067:         IF NOT get_num( start, 1, msc_lastrec )
068:           THEN
069:             err_code := 25                { Interrupted by user }
070:           ELSE
071:             BEGIN
072:                 writeln( 'Indexing' );
073:                 err_code := 0;
074:                 rn := start - 1;
075:                 WHILE ( rn < msc_lastrec ) AND ( err_code = 0 ) DO
076:                 BEGIN
077:                     rn := rn + 1;
078:                     IF keypress
079:                       THEN
080:                         err_code := 25
081:                       ELSE
082:                         err_code := seek_rec( fn, rn );
083:                     IF err_code = 0
084:                       THEN
085:                         BEGIN
086:                             get_field( fn, inx.field, s );
087:                             IF case_switch
088:                                THEN bumpstrup( s );
089:                             err_code := insert_index( inx, s, rn )
090:                         END;
091:                     write( '.' )          { Console feedback }
092:                 END; { while }
093:                 writeln
094:             END { else }
095:     END; { else / with }
096:     update_index := err_code
097: END; { update_index }
098:
099:
100: BEGIN
101:     clrscrn;
102:     WHILE get_file_name( 'Index what file? ', file_name ) DO
103:     BEGIN
104:         IF executed( open_file( file_number, file_name ) ) THEN
105:         BEGIN
106:             clreosc;
107:             mode := no_update;           { Unless all operations completed }
108:             IF get_file_name( 'To what file? ', index_name ) THEN
109:             IF load_order( 'On what field?', file_number, order ) THEN
110:             IF executed( make_index( index_file, file_number,
111:                                      order[1], index_name ) ) THEN
112:             IF executed( update_index( index_file, file_number ) )
113:                 THEN mode := update;
114:             IF ( executed( close_index( index_file, mode ) ) ) AND
115:                ( mode = update )
116:                THEN write( file_name, ' indexed to ', index_name, ' on ',
117:                 fil_recs[ file_number ].fil_msc.msc_flds[ order[1] ].fld_name );
118:             IF NOT executed( close_file( file_number, no_update ) )
119:                 THEN exit( PROGRAM )     { Extremely unlikely }
120:         END; { if }
121:         gotoxy( 0, 0 )
122:     END { while }
123: END.
```

FIND

Find uses an index file, created by the *index* program, to quickly locate records in a data file. You can use *find* in two ways. The first and primary use of find is to search for the first occurrence of some record in a data file. But you can also use *find* to list a file in sorted order by using a partial search argument or key. For example, you could search for all records starting with "SAN" to find "SAN SEBASTIAN," "SANTA CLAUS," and "SANTANA." These records are located quickly by *find* even though they may be stored in widely-separated locations in the data file.

In Fig. 6-9, *find* is used to list part of a file I have been keeping. The file is called HOUSEPLANS.PDBF. I have indexed the file, using the *index* program, on the NAME field, storing the index in a file named NAMES.INDX. As you can see in the dialogue of Fig. 6-9, *find* reads and lists the records in the order "imposed" by the index.

As explained in the instructions to the *index* program, locating the first occurrence of a record with the help of a multiway tree index is very fast. But what about subsequent records?

Here we run into the one big disadvantage of using indexes as alternatives to sorting. Listing large files in indexed order, especially if their physical ordering is very much different from their indexed order, will be much slower than the output of the *list* program. This is because the next record to display may be anywhere in the file, causing more disk swapping to occur when browsing through the records. When such disk use grows heavy, it is called "thrashing," a condition to be avoided if possible.

```
Find records in what file? HOUSEPLANS
Using what index file? NAMES
Giving what fields? [<field>,<field>,..,|ret|?]
NAME, CITY, STATE
Output report to? <cr>

Find NAME         equal to? GARDEN
00002   Garden Way Sunroom/Solar Greenhouse        Charlotte            VT

Find NAME         equal to? GR
00003   Green Mountain Homes                       Royalton             VT
00012   Green Mountain Log Homes                   Chester              VT
00009   Green River Trading Company                Millerton            NY

Find NAME         equal to? Vermont
00006   Vermont Frames                             Hinesburg            VT
00007   Vermont Log Buildings, Inc.                Hartland             VT

Find NAME         equal to? <cr>
```

Fig. 6-9. *A dialogue with the* find *program shows how records can be quickly located and listed in indexed order. Notice that the record numbers along the left edge of the list are out of numerical sequence.*

Using the Find Program

Find will attempt to locate the first occurrence of as much of the search key as you supply. For example, you could begin listing from the Ts in a file by just typing the letter "T" and pressing return.

If *find* doesn't locate a matching record, it will repeat its prompt for another search argument. Press the return key if you want to stop searching.

If more matches are found than can be displayed at once on the screen, you will see the prompt:

Press <space> to continue <esc> to quit

Tap the space bar to view more records. Press the escape key to stop listing. At that point you can enter something else that you want to find or press the return key twice to end the program.

Modifying the Program

The function *process_rec* has been separated from the program as much as possible so that it may be replaced with any other function you want. *Find*, then, can serve as a shell for the design of any program that needs to process records in an indexed order. For example, you could use *find* as the basis for a new report program that prints reports on a data file in indexed order matching some search key.

The current version of the *process_rec* function in *find* makes use of a global variable, *count*. This variable is only used to pause the display between groups of records and can be removed without harming the action of the program. Except for that, *process_rec* is completely modular and is replaceable. It is called once for each record by the *peruse* function beginning at line 83.

```
001: {$S+,I-}              { Compiler swapping on; I/O error checking off }
002:
003: PROGRAM find; uses pdbsunit, indexunit;
004:
005: {----------------------------------------------------------------------}
006: {                                                                      }
007: {    PROGRAM          :  Find indexed records                          }
008: {    LANGUAGE         :  UCSD Pascal / Apple Pascal 1.1                 }
009: {                                                                      }
010: {    Copyright (C) 1983 by Tom Swan. All commercial rights reserved.   }
011: {                                                                      }
012: {----------------------------------------------------------------------}
013:
014: VAR
015:     count            : integer;             { Display pause counter }
016:     file_name        : pdbs_fname;          { Data file name }
017:     file_number      : integer;             { Data file number }
018:     index_file       : index_rec;           { Index descriptor record }
019:     index_name       : pdbs_fname;          { Index file name }
020:     max_count        : integer;             { Pause every n records }
021:
022:
023: PROCEDURE input_key( fn, field : integer; VAR skey : string );
```

```
024: { Prompt for and return a search key }
025: BEGIN
026:    WITH fil_recs[fn].fil_msc.msc_flds[ field ] DO
027:    BEGIN
028:       write( chr(ret), 'Find ', fld_name, ' equal to ? ' );
029:       readln( skey );
030:       IF length( skey ) > 0 THEN
031:       BEGIN
032:          IF case_switch
033:             THEN bumpstrup( skey );
034:          IF fld_type = dat_number THEN
035:          BEGIN
036:             normalize( skey, fld_decimals );
037:             WHILE length( skey ) < fld_len DO
038:                insert( ' ', skey, 1 )
039:          END
040:       END { if }
041:    END { if / with }
042: END; { input_key }
043:
044:
045: FUNCTION process_rec(      fn,                      { PDBS file number }
046:                            rn    : integer;         { Record number }
047:                        VAR order : fld_order;       { Fields to process }
048:                        VAR pf    : text             { Output "Print File" }
049:                                            ) : pdbs_err;
050: { Process record number rn of file fn ignoring deleted entries (rn <= 0) }
051: { Uses global line_count }
052: CONST
053:    esc      = 27;              { ASCII value for escape char }
054: VAR
055:    ch       : char;           { Keyboard input char }
056:    err_code : pdbs_err;
057: BEGIN
058:    err_code := 0;             { Unless something goes wrong }
059:    IF rn > 0 THEN
060:    BEGIN
061:       IF ( count >= max_count ) THEN
062:       BEGIN
063:          write( chr(ret), 'Press <space> to continue <esc> to quit' );
064:          WHILE NOT( get_ch( ch ) IN [ chr(blank), chr(esc) ] ) DO
065:             beep;
066:          writeln( chr(ret) );        { One cr plus a blank line }
067:          IF ch = chr(esc)
068:             THEN err_code := 25;     { Interrupted by user }
069:          count := 0
070:       END; { if }
071:       IF err_code = 0 THEN
072:       BEGIN
073:          err_code := seek_rec( fn, rn );
074:          IF err_code = 0
075:             THEN display_rec( pf, fn, order );
076:          count := count + 1
077:       END { if }
078:    END; { if }
079:    process_rec := err_code
080: END; { process_rec }
081:
082:
083: FUNCTION peruse(      dfn   : integer;       { Data file number }
084:                  VAR inx   : index_rec;      { Index descriptor }
085:                  VAR skey  : string;         { Search key }
086:                  VAR order : fld_order;      { Fields to process }
087:                  VAR pf    : text            { Output "Print File" }
088:                                     ) : pdbs_err;
089: { Search and process closest match(es) to search key }
090: VAR
```

```
091:    err_code           : pdbs_err;
092:    ready              : boolean;          { True = ready to process recs }
093:
094:    PROCEDURE search( pn : integer );
095:    { Search page pn }
096:    VAR
097:       entry : index_entry;                { Single index key entries }
098:       found : boolean;                     { True if possible match located }
099:       missed : boolean;                    { True if key > search key }
100:       ix    : index_xchng;                 { Binary / index page exchanger }
101:       k     : integer;                     { Index entries index }
102:    BEGIN
103:       IF err_code = 0 THEN
104:       IF pn > 0 THEN WITH inx DO
105:       BEGIN
106:          err_code := read_rec( fn, pn, ix.bp );
107:          IF err_code = 0 THEN WITH ix.ip DO
108:          BEGIN
109:             k := 1;
110:             found := false;
111:             missed := false;
112:             entry.p := p0;
113:
114:          { Rough search locates probable starting point. }
115:
116:             WHILE ( k <= n ) AND ( NOT found ) AND ( NOT missed ) DO
117:             BEGIN
118:                moveleft( entries[ (k-1)*keylen ],    { Source }
119:                          entry,                       { Destination }
120:                          keylen );                    { Count }
121:                found := pos( skey, entry.key ) = 1;
122:                IF NOT found THEN
123:                   missed := entry.key > skey;
124:                IF ( NOT found ) AND ( NOT missed )
125:                   THEN k := k + 1
126:             END; { while }
127:
128:             IF k = 1
129:                THEN search( p0 )               { Follow leftmost pointers }
130:                ELSE k := k - 1;                { First key < skey }
131:
132:          { Fine tune search locates first and subsequent matches. }
133:
134:             missed := false;
135:             WHILE ( k <= n ) AND ( err_code = 0 ) AND ( NOT missed ) DO
136:             BEGIN
137:                moveleft( entries[ (k-1)*keylen ],    { Source }
138:                          entry,                       { Destination }
139:                          keylen );                    { Count }
140:                found := pos( skey, entry.key ) = 1;
141:                IF found
142:                   THEN err_code := process_rec( dfn, entry.rn, order, pf )
143:                   ELSE missed := entry.key > skey;
144:                search( entry.p );              { Follow all other branches }
145:                k := k + 1
146:             END { while }
147:          END { if }
148:       END { if }
149:    END; { search }
150:
151: BEGIN { peruse }
152:    err_code := 0;            { Initialize error code variable }
153:    search( inx.root );       { Search recursively starting at root page }
154:    peruse := err_code        { Return resulting error code }
155: END; { peruse }
156:
157:
```

```
158: PROCEDURE look_up(     fn    : integer;
159:                      VAR inx   : index_rec );
160: { Prompt for search keys and display closest matching records }
161: VAR
162:     done     : boolean;       { Repeat loop exit flag }
163:     err_code : pdbs_err;
164:     i        : integer;       { Field order array index }
165:     order    : fld_order;     { Fields to list }
166:     out_name : string;        { Output file name }
167:     pf       : text;          { Output "Print File" }
168:     recsize  : integer;       { Display-size of record }
169:     skey     : string;        { Search key }
170: BEGIN
171:
172:     clreosc;
173:     IF load_order( 'Giving what fields? ', fn, order ) THEN
174:     BEGIN
175:
176:        REPEAT
177:           IF NOT get_file_name( 'Output report to ? ', out_name )
178:              THEN out_name := 'CONSOLE:'; { Default to console }
179:           remove_ext( out_name ); { Disallow PDBS file name }
180:           rewrite( pf, out_name )
181:        UNTIL executed( ioresult );        { i.e. until no error }
182:
183:        WITH fil_recs[fn].fil_msc DO
184:        BEGIN
185:
186:        { Calculate how many records will fit on screen at one time. }
187:        { Listing will pause after "max_count" records are shown. }
188:
189:        { 1. max_count <-- number characters in each listing record }
190:
191:           max_count := 0;
192:           FOR i := 1 TO order[0] DO
193:              max_count := max_count + msc_flds[ order[i] ].fld_len + 2;
194:
195:        { 2. max_count <-- number of screen lines for each listing record }
196:
197:           max_count := ( max_count DIV screenwidth ) +
198:                        ( ord( ( max_count MOD screenwidth ) > 0 ) );
199:
200:        { 3. max_count <-- number of listing records per screen full }
201:
202:           max_count := ( 23 DIV max_count ) -
203:                        ( ord( ( 23 MOD max_count ) = 0 ) )
204:        END; { with }
205:
206:     { Find records on command, listing exact and partial matches }
207:
208:        REPEAT
209:           count := 0;                      { Initialize global pause counter }
210:           input_key( fn, inx.field, skey );
211:           done := ( length( skey ) = 0 );
212:           IF NOT done THEN
213:           BEGIN
214:              err_code := peruse( fn, inx, skey, order, pf );
215:              IF err_code = 25
216:                 THEN err_code := 0;    { Trap "interrupted by user" error }
217:              done := NOT executed( err_code )
218:           END; { if }
219:           writeln
220:        UNTIL done;
221:
222:        close( pf, lock )          { Lock in case it's a disk text file }
223:
224:     END { if }
225: END; { look_up }
```

```
226:
227:
228: BEGIN
229:    clrscrn;
230:    WHILE get_file_name( 'Find records in what file? ', file_name ) DO
231:    BEGIN
232:       IF executed( open_file( file_number, file_name ) ) THEN
233:       BEGIN
234:          IF get_file_name( 'Using what index file? ', index_name ) THEN
235:          IF executed( open_index( index_file, index_name ) )
236:             THEN look_up( file_number, index_file );
237:          IF NOT ( executed( close_index( index_file, no_update ) ) AND
238:                   executed( close_file( file_number, no_update ) ) )
239:             THEN exit( PROGRAM )        { Extremely unlikely }
240:       END; { if }
241:       gotoxy( 0, 0 )
242:    END { while }
243: END.
```

UPDATE

Records marked for deletion from a data file but not actually removed will still be found during an indexed search. The *find* program processes both marked and unmarked data records, indicating marked records with a star (*) to the left of their record numbers.

If you want to remove marked records from the index, and have *find* ignore them, use this program, *update*. (See Fig. 6-10.) The program reads through all records in the data file, selecting the ones marked for deletion and deleting the index entries for those records. The records themselves are not removed from the data file—only their index entries are affected. You can still edit and list the marked records, but they will not show up during an indexed search such as that performed by the *find* program.

The *update* program also demonstrates how to use the *indexunit* delete function (see line 55 in the listing), explained in more detail in Part Two.

```
Update what data file? HOUSEPLANS
Using what index file? NAMES
Updating index
....................
Deleted entries removed from NAMES.INDX
```

Fig. 6-10. *Use the* update *program to remove marked records in the data file from an index. After updating, the* find *program will ignore the marked records.*

```
001: {$S+,I-}              { Compiler swapping on; I/O error checking off }
002:
003: PROGRAM update_index; uses applestuff, pdbsunit, indexunit;
004:
005: {-----------------------------------------------------------------}
006: {                                                                 }
007: {     PROGRAM       : Update index file, deleting marked records  }
008: {     LANGUAGE      : UCSD Pascal / Apple Pascal 1.1              }
009: {                                                                 }
010: {     Copyright (C) 1983 by Tom Swan. All commercial rights reserved. }
011: {                                                                 }
012: {-----------------------------------------------------------------}
013:
014: VAR
015:     file_name      : pdbs_fname;       { Data file name }
016:     file_number    : integer;          { Data file number }
017:     index_file     : index_rec;        { Index file info }
018:     index_name     : pdbs_fname;       { Index file name }
019:     mode           : close_option;     { Update / no update }
020:
021:
022: FUNCTION del_index( VAR inx : index_rec;
023:                         fn  : integer ) : pdbs_err;
024: { Delete index entries for all deleted data records }
025: VAR
026:     err_code : pdbs_err;
027:     rn       : integer;       { Running record number }
028:     s        : string;        { Key field as a string }
029: BEGIN
030:     IF file_empty( fn )
031:       THEN
032:         err_code := 23                 { File empty error }
033:       ELSE
034:       WITH fil_recs[fn].fil_msc DO
035:       BEGIN
036:         writeln( 'Updating index' );
037:         err_code := 0;
038:         rn := 0;
039:         WHILE ( rn < msc_lastrec ) AND ( err_code = 0 ) DO
040:         BEGIN
041:           rn := rn + 1;
042:           IF keypress
043:             THEN
044:               err_code := 25
045:             ELSE
046:               err_code := seek_rec( fn, rn );
047:           IF err_code = 0
048:             THEN
049:               IF rec_status( fn ) = deleted
050:                 THEN
051:                   BEGIN
052:                     get_field( fn, inx.field, s );
053:                     IF case_switch
054:                       THEN bumpstrup( s );
055:                     err_code := delete_index( inx, s, rn );
056:                     IF err_code = 26            { No such record }
057:                       THEN err_code := 0        { Trap previously }
058:                                                 { deleted entries }
059:                   END; { if }
060:           write( '.' )            { Console feedback }
061:         END; { while }
062:         writeln
063:       END; { else / with }
064:       del_index := err_code
065: END; { del_index }
066:
```

```
067:
068: BEGIN
069:    clrscrn;
070:    WHILE get_file_name( 'Update what data file? ', file_name ) DO
071:    BEGIN
072:       IF executed( open_file( file_number, file_name ) ) THEN
073:       BEGIN
074:          clreosc;
075:          mode := no_update;              { Unless all operations completed }
076:          IF get_file_name( 'Using what index file? ', index_name ) THEN
077:          IF executed( open_index( index_file, index_name ) ) THEN
078:          IF executed( del_index( index_file, file_number ) )
079:             THEN mode := update;
080:          IF ( executed( close_index( index_file, mode ) ) ) AND
081:             ( mode = update )
082:           THEN write( 'Deleted entries removed from ',
083:                            fil_recs[ index_file.fn ].fil_name );
084:          IF NOT executed( close_file( file_number, no_update ) )
085:             THEN exit( PROGRAM )    { Extremely unlikely }
086:       END; { if }
087:       gotoxy( 0, 0 )
088:    END { while }
089: END.
```

7

Other Data Base Operations

UPCASE / MARK / ACTIVATE / DELETE
MINIMIZE / ERASE / CONVERT

UPCASE

The seven programs in Chapter Seven (now isn't that a lucky coincidence) are short utilities that you will find to be invaluable additions to the PDBS group. Each is under 100 lines, except for *convert*, which weighs in at 103. They may not be long, but they all pull their own weights.

Upcase converts any field or series of fields in a file from mixed upper- and lower-case to all upper-case letters. Only lower-case a through z are affected by *upcase*. Punctuation and the digits 0 through 9 pass through the program unchanged. An example of the program in use is in Fig. 7-1.

Upcase will also fix typing errors in fields that should have been entered in all upper case. State fields in a name-and-address file such as C.STATE in The Company's CUSTOMERS.PDBF file and key fields such as C.NUM in that same file are examples where a common error during data entry is to forget to capitalize every letter.

```
Convert case in what file? CUSTOMERS
Convert fields? [<field>,<field>,..,|ret|?]
C.STATE
Converting
...........
CUSTOMERS.PDBF converted
```

Fig. 7-1. To fix possible entry errors, upcase is used on the state field in the customer file to convert all state abbreviations to upper-case letters.

Another reason you may want to convert a field to all upper case is to speed up searching and sorting. By processing a file with *upcase* and then entering this statement:

case_switch : = false;

into any PDBS program, the time for most searches and sorts can be cut by as much as fifty percent. When *case_switch,* a boolean variable, is set to *false,* fields are not automatically converted to upper case before comparisons are made. The longer the field, the better the improvement.

Once converted, there is no recovering the original form of the data in mixed upper and lower case. To avoid accidents, keep a backup copy of your data file before using *upcase*.

Converting fields to upper case has no effect on indexed searches using the *find* program. However, you may gain a little speed when building the .INDX file with the *index* program if the data are all in upper case and you set the *case_switch* to false in the *index* program.

```
001: {$S+,I-}              { Compiler swapping on; I/O error checking off }
002:
003: PROGRAM upcase; uses pdbsunit;
004:
005: {---------------------------------------------------------------------}
006: {                                                                     }
007: {     PROGRAM       :  Convert selected fields to all upper case      }
008: {     LANGUAGE      :  UCSD Pascal / Apple Pascal 1.1                  }
009: {                                                                     }
010: {     Copyright (C) 1983 by Tom Swan. All commercial rights reserved. }
011: {                                                                     }
012: {---------------------------------------------------------------------}
013:
014: VAR
015:     file_name        : pdbs_fname;              { PDBS data file name }
016:     file_number      : integer;                 { PDBS file number }
017:     mode             : close_option;
018:     order            : fld_order;
019:
020:
021: FUNCTION bump_file( fn : integer; VAR order : fld_order ) : boolean;
022: { True if fields specified in order array converted to all upper case }
023: VAR
024:     field,                          { Field number }
025:     rn               : integer;     { Record number }
026:     s                : string;      { Fields as strings }
027: BEGIN
028:     writeln( 'Converting' );
029:     bump_file := false;        { Unless operation is successfull }
030:     FOR rn := 1 TO fil_recs[fn].fil_msc.msc_lastrec DO
031:     BEGIN
032:        IF NOT executed( seek_rec( fn, rn ) )
033:           THEN exit( bump_file );              { Returning function = false }
034:        FOR field := 1 TO order[0] DO           { Order[0] = number of fields }
035:           BEGIN
036:              get_field( fn, order[field], s );     { Read field }
037:              bumpstrup( s );                        { Convert case }
038:              put_field( fn, order[field], s )       { Write field }
```

```
039:           END; { for }
040:           write( '.' )               { Feedback }
041:        END; { for }
042:        writeln;
043:        bump_file := true             { No errors }
044: END; { bump_file }
045:
046:
047: BEGIN
048:     clrscrn;
049:     WHILE get_file_name( 'Convert case in what file? ', file_name ) DO
050:     BEGIN
051:        clreosc;
052:        mode := no_update;        { Unless operations completed }
053:        IF executed( open_file( file_number, file_name ) ) THEN
054:        BEGIN
055:           IF load_order( 'Convert fields?', file_number, order ) THEN
056:           IF bump_file( file_number, order )
057:              THEN mode := update;
058:           IF ( executed( close_file( file_number, mode ) ) ) AND
059:              ( mode = update )
060:              THEN write( file_name, ' converted' )
061:        END; { if }
062:        gotoxy( 0, 0 )
063:     END
064: END.
```

MARK

When using the change operation in the *editor* program, a control E (^E) command can be used to mark an individual record for later deletion. When you have a lot of deletions to make, however, you may want to use the *mark* program instead.

To mark all customers in Pennsylvania for deletion from The Company's CUSTOMERS.PDBF file, for example, follow the dialogue in Fig. 7-2. On your own data, you can use any search argument to process a subset of your file for deletion.

Marking records doesn't change their contents in any way. Records are never removed by marking, and can be easily unmarked using the *editor* or the *activate* program, described next. You can still search, edit, index, and find records that have been marked.

Mark gives you the option of choosing if you want to be prompted before

```
Mark what file? CUSTOMERS
Mark what records? [<expr>|ret|?]
C.STATE=PA
Prompt before each marking? (y/n) N
00002  C9    Bell, Liber T.
00003  C10   Crockett, D. V.
00004  C3    Danzig, Irving
00006  C4    Franklin, Benjamin
CUSTOMERS.PDBF:C.STATE=PA --> marked
```

Fig. 7-2. *In one mark operation, customer records in Pennsylvania are marked for deletion.*

```
CUSTOMERS.PDBF :
           C.NAME--------------------------   C.STATE
  00001   Bear, Theodore Edward               OH
 *00002   Bell, Liber T.                      PA
 *00003   Crockett, D. V.                     PA
 *00004   Danzig, Irving                      PA
  00005   Diffenforker, Cecil                 CA
 *00006   Franklin, Benjamin                  PA
  00007   Pascal, Blaise                      WA
  00008   Quick, Jack B.                      CA
  00009   Slumgullion, Stewart                OH
  00010   Stallion, Horace                    TX
  00011   Venus, Gypsy                        MD
  00012   West, Martin Quincy                 MD
```

Fig. 7-3. *Marked records show up in a list with asterisks next to their record numbers. In this list, records 2, 3, 4, and 6 are marked for deletion.*

each marking. If you answer ''Y,'' then you will be shown each record that matches your search argument and will be asked:

Mark this record? (y/n)

Answering ''Y'' marks that record. Answering ''N'' skips marking the record and advances to the next one until all records are processed.

A quick way to go through the entire file, marking only those records you want, is to press return when you are asked:

Mark what records? [<expr>¦ret¦?]

When you *list* the records in a file, those records that have been marked will be shown with an asterisk to the immediate left of the record number. Figure 7-3 lists the names from the customer file. All the records with states equal to PA have been marked for deletion.

```
001: {$S+,I-}             { Compiler swapping on; I/O error checking off }
002:
003: PROGRAM mark; uses applestuff, pdbsunit, evalunit;
004:
005: {-----------------------------------------------------------------}
006: {                                                                 }
007: {     PROGRAM        :  Mark selective records for deletion       }
008: {     LANGUAGE       :  UCSD Pascal / Apple Pascal 1.1            }
009: {                                                                 }
010: {     Copyright (C) 1983 by Tom Swan. All commercial rights reserved. }
011: {                                                                 }
012: {-----------------------------------------------------------------}
013:
014: VAR
015:     arg               : string;            { Search arguments }
016:     file_name         : pdbs_fname;        { Data file name }
017:     file_number       : integer;           { Data file number }
018:     mode              : close_option;
019:     prompting         : boolean;           { True for prompted delete }
020:
```

```
021:
022: PROCEDURE set_up_order( fn : integer; VAR order : fld_order );
023: { Insert fields to display in order array. }
024: VAR
025:     i : integer;      { Order array index }
026: BEGIN
027:     WITH fil_recs[fn].fil_msc DO
028:     BEGIN
029:         order[0] := msc_nflds;
030:         FOR i := 1 TO msc_nflds DO
031:             order[i] := i
032:     END; { with }
033: END; { set_up_order }
034:
035:
036: FUNCTION mark_recs( fn : integer; prompting : boolean ) : pdbs_err;
037: { Mark records in file fn for deletion pausing if prompting = true }
038: VAR
039:     err_code            : pdbs_err;
040:     ok_to_mark          : boolean;       { True to mark for deletion }
041:     order               : fld_order;     { Fields to display for feedback }
042:     rn                  : integer;       { Record number }
043: BEGIN
044:     set_up_order( fn, order );
045:     err_code := 0;
046:     ok_to_mark := true;      { Changes only if prompting = true }
047:     rn := 0;
048:     WHILE ( rn < fil_recs[fn].fil_msc.msc_lastrec ) AND
049:           ( err_code = 0 ) DO
050:     BEGIN
051:       rn := rn + 1;
052:       IF keypress
053:           THEN err_code := 25          { Interrupted by user }
054:           ELSE err_code := seek_rec( fn, rn );
055:       IF err_code = 0 THEN
056:           IF match( fn ) THEN
057:               BEGIN
058:                   display_rec( output, fn, order );
059:                   IF prompting THEN
060:                       ok_to_mark := verified( ' Mark record' );
061:                   IF ok_to_mark
062:                       THEN err_code := mark_rec( fn, deleted )
063:               END { if }
064:     END; { while }
065:     mark_recs := err_code
066: END; { mark_recs }
067:
068:
069: BEGIN
070:     clrscrn;
071:     WHILE get_file_name( 'Mark what file? ', file_name ) DO
072:     BEGIN
073:         IF executed( open_file( file_number, file_name ) ) THEN
074:         BEGIN
075:             clreosc;
076:             load_arg( 'Mark what records?', file_number, arg );
077:             prompting := verified( 'Prompt before each marking' );
078:             IF executed( mark_recs( file_number, prompting ) )
079:                 THEN mode := update
080:                 ELSE mode := no_update;
081:             IF ( executed( close_file( file_number, mode ) ) ) AND
082:                ( mode = update )
083:                 THEN write( file_name, ':', arg, ' --> marked' )
084:         END; { if }
085:         gotoxy( 0, 0 )
086:     END { while }
087: END.
```

```
Activate what file? CUSTOMERS
Setting all records = active
............
12 --> records reactivated
```

Fig. 7-4. *Marks can be removed from all records in a file by using the activate program.*

ACTIVATE

Activate removes all marks from all records in a data file.

It is a good idea to use *activate* on a file before using *mark*. There will be no marked records in the file after processing with *activate*.

The Company's Pennsylvania records are reactivated with the dialogue in Fig. 7-4. If you are following along, try listing the file after activating. The asterisks shown in Fig. 7-3 should be gone.

```
001: {$S+,I-}              { Compiler swapping on; I/O error checking off }
002:
003: PROGRAM activate; uses applestuff, pdbsunit;
004:
005: {--------------------------------------------------------------------}
006: {                                                                    }
007: {    PROGRAM        :   Re-activate all deleted records              }
008: {    LANGUAGE       :   UCSD Pascal / Apple Pascal 1.1               }
009: {                                                                    }
010: {    Copyright (C) 1983 by Tom Swan. All commercial rights reserved. }
011: {                                                                    }
012: {--------------------------------------------------------------------}
013:
014: VAR
015:     file_name       : pdbs_fname;         { Data file name }
016:     file_number     : integer;            { Data file number }
017:     mode            : close_option;
018:     recs_done       : integer;            { Number records done }
019:
020:
021: FUNCTION reactivate( fn : integer; VAR rn : integer ) : pdbs_err;
022: { Set all records in file to active status. }
023: { Rn = number of records processed }
024: VAR
025:     err_code        : pdbs_err;
026: BEGIN
027:     writeln( 'Setting all records = active' );
028:     err_code := 0;
029:     rn := 0;
030:     WHILE ( rn < fil_recs[fn].fil_msc.msc_lastrec ) AND
031:           ( err_code = 0 ) DO
032:       BEGIN
033:         rn := rn + 1;
034:         IF keypress
035:            THEN err_code := 25        { Interrupted by user }
036:            ELSE err_code := seek_rec( fn, rn );
037:         IF err_code = 0
038:            THEN err_code := mark_rec( fn, active );
```

```
039:        write( '.' )              { Console feedback }
040:     END;
041:     writeln;
042:     reactivate := err_code
043: END; { reactivate }
044:
045:
046: BEGIN
047:     clrscrn;
048:     WHILE get_file_name( 'Activate what file? ', file_name ) DO
049:     BEGIN
050:        IF executed( open_file( file_number, file_name ) ) THEN
051:        BEGIN
052:           IF executed( reactivate( file_number, recs_done ) )
053:              THEN mode := update
054:              ELSE mode := no_update;
055:           IF ( executed( close_file( file_number, mode ) ) ) AND
056:              ( mode = update )
057:              THEN write( recs_done, ' --> records reactivated' )
058:        END; { if }
059:        gotoxy( 0, 0 )
060:     END { while }
061: END.
```

DELETE

After marking records for deletion, the *delete* program can be used to remove those records. *Delete* makes a permanent change to the data file, and you should always make a backup copy of your file before executing *delete*.

The program can be seen in action in Fig. 7-5. The four marked customer records shown in Fig. 7-3 are removed from the file.

Deletions from a data file cause subsequent records to be moved up into the "holes" created by the removed records. Because of this, record numbers will change for all the records that follow, in record number sequence, the first marked record found.

After deleting, you should rebuild any indexes that exist for the file. Old indexes will give false and even unusual results if used on a file where records have been deleted.

Deleting does not change the size of the file on disk although the deleted space will be used by new records before the file is expanded again. To decrease

```
Delete from what file? CUSTOMERS
Deleting
. . . . . . . . . . . .
4 record(s) deleted
File updated
```

Fig. 7-5. *Marked records are permanently removed from The Company's customer file using* delete.

the actual storage size of a file, follow a *delete* with an *append* onto a *copy* of the file. This sequence can be used to reduce any file to its minimum required size.

```
001: {$S+,I-}              { Compiler swapping on; I/O error checking off }
002:
003: PROGRAM delete; uses pdbsunit;
004:
005: {-----------------------------------------------------------------------}
006: {                                                                       }
007: {     PROGRAM          :  Remove records marked for deletion.           }
008: {     LANGUAGE         :  UCSD Pascal / Apple Pascal 1.1                 }
009: {                                                                       }
010: {     Copyright (C) 1983 by Tom Swan. All commercial rights reserved.   }
011: {                                                                       }
012: {-----------------------------------------------------------------------}
013:
014: VAR
015:     file_name         : pdbs_fname;    { PDBS data file name }
016:     file_number       : integer;       { PDBS data file number }
017:     mode              : close_option;
018:     nrecs             : integer;       { Number of records deleted }
019:
020:
021: FUNCTION delete_recs( fn : integer; VAR nrecs : integer ) : pdbs_err;
022: { Delete marked records from file fn.  Size of file not changed, }
023: { but space occupied by marked records is released for new appends. }
024: { File fn assumed open.  Record numbers are changed by procedure. }
025: { Report nrecs = number of deletions made. }
026: VAR
027:     krunch_to,
028:     recnum            : integer;
029:     work_area         : binary_page;
030:
031:     PROCEDURE perform( n : pdbs_err );
032:     { Perform function returning error code.  Exit on any error. }
033:     BEGIN
034:        IF n <> 0 THEN
035:           BEGIN
036:              delete_recs := n;
037:              exit( delete_recs )
038:           END
039:     END; { perform }
040:
041: BEGIN
042:     writeln( 'Deleting' );
043:     nrecs := 0;
044:     krunch_to := 1;
045:     FOR recnum := 1 TO fil_recs[fn].fil_msc.msc_lastrec DO
046:     BEGIN
047:        write( '.' );              { Feedback }
048:        perform( seek_rec( fn, recnum ) );
049:        IF ( rec_status( fn ) = active ) THEN
050:        BEGIN
051:           IF ( krunch_to < recnum ) THEN
052:           BEGIN
053:              perform( get_rec( fn, work_area ) );
054:              perform( write_rec( fn, krunch_to, work_area ) )
055:           END; { if }
056:           krunch_to := krunch_to + 1
057:        END { if }
058:     END; { for }
059:
060:     WITH fil_recs[fn].fil_msc DO
061:       BEGIN   { Update msc record }
062:             nrecs := msc_lastrec - krunchto + 1;   { Records deleted }
063:             msc_lastrec := krunch_to - 1           { New end of file }
```

```
064:       END; { if }
065:     writeln;
066:     delete_recs := 0          { No errors }
067: END; { delete_recs }
068:
069:
070: BEGIN
071:    clrscrn;
072:    WHILE get_file_name( 'Delete from what file? ', file_name ) DO
073:    BEGIN
074:       clreosc;
075:       mode := no_update;    { Unless all operations completed }
076:       IF executed( open_file( file_number, file_name ) ) THEN
077:       BEGIN
078:          IF ( executed( delete_recs( file_number, nrecs ) ) ) THEN
079:          IF ( nrecs > 0 )
080:             THEN mode := update;
081:          writeln( nrecs, ' record(s) deleted.' );
082:          IF ( executed( close_file( file_number, mode ) ) ) AND
083:             ( mode = update )
084:             THEN write( 'File updated' )
085:       END; { if }
086:       gotoxy( 0, 0 )
087:    END { while }
088: END.
```

MINIMIZE

Like *mark, minimize* marks a set of records for eventual deletion with the *delete* program. The set of records marked by *minimize* are those records that have duplicated values in fields throughout the file.

Similar to *subtotal* in Chapter Five, *minimize* requires that the file be sorted on the field or fields to be marked. You can use either *sort* or *mergesort* to sort the file before minimizing.

The usefulness of this program is demonstrated in Figs. 7-6 through 7-9. For this example, a new file called STATES.PDBF was first created. Then, the C.STATE field from the CUSTOMERS.PDBF file was merged into this new file. (See Fig. 7-6.) Next, the STATES.PDBF file was sorted by state and was proc-

```
STATES.PDBF :
            C.STATE
   00001   CA
   00002   CA
   00003   MD
   00004   PA
   00005   PA
   00006   OH
   00007   OH
   00008   MD
   00009   PA
   00010   TX
   00011   WA
   00012   PA
```

Fig. 7-6. *The states before minimizing.*

```
        STATES.PDBF :
                 C.STATE
         00001  CA
        *00002  CA
         00003  MD
        *00004  MD
         00005  OH
        *00006  OH
         00007  PA
        *00008  PA
        *00009  PA
        *00010  PA
         00011  TX
         00012  WA
```

Fig. 7-7. *After sorting and minimizing, duplicate states are marked for deletion.*

```
        STATES.PDBF :
                 C.STATE
         00001  CA
         00002  MD
         00003  OH
         00004  PA
         00005  TX
         00006  WA
```

Fig. 7-8. *The delete program was used to remove the duplicated states marked by minimize.*

```
Minimize what file? STATES
Over what field? [<field>,<field>,..,|ret|?]
C.STATE
Is the file sorted by those fields ? (y/n) Y
Marking duplicates
...........
STATES.PDBF minimized
```

Fig. 7-9. *The dialogue with minimize that produces the marked list shown in Fig. 7-7.*

essed by *minimize,* which marked the duplicates in the file. (See Fig. 7-7.) Finally, *delete* was used to remove the duplicated records. (See Fig. 7-8.) The dialogue with the *minimize* program is shown in Fig. 7-9.

The same effect could have been achieved in this example by projecting the customer file onto a new file containing only the states. *Minimize,* however, gives you the opportunity to preview the duplications before they are removed. The program is therefore sometimes useful when you want to find duplicated fields without going to the trouble of projecting the file and without actually deleting anything.

```
001: {$S+,I-}                   { Compiler swapping on; I/O error checking off }
002:
003: PROGRAM minimize; uses applestuff, pdbsunit;
004:
005: {--------------------------------------------------------------------}
006: {                                                                    }
007: {    PROGRAM          :  Mark duplicated fields for deletion         }
008: {    LANGUAGE         :  UCSD Pascal / Apple Pascal 1.1              }
009: {                                                                    }
010: {    Copyright (C) 1983 by Tom Swan. All commercial rights reserved. }
011: {                                                                    }
012: {--------------------------------------------------------------------}
013:
014: VAR
015:     file_name          : pdbs_fname;
016:     file_number        : integer;
017:     mode               : close_option;
018:     order              : fld_order;
019:
020:
021: FUNCTION mark_dups( fn : integer; order : fld_order ) : pdbs_err;
022: { Mark duplicated fields in file fn }
023: VAR
024:     err_code           : pdbs_err;
025:     rn                 : integer;          { Record number }
026:     s                  : string;           { Fields as strings }
027:     same_thing         : string;           { Duplicate to look for }
028: BEGIN
029:     IF file_empty( fn )
030:         THEN err_code := 23              { File empty error }
031:         ELSE
032:     BEGIN
033:         writeln( 'Marking duplicates' );
034:
035:     { Initialize "same_thing" string for first record }
036:         rn := 1;
037:         err_code := seek_rec( fn, rn );
038:         IF err_code = 0
039:             THEN make_key( fn, order, same_thing );
040:
041:         WHILE ( rn < fil_recs[fn].fil_msc.msc_lastrec ) AND
042:               ( err_code = 0 ) DO
043:         BEGIN
044:             rn := rn + 1;
045:             IF keypress
046:                 THEN err_code := 25      { Interrupted by user }
047:                 ELSE err_code := seek_rec( fn, rn );
048:             IF err_code = 0 THEN
049:                 BEGIN
050:                     make_key( fn, order, s );
051:                     IF s = same_thing
052:                         THEN err_code := mark_rec( fn, deleted )
```

```
053:                    ELSE same_thing := s
054:              END; { if }
055:          write( '.' )                    { Console feedback }
056:        END; { while }
057:          writeln
058:      END; { else }
059:      mark_dups := err_code
060: END; { mark_dups }
061:
062:
063: BEGIN
064:     clrscrn;
065:     WHILE get_file_name( 'Minimize what file? ', file_name ) DO
066:     BEGIN
067:       IF executed( open_file( file_number, file_name ) ) THEN
068:       BEGIN
069:         clreosc;
070:         mode := no_update;            { Unless operations completed }
071:         IF load_order( 'Over what fields?', file_number, order ) THEN
072:         IF verified( 'Is file sorted by those fields' ) THEN
073:         IF executed( mark_dups( file_number, order ) )
074:             THEN mode := update;
075:         IF ( executed( close_file( file_number, mode ) ) ) AND
076:            ( mode = update )
077:            THEN write( filename, ' minimized' )
078:       END; { if }
079:       gotoxy( 0, 0 )
080:     END { while }
081: END.
```

ERASE

Erase removes all the records from a data file. Although there are other ways in PDBS to do the same thing, the program comes in handy from time to time.

The dialogue in Fig. 7-10 erases all records in the STATES.PDBF file, created for use with the last program, *minimize*. You are given a chance to change your mind about the erasure before it is made permanent. If you answer "N" to the "Update file?" prompt, then no changes will be made to your data.

The actual size of the file erased is not changed. Before the file is expanded again, new records will be inserted into the empty spaces left by erasing.

```
Erase records in what file? STATES
STATES.PDBF --> 6 records erased.
Update file ? (y/n) Y
All records removed
```

Fig. 7-10. *Using the erase progam to remove all records from the STATES.PDBF file.*

```
001: {$S+,I-}              { Compiler swapping on; I/O error checking off }
002:
003: PROGRAM erase; uses pdbsunit;
004:
005: {-----------------------------------------------------------------------}
006: {                                                                       }
007: {     PROGRAM         :  Erase all records in a data file               }
008: {     LANGUAGE        :  UCSD Pascal / Apple Pascal 1.1                  }
009: {                                                                       }
010: {     Copyright (C) 1983 by Tom Swan. All commercial rights reserved.   }
011: {                                                                       }
012: {-----------------------------------------------------------------------}
013:
014: VAR
015:     file_name         : pdbs_fnamr;    { PDBS data file name }
016:     file_number       : integer;       { PDBS data file number }
017:     mode              : close_option;
018:
019:
020: PROCEDURE warn_user( fn : integer );
021: { Display confirmation of what will happen to file fn if you proceed. }
022: BEGIN
023:     WITH fil_recs[ fn ] DO
024:     BEGIN
025:        write( fil_name );
026:        IF screen_width < 80
027:           THEN writeln;
028:        writeln( ' --> ', fil_msc.msc_lastrec, ' records erased.' )
029:     END
030: END; { warn_user }
031:
032:
033: BEGIN
034:     clrscrn;
035:     WHILE get_file_name( 'Erase records in what file? ', file_name ) DO
036:     BEGIN
037:        mode := no_update;    { Unless erasure confirmed }
038:        clreosc;
039:        IF executed( open_file( file_number, file_name ) ) THEN
040:        BEGIN
041:           IF file_empty( file_number )
042:              THEN
043:                writeln( 'File is empty' )
044:              ELSE
045:                BEGIN
046:                   warn_user( file_number );
047:                   IF executed( zero_file( file_number ) ) THEN
048:                   IF verified( 'Update file' )
049:                      THEN mode := update
050:                END; { else }
051:           IF ( executed( close_file( file_number, mode ) ) ) AND
052:              ( mode = update )
053:                THEN writeln( 'All records removed' )
054:        END; { if }
055:        gotoxy( 0, 0 )
056:     END { while }
057: END.
```

```
Update what file? VENDORS
Version is = 1.0
Update version to 1.1 ? (y/n) Y
Updating records
..........................
VENDORS.PDBF updated to 1.1
```

Fig. 7-11. *This imaginary dialogue with the* convert *program shows how a data file might be updated to new versions of the PDBS software.*

CONVERT

The last PDBS program in the group is a shell that demonstrates how the version number stored in each PDBS file may be updated to reflect modifications in the underlying *pdbsunit* software. (See Part Two.)

An imaginary use of the program is dialogued in Fig. 7-11. The example has to be imaginary because there is, as of this writing, no version 1.1 of the software in existence.

It may seem trivial to include this program, but having a way to *convert* version numbers is more important than you may think. Each PDBS data file has the current release number of *pdbsunit* stored along with other vital facts about the file in its first disk block (block 0 to be exact).

When a file is opened by PDBS, this version number is checked against the version number of the PDBS operating system in the computer's memory. If the numbers do not match, the data file will be closed without updating and no processing will be allowed on the records in the file.

This procedure guards against using future versions of the software with files that may not be in compatible formats. The *convert* program would be used on those files to bring them up to date.

A second reason why the version number is so carefully checked by PDBS can be understood by thinking about what might happen if a code or text file were accidentally opened and updated by a PDBS program. Because the current date and various other information are automatically maintained by PDBS, writing that information to a code file could damage that file beyond repair. Finding a correct version number in a known position of a PDBS data file at least gives a high degree of probability that the file is indeed a PDBS data file, and not something else.

A Note to Programmers

Function *update_recs* at line 77 in *convert* has been left blank intentionally. If you change the storage format for PDBS records, this function should be written to update previous storage formats to yours for all records in a file. The function value returned is a *pdbs_err* error code number according to the instructions in Part Two for using *pdbsunit* and in the appendix. This number should indicate the success (0) or failure (1 . . . 99) of the conversion.

Although I realize that publishing this software in a book could lead to a morass of custom versions, I will take a stab at preserving compatibility by reserving version numbers 1.0 through 4.9 for "official" releases. Please do not use these numbers in your own versions of PDBS.

```
001: {$S+,I-}                { Compiler swapping on; I/O error checking off }
002:
003: PROGRAM convert; uses pdbsunit;
004:
005: {---------------------------------------------------------------------}
006: {                                                                     }
007: {    PROGRAM         :  Version convert shell                         }
008: {    LANGUAGE        :  UCSD Pascal / Apple Pascal 1.1                 }
009: {                                                                     }
010: {    Copyright (C) 1983 by Tom Swan. All commercial rights reserved.  }
011: {                                                                     }
012: {---------------------------------------------------------------------}
013:
014: CONST
015:    block_size       = 512;          { Bytes in a disk block }
016:    previous_version = '1.0';        { Last version release }
017:
018: VAR
019:    file_name        : pdbs_fname;   { PDBS data file name }
020:    file_number      : integer;      { PDBS data file number }
021:    mode             : close_option; { PDBS close file option }
022:
023:
024: { ------------------------------------------------------ }
025: { NOTE : there should be an convert program supplied with }
026: {        each version change with the previous_version    }
027: {        constant set to the last known release number.   }
028: { ------------------------------------------------------ }
029:
030:
031: FUNCTION version_check( VAR msc_rec : msc_descriptor ) : boolean;
032: { True if file was created under previous version }
033: { Prevents accidental conversion of non-PDBS files }
034: { as well as unrecognized versions. }
035: BEGIN
036:    WITH msc_rec DO
037:       version_check := ( msc_id = previous_version )
038: END; { version_check }
039:
040:
041: FUNCTION update_version( file_name : pdbs_fname ) : pdbs_err;
042: { Update the version number of this named file }
043: VAR
044:    buffer   : PACKED ARRAY[ 1 .. block_size ] OF byte;
045:    err_code : pdbs_err;
046:    f        : FILE;
047:    msc_rec  : msc_descriptor;
048: BEGIN
049:    reset( f, file_name );
050:    err_code := ioresult;
051:    IF err_code = 0
052:      THEN
053:        IF blockread( f, buffer, 1, 0 ) <> 1
054:          THEN
055:            err_code := 18      { Disk read error }
056:          ELSE
057:            BEGIN
```

```
058:                moveleft( buffer, msc_rec, sizeof( msc_rec ) );
059:                IF NOT version_check( msc_rec )
060:                   THEN
061:                      err_code := 24        { Wrong version error }
062:                   ELSE
063:                   BEGIN
064:                      writeln( 'Version is = ', msc_rec.msc_id );
065:                      IF NOT verified( concat( 'Update version to ', version ) )
066:                         THEN exit( PROGRAM );        { Cancel update }
067:                      msc_rec.msc_id := version;
068:                      moveleft( msc_rec, buffer, sizeof( msc_rec ) );
069:                      IF blockwrite( f, buffer, 1, 0 ) <> 1
070:                         THEN err_code := 19    { Disk write error }
071:                   END
072:            END; { else }
073:      update_version := err_code
074: END; { update_version }
075:
076:
077: FUNCTION update_recs( fn : integer ) : pdbs_err;
078: { Update all records in the file as necessary. }
079: { The "guts" to this routine are the responsibility }
080: {   of the new version supplier. }
081: BEGIN
082:      update_recs := 0          { Stub returns no error }
083: END; { update_recs }
084:
085:
086: BEGIN
087:      clrscrn;
088:      WHILE get_file_name( 'Update what file? ', file_name ) DO
089:      BEGIN
090:         IF executed( update_version( file_name ) ) THEN
091:         IF executed( open_file( file_number, file_name ) ) THEN
092:         BEGIN
093:            clreosc;
094:            mode := no_update;        { Unless conversion completed }
095:            IF executed( update_recs( file_number ) )
096:               THEN mode := update;
097:            IF executed( close_file( file_number, mode ) ) THEN
098:            IF mode = update
099:               THEN writeln( file_name, ' updated to ', version )
100:         END;
101:         gotoxy( 0, 0 )
102:      END
103: END.
```

P A R T

TWO

The Computer's Point of View

To the computer, of course, there are no such things as number and character fields, or records, or row-and-column relational data base tables. It's all a jumble of bits and bytes, with the format—or "logical view"—imposed on what the computer actually sees and processes. Here we present the "physical view" of data; the way things really are.

In Part Two, the routines needed by the computer to access information on its own level, the computer's point of view, are listed. You need these routines to access the data, but you do not need to understand how they operate in order to work with the information stored in data files. I will, of course, go into the intricacies of physical storage in some detail.

ENTERING AND USING LIBRARY UNITS

Most of the programming in Part Two is in the form of library "units," groups of routines and other information that can be compiled ahead of time and used by any number of programs. This saves time and disk space and makes modifying the individual programs in Part One simple and easy.

After compiling a unit, it must be installed in the disk file named SYSTEM-.LIBRARY on the boot disk. In Apple Pascal 1.1, the following sequence can be used to install a unit in the library.

(Single disk drive note: instead of following step 5 below, transfer the unit's code file to your boot disk before running the library program. If you do not have enough room on your boot disk, make a copy of the disk and remove the SYS-TEM.EDITOR and SYSTEM.FILER programs. You can then use your original disk for entry and editing and the copy for compiling and running the programs in this book.)

1. Execute (run) the program *library*. In the Apple Pascal system, the *library* program is found on the disk volume named Apple3:.
2. When prompted with "Output code file—>", respond with "*SYSTEM-.LIBRARY". This tells the program where to direct the output. If you receive a "Disk full" error message, send the output to some other disk, "#5:SYSTEM.LIBRARY" for example, and transfer that file to the boot disk later.
3. When prompted with "Link code file—>", respond with "*SYSTEM-.LIBRARY".
4. Type an equals sign (=) to copy all existing routines in the SYSTEM.LI-BRARY to the new file.
5. Insert the disk containing the code file of the unit to be installed.
6. Type "N" to select a new code file. When prompted "Link code file—>", respond with the name of the unit.
7. Copy all entries listed in the top part of the display to any of the empty slots in the bottom part. To do this, enter the number of the entry in the top, press the space bar, enter the number of an empty slot in the bottom, and press the space bar again to copy that entry.
8. Repeat steps 5, 6, and 7 for each library unit to be installed. Enter "Q" to quit the library program. When prompted with "Notice ?", enter the date, the time, and your initials. You may press the return key instead if you do not want to enter a notice.
9. Krunch the boot disk using the filer's K(runch command. You can now compile and run all of the programs that use the units you installed.

INTRINSIC VS. REGULAR UNITS

In Apple Pascal 1.1, a unit may be intrinsic or regular. Intrinsic units must be in SYSTEM.LIBRARY when a program that uses the unit is compiled and every time the program is executed. Regular units need to be in SYSTEM.LIBRARY only when the program is compiled, but also must be linked into the program's code file before the program will run. It is also possible to have units outside SYS-TEM.LIBRARY, even compiled directly along with a program, but these methods are not used here.

Any of the units in Part Two of this book may be converted into regular or intrinsic units. An intrinsic unit requires code and data segment numbers to be specified in the unit declaration line (see line 3 of PDBSUNIT.TEXT). To make an intrinsic unit into the regular kind, remove everything after the unit name and semi-colon. For comparison, *indexunit* in Chapter Nine is a regular unit. All others are intrinsic.

To turn a regular unit into the intrinsic kind, add code and data segment numbers to the declaration line. You must use unique segment numbers for all intrinsic units installed in SYSTEM.LIBRARY.

Intrinsic units are usually preferred because they are linked only when the program is executed. This saves disk space, especially when the unit is as large as *pdbsunit,* and eliminates the need to execute the Pascal linker after compiling a program. Regular units, because their code is copied into every using program, tend to produce large code files which must be linked using SYSTEM.LINKER before running the first time.

8

Pascal Data Base System Library Unit

PDBSUNIT / CRTSETUP / TESTUNIT

PDBSUNIT

All programs in the Pascal Data Base System (PDBS) group use most of the routines in the library unit, *pdbsunit*. Before compiling and running any of the programs in Part One of this book, you must first enter and compile *pdbsunit* and install the resulting code in SYSTEM.LIBRARY. You will also need to complete the *crtsetup* program presented later in this chapter.

If your text editor cannot handle the entire unit in a single file, you will have to enter the programming into separate text files and then have the compiler "include" each file at the proper position. The compiler *include* commands at lines 316–321 in the main PDBSUNIT.TEXT file show how this can be done.

Comments are included throughout *pdbsunit* to show what is happening at various stages. The purpose of this chapter is to describe the format used for PDBS files and to explain how you can write custom data base applications using *pdbsunit* routines. I'll also suggest a few modifications to the unit you may want to try.

PDBS File Structure

Figure 8-1 shows how a PDBS data file is organized. Block 0 of every file contains the field descriptors and other information needed by PDBS programs to access the data in the file. The data in block 0 corresponds to the structured record type *msc_descriptor* declared at line 136 in PDBSUNIT.TEXT. A PDBS file is, therefore, "self-defining," allowing programs to be written for all files, regardless of the format or type of data in them.

Records are stored in pages, with one page composed of two disk blocks each 512 bytes long. Usually, many records will be stored in one disk page. PDBS al-

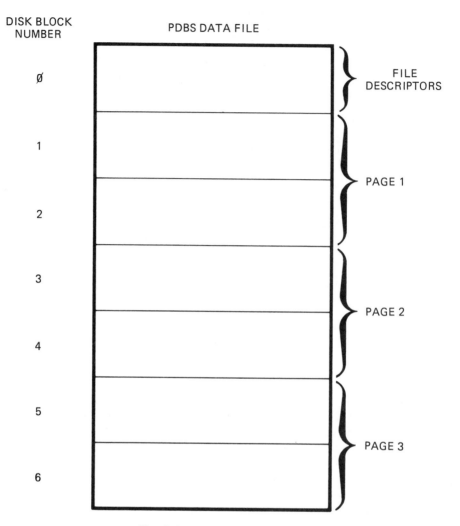

Fig. 8-1. *PDBS data file format.*

ways reads and writes full pages at a time. In the current version, there can be from 1 to 512 records per page.

As many records as possible are inserted into each page, but no record is allowed to cross the boundary of two pages. (See Fig. 8-2.) This can result in wasted space at the end of a disk page that can be as great as 511 bytes. You can avoid waste by using record sizes that are powers of two. For example, the most efficient record lengths are 2, 4, 8, 16, 32, 64, 128, 512, and 1,024. There will be no wasted space in a PDBS data file containing records of those sizes.

A record is further decomposed into fields according to a layout or plan described by the structured type, *fld_descriptor* (line 127 of PDBSUNIT.TEXT). Each field is described by name, type, length, relative byte position, and, in the

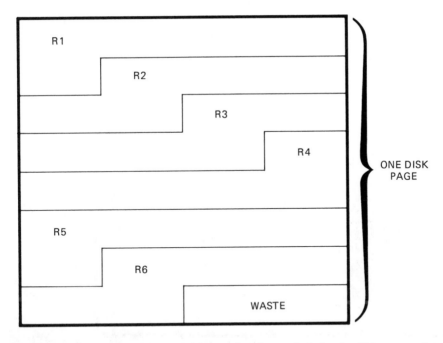

Fig. 8-2. *As many records as possible are stored in each disk page. This can result in some wasted space at the end of the page.*

case of a numeric field, the number of decimal places. Together, an array of field descriptors makes up the design of a record. (See Fig. 8-3.) This array is stored as part of the *msc_descriptor* (line 144) in block 0 of every file. In this version, there can be from 1 to 35 fields in a single record.

The first byte of a record indicates its status. The status of a record can be either *active* or *deleted* according to the subrange type *stat* declared at line 87 in PDBSUNIT.TEXT. If the status is set to *deleted,* the record is marked in the way explained in Chapter Seven. (See program *mark.)* The status byte can be set and reset without affecting the contents of the record.

Fields in a PDBS record are composed of characters, whether the data is actually defined to be a character string, a number, or a logical type. Numeric fields are padded at the left with spaces. Character strings are padded at the right with spaces. Logical fields are always represented by single characters. Each character in a field is significant. There are no length attribute or separator bytes used.

The maximum record number in a PDBS data file is limited to 32,767. To actually create a file containing that many records, however, your system has to be able to handle a file large enough to contain 32,767 records. The number of records per two-block disk page can be calculated using the formula:

$$recs\_per\_page = (page\_size + 1) \text{ div } rec\_size$$

STATUS

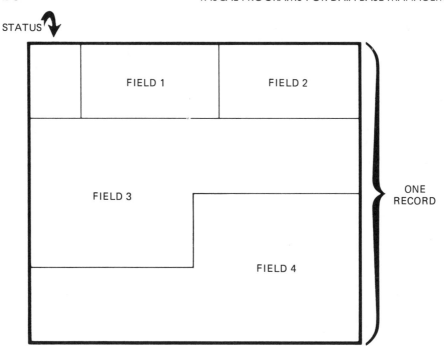

Fig. 8-3. *A record is composed of fields, usually of different lengths. The first byte of a record indicates its status, active or deleted.*

Virtual Memory

Perhaps the most important group of functions and procedures in *pdbsunit* are those that make up the Virtual Memory Operating System (VMOS) listed in the two text files, PDBS2.TEXT and PDBS3.TEXT. All accesses to records and files are controlled by VMOS.

Virtual memory, also called virtual paging, lets application programs ignore whether a record is on disk or in the computer's memory. To the program, it appears as though all the records are in memory, when in fact, most records are on disk while only a portion of the file is in the computer's memory at any one time.

Figure 8-4 shows the relationship between a disk file and the computer's memory. Disk pages that are currently in memory are linked together in a bidirectional list or chain. Each virtual page has two pointers, *vir_next* and *vir_last*, which are declared at lines 119–120 in PDBSUNIT.TEXT. *Vir_next* points forward to the next page in memory, while *vir_last* points back to a previous page. This ordering may be and usually is different from the physical ordering of the same pages as stored on disk. The virtual page list is circular in the sense that it has no beginning or end, a fact that can be verified by tracing the pointers, drawn as arrows, in Fig. 8-4.

When a program requests another record, VMOS first checks the virtual page

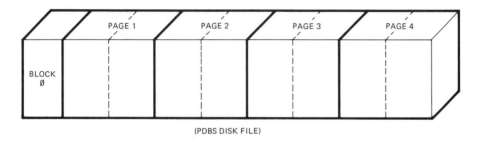

(PDBS DISK FILE)

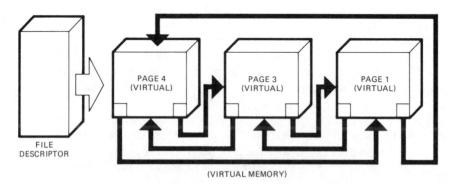

(VIRTUAL MEMORY)

Fig. 8-4. *At any one moment, pages of data stored in a disk file (top) may be held as virtual pages linked together in the computer's memory (bottom).*

list to see if the disk page containing that record is already in memory. If so, there is no need to read that page again. Instead, a pointer is set to the location of the record, which could be anywhere at all in memory. Accessing the same record repeatedly, therefore, only requires one disk read operation.

When a page does have to be read into memory, VMOS checks to see if enough free memory space exists to hold another virtual page. (See function *load_page* at line 176 in PDBS2.TEXT.)

If memory is full, controlled by the local *pdbsunit* constant *min_mem* at lines 143–147 in PDBS2.TEXT, then one of the current virtual memory pages must be released to make room for the new page to be read from disk. VMOS accomplishes this with the help of a count variable, named *vir_count*. (See line 121 of the *virtual_page* declaration in PDBSUNIT.TEXT.) Each read or write access to records in a virtual page held in memory advances *vir_count* by one. To decide which of the many pages in memory to release next, VMOS attempts to find the page with the lowest *vir_count* on the theory that this page is receiving the least amount of use and is the best one to let go.

There are other schemes you can try by rewriting function *least_used* at line 152 in PDBS2.TEXT to select pages for release using some other formula. If your system has a clock, for example, you could store the *time* of last access in each page and select pages to be released based on a "least-recently-used" plan. Be careful, though. Indexes may benefit from a "most-recently-used" release plan in order to keep the root page in memory. Whatever scheme you use, keeping the most heavily accessed pages in memory will almost always increase the speed of a program.

Writing Programs That Use PDBSUNIT

Of course the best examples for writing PDBS programs are in Part One of this book. I encourage you to add to this set but suggest that you avoid writing programs that work on only one file structure. To qualify as a PDBS program, it should operate correctly on any PDBS file. These instructions will help.

A *fil_descriptor* in PDBS is a structured record. (See lines 149–161 in PDBSUNIT.TEXT.) Each open file is described by holding in this record the name of the file *(fil_name)*, a pointer to the start of the file's virtual page list in memory *fil_page)*, the current record number *(fil_recptr)*, and other information.

The global array *fil_recs* at line 169 is an array of these *fil_descriptors*. To access any open file, then, the only thing your program needs to keep track of is a single integer number, usually called *file_number* or just *fn* in most of this software. File numbers are automatically chosen when a file is opened. (See function *open__file* at line 82 in PDBS3.TEXT.)

Error Handling

Most PDBS functions return an error code indicating the success or failure of the operation. Error handling in PDBS is automatic if you follow a few simple rules. This eliminates the need to construct complex error handlers and keeps all error messages consistent throughout the system. You can add your own error handlers, but I don't recommend it.

The function *executed* (see lines 75–116 in PDBS5.TEXT) is used to execute a PDBS function that returns an error code of the type *pdbs_err*. Because *executed* is a boolean function, it can be placed in an *if* statement. Examples of *executed* can be seen throughout the main bodies of any PDBS program in Part One.

Most PDBS programs consist of many *if* statement sequences. At any point, if a PDBS function fails, the sequence of events will be interrupted. The *executed* function returns true if the function performed *open_file* (for example) and passed back an error code of 0, indicating no error in that process. If the error code passed back by a PDBS function is not 0, then *executed* displays an appropriate error message and returns false.

Another way to execute PDBS functions is to first declare an error code variable.

```
VAR
  err_code : pdbs_err;
```

To execute a function, assign it to this variable with a statement such as this.

```
err_code : = seek_rec ( fn, rn );
```

In this case, it is up to you to check the value of *err_code* to see what the result of *seek_rec* was. This is called "error trapping." The possible error is trapped, with an appropriate response delayed for the time being until other steps can be taken.

A final way to execute PDBS functions is to build a procedure called *perform*. Examples of this method appear in many PDBS programs. (See the *sort_up* function at line 22 in the *sort* program in Chapter Six.)

Opening and Closing PDBS Files

Before reading or writing data in a file, the file must be opened. For speed, not all of the PDBS functions guard against accessing closed files. You are responsible for opening a file before permitting records to be read and written. (The most critical operations, such as trying to write a disk page to a closed file, are fully protected, however.)

To open a file for input or output, use the *open_file* function (line 82 of PDBS3.TEXT). To close a file, use *close_file* seen at line 120.

Open_file requires an integer file number variable and a file name. The file name can be variable or literal. For example, this code would open The Company's customer file for reading and writing.

```
IF executed ( open_file ( fn, 'CUSTOMERS. PDBF' ) )
    THEN { continue with program here }
```

Such a statement violates the PDBS principle of writing programs to work on all PDBS data files, not just on a particular file.

If the *open_file* is successfully executed, then variable *fn* is automatically set to the file number used. Future references to the file are made with this number. The file name is not needed again.

To close a file, the process is similar. There are two ways to close a file in PDBS—with or without an update. Closing with an update writes any changed information held in memory to the disk file and sets the date last updated to the current system date. Closing without an update does not alter the date last updated, and any changes held in memory are thrown away. In both cases, all virtual pages held in memory are deallocated and are available for use by other files. The following statements demonstrate the safest way to close files in PDBS.

```
WHILE NOT executed ( close_file ( fn, update ) ) DO
    IF NOT verified ( 'Try again' )
        THEN exit ( program )      { Fatal error }
```

Not all the PDBS programs in Part One use this method, which, if an error is discovered upon closing a file, gives the operator the chance to fix whatever is wrong and try again. Answering ''N'' to the ''Try again'' prompt ends the program with the possible loss of data.

Reading and Writing Records

Records can be manipulated as units or accessed field by field as strings. To process an entire file, the following sequence can be used.

```
FOR rn := 1 TO fil_recs[fn].fil_msc.msc_lastrec DO
BEGIN
   IF executed ( read_rec ( fn, rn, bp ) )
      THEN process_record
      ELSE exit ( program )
END;
```

The *for* statement is kept in bounds of the current range of active record numbers. It is your responsibility to ensure that records outside the current last record number *(msc_lastrec)* are not accessed with either *read_rec* or *write_rec*.

The variable *bp* is of the type *binary_page* declared at line 98 of PDBSUNIT-.TEXT. A *binary_page* is the same length as a disk page. When used internally as part of VMOS, a *binary_page* may hold many records. When used with *read_rec* and *write_rec*, a *binary_page* holds exactly one record.

After reading a record, the first byte in a *binary_page* is the status byte of the record. The first character of the first field in the record is at *bp[1]*. You can use the field descriptor *fld_pos* to locate the start of each field in a record after using *read_rec*. (See Fig. 8-3.)

Writing records is just as simple. The following code reads records from a file, then writes them back to the file after they are processed.

```
FOR rn := 1 TO fil_recs[fn].fil_msc.msc_lastrec DO
BEGIN
   IF NOT executed ( read_rec ( fn, rn, bp ) )
      THEN exit ( program );
   process_record;
   IF NOT executed ( write_rec (fn, rn, bp ) )
      THEN exit ( program )
END;
```

You will probably want more elegant error control than demonstrated here, of course. To complete the example, you should also close the file as described earlier.

To add new records to the end of a file, you must use *append_rec*. Never use *write_rec* to increase the size of a file. The following code can be used to transfer the contents of one file *(sn)* to another *(dn)*.

```
FOR rn := 1 TO fil_recs[sn].fil_msc.msc_lastrec DO
BEGIN
  IF NOT executed ( read_rec ( sn, rn, bp ) )
    THEN exit ( program );
  IF NOT executed ( append_rec ( dn, bp ) )
    THEN exit ( program )
END;
```

Function *insert_rec* can be used in a similar way. In that case, records are moved forward to make room for the insertion. *Append_rec* is, for that reason, faster.

Reading and Writing Fields

Individual fields can be read and written as string variables for further processing by your program.

Get_field reads one field from the current record into a string variable. Before using *get_field*, the current record must be located in a virtual page by VMOS. This is best accomplished by the function *seek_rec*, although *read_rec* can also be used.

The following code seeks the fourth record and reads the second field from that record into string variable *s*.

```
IF executed ( seek_rec ( fn, 4 ) )
  THEN get_field ( fn, 2, s );
```

Notice that *get_field* has three parameters—the file number, the field number, and a string variable. When read in this way, the extra spaces that might be in the field will also be read into the string. To remove all leading and trailing spaces from a string, use the *strip* procedure. You may also observe the *case_switch* boolean variable using *bumpstrup* (''BUMP STRing to UPper case'').

```
strip ( s );
IF case_switch
  THEN bumpstrup ( s );
```

You should always precede a *get_field* with a *seek_rec* or a *read_rec* operation. For speed, *get_field* does little error checking and will not prevent illegal accesses to non–existent files, records, or fields. It is your responsibility to make sure that only declared fields are read by *get_field*. The number of fields in a record can be accessed by this statement.

```
num_fields := fil_recs[fn].fil_msc.msc_nflds;
```

This sets an integer variable *num_fields* equal to the number of fields in the records of file *fn*. At no time should *get_field* or *put_field* be allowed to specify a field number less than one or greater than *num_fields*.

Writing fields into records is just as easy. Normally, a *put_field* is also preceded by a seek.

```
IF executed ( seek_rec ( fn, 2 ) )
   THEN put_field ( fn, 2, s );
```

If this example followed the *get_field* example, the effect would be to transfer the second field in the fourth record to the second field in the second record.

Reading and Writing Numeric Fields

Numbers in PDBS files are stored as strings, just as every other piece of data is stored. To make sure that numbers can be searched and sorted properly, they must be right-justified within the length of the field. This can be accomplished with the following code.

```
WITH fil_recs[fn].fil_msc do
WHILE length(s) < msc_flds[n].fld_len DO
   insert ( ' ', s, 1 );
```

This assumes that the variable *n* is set to the field number where this string is to be stored. The *while* loop inserts spaces at the left of the first character in the string until the string is equal to the declared length of the field.

You should also make sure that the number of decimals in the string is the same for all fields. This can be accomplished by normalizing the string.

```
WITH fil_recs[fn].fil_msc DO
   normalize ( s, msc_flds[n].fld_decimals );
```

Also see the *calc* program and *calcunit* library unit for additional details on handling numeric fields in PDBS.

Pascal vs. PDBS Seek

The UCSD Pascal intrinsic *seek* is not the same as the PDBS *seek_rec* function. The old *seek* can be used in your programs, but should not be used to access PDBS data files. Use *seek_rec* instead.

Seek_rec sets the current record pointer in the file descriptor for this file. This value is stored in the variable *fil_recptr* declared at line 154 of PDBSUNIT.TEXT. Using *seek_rec* initiates a search of the virtual pages in memory and triggers all VMOS actions described earlier.

Reading and writing records or fields do not change the position of the current record pointer *(fil_recptr)*. To read the next record in sequence, you must perform another *seek_rec*. You can also use *next_rec* and *last_rec* to go forward and back in the file. (See the *editor* function *browse* at line 557 in file EDITOR1.TEXT in Chapter One.)

Never seek records outside the range of active record numbers in the file. Doing otherwise is illegal and can result in the loss of data. The last active record number in the file can be determined with this statement.

last := fil_recs[fn].fil_msc.msc_lastrec;

That sets an integer variable *last* in your program to the last record number. Every record from one to *last* can be accessed by *seek_rec*, *read_rec*, *write_rec*, *get_field*, and *put_field*. If the value of *last* is 0, then the file is empty.

Modifying PDBSUNIT

There are a number of modifications you can make to the unit, many of which will not affect data you have already stored in files. This section will also help if you are attempting to convert PDBS to another Pascal compiler.

The *pdbs_init* procedure at line 240 in PDBS6.TEXT reads the system date from the boot disk. The procedure *read_date* at line 246 is dependent on the directory structure of a UCSD/Apple Pascal diskette and may not work properly in other systems. You can replace the procedure with code that reads a system clock or just lets the operator enter the current date from the console.

Changing the Constants

Constants have been used religiously throughout PDBS to simplify changes. You can change all of the file name extensions in lines 21 through 26 of PDBSUNIT.TEXT if any of these conflict with other software you may have.

Max_digits can be increased to allow larger numbers to be stored in numeric fields. If you change *max_digits*, you must also change *max_long* to the highest possible value, equal to a number containing the digit "9" *max_digits* times.

You can change *page_size* to use larger or smaller disk pages. The value of *page_size* must be one less than a multiple of the disk block size. An alteration to *page_size* requires all data currently stored to be reorganized to the new page format. The conversion could be handled in your own version of the *convert* program (Chapter Seven). VMOS will operate correctly with new page sizes.

Max_files is set to six. This is the maximum number of PDBS files that can be open at one time and managed by VMOS. You can set *max_files* to new positive values, higher or lower, without requiring any other changes. Data in existing files are not affected. Setting *max_files* too large can result in the rare out-of-memory error discussed in the program comments at line 234 in PDBS2.TEXT. Such an error will usually show up when trying to open a new file. As long as a file can be opened, at least one virtual memory page will be available for processing data in the file.

Changing *max_fld,* the maximum number of fields in a record, may require a rewrite of VMOS. *Max_fld* must not be set to a value that would result in *msc_descriptor* at line 136 in PDBSUNIT.TEXT to grow larger than one disk block. If this is done, serious problems will develop, and data can be lost.

If you ever receive a stack overflow error during the execution of a program, try setting the local constant *min_mem* at line 288 in PDBSUNIT.TEXT a little higher. You may also make *min_mem* an integer variable. Setting *min_mem* to the amount of memory available *(min_mem: = memavail* in Apple Pascal) will then temporarily prevent VMOS from allocating new virtual pages. (See lines 143–147 in PDBS2.TEXT.)

Any changes to *pdbsunit* should be followed by recompiling the *testunit* program presented last in this chapter. Never use PDBS programs on your data files without first checking the new software configuration with *testunit.*

```
001: {$S+,I-}              { Compiler swapping on; I/O error checking off }
002:
003: unit pdbsunit; intrinsic code 23 data 24;
004:
005: {--------------------------------------------------------------------}
006: {                                                                    }
007: {     PROGRAM        :  PDBSunit -- Pascal Data Base Library Unit     }
008: {     LANGUAGE       :  UCSD Pascal / Apple Pascal 1.1               }
009: {                                                                    }
010: {     Copyright (C) 1983 by Tom Swan. All commercial rights reserved. }
011: {                                                                    }
012: {--------------------------------------------------------------------}
013:
014: interface            { Parts accessible to programs }
015:
016: CONST
017:     active      = 0;            { Value for record status = active }
018:     alpha_size  = 9;            { Length (-1) of field names }
019:     blank       = 32;           { ASCII blank character }
020:     deleted     = 1;            { Value for record status = deleted }
021:     ext_indx    = '.INDX';      { Index file name extension }
022:     ext_pdbf    = '.PDBF';      { Data file name extension }
023:     ext_rprt    = '.RPRT';      { Report format file name extension }
024:     ext_scrn    = '.SCRN';      { Screen format file name extension }
025:     ext_spec    = '.SPEC';      { Output spec file name extension }
026:     ext_strc    = '.STRC';      { Structure file name extension }
027:     fname_len   = 23;           { Length of a file name }
028:     max_digits  = 13;           { Maximum digits in a number }
029:     max_files   = 6;            { Files allowed open at a time }
030:     max_fld     = 35;           { Fields per record (max) }
031:     max_long    = 9999999999999;{ Maximum long integer (max_digits 9s) }
032:     page_size   = 1023;         { Length (-1) of a binary page (record) }
033:     ret         = 13;           { ASCII return character }
034:     screen_width = 80;          { Character width of display }
035:     string_size = 255;          { Max string len }
036:     version     = '1.0';        { Version number as a 3-char string }
037:
038: TYPE
039:
040: {--------------------------------------------------------------------}
041: {   Non-standard Pascal (UCSD format) types                          }
042: {--------------------------------------------------------------------}
```

```
043:
044:     ucsd_string =                { Preserve original default string type }
045:        string;
046:
047:     string =                     { Redefine string type to maximum length }
048:        ucsd_string[ string_size ];
049:
050:     pdbs_fname =                 { File names }
051:        ucsd_string[ fname_len ];
052:
053:     long_integer =               { Binary coded decimal numbers }
054:        integer[ max_digits ];
055:
056:     ucsd_date =                  { Date format }
057:        PACKED RECORD
058:           month  : 0 .. 12;                { 0 = date not set }
059:           day    : 0 .. 31;
060:           year   : 0 .. 100
061:        END; { ucsd_date }
062:
063:
064: {-------------------------------------------------------------------------}
065: {    Scalar (enumerated) types                                            }
066: {-------------------------------------------------------------------------}
067:
068:     close_option =               { File closing option }
069:        ( update, no_update );
070:
071:     dat_descriptor =             { Describes each data type }
072:        ( dat_char,                  { Alphabetic characters }
073:          dat_number,                { Fixed decimal integer }
074:          dat_logical );             { Logical true or false }
075:
076:
077: {-------------------------------------------------------------------------}
078: {    Subrange types                                                       }
079: {-------------------------------------------------------------------------}
080:
081:     byte =                       { One eight-bit byte }
082:        0 .. 255;
083:
084:     pdbs_err =                   { PDBS function error result }
085:        0 .. 99;
086:
087:     stat =                       { Record status.  First byte of each record. }
088:        active .. deleted;
089:
090:
091: {-------------------------------------------------------------------------}
092: {    Array types                                                          }
093: {-------------------------------------------------------------------------}
094:
095:     alpha =                      { Field names and other misc strings }
096:        PACKED ARRAY[ 0 .. alpha_size ] OF char;
097:
098:     binary_page =                { Holds disk page / records in binary form }
099:        PACKED ARRAY[ 0 .. page_size ] OF byte;
100:
101:     fld_order =                  { Field numbers in selected order }
102:        ARRAY[ 0 .. max_fld ] OF integer;       { [0] = number of entries }
103:
104:
105: {-------------------------------------------------------------------------}
106: {    Pointer types                                                        }
107: {-------------------------------------------------------------------------}
108:
```

```
109:    vir_ptr =
110:       ^virtual_page;          { Pointer to virtual pages }
111:
112:
113: {----------------------------------------------------------------------}
114: {   Record (structured) types                                          }
115: {----------------------------------------------------------------------}
116:
117:    virtual_page =            { Virtual (in memory) disk pages }
118:       RECORD
119:          vir_next,                           { Pointer to next page }
120:          vir_last      : vir_ptr;            { Pointer to last page }
121:          vir_count     : integer;            { Times page accessed }
122:          vir_changed   : boolean;            { True if changes made }
123:          vir_blknum    : integer;            { Actual disk block number }
124:          vir_page      : binary_page         { Disk page contents }
125:       END; { virtual_page }
126:
127:    fld_descriptor =          { Describes each field in a record }
128:       PACKED RECORD
129:          fld_name      : alpha;              { Name of field }
130:          fld_type      : dat_descriptor;     { Data type }
131:          fld_len       : 1 .. page_size;     { Length in bytes }
132:          fld_pos       : 0 .. page_size;     { Relative position }
133:          fld_decimals  : 0 .. max_digits     { Number of decimals }
134:       END; { fld_descriptor }
135:
136:    msc_descriptor =          { Miscellaneous file descriptor (block 0) }
137:       RECORD
138:          msc_recsize,                        { Length each record }
139:          msc_maxrec,                         { Maximum record number }
140:          msc_lastrec : integer;              { Last record in file }
141:          msc_created,                        { Date created }
142:          msc_updated : ucsd_date;            { Date last updated }
143:          msc_nflds : 0 .. max_fld;           { Fields in the record }
144:          msc_flds : ARRAY[ 1 .. max_fld ]    { Field descriptors }
145:                          OF fld_descriptor;
146:          msc_id : ucsd_string[3]             { Version id stamp }
147:       END; { msc_descriptor }
148:
149:    fil_descriptor =          { Describes an active (open) file }
150:       RECORD
151:          fil_name      : pdbs_fname;         { Name of file }
152:          fil_ptr       : ^ucsd_file;         { System "file" }
153:          fil_page      : vir_ptr;            { Head of virtual page list }
154:          fil_recptr,                         { Current record pointer }
155:          fil_relptr,                         { Record relative position }
156:          fil_bpp,                            { Blocks per page }
157:          fil_rpp       : integer;            { Records per page }
158:          fil_eof,                            { True if at last record }
159:          fil_open      : boolean;            { True if file open }
160:          fil_msc       : msc_descriptor      { Block 0 info rec }
161:       END; { fil_descriptor }
162:
163:    ucsd_file = FILE;         { Untyped file for system I/O }
164:
165:
166: VAR
167:    case_switch     : boolean;    { Mixed case strings switch }
168:    f               : FILE;       { Untyped misc file }
169:    fil_recs        :             { PDBS data files }
170:     ARRAY[ 1 .. max_files ] OF fil_descriptor;
171:    page_pool       : vir_ptr;    { Disposed virtual pages pointer }
172:    today           : ucsd_date;  { Today's date }
173:
174:
175: {----------------------------------------------------------------------}
```

```
176: {    PDBS1.TEXT -- Screen output routines                              }
177: {------------------------------------------------------------------------}
178:
179:    PROCEDURE evon;
180:    PROCEDURE evoff;
181:    PROCEDURE goright;
182:    PROCEDURE goup;
183:    PROCEDURE beep;
184:    PROCEDURE clreoln;
185:    PROCEDURE clreosc;
186:    PROCEDURE clrscrn;
187:    PROCEDURE prompt( s : string );
188:    PROCEDURE promptln( s : string );
189:    PROCEDURE promptat( x, y : integer; s : string );
190:    PROCEDURE show_string( s : string; x, y, width : integer );
191:    PROCEDURE clear_col( x, y, width, len : integer );
192:
193:
194: {------------------------------------------------------------------------}
195: {   PDBS2.TEXT -- Virtual Memory Operating System (VMOS)                 }
196: {------------------------------------------------------------------------}
197:
198:    FUNCTION seek_rec( fn, rn : integer ) : pdbs_err;
199:    FUNCTION get_rec( fn  : integer; VAR bp : binary_page ) : pdbs_err;
200:    FUNCTION put_rec( fn  : integer; VAR bp : binary_page ) : pdbs_err;
201:    FUNCTION next_rec( fn : integer ) : pdbs_err;
202:    FUNCTION last_rec( fn : integer ) : pdbs_err;
203:    PROCEDURE get_field( fn, fld_num : integer; VAR s : string );
204:    PROCEDURE put_field( fn, fld_num : integer; VAR s : string );
205:
206:
207: {------------------------------------------------------------------------}
208: {   PDBS3.TEXT -- VMOS continued                                         }
209: {------------------------------------------------------------------------}
210:
211:    FUNCTION read_rec( fn, rn : integer; VAR bp : binary_page ) : pdbs_err;
212:    FUNCTION write_rec( fn, rn : integer; VAR bp : binary_page ) : pdbs_err;
213:    FUNCTION append_rec( fn : integer; VAR bp : binary_page ) : pdbs_err;
214:    FUNCTION insert_rec( fn : integer; VAR bp : binary_page ) : pdbs_err;
215:    FUNCTION open_file( VAR fn : integer; fname : pdbs_fname ) : pdbs_err;
216:    FUNCTION close_file( fn : integer; option : close_option ) : pdbs_err;
217:    FUNCTION make_file(     fname    : pdbs_fname;
218:                        VAR msc_rec : msc_descriptor ) : pdbs_err;
219:    FUNCTION expand_file( fn, rn : integer ) : pdbs_err;
220:
221:
222: {------------------------------------------------------------------------}
223: {   PDBS4.TEXT -- Miscellaneous file and record routines                 }
224: {------------------------------------------------------------------------}
225:
226:    PROCEDURE init_msc( VAR msc_rec : msc_descriptor );
227:    FUNCTION rec_status( fn : integer ) : stat;
228:    FUNCTION mark_rec( fn : integer; stat_byte : stat ) : pdbs_err;
229:    FUNCTION file_empty( fn : integer ) : boolean;
230:    FUNCTION file_end( fn : integer ) : boolean;
231:    FUNCTION file_not_in_use( fname : pdbs_fname ) : boolean;
232:    PROCEDURE zero_rec( fn : integer; VAR bp : binary_page );
233:    FUNCTION zero_file( fn : integer ) : pdbs_err;
234:    PROCEDURE display_rec( VAR pf : text; fn : integer; order : fld_order );
235:    FUNCTION fld_number( VAR msc_rec   : msc_descriptor;
236:                             field_name : alpha ) : integer;
237:    PROCEDURE list_fields( fn : integer );
238:    FUNCTION load_order(     ps    : ucsd_string;
239:                             fn    : integer;
240:                         VAR order : fld_order ) : boolean;
241:    PROCEDURE make_key(     fn    : integer;
242:                        VAR order : fld_order;
```

```
243:                         VAR key   : string );
244:
245:
246: {------------------------------------------------------------------}
247: {   PDBS5.TEXT -- General purpose functions                        }
248: {------------------------------------------------------------------}
249:
250:    FUNCTION getch( VAR ch : char ) : char;
251:    FUNCTION inrange( n, low, hi : integer ) : boolean;
252:    FUNCTION value( s : string ) : integer;
253:    FUNCTION verified( s : string ) : boolean;
254:    FUNCTION executed( err_code : pdbs_err ) : boolean;
255:    FUNCTION max( a, b : integer ) : integer;
256:    FUNCTION min( a, b : integer ) : integer;
257:    FUNCTION tf( b : boolean ) : char;
258:    FUNCTION cap( ch : char ) : char;
259:    FUNCTION getnum( VAR n : integer; low, hi : integer ) : boolean;
260:    FUNCTION common_fields(     fn1, fn2 : integer;
261:                            VAR order    : fld_order ) : boolean;
262:    FUNCTION get_file_name( s : string; VAR fname : pdbs_fname ) : boolean;
263:
264:
265: {------------------------------------------------------------------}
266: {   PDBS6.TEXT -- General purpose procedures                       }
267: {------------------------------------------------------------------}
268:
269:    PROCEDURE normalize( VAR s : string; decimals : integer );
270:    PROCEDURE bumpstrup( VAR s : string );
271:    PROCEDURE lvalue(   VAR s        : string;
272:                            decimals : integer;
273:                        VAR long     : long_integer );
274:    PROCEDURE num2string( n, d : integer; pad : char; VAR s : string );
275:    PROCEDURE strip( VAR s : string );
276:    PROCEDURE next_token( VAR s, t : string );
277:    PROCEDURE str2alpha( s : string; VAR a : alpha );
278:    PROCEDURE remove( VAR s : string; substr : string );
279:    PROCEDURE remove_ext( VAR fname : pdbs_fname );
280:    PROCEDURE date2string( date : ucsd_date; VAR date_string : string );
281:
282:
283: implementation        { Parts not accessible to programs }
284:
285:
286: CONST
287:    block_size   = 512;          { Bytes in one disk block }
288:    min_mem      = 2048;         { Minimum words memory maintained }
289:    month_names  = '???JanFebMarAprMayJunJulAugSepOctNovDec';
290:
291: TYPE
292:    crt_command  =
293:       ( crt_evon,               { Enhanced video on }
294:         crt_evoff,              { Enhanced video off }
295:         crt_goright,            { Move cursor non-destructively right }
296:         crt_goup,               { Move cursor non-destructively up }
297:         crt_bell,               { Ring bell }
298:         crt_cleoln,             { Clear from cursor to end of line }
299:         crt_cleosc,             { Clear from cursor to end of screen }
300:         crt_clscrn       );     { Clear entire screen }
301:
302:    crt_rec      =               { PDBS Cathode Ray Tube (display) record }
303:       RECORD
304:          crt_n : 0 .. 4;
305:          crt_ch : PACKED ARRAY[ 0 .. 3 ] OF char
306:          END; { crt_rec }
307:
308: VAR
309:    crt_info     :               { Array of crt command sequences }
```

```
310:          ARRAY[ crt_command ] OF crt_rec;
311:
312:
313: (*---------------------------------------------------------------*)
314: (*   Include files stored separately                             *)
315: (*---------------------------------------------------------------*)
316: (*$I PDBS1.TEXT *)     (* Screen output routines                 *)
317: (*$I PDBS2.TEXT *)     (* Virtual Memory Operating System (VMOS) *)
318: (*$I PDBS3.TEXT *)     (* VMOS continued                         *)
319: (*$I PDBS4.TEXT *)     (* Miscellaneous file and record routines *)
320: (*$I PDBS5.TEXT *)     (* General purpose functions              *)
321: (*$I PDBS6.TEXT *)     (* General purpose procedures             *)
322: (*---------------------------------------------------------------*)
323:
324:
325: BEGIN
326:    pdbs_init
327: END. { unit }

001: {---------------------------------------------------------------}
002: {                                                               }
003: {    PDBS1.TEXT -- Screen output routines                       }
004: {                                                               }
005: {---------------------------------------------------------------}
006:
007:
008: PROCEDURE send_crt( c : crt_command );
009: { Perform a crt command using crt_info variables }
010: { Local to unit }
011: BEGIN
012:    WITH crt_info[c] DO
013:        unitwrite( 1, crt_ch, crt_n )
014: END; { send_crt }
015:
016:
017: PROCEDURE evon;
018: { Switch on enhanced video }
019: BEGIN
020:    send_crt( crt_evon )
021: END; { evon }
022:
023:
024: PROCEDURE evoff;
025: { Switch off enhanced video }
026: BEGIN
027:    send_crt( crt_evoff )
028: END; { evoff }
029:
030:
031: PROCEDURE goright;
032: { Move cursor non-destructively right }
033: BEGIN
034:    send_crt( crt_goright )
035: END; { goright }
036:
037:
038: PROCEDURE goup;
039: { Move cursor non-destructively up }
040: BEGIN
041:    send_crt( crt_goup )
042: END; { goup }
043:
044:
045: PROCEDURE beep;
046: { Sound the alarm! }
047: BEGIN
048:    send_crt( crt_bell )
049: END; { beep }
```

```
050:
051:
052: PROCEDURE clreoln;
053: { Clear from cursor to end of line }
054: BEGIN
055:    send_crt( crt_cleoln )
056: END; { clreoln }
057:
058:
059: PROCEDURE clreosc;
060: { Clear from cursor to end of screen }
061: BEGIN
062:    send_crt( crt_cleosc )
063: END; { clreosc }
064:
065:
066: PROCEDURE clrscrn;
067: { Clear screen }
068: BEGIN
069:    send_crt( crt_clscrn )
070: END; { clrscrn }
071:
072:
073: PROCEDURE prompt{ s : string };
074: { Clear line and write string at present cursor position }
075: BEGIN
076:    clreoln;
077:    write( s )
078: END; { prompt }
079:
080:
081: PROCEDURE promptln{ s : string };
082: { Clear line and writeln string at present cursor position }
083: BEGIN
084:    clreoln;
085:    writeln( s )
086: END; { promptln }
087:
088:
089: PROCEDURE promptat{ x, y : integer; s : string };
090: { Write string @ X,Y and clear to end of line }
091: BEGIN
092:    gotoxy( x, y );
093:    prompt( s )
094: END; { promptat }
095:
096:
097: PROCEDURE show_string{ VAR s : string; x, y, width : integer };
098: { Display string s in a column at these coordinates and parameters. }
099: { This procedure is similar to show_from in function edit, but does }
100: { not include the mechanism to simulate keyboard interrupts. }
101: VAR
102:    i, k : integer;
103: BEGIN
104:    i := 1;                              { First char at s[1] }
105:    WHILE i <= length( s ) DO
106:    BEGIN
107:       gotoxy( x, y );
108:       k := i;                { Save old "i" value in "k" }
109:       i := i + width;        { Equivalent to a line feed }
110:       IF i > length( s )
111:         THEN unitwrite( 1, s[k], length( s ) - k + 1 )  { Last line }
112:         ELSE unitwrite( 1, s[k], width   );             { Full line }
113:       y := y + 1
114:    END  { while }
115: END; { show_string }
116:
```

```
117:
118: PROCEDURE clear_col{ x, y, width, len : integer };
119: { Clear column at these coordinates, and parameters }
120: VAR
121:    a : PACKED ARRAY[ 0 .. screen_width ] OF char;
122: BEGIN
123:    fillchar( a, width, chr( blank ) );
124:    WHILE len > 0 DO
125:    BEGIN
126:       gotoxy( x, y );
127:       write( a : width );
128:       len := len - width;          { Decrease length remaining }
129:       y := y + 1                   { Advance to next row down }
130:    END { while }
131: END; { clear_col }

001: {---------------------------------------------------------------------}
002: {                                                                     }
003: {    PDBS2.TEXT -- Virtual Memory Operating System (VMOS)             }
004: {                                                                     }
005: {---------------------------------------------------------------------}
006: {                                                                     }
007: {    Note :        fn = file_number          bp = binary_page         }
008: {                  rn = record_number        vp = virtual_page        }
009: {                  bn = block_number                                  }
010: {                  pn = page_number                                   }
011: {                                                                     }
012: {---------------------------------------------------------------------}
013:
014:
015: { ----- Local Procedures.  Not accessible to user programs. ----- }
016:
017:
018: FUNCTION read_page( fn, bn : integer; vp : vir_ptr ) : pdbs_err;
019: { Read from disk at bn into fn's virtual page (vp) }
020: { Local to unit }
021: BEGIN
022:    WITH fil_recs[ fn ] DO WITH vp^ DO
023:       IF blockread( fil_ptr^,                { UCSD file }
024:                     vir_page,                { Virtual page area }
025:                     fil_bpp,                 { Number blocks }
026:                     bn ) = fil_bpp           { Block number }
027:          THEN
028:             BEGIN
029:                vir_blknum := bn;             { Remember block number }
030:                vir_count := 0;               { Reset frequency count }
031:                vir_changed := false;         { Disk = memory }
032:                read_page := 0;               { No error }
033:             END
034:          ELSE
035:             read_page := 18     { Disk read error }
036: END; { read_page }
037:
038:
039: FUNCTION write_page( fn : integer; vp : vir_ptr ) : pdbs_err;
040: { Write current virtual page (vp) to fn's disk file }
041: { Local to unit }
042: BEGIN
043:    WITH fil_recs[ fn ] DO WITH vp^ DO
044:       IF blockwrite( fil_ptr^,               { UCSD file }
045:                      vir_page,               { Virtual page area }
046:                      fil_bpp,                { Number blocks }
047:                      vir_blknum ) = fil_bpp
048:          THEN
049:             BEGIN
050:                write_page := 0;              { No error }
051:                vir_changed := false          { Disk = memory }
052:             END
```

```
053:          ELSE
054:              write_page := 19    { Disk write error }
055: END; { write_page }
056:
057:
058: PROCEDURE link( VAR fil_page, vp : vir_ptr );
059: { Link vp^ into fil_page virtual page list }
060: { Local to unit }
061: BEGIN
062:     IF fil_page = NIL THEN
063:         BEGIN { Start a new list }
064:             fil_page := vp;
065:             vp^.vir_next := vp;    { New lists start by pointing }
066:             vp^.vir_last := vp     {  to themselves. }
067:         END ELSE
068:         BEGIN { Link vp^ into existing list }
069:             vp^.vir_next := fil_page^.vir_next;
070:             vp^.vir_last := fil_page;
071:             vp^.vir_next^.vir_last := vp;
072:             vp^.vir_last^.vir_next :=vp;
073:             fil_page := vp
074:         END { else }
075: END; { link }
076:
077:
078: PROCEDURE unlink( VAR fil_page, vp : vir_ptr );
079: { Unlink the page addressed by fil_page }
080: { Returns address of unlinked page in vp }
081: { Local to unit }
082: BEGIN
083:     vp := fil_page;
084:     IF vp^.vir_next = vp
085:       THEN
086:         fil_page := NIL   { Unlink single page }
087:       ELSE
088:         BEGIN
089:             vp^.vir_last^.vir_next := vp^.vir_next;
090:             vp^.vir_next^.vir_last := vp^.vir_last;
091:             fil_page := vp^.vir_next
092:         END { else }
093: END; { unlink }
094:
095:
096: FUNCTION deallocated( fn : integer; must_write : boolean ) : pdbs_err;
097: { Dispose of the page addressed by fil_page, linking the space into }
098: { the available storage pool, writing to disk if necessary. }
099: { Local to unit }
100: VAR
101:     err_code : pdbs_err;
102:     tp : vir_ptr;          { Temporary pointer variable }
103: BEGIN
104:
105:     { Write page to disk if any changes to it had been made. }
106:
107:     WITH fil_recs[ fn ] DO
108:       BEGIN
109:         IF ( fil_page^.vir_changed ) AND ( must_write )
110:           THEN err_code := write_page( fn, fil_page )
111:           ELSE err_code := 0;
112:
113:     { Provided no errors were received, unlink the virtual page }
114:     { from its current linked list, and insert into the storage }
115:     { pool for future use. }
116:
117:         IF err_code = 0 THEN
118:           BEGIN
119:             unlink( fil_page, tp );   { Remove fil_page from list }
120:             tp^.vir_next := page_pool; { Pool uses one-way links only }
```

```
121:                page_pool := tp              { Link into storage pool }
122:            END { if }
123:
124:      END; { with }
125:      deallocated := err_code
126: END; { deallocated }
127:
128:
129: FUNCTION allocated( VAR vp : vir_ptr ) : pdbs_err;
130: { Allocate a new virtual page area to prepare for loading }
131: { Local to unit }
132: BEGIN
133:      allocated := 0;  { No error unless operation fails }
134:
135:      IF page_pool <> NIL
136:        THEN
137:          BEGIN { Use a previously disposed virtual page if possible }
138:              vp := page_pool;
139:              page_pool := page_pool^.vir_next
140:          END
141:        ELSE
142:
143:      IF memavail > min_mem + min_mem
144:        THEN
145:          new( vp )       { Allocate fresh memory space if there is room }
146:        ELSE
147:          allocated := 21        { Out of memory error }
148:
149: END; { allocated }
150:
151:
152: FUNCTION least_used( vp : vir_ptr ) : vir_ptr;
153: { Starting at this virtual page, return the address of the least used }
154: { page in the list.  Assumes vp <> nil, and at least one page in list. }
155: { Local to unit }
156: VAR
157:      count : integer;           { Low count holder }
158:      tp : vir_ptr;              { Temporary pointer }
159: BEGIN
160:      tp := vp;                  { Sentinel marks position }
161:      count := vp^.vir_count;    { Initialize count = first page }
162:      least_used := vp;          { Initialize function value }
163:      vp := vp^.vir_next;        { Advance to next page in list }
164:      WHILE ( vp <> tp ) DO
165:          BEGIN
166:              IF vp^.vir_count < count THEN
167:                  BEGIN
168:                      least_used := vp;            { Lowest so far }
169:                      count := vp^.vir_count       { Remember new low value }
170:                  END; { if }
171:              vp := vp^.vir_next { Advance to next page in list }
172:          END   { while }
173: END; { least_used }
174:
175:
176: FUNCTION load_page( fn, pn : integer ) : pdbs_err;
177: { Load page into this file's virtual page list }
178: { Local to unit }
179: VAR
180:      count,
181:      bn       : integer;
182:      err_code : pdbs_err;
183:      found    : boolean;
184:      tp       : vir_ptr;        { Temporary pointer }
185: BEGIN
186:      WITH fil_recs[ fn ] DO
187:       IF NOT fil_open
```

```
188:        THEN
189:           err_code := 13        { Attempt to access a closed file }
190:        ELSE
191:           BEGIN
192:              err_code := 0;
193:              bn := ( ( pn - 1 ) * fil_bpp ) + 1;
194:
195:              { Check if this bn is already in memory as }
196:              { a virtual page in the file's linked list. }
197:
198:              tp := fil_page;  { Sentinel shows where to stop }
199:              found := false;
200:              WHILE ( tp <> NIL ) AND ( NOT found ) DO
201:                 BEGIN
202:                    found := fil_page^.vir_blknum = bn;
203:                    IF NOT found
204:                       THEN fil_page := fil_page^.vir_next;
205:                    IF fil_page = tp
206:                       THEN tp := NIL  { Stop when we come full circle }
207:                 END; { while }
208:
209:              { If virtual page was in memory, then fil_page is equal to }
210:              { the in memory address where that page is stored. }
211:              { Otherwise, the page is not in memory and must now be }
212:              { read from disk into a newly allocated virtual page. }
213:
214:              IF NOT found THEN
215:                 BEGIN
216:
217:                    { Attempt to allocate a fresh virtual page. }
218:
219:                    err_code := allocated( tp );
220:
221:                    { If fresh space was not available, then deallocate }
222:                    { the least-used virtual page on this file's list, }
223:                    { writing to disk if changes were made to the page. }
224:                    { Then, try to allocate tp again. }
225:
226:                    IF ( err_code <> 0 ) AND ( fil_page <> NIL ) THEN
227:                       BEGIN
228:                          fil_page := least_used( fil_page );
229:                          err_code := deallocated( fn, true );
230:                          IF err_code = 0
231:                             THEN err_code := allocated( tp )
232:                       END; { if }
233:
234:                    { tp now addresses a free virtual page.  If err_code }
235:                    { is still <> 0, however, we are out of room, and   }
236:                    { must return an error with regrets to the caller. }
237:                    { This kind of difficulty should be rare. }
238:
239:                    IF err_code = 0 THEN
240:                       BEGIN
241:                          err_code := read_page( fn, bn, tp );
242:                          IF err_code = 0
243:                             THEN link( fil_page, tp )
244:                       END   { if }
245:
246:                 END { if }
247:
248:           END; { with / if }
249:        load_page := err_code
250: END; { load_page }
251:
252:
253: FUNCTION read_msc( fn : integer ) : pdbs_err;
254: { Read miscellaneous file information for file fn }
```

```
255: { Local to unit }
256: VAR
257:    msc_buff : PACKED ARRAY[ 1 .. block_size ] OF byte;
258: BEGIN
259:    WITH fil_recs[ fn ] DO
260:       IF blockread( fil_ptr^, msc_buff, 1, 0 ) <> 1
261:          THEN
262:             read_msc := 18        { Disk read error }
263:          ELSE
264:            BEGIN
265:              moveleft( msc_buff, fil_msc, sizeof( fil_msc ) );
266:              IF fil_msc.msc_id <> version
267:                 THEN read_msc := 24        { Version error }
268:                 ELSE read_msc := 0         { No error }
269:            END { else }
270: END; { read_msc }
271:
272:
273: FUNCTION write_msc( fn : integer ) : pdbs_err;
274: { Write miscellaneous file information for this file number }
275: { Local to unit }
276: VAR
277:    msc_buff : PACKED ARRAY[ 1 .. block_size ] OF byte;
278: BEGIN
279:    fillchar( msc_buff, sizeof( msc_buff ), chr(0) );
280:    WITH fil_recs[ fn ] DO
281:       BEGIN
282:         moveleft( fil_msc, msc_buff, sizeof( fil_msc ) );
283:         IF blockwrite( fil_ptr^, msc_buff, 1, 0 ) <> 1
284:            THEN
285:              write_msc := 19 { Disk write error }
286:            ELSE
287:              write_msc := 0   { No error }
288:       END { with }
289: END; { write_msc }
290:
291:
292: FUNCTION new_file( VAR fn : integer ) : pdbs_err;
293: { Return next unused file number }
294: { Local to unit }
295: BEGIN
296:    new_file := 0;             { Presume no error }
297:    fn := 0;
298:    WHILE fn < max_files DO
299:       BEGIN
300:         fn := fn + 1;
301:         IF NOT fil_recs[ fn ].fil_open
302:            THEN exit( new_file )    { Leaving file number set }
303:       END; { while }
304:    new_file := 17              { Too many files error }
305: END; { new_file }
306:
307:
308: { ----- End of local (private) procedures. ----- }
309:
310:
311: FUNCTION seek_rec{ fn, rn : integer ) : pdbs_err };
312: { Position fil_recptr to this record number (rn) }
313: VAR
314:    err_code : pdbs_err;
315:    pn       : integer;
316: BEGIN
317:    WITH fil_recs[ fn ] DO WITH fil_msc DO
318:       BEGIN
319:         IF ( rn < 1 )
320:            THEN err_code := 3         { Illegal operation }
321:            ELSE IF ( rn > msc_maxrec )
```

```
322:                    THEN err_code := expand_file( fn, rn ) { Add new page(s) }
323:                    ELSE err_code := 0;                     { No error }
324:          IF err_code = 0 THEN
325:          BEGIN
326:             pn := ( ( rn - 1 ) DIV fil_rpp ) + 1;
327:             err_code := load_page( fn, pn );
328:             IF err_code = 0 THEN
329:             BEGIN
330:                fil_recptr := rn;
331:                fil_relptr := ( ( rn - 1 ) MOD fil_rpp ) * msc_recsize;
332:                fil_eof := ( rn >= fil_msc.msc_lastrec );
333:
334:                { Initialize new file page buffer if }
335:                { never used before. }
336:
337:                IF ( fil_recptr > fil_msc.msc_lastrec ) AND
338:                   ( fil_relptr = 0 )
339:                   THEN fillchar( fil_page^.vir_page,
340:                                 page_size + 1, chr( 0 ) )
341:             END { if }
342:          END { if }
343:       END; { with }
344:       seek_rec := err_code
345: END; { seek_rec }
346:
347:
348: FUNCTION next_rec{ fn : integer ) : pdbs_err };
349: { Advance to next record in sequence }
350: BEGIN
351:    WITH fil_recs[ fn ] DO
352:       IF fil_recptr < fil_msc.msc_lastrec  { Not at end of file }
353:          THEN
354:             next_rec := seek_rec( fn, fil_recptr + 1 )
355:          ELSE
356:             next_rec := 20           { Out of range error }
357: END; { next_rec }
358:
359:
360: FUNCTION last_rec{ fn : integer ) : pdbs_err };
361: { Go back to previous record in sequence }
362: BEGIN
363:    WITH fil_recs[ fn ] DO
364:       IF fil_recptr > 1               { i.e. not at top of physical file }
365:          THEN
366:             last_rec := seek_rec( fn, fil_recptr - 1 )
367:          ELSE
368:             last_rec := 20           { Out of range error }
369: END; { last_rec }
370:
371:
372: FUNCTION get_rec{ fn : integer; VAR bp : binary_page ) : pdbs_err};
373: { Transfer current record to bp in binary form }
374: { After, status byte is at bp[0]; first byte at bp[1] }
375: { Record position pointer (fil_recptr) is not changed }
376: BEGIN
377:    WITH fil_recs[ fn ] DO
378:       IF NOT fil_open
379:          THEN
380:             get_rec := 13              { Attempt to access a closed file }
381:          ELSE
382:             WITH fil_page^ DO          { Use this virtual in-memory page }
383:                BEGIN
384:                   moveleft( vir_page[ fil_relptr ],    { Source }
385:                             bp,                         { Dest }
386:                             fil_msc.msc_recsize   );   { Count }
```

```
387:                          vir_count := vir_count + 1;  { Update use-frequency count }
388:                          get_rec := 0              { No error }
389:                      END { else }
390: END; { get_rec }
391:
392:
393: FUNCTION put_rec{ fn : integer; VAR bp : binary_page ) : pdbs_err};
394: { Transfer record at bp[0] to current record of this file }
395: { Record position pointer (fil_recptr) is not changed }
396: BEGIN
397:     WITH fil_recs[ fn ] DO
398:         IF NOT fil_open
399:             THEN
400:                 put_rec := 13                { Attempt to access a closed file }
401:             ELSE
402:                 WITH fil_page^ DO            { Use this virtual in-memory page }
403:                     BEGIN
404:                         moveleft( bp,                           { Source }
405:                                   vir_page[ fil_relptr ],    { Dest }
406:                                   fil_msc.msc_recsize   );  { Count }
407:                         vir_changed := true;           { Must write page to disk }
408:                         vir_count := vir_count + 1;  { Update use-frequency count }
409:                         put_rec := 0              { No error }
410:                     END { else }
411: END; { put_rec }
412:
413:
414: PROCEDURE get_field{ fn, fld_num : integer; VAR s : string };
415: { Return field fld_num from current record in file fn as a string }
416: { Note: for speed, no error check done on field number. }
417: BEGIN
418:     WITH fil_recs[ fn ] DO
419:      WITH fil_msc.msc_flds[ fld_num ] DO
420:       WITH fil_page^ DO
421:         BEGIN
422: {$r-}            { Range checking off }
423:         s[0] := chr( fld_len );       { String length = field length }
424: {$r+}            { Range checking on }
425:         moveleft( vir_page[ fil_relptr + fld_pos ],      { Source }
426:                   s[1],                               { Dest }
427:                   fld_len );                          { Count }
428:         vir_count := vir_count + 1    { Update use-frequency count }
429:       END { else / with }
430: END; { get_field }
431:
432:
433: PROCEDURE put_field{ fn, fld_num : integer; VAR s : string };
434: { Insert string s into field fld_num of current record in file fn. }
435: { Note: for speed, no error check done on field number. }
436: { WARNING: string will be truncated if longer than field length. }
437: VAR
438:     first_byte      : integer;      { First byte of field }
439: BEGIN
440:     WITH fil_recs[ fn ] DO
441:      WITH fil_msc.msc_flds[ fld_num ] DO
442:       WITH fil_page^ DO
443:         BEGIN
444:         first_byte := fil_relptr + fld_pos;        { Find field in page }
445:         fillchar( vir_page[ first_byte ], fld_len, chr( blank ) );
446:         IF length( s ) > 0 THEN
447:             moveleft( s[1],                         { Source }
448:                       vir_page[ first_byte ],      { Destination }
449:                       min( length(s), fld_len ) );  { Count }
450:         vir_changed := true;           { Must write page to disk }
451:         vir_count := vir_count + 1    { Update use-frequency count }
```

```
452:        END { else / with }
453: END; { put_field }
001: {---------------------------------------------------------------------}
002: {                                                                     }
003: {    PDBS3.TEXT -- VMOS continued.                                    }
004: {                                                                     }
005: {---------------------------------------------------------------------}
006:
007:
008: FUNCTION read_rec{ fn, rn : integer; VAR bp : binary_page ) : pdbs_err };
009: { Read record number rn from file fn into bp }
010: VAR
011:    err_code : pdbs_err;
012: BEGIN
013:    err_code := seek_rec( fn, rn );
014:    IF err_code = 0
015:       THEN err_code := get_rec( fn, bp );
016:    read_rec := err_code
017: END; { read_rec }
018:
019:
020: FUNCTION write_rec{ fn, rn : integer; VAR bp : binary_page ) : pdbs_err };
021: { Write record number rn in bp to file fn }
022: VAR
023:    err_code : pdbs_err;
024: BEGIN
025:    err_code := seek_rec( fn, rn );
026:    IF err_code = 0
027:       THEN err_code := put_rec( fn, bp );
028:    write_rec := err_code
029: END; { write_rec }
030:
031:
032: FUNCTION append_rec{ fn : integer; VAR bp : binary_page ) : pdbs_err };
033: { Add record in bp to end of data file fn }
034: VAR
035:    err_code : pdbs_err;
036: BEGIN
037:    WITH fil_recs[ fn ].fil_msc DO
038:       BEGIN
039:          err_code := write_rec( fn, msc_lastrec + 1, bp );
040:          IF err_code = 0
041:             THEN msc_lastrec := msc_lastrec + 1
042:       END; { else }
043:    append_rec := err_code
044: END; { append_rec }
045:
046:
047: FUNCTION insert_rec{ fn : integer; VAR bp : binary_page ) : pdbs_err };
048: { Insert record in work area ahead of current position in file. }
049: { Because records must be moved before the insertion can }
050: { be made, this operation can be lengthy. Warn user beforehand! }
051: VAR
052:    expand_from,
053:    recnum          : integer;
054:    err_code        : pdbs_err;
055:    temp            : binary_page;
056: BEGIN
057:    WITH fil_recs[fn] DO WITH fil_msc DO
058:    IF NOT inrange( fil_recptr, 1, msc_lastrec )
059:       THEN err_code := 3              { Illegal operation }
060:       ELSE
061:    BEGIN
062:       expand_from := fil_recptr;    { Current record position }
063:       recnum := msc_lastrec;        { Current end of file }
064:       zero_rec( fn, temp );         { Prepare a blank record }
065:       err_code := append_rec( fn, temp );   { Append blank to file }
```

```
066:        WHILE ( recnum >= expand_from ) AND ( err_code = 0 ) DO
067:        BEGIN          { Create a "hole" by moving records down }
068:           err_code := read_rec( fn, recnum, temp );
069:           IF err_code = 0 THEN
070:           BEGIN
071:              err_code := write_rec( fn, recnum + 1, temp );
072:              recnum := recnum - 1
073:           END { if }
074:        END; { while }
075:        IF err_code = 0        { Insert record into the "hole" }
076:           THEN err_code := write_rec( fn, expand_from, bp )
077:     END; { if }
078:     insert_rec := err_code
079: END; { insert_rec }
080:
081:
082: FUNCTION open_file{ VAR fn : integer; fname : pdbs_fname ) : pdbs_err };
083: { Attempt to open this file for I/O. }
084: { Variable fn returned is the fil_rec array index of the  }
085: {  file descriptor record used to open fname.  }
086: VAR
087:    err_code : pdbs_err;
088: BEGIN
089:    err_code := new_file( fn );
090:    IF err_code = 0
091:     THEN
092:        WITH fil_recs[ fn ] DO
093:        BEGIN
094:           reset( fil_ptr^, fname );   { UCSD "open existing file" }
095:           err_code := ioresult;
096:           IF err_code = 0
097:              THEN err_code := read_msc( fn );
098:           IF err_code = 0
099:            THEN
100:              BEGIN              { Set up file descriptor variable }
101:                 fil_open := true;
102:                 fil_name := fname;
103:                 fil_page := NIL;    { No virtual pages in memory }
104:                 fil_bpp :=          { Blocks per page }
105:                    ( ( page_size + 1 ) DIV block_size );
106:                 fil_rpp :=          { Records per page }
107:                    ( ( page_size + 1 ) DIV fil_msc.msc_recsize );
108:                 err_code := seek_rec( fn, 1 )
109:              END; { if }
110:           IF err_code <> 0 THEN
111:              BEGIN   { If error, prevent use of file }
112:                 fil_open := false;
113:                 close( fil_ptr^ )   { Ignoring error if not open here }
114:              END { if }
115:        END; { if / with }
116:     open_file := err_code              { Report any errors received }
117: END; { open_file }
118:
119:
120: FUNCTION close_file{ fn : integer; option : close_option ) : pdbs_err };
121: { Attempt to close this file writing all held information to disk }
122: VAR
123:    err_code : pdbs_err;
124: BEGIN
125:    err_code := 0;
126:    IF inrange( fn, 1, max_files ) THEN
127:    WITH fil_recs[ fn ] DO
128:    IF fil_open THEN                { No error if already closed }
129:     BEGIN
130:
131:        { Write out, if option = update, any changed pages held }
132:        { in memory, and collect all virtual pages for use }
```

```
133:          { by other files. }
134:
135:          WHILE ( fil_page <> NIL ) AND ( err_code = 0 ) DO
136:             err_code := deallocated( fn, ( option = update ) );
137:
138:          { Update file's miscellaneous information block }
139:
140:          IF ( option = update ) AND ( err_code = 0 ) THEN
141:             BEGIN
142:                fil_msc.msc_updated := today;
143:                err_code := write_msc( fn )
144:             END; { if }
145:
146:          IF err_code = 0 THEN
147:             BEGIN
148:                close( fil_ptr^, lock );     { System "close" }
149:                err_code := ioresult;
150:                IF err_code = 0
151:                    THEN fil_open := false    { Officially closed }
152:             END { if err_code = 0 }
153:
154:      END; { with / if }
155:    close_file := err_code
156: END; { close_file }
157:
158:
159: FUNCTION make_file{     fname    : pdbs_fname;
160:                     var msc_rec : msc_descriptor ) : pdbs_err };
161: { Create a new minimum-size data base file }
162: VAR
163:    err_code : pdbs_err;
164:    nblks    : integer;       { Disk blocks to allocate }
165:    msc_buff : PACKED ARRAY[ 1 .. block_size ] OF byte;
166: BEGIN
167:    rewrite( f, fname );
168:    err_code := ioresult;
169:    IF err_code = 0 THEN WITH msc_rec DO
170:    BEGIN
171:       msc_maxrec := ( page_size + 1 ) DIV msc_recsize;
172:       msc_lastrec := 0;           { File starts out empty }
173:       msc_created := today;
174:       msc_updated := today;
175:       msc_id := version;
176:       nblks := ( page_size + 1 ) DIV block_size; { Single page }
177:       IF blockwrite( f, msc_buff, 1, nblks ) <> 1
178:          THEN
179:             err_code := 8         { No room }
180:          ELSE
181:             BEGIN { Format block 0 of file for PDBS access }
182:                moveleft( msc_rec, msc_buff, sizeof( msc_rec ) );
183:                IF blockwrite( f, msc_buff, 1, 0 ) <> 1
184:                    THEN err_code := 19  { Disk write error }
185:             END { else }
186:    END; { if }
187:    IF err_code { is still } = 0
188:       THEN close( f, lock )            { Fix file in directory }
189:       ELSE close( f );                 { Do not save file }
190:    make_file := err_code               { Return error code }
191: END; { make_file }
192:
193:
194: FUNCTION expand_file{ fn, rn : integer ) : pdbs_err };
195: { Expand file fn to hold at least rn records }
196: VAR
197:    buffer              : PACKED ARRAY[ 1 .. block_size ] OF byte;
198:    new_last_page,
199:    new_max_rec         : integer;
```

```
200: BEGIN
201:     WITH fil_recs[fn] DO WITH fil_msc DO
202:     BEGIN
203:       new_last_page := rn DIV fil_rpp;
204:       IF rn MOD fil_rpp <> 0
205:        THEN
206:          new_last_page := new_last_page + 1;
207:       new_max_rec := new_last_page * fil_rpp;
208:       IF new_max_rec < 0
209:        THEN
210:          new_max_rec := maxint;
211:       IF new_max_rec > msc_maxrec
212:        THEN
213:          IF blockwrite( fil_ptr^, buffer, 1, new_last_page * fil_bpp ) <> 1
214:           THEN
215:             expand_file := 8         { No room on disk }
216:           ELSE
217:             BEGIN
218:               msc_maxrec := new_max_rec;
219:               expand_file := 0     { No error }
220:             END
221:        ELSE
222:          expand_file := 22              { File is full }
223:     END { with }
224: END; { expand_file }

001: {------------------------------------------------------------------------}
002: {                                                                        }
003: {    PDBS4.TEXT --   Miscellaneous file and record routines              }
004: {                                                                        }
005: {------------------------------------------------------------------------}
006:
007:
008: PROCEDURE init_msc{ var msc_rec : msc_descriptor };
009: { Initialize a new miscellaneous information record }
010: BEGIN
011:     WITH msc_rec DO
012:     BEGIN
013:       msc_recsize := 1;      { Reserve status byte }
014:       msc_nflds := 0;        { Number of fields in record }
015:       fillchar( msc_flds, sizeof( msc_flds ), chr( 0 ) ) { Zero fields }
016:     END { with }
017: END; { init_msc }
018:
019:
020: FUNCTION rec_status{ fn : integer ) : stat };
021: { Return status byte of current record }
022: BEGIN
023:     WITH fil_recs[ fn ] DO
024:       rec_status := fil_page^.vir_page[ fil_relptr ]
025: END; { rec_status }
026:
027:
028: FUNCTION mark_rec{ fn : integer; stat_byte : stat ) : pdbs_err };
029: { Mark current record with this status value }
030: BEGIN
031:     WITH fil_recs[ fn ] DO
032:     IF NOT fil_open
033:      THEN
034:        mark_rec := 13              { File not open error }
035:      ELSE
036:       WITH fil_page^ DO
037:        BEGIN
038:          vir_page[ fil_relptr ] := stat_byte;        { First byte of rec }
039:          vir_changed := true;                        { Must write to disk }
040:          mark_rec := 0                               { Report no error }
041:        END { else }
```

```
042: END; { mark_rec }
043:
044:
045: FUNCTION file_empty{ fn : integer ) : boolean };
046: { True if no records in file }
047: BEGIN
048:    file_empty :=
049:     fil_recs[ fn ].fil_msc.msc_lastrec <= 0
050: END; { file_empty }
051:
052:
053: FUNCTION file_end{ fn : integer ) : boolean };
054: { True if at or past last record in the file }
055: BEGIN
056:    file_end :=
057:     fil_recs[ fn ].fil_eof
058: END; { file_end }
059:
060:
061: FUNCTION file_not_in_use{ fname : pdbs_fname ) : boolean };
062: { Return true if no file by this name found, else return false }
063: { and print an appropriate error message. }
064: VAR
065:    err_code : pdbs_err;
066: BEGIN
067:    reset( f, fname );                  { File "f" declared globally }
068:    err_code := ioresult;
069:    IF err_code = 0                     { File was found; }
070:       THEN err_code := 11              {  duplicate file error. }
071:       ELSE IF err_code = 10            { No file, which is what we want; }
072:              THEN err_code := 0;       {  no error, else use ioresult. }
073:    file_not_in_use := executed( err_code );
074:    close( f )
075: END; { file_not_in_use }
076:
077:
078: PROCEDURE zero_rec{ fn : integer; VAR bp : binary_page };
079: { Initialize a blank record in bp for file fn }
080: BEGIN
081:    WITH fil_recs[ fn ].fil_msc DO
082:     fillchar( bp,                                    { Destination }
083:               min( msc_recsize, page_size + 1 ),     { Count }
084:               chr( blank ) );                        { Fill with }
085:    bp[0] := active    { Set status byte }
086: END; { zero_rec }
087:
088:
089: FUNCTION zero_file{ fn : integer ) : pdbs_err };
090: { Erase all records in the file }
091: BEGIN
092:    WITH fil_recs[ fn ] DO
093:    IF NOT fil_open
094:     THEN
095:       zero_file := 13        { File not open error }
096:     ELSE
097:       BEGIN
098:         fil_msc.msc_lastrec := 0;
099:         zero_file := 0     { No error }
100:       END { else }
101: END; { zero_file }
102:
103:
104: PROCEDURE display_rec(*VAR pf       : text;          { Output file }
105:                            fn       : integer;       { File number }
106:                            order    : fld_order*);  { Fields to list }
```

```
107: { Read and display current record contents to pf output file }
108: VAR
109:    field      : integer;      { Field number }
110:    s          : string;       { Miscellaneous string variable }
111: BEGIN
112:    IF rec_status( fn ) = active
113:       THEN write( pf, chr( blank ) )       { Not a deleted record }
114:       ELSE write( pf, '*' );               { Marked for deletion }
115:    num2string( fil_recs[fn].fil_recptr,    { Record number to string }
116:                5, '0', s );
117:    evon;                                   { Turn on enhanced video }
118:    write( pf, s );                         { Show record number }
119:    evoff;                                  { Turn off enhanced video }
120:    FOR field := 1 TO order[0] DO           { Order[0] = number of fields }
121:       BEGIN                                {  to be listed this time. }
122:          get_field( fn, order[field], s ); { Read field as a string }
123:          write( pf, chr( blank ) : 2, s )  { Two leading spaces in front }
124:       END; { for }
125:    writeln( pf )
126: END; { display_rec }
127:
128:
129: FUNCTION fld_number{ VAR msc_rec    : msc_descriptor;
130:                          field_name : alpha ) : integer };
131: { Return field number with this name in msc_rec.  0 = no such field. }
132: VAR
133:    i : integer;
134: BEGIN
135:    WITH msc_rec DO
136:       FOR i := 1 TO msc_nflds DO
137:          IF msc_flds[ i ].fld_name = field_name THEN
138:             BEGIN                { Found name in record descriptor }
139:                fld_number := i;     { Report field number }
140:                exit( fld_number )   { Exit procedure early }
141:             END;
142:    fld_number := 0          { Field name not found }
143: END; { fld_number }
144:
145:
146: PROCEDURE list_fields{ fn : integer };
147: { List file fn's field names to console }
148: VAR
149:    i          : integer;      { Character count and index }
150: BEGIN
151:    clreoln;
152:    WITH fil_recs[ fn ].fil_msc DO
153:    FOR i := 1 TO msc_nflds DO
154:    BEGIN
155:       write( msc_flds[i].fld_name, chr( blank ):2 );
156:       IF ( i MOD 6 ) = 0 THEN
157:       BEGIN
158:          writeln;            { Start a new line }
159:          clreoln
160:       END
161:    END; { for }
162:    writeln
163: END; { list_fields }
164:
165:
166: FUNCTION load_order{     ps   : ucsd_string;
167:                          fn   : integer;
168:                     VAR order : fld_order ) : boolean };
169: { True if operator enters valid field names list. ps = prompt string }
170: VAR
171:    i, n : integer;
172:    token, s : string;
```

```
173:    name : alpha;
174: BEGIN
175:    REPEAT
176:
177:    { Note: if your terminal doesn't have the vertical bar '|' }
178:    {        character, use a slash in its place in the next line. }
179:
180:       promptln( concat( ps, ' [<field>,<field>,..,|ret|?]' ) );
181:
182:       readln( s );
183:       n := pos( '?', s );
184:       IF n <> 0
185:          THEN list_fields( fn )
186:    UNTIL n = 0;
187:    bumpstrup( s );
188:    IF length( s ) = 0        { Return key or "ALL" gives all fields }
189:       THEN s := 'ALL';
190:    fillchar( order, sizeof( order ), chr(0) );      { Zero order array }
191:    i := 0;
192:    WITH fil_recs[fn] DO
193:    WHILE ( length(s) > 0 ) AND ( i < fil_msc.msc_nflds ) DO
194:       BEGIN
195:          IF s = 'ALL'
196:             THEN
197:             n := i + 1      { Use index as field number }
198:             ELSE
199:                BEGIN
200:                   nexttoken( s, token );        { Search file for name }
201:                   str2alpha( token, name );
202:                   n := fld_number( fil_msc, name )
203:                END; { else }
204:          IF n > 0
205:             THEN
206:                BEGIN        { Save this field number in array }
207:                   i := i + 1;
208:                   order[ i ] := n
209:                END
210:             ELSE
211:                BEGIN
212:                   writeln( 'No field ', token );
213:                   s := '';    { Forcing exit from "while" loop }
214:                   i := 0      { Deleting any entries made so far }
215:                END { else }
216:       END; { while }
217:    order[ 0 ] := i;
218:    load_order := ( i > 0 )  { True if at least one correct entry }
219: END; { load_order }
220:
221:
222: PROCEDURE make_key(*    fn    : integer;               { File number }
223:                        VAR order : fld_order;          { Fields }
224:                        VAR key   : string *);          { Result }
225: { Construct a concatenated key from fields specified in order array }
226: { For speed, no check for overflow is done on the string. }
227: VAR
228:    field      : integer;
229:    s          : string;
230: BEGIN
231:    key := '';
232:    FOR field := 1 TO order[0] DO   { Order[0] = number of fields }
233:    BEGIN
234:       get_field( fn, order[ field ], s );
235:       key := concat( key, s )    { Possible overflow here }
236:    END;
237:    IF case_switch
238:       THEN bumpstrup( key )
239: END; { make_key }
```

```
001: {------------------------------------------------------------------}
002: {                                                                  }
003: {    PDBS5.TEXT -- General purpose functions                       }
004: {                                                                  }
005: {------------------------------------------------------------------}
006:
007:
008: FUNCTION getch{ VAR ch : char ) : char };
009: { Input char from keyboard returning as function and variable char }
010: BEGIN
011:    read( keyboard, ch );
012:    IF eoln( keyboard )
013:       THEN ch := chr( ret );         { Otherwise, ret = blank }
014:    IF NOT case_switch                { If mixed case not allowed }
015:       THEN ch := cap( ch );          {   then convert to capital }
016:    getch := ch                       { Return function value }
017: END; { getch }
018:
019:
020: FUNCTION inrange{ n, low, hi : integer ) : boolean };
021: { True if low <= n <= hi }
022: BEGIN
023:    inrange := ( low <= n ) AND ( n <= hi )
024: END; { inrange }
025:
026:
027: FUNCTION value{ s : string ) : integer };
028: { Return integer value of string s }
029: VAR
030:    a:      real;
031:    i:      integer;
032:    ch:     char;
033:    neg:    boolean;
034: BEGIN
035:    a := 0.0;
036:    neg := false;
037:    i := 1;
038:    WHILE i <= length( s ) DO
039:       BEGIN
040:          ch := s[ i ];
041:          CASE ch OF
042:             '-' : neg := true;
043:             '0','1','2','3','4','5','6','7','8','9' :
044:                a := 10 * a + ord( ch ) - ord( '0' )
045:          END; { case }
046:          i := i + 1
047:       END; { while }
048:    IF neg
049:       THEN a := -a;
050:
051:    { Check range of result (a) before returning as function value }
052:
053:    IF ( a >= -maxint ) AND ( a <= maxint )
054:       THEN
055:          value := trunc( a )
056:       ELSE
057:          value := 0
058: END; { value }
059:
060:
061: FUNCTION verified{ s : string ) : boolean };
062: { True if 'Y' or 'y' typed in response to s }
063: VAR
064:    ch : char;
065: BEGIN
066:    prompt( concat( s, ' ? (y/n) ') );
067:    WHILE ( NOT ( getch( ch )
```

```
068:      IN [ 'Y', chr(121), 'N', chr(110) ] ) ) DO      { [ 'Y','y','N','n' ]
069:        beep;
070:     writeln( ch );
071:     verified := ( ch = 'Y' ) OR ( ch = 'y' )
072: END; { verified }
073:
074:
075: FUNCTION executed{ err_code : pdbs_err ) : boolean };
076: { Execute any function that returns a pdbs error code. }
077: { Returns true if no error, else prints message and returns false. }
078:
079:    PROCEDURE show_error( err_code : pdbs_err );
080:    { Display message according to err_code.   }
081:    { Error messages can optionally be kept in }
082:    { a .PDBF data file, with one string field }
083:    { of any length in each record.  Record    }
084:    { numbers and error codes are equivalent.  }
085:    { If the file does not exist, then error    }
086:    { numbers will be shown without messages.  }
087:    { Local to function "executed." }
088:    CONST
089:       file_name = '*ERRORS.PDBF';       { The * = boot disk }
090:    VAR
091:       s          : string;              { Holds error message }
092:       fn         : integer;             { PDBS file number }
093:    BEGIN
094:       { Note : To avoid an inevitable stack overflow,  }
095:       {        do NOT call function "executed" in this }
096:       {        procedure.  (See next function.)        }
097:       clreoln;
098:       write( 'Error ', err_code );
099:       IF open_file( fn, file_name ) = 0 THEN
100:       BEGIN
101:          IF seek_rec( fn, err_code ) = 0 THEN
102:             BEGIN
103:                get_field( fn, 1, s );            { Use field #1 }
104:                IF length( s ) > 0
105:                   THEN write( ' : ', s )
106:             END; { if }
107:          err_code := close_file( fn, no_update )  { Ignore any error here }
108:       END; { if }
109:       writeln
110:    END; { show_error }
111:
112: BEGIN { executed }
113:    IF err_code <> 0
114:       THEN show_error( err_code );
115:    executed := ( err_code = 0 )
116: END; { executed }
117:
118:
119: FUNCTION max{ a, b : integer ) : integer };
120: { Return the larger value of the two integers a, b }
121: BEGIN
122:    IF a > b
123:       THEN max := a
124:       ELSE max := b
125: END; { max }
126:
127:
128: FUNCTION min{ a, b : integer ) : integer };
129: { Return the smaller value of the two integers a, b }
130: BEGIN
131:    IF a < b
132:       THEN min := a
133:       ELSE min := b
134: END; { min }
```

```
135:
136:
137: FUNCTION tf{ b : boolean ) : char };
138: { Return 'T' for true, 'F' for false boolean value }
139: BEGIN
140:    IF b THEN tf := 'T'
141:         ELSE tf := 'F'
142: END; { tf }
143:
144:
145: FUNCTION cap{ ch : char ) : char };
146: { If ch is lower case then return capital, else return ch }
147: BEGIN
148:    IF ch IN [ chr( 97 ) .. chr( 122 ) ]      { [ 'a' .. 'z' ] }
149:       THEN cap := chr( ord( ch ) - 32 )
150:       ELSE cap := ch
151: END; { cap }
152:
153:
154: FUNCTION getnum{ VAR n : integer; low, hi : integer ) : boolean };
155: { Input integer value in low..hi range with no danger of I/O error. }
156: { Returns false if operator just presses return key or out of range. }
157: VAR
158:    s : string;      { Input string }
159: BEGIN
160:    readln( s );
161:    n := value( s );
162:    getnum := ( length( s ) > 0 ) AND ( inrange( n, low, hi ) )
163: END; { getnum }
164:
165:
166: FUNCTION common_fields{     fn1, fn2 : integer;
167:                         VAR order    : fld_order ) : boolean };
168: { For each field in fn1, find its match in fn2 storing results in order. }
169: { Returns true if at least one match found, else returns false. }
170: { Matched fields must be identical in type and length as well as name. }
171: { Unmatched fields in fn1 are set to zero in order array. }
172: { Order[0] is always equal to number of fields in fn1. }
173: VAR
174:    i, n : integer;
175: BEGIN
176:    common_fields := false;
177:    WITH fil_recs[fn1].fil_msc DO
178:    BEGIN
179:       order[0] := msc_nflds;
180:       FOR i := 1 TO msc_nflds DO WITH msc_flds[i] DO
181:       BEGIN
182:          order[i] := 0;
183:          n := fld_number( fil_recs[fn2].fil_msc, fld_name );
184:          IF n <> 0 THEN    { Found same name; check type and length }
185:          IF ( fld_type = fil_recs[fn2].fil_msc.msc_flds[n].fld_type )
186:             AND
187:             ( fld_len = fil_recs[fn2].fil_msc.msc_flds[n].fld_len )
188:             THEN
189:                BEGIN
190:                   common_fields := true;
191:                   order[i] := n
192:                END { if }
193:       END { for }
194:    END { with }
195: END; { common_fields }
196:
197:
198: FUNCTION get_file_name{ s : string; VAR fname : pdbs_fname ) : boolean };
199: { True if file name entered.  File not checked for existence. }
200: { Operator sees prompt string (s) at current cursor position. }
201: { Defaults to file <name>.<ext_pdbf> if other extension not entered. }
```

```
202: BEGIN
203:    prompt( s );      { Display prompting message. Not used again.}
204:    readln( s );      { Use long string for easier editing. }
205:    IF length( s ) > 0 THEN
206:       BEGIN
207:          bumpstrup( s );                { Change to all upper case }
208:          IF ( length( s ) < length( ext_pdbf ) ) OR
209:             ( pos( '.', s ) <> length( s ) - 4 )
210:             THEN s := concat( s, ext_pdbf ); { Add default extension }
211:          IF length( s ) > fname_len        { Limit string length }
212:             THEN s := copy( s, 1, fname_len )
213:       END; { if }
214:    fname := s;
215:    get_file_name := ( length( fname ) > 0 )
216: END; { get_file_name }

001: {------------------------------------------------------------------------}
002: {                                                                        }
003: {    PDBS6.TEXT -- General purpose procedures                            }
004: {                                                                        }
005: {------------------------------------------------------------------------}
006:
007:
008: PROCEDURE normalize{ VAR s : string; decimals : integer };
009: { Reformat presumed number in s to fixed number of decimals }
010: { Note: string should be re-right justified before being }
011: {       stored in database. }
012: VAR
013:    tlong    : long_integer;
014: BEGIN
015:    lvalue( s, decimals, tlong );
016:    str( tlong, s );
017:    WHILE length( s ) < decimals DO
018:       insert( '0', s, 1 );                { Pad fractions with zeros }
019:    IF decimals > 0
020:       THEN insert( '.', s, ( length( s ) - decimals + 1 ) )
021: END; { normalize }
022:
023:
024: PROCEDURE bumpstrup{ VAR s : string };
025: { Shift characters in string to upper case }
026: VAR
027:    i    : integer;
028: BEGIN
029:    FOR i := 1 TO length( s ) DO
030:       BEGIN
031:          IF s[i] IN [ chr( 97 ) .. chr( 122 ) ]   { i.e. [ 'a' ..'z' ] }
032:             THEN s[i] := chr( ord( s[i] ) - 32 )
033:       END
034: END; {bumpstrup}
035:
036:
037: PROCEDURE lvalue(* var s          : string;              { Source string }
038:                     decimals : integer;              { Decimal places }
039:                 var long     : long_integer *);  { Result }
040: { Convert presumed number in cp to fixed decimal long integer }
041: VAR
042:    ch            : char;        { Holds individual characters }
043:    i,                           { String character index }
044:    dec_count,                   { Decimal count }
045:    dig_count    : integer;      { Digit count }
046:    fractional,                  { True if past decimal point }
047:    neg          : boolean;      { True if minus sign in string }
048: BEGIN
049:    long := 0;
050:    i := 1;
051:    dec_count := 0;
```

```
052:        dig_count := 0;
053:        fractional := false;
054:        neg := false;
055:        WHILE ( i <= length( s )         ) AND
056:              ( dec_count <= decimals  ) AND
057:              ( dig_count < max_digits ) DO
058:           BEGIN
059:              ch := s[ i ]; { i.e. s[ 1 .. length(s) ] }
060:              CASE ch OF
061:                 '.' : fractional := true;
062:                 '-' : neg := true;
063:                 '0','1','2','3','4','5','6','7','8','9'
064:                     : BEGIN
065:                          dig_count := dig_count + 1;
066:                          IF fractional
067:                             THEN dec_count := dec_count + 1;
068:                          IF dec_count <= decimals
069:                             THEN long := 10 * long + ord(ch) - ord('0')
070:                       END
071:              END; { case }
072:              i := i + 1
073:           END; { while }
074:
075:        { Expand number to fixed number of decimal places }
076:        { if enough places had not been entered. }
077:
078:        IF ( dec_count < decimals ) AND
079:           ( dig_count <= max_digits - decimals ) THEN
080:           FOR i := 1 TO ( decimals - dec_count ) DO long := long * 10;
081:
082:        IF neg
083:           THEN long := -long     { Convert to negative }
084:
085: END; { lvalue }
086:
087:
088: PROCEDURE num2string{ n, d : integer; pad : char; VAR s : string };
089: { Convert number n to string s padded at left to d digits with pad }
090: VAR
091:     s1 : ucsd_string[1];      { Single char string }
092: BEGIN
093:     s1 := ' ';              { Single blank space }
094:     s1[1] := pad;          { Insert pad char into short string }
095:     str( n, s );            { Raw number to string conversion }
096:     WHILE length( s ) < d DO
097:        insert( s1, s, 1 )    { Pad to desired width }
098: END; { num2string }
099:
100:
101: PROCEDURE strip{ VAR s : string };
102: { Remove trailing and leading spaces from the string }
103: BEGIN
104:     IF length( s ) > 0 THEN
105:     BEGIN
106:     {$r-}    { Range checking off }
107:        s[0] :=
108:        chr( length( s ) +
109:             scan( -length( s ), <>chr( blank ), s[ length( s ) ] ) );
110:     {$r+}    { Range checking on }
111:        IF length( s ) > 0 THEN
112:           delete( s, 1, scan( length( s ), <>chr( blank ), s[ 1 ] ) )
113:     END { if }
114: END; { strip }
115:
116:
117: PROCEDURE next_token{ VAR s, t : string };
118: { Strip next token from string and return in variable "t" }
```

```
119: VAR
120:     ch                    : char;
121:     operators             : SET OF char;
122:     p                     : integer;
123:     stopped               : boolean;
124:     terminators           : SET OF char;
125: BEGIN
126:     operators := [ '*', '/', '+', '-', '=', '<', '>', '@' ];
127:     terminators := [ ' ', ',', '"' ];
128:     strip( s );                    { Remove extraneous blanks }
129:     IF length( s ) = 0
130:       THEN
131:         t := ''
132:       ELSE
133:         BEGIN
134:             ch := s[1];
135:             IF ch = '"'
136:               THEN
137:                 BEGIN { Double quoted string }
138:                     delete( s, 1, 1 );            { Remove first quote }
139:                     p := pos( '"', s );           { Find next quote }
140:                     IF p > 0
141:                       THEN
142:                         BEGIN
143:                             delete( s, p, 1 );    { Remove second quote }
144:                             p := p - 1            { Set p = pos previous char }
145:                         END { else }
146:                 END
147:               ELSE
148:             IF ch IN operators
149:               THEN
150:                 BEGIN { Math operator }
151:                     p := 1;                       { Return single character }
152:                     IF length( s ) > 1 THEN
153:                         IF s[2] IN operators      { Unless double op (e.g.<=) }
154:                             THEN p := 2
155:                 END
156:               ELSE
157:                 BEGIN { Normal next word }
158:                     p := 0;
159:                     stopped := false;
160:                     WHILE ( p < length( s ) ) AND ( NOT stopped ) DO
161:                     BEGIN
162:                         p := p + 1;
163:                         stopped := s[p] IN operators + terminators
164:                     END;
165:                     IF stopped
166:                       THEN
167:                         BEGIN
168:                             IF s[p] IN terminators
169:                                 THEN delete( s, p, 1 );
170:                             p := p - 1
171:                         END { else }
172:                 END; { else }
173:             IF p <= 0
174:               THEN
175:                 BEGIN
176:                     t := s;
177:                     s := ''
178:                 END
179:               ELSE
180:                 BEGIN
181:                     t := copy( s, 1, p );
182:                     delete( s, 1, p )
183:                 END; { else }
184:             bumpstrup( t )
185:         END { else }
```

```
186: END; { next_token }
187:
188:
189: PROCEDURE str2alpha{ s : string; VAR a : alpha };
190: { Convert string to packed array of char (alpha). }
191: { Truncates string s to alpha_size + 1 if too long }
192: BEGIN
193:    fillchar( a, sizeof( a ), chr( blank ) );
194:    IF length( s ) > 0 THEN
195:       moveleft( s[1], a[0], min( length(s), (alpha_size+1) ) )
196: END; { str2alpha }
197:
198:
199: PROCEDURE remove{ VAR s : string; substr : string };
200: { Remove substr from s if present in s }
201: BEGIN
202:    delete( s, pos( substr, s ), length( substr ) )
203: END; { remove }
204:
205:
206: PROCEDURE remove_ext{ var fname : pdbs_fname };
207: { Remove all known extensions, if present, from file name }
208: VAR
209:    s : string;        { Temporary string }
210: BEGIN
211:    s := fname;
212:    bumpstrup( s );
213:    remove( s, ext_indx );
214:    remove( s, ext_pdbf );
215:    remove( s, ext_rprt );
216:    remove( s, ext_scrn );
217:    remove( s, ext_spec );
218:    remove( s, ext_strc );
219:    fname := s
220: END; { remove_ext }
221:
222:
223: PROCEDURE date2string{ date : ucsd_date; VAR date_string : string };
224: { Convert UCSD system date into a string s }
225: VAR
226:    day_string,
227:    year_string : string;
228: BEGIN
229:    WITH date DO
230:       BEGIN
231:          num2string( day, 2, '0', day_string );
232:          num2string( year, 2, '0', year_string );
233:          date_string := concat( day_string, '-',
234:                                 copy( month_names, ( month * 3 + 1 ), 3 ),
235:                                 '-', year_string )
236:       END { with }
237: END; { date2string }
238:
239:
240: PROCEDURE pdbs_init;
241: { Initialize PDBS unit.  Runs once before user program begins. }
242: { Local to unit }
243: VAR
244:    i : integer;
245:
246:    PROCEDURE read_date( VAR d : ucsd_date );
247:    { Read and initialize date variable from root volume }
248:    { UCSD system dependent.  Local procedure }
249:    VAR
250:       buffer  : ARRAY[ 0 .. 255 ] OF integer;
251:       daterec : RECORD CASE boolean OF
252:                       true : ( int : integer );
```

```
253:                        false: ( date : ucsd_date )
254:                END;
255:    BEGIN
256:       unitread( 4, buffer, sizeof(buffer), 2 );
257:       daterec.int := buffer[ 10 ];
258:       d := daterec.date
259:    END; { read_date }
260:
261:    PROCEDURE read_crt;
262:    { Read crt (display) commands from PDBS.MISCINFO file }
263:    CONST
264:       crt_fname = '*PDBS.MISCINFO';
265:    VAR
266:       buffer : ARRAY[ 1 .. block_size ] OF byte;
267:    BEGIN
268:       reset( f, crt_fname );
269:       IF blockread( f, buffer, 1, 0 ) <> 1 THEN
270:          BEGIN
271:             writeln( 'Can''t read ', crt_fname );
272:             halt
273:          END;
274:       moveleft( buffer, crt_info, sizeof( crt_info ) );
275:       close( f )
276:    END; { read_crt }
277:
278: BEGIN { pdbs_init }
279:    read_date( today );                  { Read today's date from boot disk }
280:    case_switch := true;                 { False if not using mixed case }
281:    read_crt;                            { Read PDBS.MISCINFO crt commands }
282:
283: { Initialize array of files variable }
284:    fillchar( fil_recs, sizeof( fil_recs ), chr(0) );
285:    FOR i := 1 TO max_files DO
286:       BEGIN  { Prepare system I/O files }
287:          new( fil_recs[ i ].fil_ptr );
288:          fillchar( fil_recs[ i ].fil_ptr^, sizeof( f ), chr(0) )
289:       END; { for }
290:    page_pool := NIL            { No disposed virtual pages }
291: END; { pdbs_init }
```

CRTSETUP

After entering and compiling *pdbsunit,* compile and execute this short program, *crtsetup*. The program initializes and edits a small file named PDBS.MISC-INFO on your boot disk.

The values stored in PDBS.MISCINFO are used by all programs to control the computer's display. This information is, unfortunately, duplicated in the UCSD Pascal system's own file named SYSTEM.MISCINFO. The reason PDBS doesn't take its control values directly from the UCSD system file is that there is no provision in that file for using enhanced or reversed video on the screen. PDBS programs, especially the *editor,* make heavy use of enhanced video, and the duplication of effort, I hope you will agree, is worth it!

To avoid making you reenter the same information twice, however, *crtsetup* reads most of the information it needs from SYSTEM.MISCINFO. The only things you need to enter are the commands for turning enhanced video on and off at your terminal (provided, of course, your terminal has this feature).

```
Number (-1 to quit)? 0
                     NC  C1   C2   C3  C4
0) CRT-EVON          2   27   112  0   0
1) CRT-EVOFF         1   14   0    0   0
2) CRT-GORIGHT       1   28   0    0   0
3) CRT-GOUP          1   31   0    0   0
4) CRT-BELL          0   0    0    0   0
5) CRT-CLEOLN        1   29   0    0   0
6) CRT-CLEOSC        1   11   0    0   0
7) CRT-CLSCRN        1   12   0    0   0

---------------------------------------------------

CRT-EVON
Number of chars? 2
ASCII (decimal) 1? 27
ASCII (decimal) 2? 112
```

Fig. 8-5. *Editing the PDBS.MISCINFO file using* crtsetup *to configure the software for a particular terminal or video card.*

In the future, if you make any changes to the SYSTEM.MISCINFO file (using the UCSD program, *setup*), you must rerun *crtsetup* before those changes will take effect for PDBS programs. As long as the old PDBS.MISCINFO file is present, you do not have to reenter the enhanced video commands. You may, of course, change those values if necessary.

Whatever you do, remember that programs using *pdbsunit* will not operate if the PDBS.MISCINFO file is missing.

Figure 8-5 shows the display you will see when using the *crtsetup* program. All of the commands can be edited before being written to disk—even the values loaded from SYSTEM.MISCINFO. To make a change, enter the number of the line you want to edit. Next, enter the number of characters in that command sequence. Finally, enter the ASCII decimal values for the command.

For example, if your terminal uses the two-character sequence "ESC-p" to switch on enhanced video (CRT-EVON), enter 0 to edit that line. Enter 2, the number of characters in the command, and then enter 27 and 112 as the ASCII decimal values of the characters in the command. This sequence is shown in the dialogue of Fig. 8-5. Figure 8-6 clarifies what each of the *crtsetup* commands does and lists the values needed by Apple II and Apple IIe computers. (Enhanced video will only be visible on Apple IIe computers with the 80-column option installed.)

If you want to switch off any command (turning off the bell, for example) or if you do not have enhanced video on your terminal, set the number of characters in that command to zero. In Fig. 8-5, the bell has been switched off. This will not affect those times the operating system may ring the bell, but will affect only the uses of the *beep* procedure by PDBS programs. (See line 45 in PDBS1.TEXT.)

You may also edit the values for clearing the screen, erasing to the end of a line, and so on. If you do change any of these items, be aware that the altered values will not be stored back in SYSTEM.MISCINFO. Except to provide enhanced video, then, it is probably best to use the UCSD *setup* program to configure your terminal and then use *crtsetup* to copy that configuration for use with PDBS.

```
Command        Value     Description
-----------    -----     ------------------------
CRT-EVON        15       Switch on enhanced video
CRT-EVOFF       14       Switch off enhanced video
CRT-GORIGHT     28       Move cursor to right
CRT-GOUP        31       Move cursor up
CRT-BELL         7       Ring the bell
CRT-CLEOLN      29       Clear to end of line
CRT-CLEOSC      11       Clear to end of screen
CRT-CLSCRN      12       Clear entire screen
```

Fig. 8-6. *A list of the* crtsetup *commands and what they do. The values shown here are correct for Apple II and Apple IIe computers. Other systems and terminals will require different values, possibly with more than one character per command.*

After entering all the commands for your terminal, enter −1 to quit editing. Press ''U'' to update the PDBS.MISCINFO file, followed by ''Q'' to quit the program. Press ''Q'' first if you want to quit without saving your changes on disk.

The CRTSETUP Listing

The two type declarations, *crt_command* and *crt_rec,* and the variable, *crt_info,* are identical to the same declarations in PDBSUNIT.TEXT at lines 292, 302, and 309. To make typing easier, you may want to copy these declarations into the *crtsetup* program instead of typing them over.

In procedure *read_info,* the SYSTEM.MISCINFO file is loaded into a buffer variable. For more information about the locations of items in that file, see page 212 of *Pascal Programs for Business* by the author.

```
001: {$S+,I-}               { Compiler swapping on; I/O error checking off }
002:
003: PROGRAM crtsetup;
004:
005: {-----------------------------------------------------------------------}
006: {                                                                       }
007: {    PROGRAM         :  Set up PDBS crt commands file                   }
008: {    LANGUAGE        :  UCSD Pascal / Apple Pascal 1.1                   }
009: {                                                                       }
010: {    Copyright (C) 1983 by Tom Swan. All commercial rights reserved.    }
011: {                                                                       }
012: {-----------------------------------------------------------------------}
013:
014:
015: (* ---------------------------------------- *)
016: (* Copied in part from PDBSUNIT.TEXT        *)
017: (* ---------------------------------------- *)
018:
019: CONST
020:    block_size   = 511;          { Bytes minus one in a disk block }
021:    screen_width = 40;           { Display screen width }
022:
023: TYPE
024:    byte =                       { Eight-bit values }
025:       0 .. 255;
026:
027:    crt_command  =
```

```
028:          ( crt_evon,                { Enhanced video on }
029:            crt_evoff,               { Enhanced video off }
030:            crt_goright,             { Move cursor non-destructively right }
031:            crt_goup,                { Move cursor non-destructively up }
032:            crt_bell,                { Ring bell }
033:            crt_cleoln,              { Clear from cursor to end of line }
034:            crt_cleosc,              { Clear from cursor to end of screen }
035:            crt_clscrn        );     { Clear entire screen }
036:
037:    crt_rec        =                 { PDBS Cathode Ray Tube (display) record }
038:       RECORD
039:          crt_n : 0 .. 4;
040:          crt_ch : PACKED ARRAY[ 0 .. 3 ] OF char
041:       END; { crt_rec }
042:
043: VAR
044:    ch            : char;            { Keyboard input character }
045:    crt_info      :                  { Array of crt command sequences }
046:       ARRAY[ crt_command ] OF crt_rec;
047:    crt_names    :                   { Array of crt command names }
048:       ARRAY[ crt_command ] OF string[11];
049:
050:
051: PROCEDURE transfer( crt_cmd  : crt_command;
052:                     prefixed : boolean;
053:                     leadin   : char;
054:                     control  : char         );
055: { Insert this crt command into the PDBS crt information array }
056: { Assumes information is coming from SYSTEM.MISCINFO }
057: BEGIN
058:    WITH crt_info[ crt_cmd ] DO
059:       BEGIN
060:          fillchar( crt_ch, sizeof(crt_ch), chr(0) );  { Zero char array }
061:          IF prefixed
062:            THEN
063:              BEGIN
064:                crt_n := 2;
065:                crt_ch[0] := leadin;
066:                crt_ch[1] := control
067:              END
068:            ELSE
069:              BEGIN
070:                crt_n := 1;
071:                crt_ch[0] := control
072:              END
073:       END { with }
074: END; { transfer }
075:
076:
077: PROCEDURE read_info;
078: { Read crt (display) commands from SYSTEM.MISCINFO file }
079: { Transfer applicable commands to PDBS crt information array }
080: CONST
081:    info_fname = '*SYSTEM.MISCINFO';
082: VAR
083:    buffer : PACKED ARRAY[ 0 .. block_size ] OF char;
084:    f : FILE;
085:    faker : RECORD    { From Pascal Programs for Business, pg 212 }
086:               CASE boolean OF
087:                 true:  ( ch : PACKED ARRAY[ 0..1 ] OF char );
088:                 false: ( bit: PACKED ARRAY[ 1..16 ] OF boolean )
089:            END; { faker }
090: BEGIN
091:    reset( f, info_fname );
092:    IF blockread( f, buffer, 1, 0 ) = 1 THEN
093:    BEGIN
094:
```

```
095:           { Transfer commands from SYSTEM.MISCINFO, now stored in buffer,  }
096:           { to the PDBS functions of the same name.  If you change the      }
097:           { commands in SYSTEM.MISCINFO using the SETUP program, you must    }
098:           { rerun CRTSETUP before the new values will take effect for PDBS. }
099:
100:           { See Pascal Programs for Business by the author page 212 for the }
101:           { source of the buffer and bit indexes used below.                }
102:
103:           faker.ch[0] := buffer[72];  faker.ch[1] := buffer[73];
104:
105:           {          PDBS function   Prefixed(T/F)   Lead-in      Ctrl-char }
106:           { --------------------     -------------   -----------  ---------- }
107:
108:           transfer( crt_goright,     faker.bit[2],   buffer[62],  buffer[66] );
109:           transfer( crt_goup,        faker.bit[1],   buffer[62],  buffer[67] );
110:           transfer( crt_bell,        false,          chr(0),      chr(7)     );
111:           transfer( crt_cleoln,      faker.bit[3],   buffer[62],  buffer[65] );
112:           transfer( crt_cleosc,      faker.bit[4],   buffer[62],  buffer[64] );
113:           transfer( crt_clscrn,      faker.bit[7],   buffer[62],  buffer[71] )
114:
115:     END { if }
116: END; { read_info }
117:
118:
119: PROCEDURE read_crt;
120: { Read crt (display) commands from PDBS.MISCINFO file }
121: CONST
122:     crt_fname = '*PDBS.MISCINFO';
123: VAR
124:     buffer : PACKED ARRAY[ 0 .. block_size ] OF byte;
125:     f : FILE;
126: BEGIN
127:     reset( f, crt_fname );
128:     IF blockread( f, buffer, 1, 0 ) = 1
129:         THEN moveleft( buffer, crt_info, sizeof( crt_info ) )
130: END; { read_crt }
131:
132:
133: PROCEDURE write_crt;
134: { Write crt (display) commands to PDBS.MISCINFO file }
135: CONST
136:     crt_fname = '*PDBS.MISCINFO';
137: VAR
138:     buffer : PACKED ARRAY[ 0 .. block_size ] OF byte;
139:     f : FILE;
140: BEGIN
141:     fillchar( buffer, sizeof( buffer ), chr(0) );
142:     moveleft( crt_info, buffer, sizeof( crt_info ) );
143:     rewrite( f, crt_fname );
144:     IF blockwrite( f, buffer, 1, 0 ) = 1
145:       THEN
146:         close( f, lock )
147:       ELSE
148:         BEGIN
149:           writeln( 'Can''t write ', crt_fname );
150:           close( f );
151:           exit( PROGRAM )
152:         END;
153: END; { write_crt }
154:
155:
156: FUNCTION n2crt( n : integer ) : crt_command;
157: { Convert number n to scalar crt command }
158: VAR
159:     x : RECORD CASE boolean OF                    { Free union "Xchange" rec }
160:             true : ( n : integer );
```

```
161:              false : ( c : crt_command )
162:          END;
163: BEGIN
164:    x.n := n;
165:    n2crt := x.c
166: END; { n2crt }
167:
168:
169: PROCEDURE clear_lines( y1, y2 : integer );
170: { Erase lines from y1 through y2 }
171: VAR
172:    a : PACKED ARRAY[ 0 .. 79 ] OF char;
173:    y : integer;
174: BEGIN
175:    y := y1;
176:    fillchar( a, sizeof(a), chr(32) );
177:    WHILE y1 <= y2 DO
178:       BEGIN
179:          gotoxy( 0, y1 );
180:          write( a : screenwidth );
181:          y1 := y1 + 1
182:       END; { while }
183:    gotoxy( 0, y )
184: END; { clear_lines }
185:
186:
187: PROCEDURE show_crt;
188: { Display crt command values }
189: VAR
190:    crt_i : crt_command;      { Array index }
191:    j : integer;             { Char index }
192: BEGIN
193:    clear_lines( 1, 12 );
194:    writeln;
195:    writeln( 'NC  C1  C2  C3  C4' : 34 );    { Two blanks between each }
196:    FOR crt_i := crt_evon TO crt_clscrn DO
197:     WITH crt_info[ crt_i ] DO
198:      BEGIN
199:        write( ord(crt_i), ') ' );                { Single blank after ")" }
200:        write( crt_names[ crt_i ] );
201:        write( crt_n : 4 );
202:        FOR j := 0 TO 3 DO
203:            write( ord( crt_ch[j] ) : 4 );
204:        writeln
205:      END; { for / with }
206:    write( '----------------------------------------' )      { 40 dashes }
207: END; { show_crt }
208:
209:
210: FUNCTION get_num( s : string; lo, hi : integer; VAR n : integer ): integer;
211: { Prompt for and return number n in range lo..hi }
212: BEGIN
213:    REPEAT
214:       write( s );
215: (*$r-*)  (* Turn off range checking *)
216:       readln( n )
217: (*$r+*)  (* Turn on range checking *)
218:    UNTIL ( lo <= n ) AND ( n <= hi );
219:    get_num := n      { Return as function value }
220: END; { get_num }
221:
222:
223: PROCEDURE edit_crt;
224: { Edit crt commands }
225: VAR
226:    i, n : integer;
```

```
227: BEGIN
228:    REPEAT
229:       show_crt;
230:       clear_line( 0, 0 );
231:       IF get_num( 'Number (-1 to quit)? ', -1, 7, n ) >= 0 THEN
232:       BEGIN
233:          clear_lines( 13, 23 );
234:          writeln( crt_names[ n2crt(n) ]);
235:          WITH crt_info[ n2crt(n) ] DO
236:          BEGIN
237:             crt_n := get_num( 'Number of chars? ', 0, 4, n );
238:             FOR i := 0 TO 3 DO
239:                crt_ch[i] := chr(0);
240:             FOR i := 1 TO crt_n DO
241:             BEGIN
242:                write( 'ASCII (decimal) ', i );
243:                crt_ch[i-1] := chr( get_num( '? ', 0, 255, n ) )
244:             END { for }
245:          END { with }
246:       END { if }
247:    UNTIL n = -1
248: END; { edit_crt }
249:
250:
251: PROCEDURE initialize;
252: { Set up global variables }
253: BEGIN
254:    fillchar( crt_info, sizeof( crt_info ), chr(0) );
255:    crt_names[ crt_evon     ] := 'CRT-EVON    ';
256:    crt_names[ crt_evoff    ] := 'CRT-EVOFF   ';
257:    crt_names[ crt_goright  ] := 'CRT-GORIGHT';
258:    crt_names[ crt_goup     ] := 'CRT-GOUP    ';
259:    crt_names[ crt_bell     ] := 'CRT-BELL    ';
260:    crt_names[ crt_cleoln   ] := 'CRT-CLEOLN ';
261:    crt_names[ crt_cleosc   ] := 'CRT-CLEOSC ';
262:    crt_names[ crt_clscrn   ] := 'CRT-CLSCRN '
263: END; { initialize }
264:
265:
266: BEGIN
267:    initialize;
268:    read_crt;                 { Read old PDBS.MISCINFO if it exists }
269:    read_info;                { Read SYSTEM.MISCINFO if it exists }
270:    edit_crt;                 { Edit all settings. (optional) }
271:    clear_lines( 13, 23 );
272:    REPEAT
273:       write( 'U(pdate disk, Q(uit ? ' );
274:       unitclear( 1 );            { Ignoring any "type-ahead" characters }
275:       read( keyboard, ch );
276:       writeln( ch );
277:       IF ch IN [ 'U', chr(117) ] THEN        { chr(117) = 'u' }
278:          BEGIN
279:             write_crt;
280:             writeln( 'Updated' )
281:          END;
282:    UNTIL ch IN [ 'Q', chr(113) ]             { chr(113) = 'q' }
283: END.
284:
285:
286: {
287:    Notes : Program is designed to attempt loading previously created
288:    PDBS.MISCINFO file.  If that fails, all commands are nulled (set to
289:    value chr(0) ).  Next, it tries to read current settings as stored
290:    in SYSTEM.MISCINFO.  If that fails, all commands are set to those
291:    in the old PDBS.MISCINFO file or nulls.  Finally, all commands are
292:    presented for editing.
293:
```

```
294:    The first time you use the program, you must insert commands for
295:    using enhanced video on and off.  If you do not want enhanced video
296:    to be used, just leave those positions set to null characters.
297: }
```

TESTUNIT

Some of the settings in *pdbsunit* are critical to the operation of the software. This program, *testunit*, checks the most important values to be sure that you do not inadvertently cause a disaster.

Before compiling any of the PDBS programs, and every time you make a change to *pdbsunit*, compile and execute *testunit*.

```
Pascal Data Base System (PDBS) V1.0
------------------------------------
Memory available = 11267 words.
------------------------------------
ID        SIZE     MAX    AVAIL   CHK

FLD         14      14       0    Ok
MSC        506     512       6    Ok
B-PAGE    1024    1024       0    Ok
STRING     255     255       0    Ok
DATE         2       2       0    Ok
VERSION      3       3       0    Ok
```

Fig. 8-7. Testunit *verifies the most critical settings in* pdbsunit. *All checks must read "OK" before using PDBS programs.*

Figure 8-7 shows a successful test. Each check ends with ''Ok''. If any check ends in ''Error'', you must fix the error before you can use the software. Most errors will be due to typing mistakes or to the improper setting of some constant.

```
001: {$S+}        { Compiler swapping mode on }
002:
003: PROGRAM testunit; uses pdbsunit;
004:
005: {-----------------------------------------------------------------------}
006: {                                                                       }
007: {    PROGRAM          :  Test Unit -- Test PDBSunit declarations        }
008: {    LANGUAGE         :  UCSD Pascal / Apple Pascal 1.1                 }
009: {                                                                       }
010: {    Copyright (C) 1983 by Tom Swan. All commercial rights reserved.    }
011: {                                                                       }
012: {-----------------------------------------------------------------------}
013:
014: VAR
015:     fld        : fld_descriptor;
016:     msc        : msc_descriptor;
017:     date       : ucsd_date;
018:     bpage      : binary_page;
019:     s          : string;
020:
021:
022: PROCEDURE check( id : string; size, max_size : integer );
```

```
023: { Verify size of this variable }
024: BEGIN
025:    writeln;
026:    write( id, size:6, ' ':2, max_size:6, ' ':2, max_size - size:6 );
027:    IF max_size - size < 0
028:       THEN write( ' Error' )
029:       ELSE write( ' Ok' )
030: END; { check }
031:
032:
033: BEGIN
034: {$r-}        { Range checking off }
035:    s[0] := chr( string_size );        { Set string to maximum length }
036: {$r+}        { Range checking on }
037:    writeln;
038:    writeln( 'Pascal Data Base System (PDBS) V', version);
039:    writeln( '---------------------------------' );
040:    writeln( 'Memory available = ', memavail, ' words.' );
041:    writeln( '---------------------------------' );
042:    writeln( 'ID        SIZE     MAX    AVAIL  CHK' );
043:
044:    check( 'FLD    ', sizeof(fld), sizeof(fld) );    { Just to display it }
045:    check( 'MSC    ', sizeof(msc), 512 );            { Must fit in block 0 }
046:    check( 'B-PAGE ', sizeof(bpage), page_size + 1 );
047:    check( 'STRING ', length(s), string_size );
048:    check( 'DATE   ', sizeof(date), 2 );             { Must be packed }
049:    check( 'VERSION ', length(version), 3 )
050: END.
```

9

Miscellaneous Library Units

EVALUNIT / CALCUNIT / INDEXUNIT

EVALUNIT

The units in this chapter all use the *pdbsunit* themselves. Therefore, before compiling these units, you must have previously compiled *pdbsunit* and installed its code file in SYSTEM.LIBRARY.

One of the main operations in data base programming is finding records that match given arguments. The routines in *evalunit* simplify entering expressions at the console and determining if records match the arguments in those expressions. The expressions are parsed or interpreted into a form that speeds the comparison process. A good example of the use of *evalunit* is in the *list* program in Chapter Two. You can also use the three main procedures in your own programs.

Parse_eval requires a file number of an open PDBS data file and a string containing the search argument entered at the keyboard. The string should be in the form described in the instructions to *list*. (In particular, see Fig. 2-3.)

You can also use a literal string. Although this breaks the PDBS principle of designing general purpose programs that will operate on all files, there may be times when it is convenient to use a statement such as this:

```
IF parse_eval ( fn, 'BALANCE > 0 AND DATE < 830601' )
   THEN {continue with program}
```

Parse_eval converts the search argument string into a form that facilitates matching records against arguments. This internal format can be seen by studying the *argument* record type declaration at line 32 in the *evalunit* listing. You and your program do not need to be aware of the internal *argument* record or its contents.

If parsing is successful, *pars_eval* returns true. If the argument string cannot

```
load_arg( 'Search for?', fn, s );
FOR rn := 1 TO fil_recs[fn].fil_msc.msc_lastrec DO
   IF executed( seek_rec( fn, rn ) ) THEN
      IF match( fn ) THEN process_record;
```

Fig. 9-1. *Use this general plan to enter a search argument and process all the records that match.*

be understood, then a false value is returned. Appropriate error messages are displayed on the terminal as needed to explain what is wrong with bad expressions.

Procedure *load_arg* shows how you might use *parse_eval* to prompt an operator for a search argument at the terminal. You may of course use *load_arg* in your own programs. In this version, a proper search argument must be entered before *load_arg* ends. If the operator presses the return key without entering a search argument, then the *match* function will return the value *true* for every record matched.

Load_arg lets you choose what prompting message you want the operator to see. For example, this statement:

load_arg ('Search for?', fn, s);

would produce the following prompt message on the operator's console. Notice that a short memory jogger is attached to the prompt message. If the operator enters a question mark instead of responding with an expression, a list of available field names is printed on the screen, and then the prompt repeats. The example field names are taken from Part One.

```
Search for? [<expr>|ret|?]
?
P.NUM  P.NAME  P.COLOR  P.REO  P.STOCK
Search for? [<expr>|ret|?]
P.COLOR = RED
```

Matching Records

After parsing an expression, the current record can be tested to see if it matches. If so, your program can decide what to do with that record. Figure 9-1 shows a generalized plan for loading a search argument and for processing all matching records in a data file. Usually, *match* will follow *seek_rec* in this way. Also see the *list* and *editor* programs for more details.

```
001: {$S+,I-}              { Compiler swapping on; I/O error checking off }
002:
003: unit evalunit; intrinsic code 25 data 26;
004:
005: {---------------------------------------------------------------}
006: {                                                               }
```

```
007: {    PROGRAM        :  Record evaluation library unit           }
008: {    LANGUAGE       :  UCSD Pascal / Apple Pascal 1.1            }
009: {                                                                }
010: {    Copyright (C) 1983 by Tom Swan. All commercial rights reserved.  }
011: {                                                                }
012: {----------------------------------------------------------------}
013:
014: interface
015:    uses pdbsunit;            { Must be in System.Library }
016:
017: FUNCTION parse_eval( fn : integer; s : string ) : boolean;
018: PROCEDURE load_arg( ps : ucsd_string; fn : integer; VAR s : string );
019: FUNCTION match( fn : integer ) : boolean;
020:
021:
022: implementation                { Parts not accessible to programs }
023:
024: CONST
025:    arg_size        = 20;              { Size of argument strings }
026:
027: TYPE
028:    operator =
029:       ( op_eq, op_neq, op_in, op_less,
030:         op_gtr, op_loe, op_goe, op_and, op_or );
031:
032:    argument =                         { Search arguments type }
033:       RECORD
034:          arg_order      : fld_order;    { Field order }
035:          arg_logic      : ARRAY[ 1 .. max_fld ] OF op_and .. op_or;
036:          arg_operations : ARRAY[ 1 .. max_fld ] OF op_eq .. op_goe;
037:          arg_var        : ARRAY[ 1 .. max_fld ] OF boolean;
038:          arg_strings    : ARRAY[ 1 .. max_fld ] OF ucsd_string[ arg_size ]
039:       END; { argument }
040:
041: VAR
042:    arg : argument;                    { Search arguments variable }
043:
044:
045: FUNCTION parse_eval{ fn : integer; s : string ) : boolean };
046: { True if operator enters search arguments into global arg record }
047: VAR
048:    arg_error       : integer;       { Parsing error code }
049:    argn            : integer;       { Number of arguments entered }
050:    name            : alpha;         { Field name }
051:    n               : integer;       { Field number }
052:    op              : operator;      { Logic or compare operator }
053:    part            : integer;       { Part of in each argument }
054:    t               : string;        { Token or word from string s }
055: BEGIN
056:    WITH arg DO
057:    BEGIN
058:       arg_error := 0;
059:       argn := 0;
060:       IF length( s ) > 0 THEN
061:       BEGIN
062:          s := concat( 'AND ', s );  { ** Note blank after "AND " ** }
063:
064:          WHILE ( length( s ) > 0 ) AND
065:                ( arg_error = 0   ) AND
066:                ( argn < max_fld  ) DO
067:          BEGIN
068:             argn := argn + 1;
069:             part := 0;
070:             WHILE ( part < 4 ) AND ( arg_error = 0 ) DO
071:             BEGIN
072:                part := part + 1;    { Parse next part of argument string }
073:                next_token( s, t );
```

```
074:                CASE part OF
075:
076:                   { <logic> <field> <operator> <argument> }
077:                   {    1       2        3          4      }
078:
079:                   1 : BEGIN { Parse comparison logic }
080:                           IF t = 'AND'
081:                               THEN op := op_and
082:                               ELSE
083:                           IF t = 'OR'
084:                               THEN op := op_or
085:                               ELSE arg_error := 1;
086:                           IF arg_error = 0
087:                               THEN arg_logic[ argn ] := op
088:                       END; { logic part }
089:
090:                   2 : BEGIN { Parse field name }
091:                           str2alpha( t, name );
092:                           n := fld_number( fil_recs[fn].fil_msc, name );
093:                           IF n > 0
094:                               THEN arg_order[ argn ] := n
095:                               ELSE arg_error := 2
096:                       END; { field part }
097:
098:                   3 : BEGIN { Parse comparison operator }
099:                           IF t = '='   THEN op := op_eq   ELSE
100:                           IF t = '<>'  THEN op := op_neq  ELSE
101:                           IF t = '@'   THEN op := op_in   ELSE
102:                           IF t = '<'   THEN op := op_less ELSE
103:                           IF t = '>'   THEN op := op_gtr  ELSE
104:                           IF t = '<='  THEN op := op_loe  ELSE
105:                           IF t = '>='  THEN op := op_goe
106:                                            ELSE arg_error := 3;
107:                           IF arg_error = 0
108:                               THEN arg_operations[ argn ] := op
109:                       END; { operator part }
110:
111:                   4 : WITH fil_recs[fn] DO
112:                       BEGIN { Parse comparison argument }
113:                           IF length( t ) > arg_size
114:                               THEN t := copy( t, 1, arg_size );
115:                           str2alpha( t, name );
116:                           n := fld_number( fil_msc, name );
117:                           IF n > 0
118:                            THEN arg_var[ argn ] := true ELSE
119:                            BEGIN
120:                               arg_var[ argn ] := false;
121:                               WITH fil_msc.msc_flds[ arg_order[ argn ] ] DO
122:                               IF fld_type = dat_number THEN
123:                               BEGIN
124:                                  normalize( t, fld_decimals );
125:                                  WHILE length( t ) < fld_len DO
126:                                      insert( ' ', t, 1 )  { Right justify }
127:                               END { if }
128:                            END; { else }
129:                           arg_strings[ argn ] := t
130:                       END   { argument part }
131:
132:              END { case }
133:           END { while }
134:        END { while }
135:     END; { if }
136:
137:     IF arg_error = 0
138:      THEN
139:        parse_eval := true                    { Even if nothing entered }
140:      ELSE
```

```
141:            BEGIN
142:              parse_eval := false;
143:              beep;
144:              promptln( concat( '>>> ', t, s ) );  { Print part that failed }
145:              CASE arg_error OF
146:                1 : prompt( 'And/Or' );
147:                2 : prompt( 'Field name' );
148:                3 : prompt( '= <> @ < > <= >=' );
149:              END;
150:              writeln( ' expected' )
151:            END; { else }
152:
153:        arg_order[0] := argn             { Number of comparisons in argument }
154:     END { with }
155:
156: END; { parse_eval }
157:
158:
159: PROCEDURE load_arg{ ps : ucsd_string; fn : integer; VAR s : string };
160: { Load search arguments. ps = prompt string. returns arg string = entry.}
161: VAR
162:     ok : boolean;     { True when arguments accepted }
163: BEGIN
164:     ok := false;
165:     REPEAT
166:         promptln( concat( ps, ' [<expr>|ret|?]' ) );
167:         readln( s );
168:         bumpstrup( s );
169:         IF pos( '?', s ) > 0
170:             THEN list_fields( fn )
171:             ELSE ok := parse_eval( fn, s )
172:     UNTIL ok
173: END; { load_arg }
174:
175:
176: FUNCTION match{ fn : integer ) : boolean };
177: { True if current record matches global arguments }
178: VAR
179:     i          : integer;      { Comparison index }
180:     name       : alpha;        { Field names for variable arguments }
181:     result     : boolean;      { Result as comparison progresses }
182:     s          : string;       { Fields as strings }
183:     s2         : string;       { Argument string }
184:     tb         : boolean;      { Temporary boolean variable }
185:
186:     PROCEDURE read_field( fn, field : integer; VAR s : string );
187:     { Read and return field as string minus trailing blanks }
188:     { and converted to upper case ready for comparison. }
189:     BEGIN
190:         get_field( fn, field, s );                  { Read field into string }
191:
192: {$r-}   { Range checking off }
193:         s[0] :=                                     { Remove trailing blanks }
194:       chr( length( s ) +
195:             scan( -length( s ), <>chr( blank ), s[ length( s ) ] ) );
196: {$r+}   { Range checking on }
197:
198:         IF case_switch
199:             THEN bumpstrup( s )                     { Convert to all upper case }
200:     END; { read_field }
201:
202: BEGIN { match }
203:     result := true;            { So that no arguments matches everything }
204:     WITH arg DO
205:     FOR i := 1 TO arg_order[0] DO
206:     BEGIN
207:         read_field( fn, arg_order[i], s );     { Value to compare }
```

```
208:
209:        IF arg_var[i]
210:        THEN
211:          BEGIN       { Load variable argument into s2 }
212:             str2alpha( arg_strings[i], name );
213:             read_field( fn, fld_number( fil_recs[fn].fil_msc, name ), s2 )
214:          END
215:        ELSE          { Load literal argument into s2 }
216:          s2 := arg_strings[i];
217:
218:        CASE arg_operations[i] OF
219:          op_eq      : tb := s = s2;
220:          op_neq     : tb := s <> s2;
221:          op_in      : tb := pos( s2, s ) > 0;
222:          op_less    : tb := s < s2;
223:          op_gtr     : tb := s > s2;
224:          op_loe     : tb := s <= s2;
225:          op_goe     : tb := s >= s2
226:        END; { case }
227:
228:        IF arg_logic[i] = op_and     { Note: first compare is always "and" }
229:          THEN result := result AND tb      { Using "and" logic }
230:          ELSE result := result OR tb       { Using "or" logic }
231:
232:     END; { with / for }
233:     match := result              { Pass result back as function value }
234: END; { match }
235:
236: BEGIN
237:     arg.arg_order[0] := 0      { Empties argument record }
238: END. { unit }
```

CALCUNIT

The only program to use this unit is *calc* presented in Chapter Five. You may want to use the routines in your own programming, however, to calculate formulas based on the values in selected fields of your records.

Like *evalunit, calcunit* accepts an argument or expression in the form of a string. After that, the result of applying the expression to the current record is performed by a simple procedure call. This can be repeated without having to reinterpret the same expression for each new record.

Expressions must be in the correct form, explained in the instructions to the *calc* program. The two functions, *parse_calc* and *load_expression,* can be used to interpret expressions and prompt an operator to enter expressions to be calculated.

Use *parse_calc* to load an expression for evaluation. The number of decimals in the result must be specified. The following example parses, or interprets for eventual calculations, what might be a payroll check amount in an employee data file. Two decimal places are specified for the result. The data fields in the expression must, of course, exist in the file to avoid an error message.

```
IF parse_calc ( fn, 2, 'HRS * RATE - FICA - FED - STATE' )
   THEN { process all records }
```

When the result is to be assigned to another field in the same record, use *load_expression* to prompt the operator for the argument. *Load_expression* returns an integer variable *field* set to the number of the field that is to receive the result of a calculation. This function is used in the *calc* program to interpret expressions entered at the console. Examine *calc* to see how the result is written to the record after the calculation is performed. (See especially lines 44–55.)

After successfully loading an expression with *parse_calc* or *load_expression,* the values for records can be computed using the *compute* procedure. *Compute* returns the long integer variable *result* set to the result of applying the expression to the current record. See line 44 in the *calc* program for an example of *compute.*

Modifying Calcunit

Calcunit does not allow nested expressions or parentheses. Adding these capabilities would improve the unit but is not a trivial job.

The best approach would be to convert an existing expression evaluator to the PDBS way of doing things using the routines in this version of *calcunit* as guides. A UCSD Pascal expression evaluator appears in the *Journal of Pascal and Ada,** Mar./Apr. 1983, ''An Expression Evaluator,'' by Stuart B. Greenfield, pp. 29–35, 40. The algorithm described in that article could be adapted to PDBS.

```
001: {$S+,I-}              { Compiler swapping on; I/O error checking off }
002:
003: unit calcunit; intrinsic code 16 data 17;
004:
005: {------------------------------------------------------------------}
006: {                                                                  }
007: {    PROGRAM        : Data file calculator unit                    }
008: {    LANGUAGE       : UCSD Pascal / Apple Pascal 1.1               }
009: {                                                                  }
010: {    Copyright (C) 1983 by Tom Swan. All commercial rights reserved. }
011: {                                                                  }
012: {------------------------------------------------------------------}
013:
014: interface
015:    uses pdbsunit;            { Must be in System.Library }
016:
017: FUNCTION parse_calc( fn, decimals : integer; s : string ) : boolean;
018: FUNCTION load_expression(    fn    : integer;
019:                          VAR field : integer;
020:                          VAR s     : string    ) : boolean;
021: PROCEDURE compute( fn, decimals : integer; VAR result : long_integer );
022:
023:
024: implementation
025:
026: TYPE
027:    operator =
028:       ( op_mult, op_div, op_add, op_sub );
029:
030:    calculation =
031:       RECORD
032:          calc_order    : fld_order;          { 0 = literal value }
```

*Ada is a REGISTERED TRADEMARK of the U.S. Department of Defense.

```
033:                 calc_operation : ARRAY[ 1 .. max_fld ] OF operator;
034:                 calc_values    : ARRAY[ 1 .. max_fld ] OF long_integer;
035:             END; { calculation }
036:
037: VAR
038:     calc_rec : calculation;
039:
040:
041: FUNCTION parse_calc{ fn, decimals : integer; s : string ) : boolean };
042: { True if string can be interpreted correctly as an expression. }
043: { Decimals = number of decimals expected in result. }
044: VAR
045:     calc_error        : integer;        { Parsing error code }
046:     calcn             : integer;        { Number of expressions entered }
047:     n                 : integer;        { Field number }
048:     name              : alpha;          { Field name }
049:     op                : operator;       { Arithmetic operator }
050:     part              : integer;        { Part number of expression }
051:     t                 : string;         { Token or word from string }
052:
053:     FUNCTION all_digits( VAR s : string ) : boolean;
054:     { True if string contains legal numerical digits and punctuation }
055:     VAR
056:         i : integer;
057:     BEGIN
058:         FOR i := 1 TO length( s ) DO
059:             IF NOT ( s[i] IN [ '0'..'9', '.', '-' ] ) THEN
060:                 BEGIN
061:                     all_digits := false;
062:                     exit( all_digits )
063:                 END;
064:         all_digits := true
065:     END; { all_digits }
066:
067: BEGIN { parse_calc }
068:     WITH calc_rec DO
069:     BEGIN
070:         calc_error := 0;
071:         calcn := 0;
072:         IF length( s ) > 0 THEN
073:         BEGIN
074:             s := concat( '+ ', s );     { Note space after "+ " }
075:
076:             WHILE ( length( s ) > 0 ) AND
077:                   ( calc_error = 0   ) AND
078:                   ( calcn < max_fld ) DO
079:             BEGIN
080:                 calcn := calcn + 1;
081:                 part := 0;
082:                 WHILE ( part < 2 ) AND ( calc_error = 0 ) DO
083:                 BEGIN
084:                     part := part + 1;     { Parse next part of expression }
085:                     next_token( s, t );
086:
087:                     CASE part OF
088:
089:                         { <operation> <field|literal>, ... , }
090:                         {     1                2       , ... , }
091:
092:                         1 : BEGIN  { Parse operation }
093:                                 IF t = '*'
094:                                     THEN op := op_mult
095:                                     ELSE
096:                                 IF t = '/'
097:                                     THEN op := op_div
098:                                     ELSE
099:                                 IF t = '+'
```

```
100:                              THEN op := op_add
101:                              ELSE
102:                         IF t = '-'
103:                              THEN op := op_sub
104:                              ELSE calc_error := 1;
105:                         IF calc_error = 0
106:                              THEN calc_operations[ calcn ] := op
107:                       END; { operation part }
108:
109:              2 : BEGIN   { Parse field or literal }
110:                       str2alpha( t, name );
111:                       n := fld_number( fil_recs[fn].fil_msc, name );
112:                       IF n > 0
113:                         THEN
114:                            calc_order[ calcn ] := n          { Variable }
115:                         ELSE
116:                            IF all_digits( t )
117:                              THEN
118:                                BEGIN
119:                                   calc_order[ calcn ] := 0;  { Literal }
120:                                   lvalue( t, decimals, calc_values[calcn] )
121:                                END
122:                              ELSE
123:                                calc_error := 2
124:                       END; { field or literal part }
125:
126:             END { case }
127:          END { while }
128:        END { while }
129:      END; { if }
130:
131:      IF calc_error = 0
132:        THEN
133:          parse_calc := true
134:        ELSE
135:          BEGIN
136:            parse_calc := false;
137:            beep;
138:            promptln( concat( '>>> ', t, ' ', s ) ); { Print what failed }
139:            CASE calc_error OF
140:              1 : prompt( '* / + -' );
141:              2 : prompt( 'Field name or literal' )
142:            END; { case }
143:            writeln( ' expected' )
144:          END; { else }
145:
146:      calc_order[0] := calcn
147:    END { with }
148:
149: END; { parse_calc }
150:
151:
152: FUNCTION load_expression{     fn    : integer;
153:                           var field : integer;
154:                           var s     : string    ) : boolean };
155: { True if expression entered and parsed, else false. }
156: { If true, then field = field number for result of calculation. }
157: VAR
158:    done          : boolean;       { Repeat loop flag }
159:    err           : 0 .. 2;        { Not a pdbs_err type }
160:    name          : alpha;         { Field name }
161:    part          : integer;       { Expression part expected }
162:    ts, t         : string;        { Temp and token strings }
163: BEGIN
164:    REPEAT
165:        done := false;         { Initialize repeat loop flag }
166:        REPEAT
```

```
167:              writeln(
168:               'Expression? [?|<fld> = <fld,lit> <*,/,+,-> <fld,lit>, ...,]' );
169:              readln( s );
170:              IF pos( '?', s ) > 0
171:                THEN list_fields( fn )
172:                ELSE done := true
173:          UNTIL done;   { So far }
174:          done := false;          { Reset repeat loop flag }
175:          bumpstrup( s );
176:          ts := s;
177:          IF length( ts ) = 0
178:            THEN
179:              done := true        { No expression entered. Exit. }
180:            ELSE
181:              BEGIN
182:                err := 0;
183:                part := 0;
184:                WHILE ( part < 2 ) AND ( err = 0 ) DO
185:                BEGIN
186:                   part := part + 1;
187:                   next_token( ts, t );
188:                   CASE part OF
189:
190:                      1 : BEGIN { Parse result field name }
191:                            str2alpha( t, name );
192:                            field := fld_number( fil_recs[fn].fil_msc, name );
193:                            IF field <= 0
194:                               THEN err := 1
195:                          END; { part one }
196:
197:                      2 : BEGIN
198:                            IF t <> '='
199:                               THEN err := 2
200:                          END { part two }
201:
202:                   END { case }
203:                END; { while }
204:
205:                IF err <> 0
206:                  THEN
207:                    BEGIN
208:                       beep;
209:                       CASE err OF
210:                         1 : write( 'Field name' );
211:                         2 : write( '"="' )
212:                       END; { case }
213:                       writeln( ' expected' )
214:                    END
215:                  ELSE
216:                    WITH fil_recs[fn].fil_msc.msc_flds[ field ] DO
217:                       done := parse_calc( fn, fld_decimals, ts )
218:
219:              END { else }
220:        UNTIL done;
221:        load_expression := ( length( s ) > 0 )
222: END; { load_expression }
223:
224:
225: PROCEDURE compute{ fn, decimals : integer; var result : long_integer };
226: { Perform computation on current record as specified in calc_rec }
227: { Decimals = number of decimals expected in result }
228: VAR
229:    i, j    : integer;
230:    s       : string;
231: BEGIN
232:    result := 0;
233:    WITH calc_rec DO
234:    BEGIN
```

```
235:
236:          { First load all values involved in this calculation. }
237:
238:          FOR i := 1 TO calc_order[0] DO
239:            IF calc_order[i] > 0          { i.e. is not a literal value }
240:            THEN
241:              BEGIN
242:                get_field( fn, calc_order[i], s );
243:                normalize( s, decimals );
244:                lvalue( s, decimals, calc_values[i] )
245:              END; { if }
246:
247:          { Next, perform the calculation on the values loaded. }
248:
249:          FOR i := 1 TO calc_order[0] DO
250:            CASE calc_operations[i] OF
251:              op_mult : BEGIN
252:                          result := result * calc_values[i];
253:                          FOR j := 1 TO decimals DO
254:                            result := result DIV 10
255:                        END;
256:              op_div  : BEGIN
257:                          FOR j := 1 TO decimals DO
258:                            result := result * 10;
259:                          result := result DIV calc_values[i]
260:                        END;
261:              op_add  : result := result + calc_values[i];
262:              op_sub  : result := result - calc_values[i]
263:            END { case }
264:
265:      END { with }
266: END; { compute }
267:
268: BEGIN
269:    calc_rec.calc_order[0] := 0          { Empties calculation record }
270: END. { unit }
```

INDEXUNIT

The programs *index, find,* and *update* use this library unit to create and maintain index files for quick searches of PDBS records.

Indexunit organizes an index as a multiway B-tree. (See references at end of this chapter.) One reason why this method works so well is because of the way the tree structure drastically limits disk reads, potentially the slowest action in a search.

For each index in use, you must declare an index record variable of the type *index_rec* shown at line 21 in the listing. You can have multiple indexes in use at one time up to the number of PDBS files available. In the current version of *pdbsunit,* there can be a maximum of one data file and five indexes open at one time.

To open an index file for searching, use function *open_index. Index* is a variable of the type *index_rec. File_name* is a string equal to the name of an existing PDBS data file with or without an extension, .PDBF (Pascal Data Base File), for example. *Open_index* will replace any such extension with .INDX, the required name suffix for an index file.

IF executed(open_index(index, file_name))
    THEN { continue processing }

Closing an index must be accomplished with the *close_index* function. Do not attempt to close the index file using the *pdbsunit* function *close_file*. You could lose data in the index if it is not closed properly. To be safe, use this method when closing an index.

WHILE NOT executed(close_index(index, update)) DO
    IF NOT verified('Try again')
        THEN exit(program);

Searching is accomplished in one of two ways. Use the *peruse* procedure described in Chapter Six in the *find* program to locate all occurrences matching or partially matching a search key or use the *search_index* function to locate an exact match.

Imposing on PDBS

Although an index file ending in .INDX is a PDBS data file, it cannot be edited or listed using PDBS programs. This is because the data in the file are stored in a way not recognized by PDBS record and field procedures. This new structure is imposed on the file structure of PDBS to allow VMOS to control disk accesses for both data and index files. (You can use the *status* program, however, to examine the structure of an index file.)

Each disk page of an index (see Fig. 8-2) is no longer composed of PDBS records. Instead, pages are redefined to be of type *index_page*, declared at line 31 in the listing. The structure of an *index_page* is overlayed or imposed on the bytes in a disk page.

One *index_page* corresponds to one disk page. It contains a counter *n* showing how many index entries are in the page, a pointer *p0*, which addresses the page containing entries with keys less than the alphabetically lowest key on this page, and an array of index *entries*.

An *index_entry* is structured at line 39. Each *index_entry* has a pointer *p*, which addresses the page containing other entries with keys between this entry and the next one on the same page. The other parts of an *index_entry* are a record number, *rn*, and a search string labeled *key*.

When searching, the *indexunit* routines find the *index_entry* containing the *key* that most closely matches the search key. The record number *rn* is then reported to your program and can be used to read the actual record from the data file. Although this method is fast for individual searches, listing or processing a file in indexed order will probably be slowed by the cross-reference action between the index and the data file. The code in Fig. 9-2 searches for the value of the string variable *skey*.

If you want to impose other data file structures on disk pages in the way explained here, while still taking advantage of VMOS file handling, look at the way the record *index_xchng* translates a *binary_page* into an *index_page*. Using a case statement without a tag field as shown at line 48 is called a "free union," an infamous Pascal programming technique that allows a program to view one item as having two or more dissimilar structures. In that way, one structure can be imposed over another. Here, any variable declared to be of type *index_xchng* is a raw page of bytes if accessed through the identifier *bp* (see line 219) or a page of index entries when accessed through *ip* (see lines 220–244).

Inserting New Entries

To insert a new index entry, assign its value to a string variable *skey* and its record number to an integer variable *rn*. Use the method shown in Fig. 9-3 to insert the entry into an index.

When new entries are inserted into index pages that are already full, the page is split into equal numbers of records, and an item is passed upward in the tree toward the root. Due to this method of balancing the tree, each index page, except for the root page, is never less than half full of entries. The UCSD memory-move procedures *moveleft* and *moveright* are used in place of array indexing to speed up page-splitting in the function *insert_index*.

Deleting Index Entries

The routines for deleting entries in a B-tree index are complex, consume memory ravenously when called by a program, and would take several pages to present. Instead, there is a simple way to effectively remove index entries that takes far less room and works well in most cases.

Rather than actually remove the deleted entry, which would require a potentially complicated rebalancing of the B-tree, the *delete_index* function simply sets that entry's record number (*rn*) to zero. When a subsequent search returns a record number of zero, the program can assume that the record was deleted and take an

```
IF search_index( index, skey, rn ) = 0
  THEN
    BEGIN
      IF executed( read_rec( fn, rn, bp ) )
        THEN process_record
    END
  ELSE
    writeln( skey, ' not found' );
```

Fig. 9-2. *This program fragment demonstrates how to search an index file to locate the record number of a data record that can then be processed.*

```
IF executed( seek_rec( fn, rn ) ) THEN
BEGIN
   get_field( fn, index.field, skey );
   bumpstrup( skey );
   IF executed( insert_index( index, skey, rn ) )
      THEN writeln( skey, ' inserted' )
END;
```

Fig. 9-3. *These statements show how new entries can be inserted into an index. The bumpstrup procedure converts the key to upper-case letters and is optional.*

appropriate action. The *find* program's *process_rec* function (line 45) does exactly that by processing only record numbers greater than zero. All others are ignored.

To distinguish between keys with the same value, the record number is used. As an example, suppose you have five mailing list records for Marsupials Ltd. (You know the place—the one where the employees keep hopping for a raise.) You want to delete the third record while leaving the others undisturbed. If you know that this record has the PDBS record number 125, then this code will delete only that entry from the index. (*Skey* is a string; *rn* is an integer variable.)

```
skey := 'Marsupials Ltd.'; rn := 125;
IF executed( delete_index( index, skey, rn ) )
   THEN { continue program }
```

Of course the actual entry stays in the index. Except for its record number, it is not disturbed. You may think that all those deleted entries would eventually clutter up the works, and if you make a lot of deletions, you would be right. In practice, the number of deletions made from typical data files is proportionally small, although there are certainly exceptions—an airline reservation system, for example, in which it would not be surprising to find the total number of cancellations exceeding the number of new reservations.

As a rule of thumb, after about 10 percent of the entries in the index have been marked for deletion, it is a good idea to rerun the *index* program and rebuild the index. Most people schedule such maintenance chores during off hours.

Keys

Indexunit allows multiple key values to be inserted into the index. Although this requires a sequential search on the index entries in a page (see lines 225–234 and 373–382), the search is still very fast because of the way VMOS works to keep at least the root page of the index tree in memory at most times.

The value assigned to an index is usually the contents of a data field. If the field is a character string, you will probably want to convert the characters of the field to upper case before inserting it as a key in the index. Alternatively, you could insert something other than a data field into the index, perhaps that field's soundex number for performing data searches based on the sound instead of the spelling of names.

More information on the use and organization of multiway B-trees can be found in the following references.

Date, C. J., *An Introduction to Database Systems,* Third edition (Mass: Addison-Wesley, 1981), pp. 47–50.

Knuth, D. E., *Sorting and Searching,* The Art of Computer Programming Vol. 3 (Mass: Addison-Wesley, 1973), pp. 471–479.

Wirth, N., *Algorithms + Data Structures = Programs,* (N.J.: Prentice-Hall, Inc., 1976), pp. 242–257.

```
001: {$S+,I-}              { Compiler swapping on; I/O error checking off }
002:
003: unit indexunit;
004:
005: {-------------------------------------------------------------------}
006: {                                                                   }
007: {     PROGRAM        :  B-Tree Index Library Unit                   }
008: {     LANGUAGE       :  UCSD Pascal / Apple Pascal 1.1              }
009: {                                                                   }
010: {     Copyright (C) 1983 by Tom Swan. All commercial rights reserved. }
011: {                                                                   }
012: {-------------------------------------------------------------------}
013:
014: interface
015:     uses pdbsunit;             { Must be in System.Library }
016:
017: CONST
018:     index_size      = 1019;         { Page_size - 4 }
019:
020: TYPE
021:     index_rec =                { Describes an open index file }
022:         RECORD
023:             fn,                       { Index file number }
024:             root,                     { Root page number }
025:             field,                    { Data file field number }
026:             keylen,                   { Length of key entries }
027:             kpp,                      { Keys per page }
028:             kppd2      : integer      { Keys per page div 2 }
029:         END; { index_rec }
030:
031:     index_page =               { Format overlayed onto PDBS pages }
032:         RECORD
033:             n,                        { Number entries on this page }
034:             p0         : integer;     { Left most page pointer }
035:             entries    :              { Array of index entries }
036:                 PACKED ARRAY[ 0 .. index_size ] OF byte
037:         END; { index_page }
038:
039:     index_entry =              { Single entry stored in index pages }
040:         RECORD
041:             p,                        { Node pointer }
042:             rn         : integer;     { Data file record number }
043:                                       {  rn = 0 indicates deleted entry }
044:             key        : string       { Matching key field }
045:         END; { index_entry }
046:
047:     index_xchng =              { Index exchange record (free union) }
048:         RECORD CASE boolean OF
```

```
049:           true  : ( bp : binary_page );        { Viewed as binary page }
050:           false : ( ip : index_page )          { Or as an index page }
051:         END; { index_xchng }
052:
053:
054: FUNCTION open_index( VAR index : index_rec;
055:                          fname : pdbs_fname ) : pdbs_err;
056: FUNCTION close_index( VAR index : index_rec;
057:                          mode  : close_option ) : pdbs_err;
058: FUNCTION create_index( VAR index   : index_rec;
059:                            dfn,
060:                            dfield,
061:                            dlen    : integer;
062:                        VAR fname   : pdbs_fname ) : pdbs_err;
063: FUNCTION search_index( VAR index : index_rec;
064:                        VAR skey  : string;
065:                        VAR drn   : integer     ) : pdbs_err;
066: FUNCTION insert_index( VAR index : index_rec;
067:                        VAR skey  : string;
068:                        VAR drn   : integer     ) : pdbs_err;
069: FUNCTION delete_index( VAR index : index_rec;
070:                        VAR skey  : string;
071:                            drn   : integer     ) : pdbs_err;
072:
073:
074: implementation               { Parts not accessible to programs }
075:
076:
077: FUNCTION open_index{ VAR index : index_rec;
078:                          fname : pdbs_fname ) : pdbs_err };
079: { Open existing index for i/o }
080: VAR
081:    bp        : binary_page;  { For reading index miscellaneous info }
082:    err_code : pdbs_err;
083:    xfn       : integer;       { Temporary index file number }
084: BEGIN
085:    remove_ext( fname );
086:    fname := concat( fname, ext_indx );
087:    err_code := open_file( xfn, fname );
088:    IF err_code = 0 THEN
089:    BEGIN
090:       err_code := read_rec( xfn, 1, bp );   { Read misc. info }
091:       IF err_code = 0
092:         THEN
093:           BEGIN
094:             moveleft( bp[1],                 { Source }
095:                       index,                 { Destination }
096:                       sizeof( index ) );     { Count }
097:             index.fn := xfn
098:           END
099:         ELSE
100:           IF NOT executed( close_file( xfn, no_update ) )
101:              THEN halt       { Extremely unlikely }
102:    END; { if }
103:    open_index := err_code
104: END; { open_index }
105:
106:
107: FUNCTION close_index{ VAR index : index_rec;
108:                           mode : close_option ) : pdbs_err };
109: { Close index file, saving miscellaneous information for next time }
110: VAR
111:    bp        : binary_page;  { For reading index miscellaneous info }
112:    err_code : pdbs_err;
113: BEGIN
114:    IF mode = update
115:      THEN
116:        BEGIN
```

```
117:                 fill_char( bp, sizeof( bp ), chr(0) );
118:                 move_left( index,                   { Source }
119:                            bp[1],                   { Destination }
120:                            sizeof( index ) );       { Count }
121:                 err_code := write_rec( index.fn, 1, bp )
122:          END
123:        ELSE
124:          err_code := 0;
125:      IF err_code = 0
126:        THEN err_code := close_file( index.fn, mode );
127:      close_index := err_code
128: END; { close_index }
129:
130:
131: FUNCTION create_index(*VAR index    : index_rec;
132:                            dfn,                          { Data file number }
133:                            dfield,                       { Data field number }
134:                            dlen    : integer;            { Data field length }
135:                       VAR fname    : pdbs_fname ) : pdbs_err*);
136: { Create new index file }
137: VAR
138:    blank_rec         : binary_page;          { For appending record #1 }
139:    err_code          : pdbs_err;
140:    msc_rec           : msc_descriptor;       { Describes PDBS file format }
141: BEGIN
142:    remove_ext( fname );
143:    fname := concat( fname, ext_indx );
144:    IF NOT fil_recs[ dfn ].fil_open
145:      THEN
146:        err_code := 13         { Data file not open error }
147:      ELSE
148:        BEGIN
149:          init_msc( msc_rec );
150:          WITH msc_rec DO
151:            BEGIN
152:              msc_recsize := page_size + 1;   { One index pg per disk pg }
153:              msc_nflds := 1;                 { ·Field = page here }
154:              WITH msc_flds[1] DO
155:                BEGIN
156:                  fld_name := 'INDEX.PAGE';   { Alpha_size characters }
157:                  fld_type := dat_char;       { But not used as such }
158:                  fld_len := page_size;       { As large as possible }
159:                  fld_pos := 1;               { Binary page index }
160:                  fld_decimals := 0
161:                END { with }
162:            END; { with }
163:          err_code := make_file( fname, msc_rec );
164:          IF err_code = 0 THEN
165:          BEGIN
166:            err_code := open_file( index.fn, fname );
167:            IF err_code = 0 THEN
168:            BEGIN
169:              fillchar( blank_rec, sizeof( blank_rec ), chr(0) );
170:              err_code := append_rec( index.fn, blank_rec );
171:              IF err_code <> 0
172:                THEN
173:                  BEGIN
174:                    IF NOT executed( close_file( index.fn, no_update ) )
175:                      THEN halt     { Extremely unlikely }
176:                  END
177:                ELSE
178:                  WITH index DO
179:                    BEGIN
180:                      root := 0;
181:                      field := dfield;
182:                      keylen := dlen + 5;
183:                      IF odd( keylen )
```

```
184:                         THEN keylen := keylen + 1;
185:                         kpp := ( page_size - 4 ) DIV keylen;
186:                         IF odd( kpp )
187:                             THEN kpp := kpp - 1;
188:                         kppd2 := kpp DIV 2;
189:                         err_code := close_index( index, update )
190:                     END; { else / with }
191:               END { if }
192:            END { if }
193:          END; { else }
194:      create_index := err_code
195: END; { create_index }
196:
197:
198: FUNCTION search_index{ VAR index : index_rec;
199:                        VAR skey  : string;
200:                        VAR drn   : integer      ) : pdbs_err };
201: { Search for skey in this index.  If found, return drn = record number }
202: VAR
203:     entry    : index_entry;           { Index entry (key + record number) }
204:     err_code : pdbs_err;
205:     ix       : index_xchng;           { Index / binary page exchanger }
206:
207:     PROCEDURE search( pn : integer );
208:     { Perform recursive search for skey }
209:     VAR
210:         found : boolean;        { True if search key matches index key }
211:         k     : integer;        { Page index }
212:         q     : integer;        { Next page number holder }
213:     BEGIN
214:         IF pn <= 0
215:           THEN
216:             err_code := 26      { Search failed }
217:           ELSE WITH index DO
218:             BEGIN
219:               err_code := read_rec( fn, pn, ix.bp );
220:               IF err_code = 0 THEN WITH ix.ip DO
221:               BEGIN
222:                 k := 1;
223:                 found := false;
224:                 entry.p := p0;
225:                 WHILE ( k <= n ) AND ( NOT found ) DO
226:                 BEGIN
227:                    q := entry.p;
228:                    moveleft( entries[ (k-1)*keylen ],      { Source }
229:                              entry,                        { Destination }
230:                              keylen );                     { Count }
231:                    found := entry.key >= skey;
232:                    IF NOT found
233:                       THEN k := k + 1
234:                 END; { while }
235:                 IF { possibly } found THEN
236:                     found { confirmed } := entry.key = skey;
237:                 IF { definitely } found
238:                    THEN
239:                      drn := entry.rn    { Pass record number back }
240:                    ELSE
241:                      IF k > n
242:                         THEN search( entry.p )
243:                         ELSE search( q )
244:               END { if }
245:            END { else / with }
246:      END; { search }
247:
248: BEGIN { search_index }
249:     search( index.root );
250:     search_index := err_code
```

```
251: END; { search_index }
252:
253:
254: FUNCTION insert_index{ VAR index : index_rec;
255:                        VAR skey  : string;
256:                        VAR drn   : integer      ) : pdbs_err };
257: { Insert new index entry with key = skey and record number = drn }
258: VAR
259:    entry      : index_entry;         { Index key entry }
260:    err_code   : pdbs_err;
261:    insrting   : boolean;             { Purposely mizspelled }
262:    ix         : index_xchng;         { Index / binary page exchanger }
263:
264:    PROCEDURE search(    pn         : integer;
265:                    VAR insrting : boolean;
266:                    VAR entry    : index_entry );
267:    { Search index to locate position for inserting entry }
268:    VAR
269:       found : boolean;        { True if search key matches index key }
270:       item  : index_entry;    { Item to pass up through tree }
271:       k     : integer;        { Page index }
272:       q     : integer;        { Next page number holder }
273:
274:       PROCEDURE insert;
275:       { Insert item into index at page pn }
276:       VAR
277:          nx : index_xchng;              { New index page }
278:       BEGIN
279:          WITH index DO
280:          BEGIN
281:             err_code := read_rec( fn, pn, ix.bp );
282:             IF err_code = 0 THEN WITH ix.ip DO
283:             IF n < kpp
284:               THEN
285:                 BEGIN          { Normal insert into partially full page }
286:                   IF k <= n
287:                     THEN moveright( entries[ (k-1)*keylen ],
288:                                     entries[ k*keylen ],
289:                                     ((n-k+1)*keylen) );
290:                   moveleft( item,
291:                             entries[ (k-1)*keylen ],
292:                             keylen );
293:                   n := n + 1;
294:                   insrting := false
295:                 END
296:               ELSE
297:                 BEGIN          { Split full page and insert }
298:                   zero_rec( fn, nx.bp );
299:                   IF k <= kppd2
300:                     THEN
301:                       BEGIN { Insert into left half of page }
302:                         IF k = kppd2
303:                           THEN
304:                             entry := item
305:                           ELSE
306:                             BEGIN
307:                               moveleft( entries[ (kppd2-1)*keylen ],
308:                                         entry,
309:                                         keylen );
310:                               IF k < kppd2
311:                                 THEN
312:                                   moveright( entries[ (k-1)*keylen ],
313:                                              entries[ k*keylen ],
314:                                              ((kppd2-k)*keylen) );
315:                               moveleft( item,
316:                                         entries[ (k-1)*keylen ],
317:                                         keylen )
```

```
318:                             END; { else }
319:                         moveleft( entries[ kppd2*keylen ],
320:                                   nx.ip.entries[0],
321:                                   kppd2 * keylen )
322:                     END { if }
323:                   ELSE
324:                     BEGIN  { Insert into right half of page }
325:                         moveleft( entries[ kppd2*keylen ],
326:                                   entry,
327:                                   keylen );
328:                         moveleft( entries[ (kppd2+1)*keylen ],
329:                                   nx.ip.entries[0],
330:                                   (kppd2-1)*keylen  );
331:                         k := k - kppd2 - 1;
332:                         IF k <= 0
333:                           THEN k := 1;
334:                         IF k < kppd2
335:                           THEN
336:                             moveright( nx.ip.entries[ (k-1)*keylen ],
337:                                        nx.ip.entries[ k*keylen ],
338:                                        ((kppd2-k)*keylen) );
339:                         moveleft( item,
340:                                   nx.ip.entries[ (k-1)*keylen ],
341:                                   keylen )
342:                     END; { else }
343:                   n := kppd2;
344:                   nx.ip.n := kppd2;
345:                   nx.ip.p0 := entry.p;
346:                   err_code := append_rec( fn, nx.bp );
347:                   IF err_code = 0
348:                     THEN entry.p := fil_recs[fn].fil_msc.msc_lastrec
349:                 END; { else }
350:             IF err_code = 0
351:               THEN err_code := write_rec( fn, pn, ix.bp )
352:         END { with }
353:     END; { insert }
354:
355:   BEGIN { search }
356:     IF err_code = 0 THEN
357:     IF pn <= 0
358:       THEN WITH entry DO
359:         BEGIN
360:           insrting := true;
361:           p := 0;                   { Equivalent to nil }
362:           rn := drn;                { Record number }
363:           key := skey               { Search key }
364:         END
365:       ELSE WITH index DO
366:         BEGIN       { Keep searching }
367:           err_code := read_rec( fn, pn, ix.bp );
368:           IF err_code = 0 THEN WITH ix.ip DO
369:           BEGIN
370:             k := 1;
371:             found := false;
372:             entry.p := p0;
373:             WHILE ( k <= n ) AND ( NOT found ) DO
374:             BEGIN
375:               q := entry.p;
376:               moveleft( entries[ (k-1)*keylen ],      { Source }
377:                         entry,                        { Destination }
378:                         keylen );                     { Count }
379:               found := entry.key >= skey;
380:               IF NOT found
381:                 THEN k := k + 1
382:             END; { while }
383:             IF k > n
384:               THEN q := entry.p;
```

```
385:                       search( q, insrting, item );
386:                       IF insrting AND ( err_code = 0 )
387:                          THEN insert
388:                    END { if }
389:                END { else }
390:       END; { search }
391:
392: BEGIN { insert_index }
393:     insrting := false;
394:     err_code := 0;
395:     search( index.root, insrting, entry );
396:     IF insrting AND ( err_code = 0 ) THEN
397:     BEGIN     { Root page must be split.  Tree grows one level higher. }
398:        zero_rec( index.fn, ix.bp );
399:        WITH ix.ip DO
400:        BEGIN
401:          n := 1;              { Only time number of entries < kppd2 }
402:          p0 := index.root;
403:          moveleft( entry,
404:                    entries[0],       { Source }
405:                    index.keylen )    { Destination }
406:        END; { with }                 { Count }
407:        err_code := append_rec( index.fn, ix.bp );
408:        IF err_code = 0
409:         THEN
410:            index.root := fil_recs[ index.fn ].fil_msc.msc_lastrec
411:     END; { if }
412:     insert_index := err_code
413: END; { insert_index }
414:
415:
416: FUNCTION delete_index{ VAR index : index_rec;
417:                        VAR skey  : string;
418:                            drn   : integer      ) : pdbs_err };
419: { Mark index entry with this skey and data record number drn }
420: { Record number drn is used to distinguish among duplicate keys }
421: { Deletion accomplished by setting index entry rn <-- 0 indicating }
422: {   that this entry is no longer valid.  After many deletions, }
423: {   the file should be reindexed. }
424: VAR
425:     err_code : pdbs_err;
426:     ix       : index_xchng;          { Index / binary page exchanger }
427:
428:     PROCEDURE delete( pn : integer );
429:     { Search for and delete matching index entry }
430:     VAR
431:        found : boolean;     { True if search key matches index key }
432:        missed : boolean;    { True if key > search key }
433:        entry : index_entry; { Miscellaneous index entry record }
434:        k     : integer;     { Page index }
435:        q     : integer;     { Next page number holder }
436:
437:     BEGIN { delete }
438:        IF err_code = 0 THEN
439:        IF pn <= 0
440:          THEN err_code := 26  { Key not found }
441:          ELSE WITH index DO
442:            BEGIN             { Keep searching }
443:               err_code := read_rec( fn, pn, ix.bp );
444:               IF err_code = 0 THEN WITH ix.ip DO
445:               BEGIN
446:                  k := 1;
447:                  found := false;
448:                  missed := false;
449:                  entry.p := p0;
450:                  WHILE ( k <= n ) AND ( NOT found ) AND ( NOT missed ) DO
451:                  BEGIN
```

```
452:                    q := entry.p;
453:                    moveleft( entries[ (k-1)*keylen ],      { Source }
454:                              entry,                         { Destination }
455:                              keylen );                      { Count }
456:                    found := ( entry.key = skey ) AND ( entry.rn = drn );
457:                    IF NOT found
458:                      THEN
459:                        missed := ( entry.key > skey )
460:                      ELSE
461:                        BEGIN          { delete entry }
462:                          entry.rn := 0;          { i.e. ignore this index }
463:                                                  { entry from now on. }
464:                          moveleft( entry,                        { Source }
465:                                    entries[ (k-1)*keylen ],      { Dest }
466:                                    keylen );                     { Count }
467:                          err_code := write_rec( fn, pn, ix.bp )
468:                        END; { else }
469:                    IF ( NOT found ) AND ( NOT missed )
470:                      THEN k := k + 1
471:                  END; { while }
472:
473:                  IF k > n
474:                    THEN q := entry.p;          { else q = p0 }
475:
476:                  IF NOT found
477:                    THEN delete( q )     { search some more }
478:
479:              END { if / with }
480:            END { else }
481:      END; { delete }
482:
483: BEGIN { delete_index }
484:     err_code := 0;
485:     delete( index.root );
486:     delete_index := err_code
487: END; { delete_index }
488:
489:
490: END. { unit }
```

10

Writing a PDBS Application

PAYCALC / PAYUPDATE / PAYCHECK /
PAYNEWYEAR

Although most of the programming in this book is designed to operate on all data files regardless of their contents, there are times you will want to write specific programs to do specific jobs. By including the PDBS library unit routines in your application program with a *uses* statement in the program header, you can easily access PDBS data file fields through simple function calls. This lets PDBS handle all file, record, and VMOS memory manipulations while you concentrate on the other details of your application.

As an example of how to write a PDBS application program, I develop in this chapter most of the programming needed for a general purpose payroll system, written entirely in PDBS format. Because this is only a sample application, you may have to modify some of the details, particularly the formulas used to compute taxes.

The payroll programs also demonstrate how to handle two common data base programming problems not covered elsewhere in the book.

One of these problems seems to arise more than others and is considered by some, the author included, as an axiom of data base programming.

Axiom: You will always need at least one more field than the maximum number of fields allowed.

Because PDBS allows up to six files to be open at one time, you can easily increase the number of apparent fields available—up to 210 in the current version—by treating two or more files as though they were one. In the payroll system here, I keep employee information apart from hours and wages information, but the programs will connect the two files automatically.

A second common problem is designing reports to fill out pre-printed forms. There is a very simple way to solve this detail, as seen in the *paycheck* program.

The same method shown here could be used to program a variety of PDBS "forms" reports to print out insurance forms, invoices, inventory reports—or any pre-printed form that fits into your printer.

Designing the Application

Figures 10-1 and 10-2 are *status* reports for the two data files in the PDBS payroll system. Although you may want to make changes to the structures of these files, enter them for now with the *create* program exactly as shown here. Unless they too are modified, the four payroll programs that do all payroll calculations and print the checks expect these files to be exactly as listed.

Year-to-date totals for wages, hours, and deductions are stored in fields 13 through 20 in the employee data file (see Fig. 10-1). In this same file are the names and addresses of all employees along with other general information, including phone numbers, dates hired, and so forth.

The first field, SS.NUM (social security number), is the same in both the employee and payroll data files. In this system, the SS.NUM field is used as a "key" to link the two files together. You need to maintain the social security numbers of employees anyway, so you may as well use them as your search keys. You can use the same method to link more than two PDBS files together.

```
EMPLOYEE.PDBF
Record size ............ 185
Number of fields ........ 20
Maximum record number ... 5
Records in use .......... 0
Records not used ........ 5
Date created ........... 07-Nov-83
Date last updated ....... 11-Nov-83

 #   NAME          TYPE      LEN DEC POS

 1   SS.NUM        Char       11   0   1
 2   NAME          Char       30   0  12
 3   ADDRESS       Char       30   0  42
 4   CITY          Char       15   0  72
 5   STATE         Char        2   0  87
 6   ZIP           Char        5   0  89
 7   PHONE         Char       12   0  94
 8   ACTIVE        Logical     1   0 106
 9   HIRED         Number      6   0 107
10   TERMINATED    Number      6   0 113
11   FULL.TIME     Logical     1   0 119
12   PAY.RATE      Number      5   2 120
13   YTD.WAGES     Number      8   2 125
14   YTD.FEDTAX    Number      8   2 133
15   YTD.FICA      Number      8   2 141
16   YTD.STTAX     Number      8   2 149
17   YTD.REG       Number      7   2 157
18   YTD.OVT       Number      7   2 164
19   YTD.SICK      Number      7   2 171
20   YTD.VAC       Number      7   2 178
```

Fig. 10-1. *The employee file for the PDBS Payroll system. Create this file, using the* create *program, exactly as shown here.*

Before entering information into the employee file, design a screen entry format following the directions to the *editor* in Chapter One. (Also see Figs. 1-8, 1-9, and 1-10.) Using the *editor*, enter the values shown in Fig. 10-3 into a file named EMPLOYEE.SCRN with the structure detailed in Fig. 1-8.

With both the EMPLOYEE.PDBF and EMPLOYEE.SCRN files on the same diskette or volume, you are ready to enter the details for each employee record. Execute the *editor* and when asked for a file name, enter *employee*. You may enter current year-to-date totals or leave those fields blank. You must enter an hourly pay rate for each employee.

Figure 10-2 shows the structure of the second of the two data files, PAYROLL.PDBF. There is no accompanying screen format for this file, but if you want a nicer entry display, you can certainly design one.

At the end of each pay period, using the PDBS *editor*, enter the number of hours into the PAYROLL.PDBF file in each of the four categories, REG.HRS (regular hours), OVRTIM.HRS (overtime hours), SICK.HRS (sick hours), and VACAT.HRS (vacation hours). Use social security numbers to identify employees. Employees who did not work during this pay period may be skipped. Every entry in the payroll file must have a corresponding record in the employee file with the same social security number or you will receive an error when using the *paycalc* program.

```
PAYROLL.PDBF
Record size ............. 112
Number of fields ........ 15
Maximum record number ... 9
Records in use .......... 0
Records not used ........ 9
Date created ............ 08-Nov-83
Date last updated ....... 11-Nov-83
```

#	NAME	TYPE	LEN	DEC	POS
1	SS.NUM	Char	11	0	1
2	REG.HRS	Number	5	2	12
3	OVRTIM.HRS	Number	5	2	17
4	SICK.HRS	Number	5	2	22
5	VACAT.HRS	Number	5	2	27
6	REG.PAY	Number	8	2	32
7	OVRTIM.PAY	Number	8	2	40
8	SICK.PAY	Number	8	2	48
9	VACAT.PAY	Number	8	2	56
10	GROSS.PAY	Number	8	2	64
11	FEDTAX	Number	8	2	72
12	FICA	Number	8	2	80
13	STTAX	Number	8	2	88
14	DEDUCTIONS	Number	8	2	96
15	NET.PAY	Number	8	2	104

Fig. 10-2. *At the end of each pay period, hours worked by each employee are entered into this file, also created with the create program. The social security number field (SS.NUM) links the employee and payroll files together as though they were one. This method allows large records to be constructed in PDBS.*

	Field	Xheader	Yheader	Xentry	Yentry	Width
	==	==	==	==	==	==
00001	1	3	4	15	4	11
00002	8	48	4	61	4	1
00003	11	64	4	76	4	1
00004	2	3	6	15	6	30
00005	3	3	7	15	7	30
00006	4	3	8	15	8	15
00007	5	3	9	15	9	2
00008	6	3	10	15	10	5
00009	7	3	12	15	12	12
00010	9	53	7	65	7	6
00011	10	53	9	65	9	6
00012	12	53	11	65	11	5
00013	13	3	15	3	16	8
00014	14	23	15	23	16	8
00015	15	43	15	43	16	8
00016	16	63	15	63	16	8
00017	17	3	18	3	19	7
00018	18	23	18	23	19	7
00019	19	43	18	43	19	7
00020	20	63	18	63	19	7

20 records processed

Fig. 10-3. *Enter these values into a PDBS data file named EMPLOYEE.SCRN with the structure shown in Fig. 1-8. The numbers in the left column here are the record numbers for each entry and are not entered. This information is used by the editor to configure a professional entry screen for the employee data file.*

To begin a new payroll, use the *erase* program to clear the old PAY-ROLL.PDBF data file. Next, for each employee enter a social security number followed by the number of regular hours, overtime hours, hours on paid sick leave, and hours on paid vacation into the appropriate fields. Leave the rest of the fields blank—they will be calculated by the payroll system automatically. Figures 10-4 and 10-5 show sample data for Mom and Pop Software, Inc., a fledgling cottage company about to take the microcomputer world by storm with its new programs. Figures 10-6 and 10-7 list the report format values used to print the sample data in Figs. 10-4 and 10-5.

Notice in Fig. 10-4, by the way, that dates are entered as six-digit integers in YYMMDD format. This format allows searching and sorting by date, although you can change the field type to a character string to enter dates in a more casual style (for example, 4/3/50 or 11-Nov-83, and so on).

Running the Payroll Application Programs

Type in the five text files at the end of this chapter, *paycommon.text, paycalc.text, payupdate.text, paycheck.text,* and *paynewyear.text.* Store these files on a diskette along with the Pascal compiler and use the UCSD filer to set the prefix to that diskette's name or drive number.

MOM AND POP SOFTWARE, INC.
Employee Report

Social Security	Employee Name	Address	City	St	Zip	Telephone	Date Hired	Date Term.	Pay Rate	Active	Ful Tim
000-12-3456	Dolittle, Raymond P.	8510 Lazy Lane Hwy	Sleepytown	TX	45233	797-555-1212	650611	0	12.55	T	F
000-76-5432	Schemer, Suzanne	955 Mystery Road	Twilight Town	TX	45233	796-555-1212	710403	0	14.55	T	F
000-99-8811	Revolta, John	1 Disco Drive	Koolsville	TX	45233	795-555-1212	600315	0	13.75	T	T

Total   40.85
Minimum   12.55
Maximum   14.55
Average   13.61

3 records processed

Fig. 10-4. Partial report of the EMPLOYEE.PDBF file, showing sample records for three employees. The report was printed by the report program using the values in Fig. 10-6 as the report format. See the instructions to the report program for creating report format (.RPRT) files.

```
Date : 14-Nov-83          MOM AND POP SOFTWARE, INC.              Page-1
                              Payroll Hours Report

================================================================================
              Social      Regular    Overtime     Sick      Vacation
             Security      Hours       Hours       Hours       Hours
           ==========   ==========  ==========  ==========  ==========
00001      000-12-3456       40.00        4.00         .00         .00
00002      000-76-5432       35.00         .00        4.50         .00
00003      000-99-8811         .00         .00         .00       40.00
                         ==========  ==========  ==========  ==========
Total                         75.00        4.00        4.50       40.00
Minimum                           0           0           0           0
Maximum                       40.00        4.00        4.50       40.00
Average                       25.00        1.33        1.50       13.33

3 records processed
```

Fig. 10-5. *The current payroll is entered into the PAYROLL.PDBF file. Only the social security and four hourly fields are entered; the rest of the fields are calculated by the paycalc program. This report was printed by the report program using the values in Fig. 10-7 entered into a report format file named HOURS.RPRT.*

Next, compile *paycalc, payupdate, paycheck,* and *paynewyear* saving the resulting code in files with the same names. You must have the *pdbsunit* installed in SYSTEM.LIBRARY before any of the payroll files will compile.

To save typing, the file *paycommon* contains some procedures that are common to all but the *paynewyear* program. This file is included during compilation by the programs that need these routines.

```
Date : 14-Nov-83                    EMPLOYEE.RPRT                     Page-1
                          (Employee Report Format Values)

================================================================================
        Field  Column  Width  TRN EOL TOT    Header.1          Header.2
          ==     ===     ===    =   =   =   ===============   ===============
00001      1       0      11     F   F   F   Social            Security
00002      2      13      20     F   F   F   Employee          Name
00003      3      35      20     F   F   F                     Address
00004      4      57      15     F   F   F                     City
00005      5      74       2     F   F   F                     St
00006      6      78       5     F   F   F                     Zip
00007      7      85      12     F   F   F                     Telephone
00008      9      99       6     F   F   F   Date              Hired
00009     10     107       6     F   F   F   Date              Term.
00010     12     115       5     F   F   T   Pay               Rate
00011      8     122       6     F   F   F                     Active
00012     11     129       4     F   F   F   Full              Time

12 records processed
```

Fig. 10-6. *Values used to print the employee report shown in Fig. 10-4. These values were entered into a report format file named EMPLOYEE.RPRT with a structure detailed in Fig. 2-4.*

```
Date : 14-Nov-83                    HOURS.RPRT                      Page-1
                           (Hours Report Format Values)

==========================================================================
           Field  Column  Width  TRN EOL TOT    Header.1          Header.2
           ==     ===     ===     =   =   =    ================  ================
00001        1      10     11     F   F   F    Social            Security
00002        2      23     10     F   F   T    Regular           Hours
00003        3      35     10     F   F   T    Overtime          Hours
00004        4      47     10     F   F   T    Sick              Hours
00005        5      59     10     F   F   T    Vacation          Hours

5 records processed
```

Fig. 10-7. *Values used to print the payroll hours report shown in Fig. 10-5. These values were entered into a report format file named HOURS.RPRT with a structure detailed in Fig. 2-4.*

Before running any of the PDBS payroll programs, make sure you have the EMPLOYEE.PDBF and PAYROLL.PDBF files on a diskette inserted in a disk drive. Use the UCSD filer to set the prefix to that diskette and then follow these instructions for using the payroll programs.

PAYCALC

With the employee and payroll files ready to go, execute the program *paycalc*. In a few minutes—longer depending on the number of employees—all payments and deductions are calculated and stored back in the payroll data file.

If you receive an error, it is probably because you incorrectly entered a social security number in the payroll file. Use the *editor* to correct the bad number, then rerun *paycalc*.

The formulas used by *paycalc* are listed in Fig. 10-8. As explained earlier, these tax formulas are simplistic and will probably need reprogramming. To help you with that job, the listing is well marked with comments.

This is a good place for a caution. Resist the temptation to write one program that computes the payroll, updates the year-to-date totals, prints the checks, writes the payroll report, takes out the garbage, milks the cows, and feeds the cat—all in one superhuman monument to your, I am sure, considerable programming skills. Better to have four separate, easily-modified programs, each with a designated purpose, than a single do-it-all version that may not do it at all!

Another reason for breaking up the functions of the payroll system into separate programs is to allow editing of the results along the way. When the *paycalc* program is done, you can examine, list, and modify the payroll file before printing the checks. After running *paycalc*, use the *editor* to examine fields 6 through 15 in the PAYROLL.PDBF file. This gives you a way to catch the odd error before wasting a lot of expensive pre-printed checks and before the janitor cashes his unexpected $25,000 bonus and takes an extended leave of absence in Acapulco.

```
PAYROLL.PDBF

FIELD            FORMULA

-------------    --------------------------------------------

REG.PAY          = PAY.RATE * REG.HRS

OVRTIM.PAY       = (PAY.RATE * 1.5) * OVRTIM.HRS

SICK.PAY         = (PAY.RATE * 0.85) * SICK.HRS

VACAT.PAY        = (PAY.RATE * 0.85) * VACAT.HRS

GROSS.PAY        = REG.PAY + OVRTIM.PAY + SICK.PAY + VACAT.PAY

FEDTAX           = GROSS.PAY * 0.15

FICA             = MAX( (GROSS.PAY * 0.0935), 3,029.40 )

STTAX            = FEDTAX * 0.5

DEDUCTIONS       = FEDTAX + FICA + STTAX

NET.PAY          = GROSS.PAY - DEDUCTIONS
```

Fig. 10-8. *Formulas used by paycalc to compute paycheck amounts and deductions. These formulas may require reprogramming to conform with current tax laws and your own requirements. Notice, for example, that the company does not pay full hourly rates for sick and vacation pay.*

Because the payroll file is a temporary file and does not change any of the year-to-date totals, you may run and rerun *paycalc* as many times as necessary until the payroll is verified and is ready to print. When you are satisfied, move on to the next program.

PAYUPDATE

After running *paycalc* and verifying the results in the payroll file, make a complete backup copy of your employee data file before proceeding. If anything should go wrong during updating, recover the original file before proceeding. This step is essential to preserving the accuracy of your employee records and must not be neglected.

After backing up, execute *payupdate*, read the warning, and answer the prompts. The information in the payroll file, calculated by *paycalc*, is added to the year-to-date totals in the employee file. This completes the entry and calculation steps for the payroll.

Payupdate should be run once and only once for each new payroll period. Updating twice would add the paycheck amounts twice and would cause the year-to-date totals to be inaccurate. When updating is done, locate the checks and proceed to the next step.

PAYCHECK

This program, as you may suppose, prints the checks using the information in both the employee and payroll data files. Before printing the checks, you must have run the *paycalc* and *payupdate* programs, in that order.

You are first asked to supply the starting check number. This can be any number with as many as 13 digits. The check number is automatically increased sequentially by one for each check, starting with the number you supply.

After entering the check number, you will be told to insert the checks and verify, by pressing "Y", that you are ready to begin printing.

It is probably a good idea to enter a few dummy records into a sample file for the purpose of aligning your checks in the printer. If you don't want to waste checks, print sample payroll runs on blank paper until you are sure you know how to register the top line of the first form.

Printing proceeds automatically as soon as you press "Y". An example of the results is shown in Fig. 10-9. *Paycheck* is designed to print on check form series 6010, available from Moore Business Center, P.O. Box 20, Wheeling, IL 60090, 800-323-6230.

The method used to create each check in the *paycheck* program can be adapted to practically any pre-printed form. The data type *form* is a simple array of lines, each exactly as long as your form is wide. Procedure *init_form* sets up a blank form, or "frame" as it is sometimes called, with all fixed information. Examples of fixed information are dates, company names, and various tags. See the listing for details on how to enter this information into the blank form.

Each new form is filled with data from the appropriate PDBS data files with calls to procedures *insert_field* and *insert_string*. Only after the entire form is filled does printing occur in procedure *print_form*.

Delaying printing by filling in a blank form in memory this way is less restrictive than requiring that each new line be formed and printed as is done in the *report* program. Fields can be read and entered into the blank form in any order. Only when the entire form is filled does printing begin. The disadvantage of this method is that a lot of memory is required to hold the blank form. An 80-column insurance form with 66 lines, for example, would take up 5,280 bytes or characters in memory, even though most positions on the page would be blank. Because the method demonstrated here uses two such forms, 10,560 bytes would be occupied by the blank forms alone. That is about one-third the available memory on an Apple II computer using Apple Pascal 1.1.

PRINTING THE PAYROLL REPORT

After the checks are done, you should print a report of the payroll for the company records. Although this is not required, and you could just keep a copy of the diskette on file, most people like to have the information on paper as well.

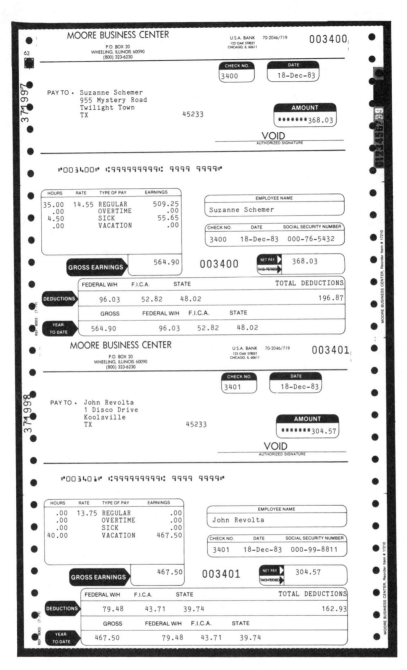

Fig. 10-9. *The paycheck program prints the actual checks using a blank form or "frame" in memory. Fields are simply inserted into the blank form, which can then be printed in one easy step. Checks (stock #17210) reproduced courtesy of Moore Business Forms, Inc.*

```
Join what file? EMPLOYEE
And what file? PAYROLL
To what file? TEMP
Join over what field? SS.NUM
Joining
  3 of 3
3 records --> TEMP.PDBF
```

Fig. 10-10. *Follow this dialogue, entering the items underlined with the join program to produce a new file called TEMP.PDBF. The information in this file is used to print the payroll report shown in Fig. 10-12.*

There is no special program for printing the report. Instead, two of the standard PDBS programs are used.

First, you have to combine the current payroll with the employee data file. This is done so that employee names—not included in the payroll file—can be printed on the report along with the paycheck amounts. Combining two files over a common field is a typical operation in any data base system.

Use the program *join* to combine the EMPLOYEE.PDBF and PAYROLL.PDBF data files to a new file named TEMP.PDBF (or to a file of any other name) over the common field, SS.NUM. To help you with this process, the dialogue for using *join* is given in Fig. 10-10.

After joining the two files, use the report format listed in Fig. 10-11 to print

```
Date : 14-Nov-83              PAYROLL.RPRT                    Page-1
                        (Payroll Report Format Values)

===================================================================
        Field  Column  Width  TRN EOL TOT    Header.1         Header.2
        ==     ===     ===    =   =   =      ===============  ===============
00001     1      0      11     F   T   F     Social Sec.      Name
00002     2      0      12     T   F   F
00003    12     13       5     F   F   T                      Rate
00004    21     19       5     F   F   T     Reg              Hrs
00005    22     25       5     F   F   T     Ovrtm            Hrs
00006    23     31       5     F   F   T     Sick             Hrs
00007    24     37       5     F   F   T     Vacat            Hrs
00008    25     43       8     F   F   T     Regular          Pay
00009    26     52       8     F   F   T     Overtime         Pay
00010    27     61       8     F   F   T     Sick             Pay
00011    28     70       8     F   F   T     Vacation         Pay
00012    29     79       8     F   F   T     Gross            Pay
00013    30     88       8     F   F   T     Federal          Tax
00014    31     97       8     F   F   T                      F.I.C.A.
00015    32    106       8     F   F   T     State            Tax
00016    33    115       8     F   F   T     Total            Deducts
00017    34    124       8     F   F   T     Net              Pay

17 records processed
```

Fig. 10-11. *Enter these values into a file called PAYROLL.RPRT using the format shown in Fig. 2-4. The report program can then be used to print the payroll report from the join of the employee and payroll files, as shown in Fig. 10-12.*

```
Date : 14-Nov-83                              MOM AND POP SOFTWARE, INC.                                              Page-1
                                                     Payroll Report
```

Social Sec. Name	Rate	Reg Hrs	Ovrtm Hrs	Sick Hrs	Vacat Hrs	Regular Pay	Overtime Pay	Sick Pay	Vacation Pay	Gross Pay	Federal Tax	F.I.C.A.	State Tax	Total Deducts	Net Pay
000-12-3456 Dolittle, Ra	12.55	40.00	4.00	.00	.00	502.00	75.30	.00	.00	577.30	98.14	53.98	49.07	201.19	376.11
000-76-5432 Schemer, Suz	14.55	35.00	.00	4.50	.00	509.25	.00	55.65	.00	564.90	96.03	52.82	48.02	196.87	368.03
000-99-8811 Revolta, Joh	13.75	.00	.00	.00	40.00	.00	.00	.00	467.50	467.50	79.48	43.71	39.74	162.93	304.57
Total	40.85	75.00	4.00	4.50	40.00	1011.25	75.30	55.65	467.50	1609.70	273.65	150.51	136.83	560.99	1048.71
Minimum	12.55	0	0	0	0	0	.00	.00	.00	467.50	79.48	43.71	39.74	162.93	304.57
Maximum	14.55	40.00	4.00	4.50	40.00	509.25	75.30	55.65	467.50	577.30	98.14	53.98	49.07	201.19	376.11
Average	13.61	25.00	1.33	1.50	13.33	337.08	25.10	18.55	155.83	536.56	91.21	50.17	45.61	186.99	349.57

3 records processed

Fig. 10-12. *The final payroll report printed with the report program using the format values in Fig. 10-11. The information for this report came from a temporary file produced by joining the employee and payroll files over the common field, SS.NUM.*

the payroll report. The values in the report format must be entered (using the PDBS *editor)* into a file named PAYROLL.RPRT according to the instructions in Chapter Two. (See Fig. 2-4 for the structure of the report format file.)

The final payroll report for our sample employee data base is listed in Fig. 10-12.

One problem you may encounter if you add fields to either the payroll or employee files used here is the restriction on the number of fields in a file. You cannot join two files if the total number of fields exceeds the maximum, set to 35 fields in this version of PDBS. If you have more than a total of 35 fields, you can first *project* or *merge* the fields you want from each file into two other temporary files and then *join* these to produce the final report.

PAYNEWYEAR

The final program in the payroll system is used once a year to reset all year-to-date totals in the employee data file. Before running the program, you will probably want to print out a final report of the year-end totals. It may also be a good idea to retain a copy of the diskette files as they existed at the end of each year before running *paynewyear*. The collection of your old payroll totals on diskette in PDBS data format is then available for invaluable historical research and reporting on your company's payroll.

```
001: { PAYCOMMON.TEXT    --  Include-file for PDBS Payroll System }
002:
003:
004: PROCEDURE process_one_record;
005:     forward;
006:
007:
008: PROCEDURE poweroften( exponent : integer; VAR long : long_integer );
009: { Return "long" = ten to the power of exponent }
010: { Long integer equivalent of the intrinsic pwroften real function }
011: { For 0 <= exponent <= max_digits - 1 }
012: BEGIN
013:     long := 1;
014:     WHILE exponent > 0 DO
015:         BEGIN
016:             long := long * 10;
017:             exponent := exponent - 1
018:         END
019: END; { poweroften }
020:
021:
022: PROCEDURE roundoff( VAR long : long_integer; places, decimals : integer );
023: { Round "long" up or down as required.  Assume that the value has }
024: { "places" decimal places.  Round the value to "decimals" places. }
025: { Note: for decimals <= places }
026: { The value 1.5550 (4 places) is rounded to 1.56 (2 decimals) }
027: { See below if you want 1.5550 to round to 1.55, and 1.5551 to 1.56 }
028: VAR
029:     original,                       { Original value passed to here }
030:     truncated,                      { Truncated portion of value }
031:     tenp : long_integer;            { Ten to the power of ... }
```

```
032: BEGIN
033:    original_value := long;
034:    poweroften( places - decimals, tenp );
035:    long := long DIV tenp;
036:    truncated := original - ( long * tenp );
037:    poweroften( places - decimals - 1, tenp );
038:    IF truncated >= 5 * tenp        { if truncated > 5 * tenp (see note)}
039:       THEN long := long + 1
040: END; { roundoff }
041:
042:
043: PROCEDURE rj( long : long_integer; columns : integer; VAR s : string );
044: { Convert long integer "long" into string "s" }
045: { right justified in "columns" spaces. }
046: BEGIN
047:    str( long, s );            { Raw UCSD long integer to string conversion }
048:    WHILE length( s ) < decimals DO          { Pad fractions with zeros }
049:       insert( '0', s, 1 );
050:    IF decimals > 0                          { Insert decimal point }
051:       THEN insert( '.', s, ( length( s ) - decimals + 1 ) );
052:    WHILE length ( s ) < columns DO          { Right justify string }
053:       insert( ' ', s, 1 )
054: END; { rj }
055:
056:
057: PROCEDURE get_value( fn, fld : integer; VAR long : long_integer );
058: { Read field "fld" from file "fn" returning integer value long }
059: VAR
060:    s : string;
061: BEGIN
062:    get_field( fn, fld, s );
063:    lvalue( s, decimals, long )
064: END; { get_value }
065:
066:
067: PROCEDURE put_value( fn, fld : integer; long : long_integer );
068: { Write integer value "long" to field "fld" in file "fn" }
069: VAR
070:    s : string;
071: BEGIN
072:    rj( long, digits, s );        { Convert long to right justified string }
073:    put_field( fn, fld, s )       { Save string in data file }
074: END; { put_value }
075:
076:
077: FUNCTION find_record(      fn  : integer;              { File number }
078:                     fld_num : integer;              { Field number }
079:                         key : string;               { Search key }
080:                     VAR rn  : integer ) : boolean;   { Record number }
081: { Search for record in file fn with key field in field number fld_num }
082: { If found, return function value true, else return false. }
083: { If function returns true, then rn equals record number }
084: {  else rn is undefined. }
085: { Note : if an index were available, you could use that to }
086: { do the search without having to change anything else in }
087: { the program.  In a very large file, this could dramatically }
088: { improve performance. }
089: VAR
090:    trn              : integer;    { Temporary record number }
091:    s                : string;     { For reading fields }
092: BEGIN
093:    IF case_switch
094:       THEN bumpstrup( key );
095:    WITH fil_recs[ fn ] DO
096:       FOR trn := 1 TO fil_msc.msc_lastrec DO
097:          IF executed( seek_rec( fn, trn ) ) THEN
098:             IF rec_status( fn ) = active THEN
```

```
099:               BEGIN
100:                  get_field( fn, fld_num, s );
101:                  IF case_switch
102:                     THEN bumpstrup( s );
103:                  IF key = s THEN
104:                  BEGIN            { Success }
105:                     rn := trn;
106:                     find_record := true;
107:                     exit( find_record )
108:                  END { if }
109:               END; { with / for / if / if }
110:       find_record := false
111: END; { find_record }
112:
113:
114: PROCEDURE process_all_records;
115: { Process all payroll and employee records. }
116: { This shows one way you can treat two separate records as though }
117: { they were one.  Using this method, a single data record can have }
118: { up to max_files x max_fld fields (210 fields) in PDBS version 1.0. }
119: VAR
120:    ern,                                      { Employee record number }
121:    prn                  : integer;           { Payroll record number }
122:    s                    : string;
123: BEGIN
124:    WITH fil_recs[ payroll ].fil_msc DO         { Using this file, }
125:    FOR prn := 1 TO msc_lastrec DO              { process all records.}
126:    BEGIN
127:
128:      writeln( prn:5, ' of ', msc_lastrec );        { Operator feedback }
129:      goup;
130:
131:      IF NOT executed( seek_rec( payroll, prn ) ) THEN
132:         BEGIN
133:            beep;
134:            writeln( chr(ret), 'Error reading payroll record # ', prn );
135:            exit( PROGRAM )
136:         END;
137:
138:      IF rec_status( payroll ) = active THEN          { i.e. not deleted }
139:      BEGIN
140:
141:      { Look up the employee record with the same social security }
142:      { number as found in the payroll file.  If no such employee }
143:      { can be found, signal an error and end the program. }
144:
145:         get_field( payroll, 1, s );                  { Payroll ssnum }
146:         IF NOT find_record( employee, 1, s, ern )    { Employee ssnum }
147:          THEN
148:            BEGIN
149:               beep;
150:               writeln( chr(ret), 'Error in payroll record # ', prn );
151:               writeln( 'Bad social security number ', s );
152:               exit( PROGRAM )
153:            END { if }
154:          ELSE
155:          IF NOT executed( seek_rec( employee, ern ) )
156:            THEN
157:            BEGIN
158:               beep;
159:               writeln( chr(ret), 'Error reading employee record # ', ern );
160:               exit( PROGRAM )
161:            END; { if }
162:
163:         process_one_record
164:
165:      END { if }
```

```
166:    END { with / for }
167: END; { process_all_records }


001: {$S+,I-}              { Compiler swapping on; I/O error checking off }
002:
003: PROGRAM paycalc; uses pdbsunit;
004:
005: {------------------------------------------------------------------------}
006: {                                                                        }
007: {      PROGRAM       :  PayCalc -- Paycheck Calculator                    }
008: {      LANGUAGE      :  UCSD Pascal / Apple Pascal 1.1                    }
009: {                                                                        }
010: {      Copyright (C) 1983 by Tom Swan. All commercial rights reserved.   }
011: {                                                                        }
012: {------------------------------------------------------------------------}
013:
014: CONST
015:    decimals          = 2;               { Number decimals for all $values }
016:    digits            = 8;               { Total digits for all $values }
017:
018: VAR
019:    employee, payroll      : 0 .. max_files;         { File numbers }
020:
021:
022: {$I PAYCOMMON.TEXT }          { Include common routines }
023:
024:
025: PROCEDURE process_one_record;
026: { Calculate check amounts for this record storing results in payroll file }
027: CONST
028:    maxfica           = 302940;          { i.e. $ 3,029.40 maximum tax. }
029:
030: { This company pays 85% of regular time for hours sick and on vacation. }
031: { Notice that simple percentages are used to figure all deductions. }
032: { In a production program, a more complicated tax table would have }
033: { to be programmed.  Integer values are used here because we assume }
034: { two decimal places for each value, except ficarate which has four. }
035:
036:    ovrtimrate        = 150;             { i.e. 1.50 x pay rate }
037:    sickrate          = 85;              { i.e. 0.85 x pay rate }
038:    vacatrate         = 85;              {       "      "       }
039:    fedtaxrate        = 17;              { i.e. 0.17 x gross pay }
040:    ficarate          = 935;             { i.e. 0.0935 x gross pay }
041:    sttaxrate         = 50;              { i.e. 0.50 x fed tax }
042:
043: VAR
044:    reghrs,                              { Regular hours worked }
045:    ovrtimhrs,                           { Overtime hours worked }
046:    sickhrs,                             { Hours out sick }
047:    vacathrs,                            { Hours on paid vacation }
048:    ytdfica,                             { Year-to-date fica withheld }
049:    payrate,                             { Employee hourly rate }
050:    regpay,                              { Amount of regular pay }
051:    ovrtimpay,                           { Amount of overtime pay }
052:    sickpay,                             { Amount of sick pay }
053:    vacatpay,                            { Amount of vacation pay }
054:    grosspay,                            { Total gross pay }
055:    fedtax,                              { Amount of federal tax }
056:    fica,                                { Amount of fica fax }
057:    sttax,                               { Amount of state tax }
058:    deductions,                          { Total deductions }
059:    netpay            : long_integer;    { Total net pay (amount of check) }
060:    s                 : string;          { Field input string }
061:
062: BEGIN
063:
```

```
064:    { Read number of hours worked in all categories.  Procedure }
065:    { get_value reads the specified field and returns its long }
066:    { integer value. }
067:
068:        get_value( payroll,  2, reghrs );
069:        get_value( payroll,  3, ovrtimhrs );
070:        get_value( payroll,  4, sickhrs );
071:        get_value( payroll,  5, vacathrs );
072:
073:    { Get the employee's pay rate and year-to-date fica }
074:    { from the employee data file. }
075:
076:        get_value( employee, 12, payrate );
077:        get_value( employee, 15, ytdfica );
078:
079:    { Compute payment amounts.  Because long integers are used, }
080:    { the results of multiplying have too many decimal places. }
081:    { These values must be properly rounded back to 2 decimal places }
082:    { before tax deductions are calculated.  See procedure roundoff.}
083:
084:        regpay     := payrate * reghrs;
085:          roundoff( regpay, 4, decimals );
086:        ovrtimpay := ( payrate * ovrtimrate ) * ovrtimhrs;
087:          roundoff( ovrtimpay, 6, decimals );
088:        sickpay    := ( payrate * sickrate ) * sickhrs;
089:          roundoff( sickpay, 6, decimals );
090:        vacatpay   := ( payrate * vacatrate ) * vacathrs;
091:          roundoff( vacatpay, 6, decimals );
092:
093:    { Gross pay is equal to all the payment amounts added together. }
094:    { Addition does not require rounding.  Taxes, however, must }
095:    { be rounded to two decimal places because of the multiplications. }
096:    { Note special handling of FICA tax.  Probably, federal and maybe }
097:    { state tax calculations will need reprogramming. If so, this is the }
098:    { place to make the modifications. }
099:
100:        grosspay  := regpay + ovrtimpay + sickpay + vacatpay;
101:
102:        fedtax := ( grosspay * fedtaxrate );
103:          roundoff( fedtax, 4, decimals );
104:
105:        fica := ( grosspay * ficarate );
106:          roundoff( fica, 6, decimals );
107:        IF ytdfica + fica > maxfica
108:          THEN fica := maxfica - ytdfica;
109:
110:        sttax := ( fedtax * sttaxrate );
111:          roundoff( sttax, 4, decimals );
112:
113:        deductions := fedtax + fica + sttax;
114:        netpay := grosspay - deductions;
115:
116:    { Now that all amounts have been calculated, they can be put }
117:    { back into the data base for editing and printing checks and }
118:    { reports.  It is usually a good idea to first calculate every- }
119:    { thing in this way and then print out the results, rather than }
120:    { calculating and printing at the same time.  If the paper tears }
121:    { on the last page, it's easier to print the last few records }
122:    { instead of going through all the calculations a second time. }
123:
124:        put_value( payroll,  6, regpay );
125:        put_value( payroll,  7, ovrtimpay );
126:        put_value( payroll,  8, sickpay );
127:        put_value( payroll,  9, vacatpay );
128:        put_value( payroll, 10, grosspay );
129:        put_value( payroll, 11, fedtax );
130:        put_value( payroll, 12, fica );
```

```
131:       put_value( payroll, 13, sttax );
132:       put_value( payroll, 14, deductions );
133:       put_value( payroll, 15, netpay )
134:
135: END; { process_one_record }
136:
137:
138: BEGIN
139:    clrscrn;
140:    writeln( chr(ret), 'Payroll Calculation' );
141:    IF executed( open_file( employee, 'EMPLOYEE.PDBF' ) ) THEN
142:    IF executed( open_file( payroll, 'PAYROLL.PDBF' ) ) THEN
143:    BEGIN
144:       process_all_records;
145:       IF ( executed( close_file( employee, no_update ) ) ) AND
146:          ( executed( close_file( payroll, update    ) ) )
147:          THEN write( chr(ret), 'Payroll calculation completed' )
148:    END { if }
149: END.
```

```
001: {$S+,I-}              { Compiler swapping on; I/O error checking off }
002:
003: PROGRAM payupdate; uses pdbsunit;
004:
005: {-------------------------------------------------------------------}
006: {                                                                   }
007: {     PROGRAM         : PayUpdate -- Updates Employee YTD totals    }
008: {     LANGUAGE        : UCSD Pascal / Apple Pascal 1.1              }
009: {                                                                   }
010: {     Copyright (C) 1983 by Tom Swan. All commercial rights reserved. }
011: {                                                                   }
012: {-------------------------------------------------------------------}
013:
014: CONST
015:    decimals          = 2;              { Number decimals for all $values }
016:    digits            = 8;              { Total digits for all $values }
017:
018: VAR
019:    employee, payroll          : 0 .. max_files;      { File numbers }
020:
021:
022: {$I PAYCOMMON.TEXT }          { Include common routines }
023:
024:
025: PROCEDURE add_fields( fn1, fld1, fn2, fld2 : integer );
026: { Add field "fld1" from file "fn1" to "fld2" of file "fn2" }
027: {   and store the result in field "fld2" of file "fn2" }
028: VAR
029:    long1,                             { Fields as integer values }
030:    long2    : long_integer;
031: BEGIN
032:    get_value( fn1, fld1, long1 );              { Read value 1 }
033:    get_value( fn2, fld2, long2 );              { Read value 2 }
034:    put_value( fn2, fld2, (long1 + long2) )     { Add and store }
035: END; { add_fields }
036:
037:
038: PROCEDURE process_one_record;
039: { Update employee ytd.total := payroll.amount + ytd.total }
040: BEGIN
041:    add_fields( payroll, 2, employee, 17 );        { reg.hrs + ytd.reg }
042:    add_fields( payroll, 3, employee, 18 );        { ovrtim.hrs + ytd.ovt }
043:    add_fields( payroll, 4, employee, 19 );        { sick.hrs + ytd.sick }
044:    add_fields( payroll, 5, employee, 20 );        { vacat.hrs + ytd.vac }
045:    add_fields( payroll, 10, employee, 13 );       { gross.pay + ytd.wages }
046:    add_fields( payroll, 11, employee, 14 );       { fedtax + ytd.fedtax }
```

```
047:     add_fields( payroll, 12, employee, 15 );    { fica + ytd.fica }
048:     add_fields( payroll, 13, employee, 16 )     { sttax + ytd.sttax }
049: END; { process_one_record }
050:
051:
052: PROCEDURE initialize;
053: { Clear screen, welcome user and print a warning }
054: BEGIN
055:     clrscrn;
056:     writeln( chr(ret), 'Payroll Year-To-Date Update', chr(ret) );
057:
058:     beep; evon;
059:     write(   ' WARNING: ' ); evoff;
060:     writeln(          ' If any errors occur during' );
061:     writeln( '           this program, recover your' );
062:     writeln( '           old employee data immediately' );
063:     writeln( '           from your backup copy.', chr(ret) );
064:
065:     IF NOT verified( 'Is your employee data file backed up' )
066:        THEN exit( PROGRAM );
067:     IF NOT verified( 'Did you run the PAYCALC program' ) THEN
068:        BEGIN
069:           writeln( 'Execute PAYCALC first, then rerun PAYUPDATE' );
070:           exit( PROGRAM )
071:        END
072: END; { initialize }
073:
074:
075: BEGIN
076:     IF executed( open_file( employee, 'EMPLOYEE.PDBF' ) ) THEN
077:     IF executed( open_file( payroll, 'PAYROLL.PDBF' ) ) THEN
078:     BEGIN
079:        initialize;              { with possible exit }
080:        writeln( 'Updating totals' );
081:        process_all_records;
082:        IF ( executed( close_file( employee, update ) ) ) AND
083:           ( executed( close_file( payroll, no_update   ) ) )
084:           THEN write( chr(ret), 'Payroll update completed' )
085:     END { if }
086: END.
```

```
001: {$S+,I-}              { Compiler swapping on; I/O error checking off }
002:
003: PROGRAM paycheck; uses pdbsunit;
004:
005: {-------------------------------------------------------------------}
006: {                                                                   }
007: {    PROGRAM       :  PayCheck -- Paycheck printer program          }
008: {    LANGUAGE      :  UCSD Pascal / Apple Pascal 1.1                }
009: {                                                                   }
010: {    Copyright (C) 1983 by Tom Swan. All commercial rights reserved.}
011: {                                                                   }
012: {-------------------------------------------------------------------}
013:
014: CONST
015:     decimals       = 2;            { Number decimals for all $values }
016:     digits         = 8;            { Total digits for all $values }
017:     line_len       = 80;           { Width of form in chars }
018:     form_len       = 42;           { Length of form in lines }
019:
020: TYPE
021:     line = PACKED ARRAY[ 1 .. line_len ] OF char;    { Single line }
022:     form = PACKED ARRAY[ 1 .. form_len ] OF line;    { One "frame" }
023:
024: VAR
025:     blank_check      : form;                         { Checks minus data }
```

```
026:      check_number     : long_integer;        { Sequential check number }
027:      employee,                               { File number }
028:      payroll          : 0 .. maxfiles;       {   "      "    }
029:      pf               : text;                { Print file }
030:
031:
032: {$I PAYCOMMON.TEXT}          { Include common routines }
033:
034:
035: PROCEDURE insert_string( VAR frm : form;       { Insert into this form }
036:                              s   : string;     { this string }
037:                              row,              { at this row }
038:                              col : integer );  { and column numbers. }
039: { Assume that the destination field is prepared or cleared }
040: VAR
041:    i : integer;              { For-loop variable }
042: BEGIN
043:    (* { Enable this line if you get value range errors.  It will
044:         help pinpoint the problem. }
045:      writeln( ' Row=', row, ' Col=',col, ' S=',s );
046:    *)
047:
048:      FOR i := 1 TO length(s) DO
049:         IF s[i] <> chr( blank ) THEN           { e.g. to print ****123.45 }
050:           frm[ row ][ col + i - 1 ] := s[ i ]
051:
052: END; { insert_string }
053:
054:
055: PROCEDURE insert_field( VAR frm  : form;       { Insert into this form }
056:                             fn,                { from this PDBS file }
057:                             fld,               { and this PDBS field }
058:                             row,               { at this row }
059:                             col : integer );   { and column numbers. }
060: VAR
061:    s          : string;
062: BEGIN
063:    get_field( fn, fld, s );
064:    insert_string( frm, s, row, col )
065: END; { insert_field }
066:
067:
068: FUNCTION leng( VAR lin : line ) : integer;
069: { Return length of a single line in form }
070: BEGIN
071:    leng := line_len + scan( -line_len, <>chr(blank), lin[ line_len ] )
072: END; { leng }
073:
074:
075: PROCEDURE print_form( VAR frm : form );
076: { Send form to output file, probably the printer }
077: VAR
078:    len, row : integer;
079: BEGIN
080:    FOR row := 1 TO form_len DO
081:       BEGIN
082:          len := leng( frm[ row ] );
083:          IF len > 0
084:             THEN writeln( pf, frm[ row ] : len )
085:             ELSE writeln( pf )              { Skip blank lines }
086:       END { for }
087: END; { print_form }
088:
089:
090: PROCEDURE init_form( VAR frm : form );
091: { Initialize a new form (i.e. a blank check) }
092: VAR
```

```
093:     s : string;
094: BEGIN
095:     fillchar( frm, sizeof( frm ), chr( blank ) );  { Fill with blanks }
096:
097: { Insert the date into both the check and stub }
098:
099:     date2string( today, s );
100:     insert_string( frm, s,  7, 57 );     { date }
101:     insert_string( frm, s, 29, 48 );     { date }
102:
103: { Prepare the check amount field to guard against forgeries. }
104:
105:     insert_string( frm, '*************', 13, 57 ); { 13 asterisks }
106:
107: { Scratch out an unused part of the stub ("This Period" field) }
108:
109:     insert_string( frm, '-----', 33, 52 );          { 5 dashes }
110:
111: { Insert some labels not pre-printed on the check stubs. }
112:
113:     insert_string( frm, 'REGULAR', 24, 15 );
114:     insert_string( frm, 'OVERTIME', 25, 15 );
115:     insert_string( frm, 'SICK', 26, 15 );
116:     insert_string( frm, 'VACATION', 27, 15 );
117:     insert_string( frm, 'TOTAL DEDUCTIONS', 35, 56 );
118:
119: { Note: if your checks are not pre-printed with the company name, }
120: {       this is the place to insert that fields, plus any other    }
121: {       information that will not change from check to check.  For}
122: {       example, you could insert "** Merry Christmas **" in some  }
123: {       unused portion of the stub.  Here's how: }
124:
125: (*
126:     insert_string( frm, '** Happy Easter !!! **', 22, 40 );
127: *)
128:
129: END; { init_form }
130:
131:
132: PROCEDURE reverse_name( VAR s : string );
133: { Assuming s is a name in "<lastname>, <firstname> [<initial>]" order, }
134: { change order to       "<firstname> [<initial>] <lastname>" }
135: VAR
136:     p : integer;
137:     firstname, lastname : string;
138: BEGIN
139:     s := concat( s, ' ' );     { Add space to string to avoid indexing errs }
140:     p := pos( ',', s );        { Find position of first comma }
141:     IF p > 0 THEN              { No change to fields without commas }
142:     BEGIN                                          {'lastname, firstname mi '}
143:         p := p + 1;                                {' firstname mi'          }
144:         firstname := copy( s, p, length(s) - p ); {' firstname mi'           }
145:         lastname := copy( s, 1, p - 2 );          {'lastname'                }
146:         strip( lastname );                         {'lastname'               }
147:         strip( firstname );                        {'firstname mi'           }
148:         s := concat( firstname, ' ', lastname )    {'firstname mi lastname'  }
149:     END { if }
150: END; { reverse_name }
151:
152:
153: PROCEDURE process_one_record;
154: { Print check for current employee / payroll records }
155: VAR
156:     check   : form;                  { Output character array }
157:     s       : string;
158: BEGIN
159:
```

```
160: { Initialize the check by assigning the blank check to the local }
161: { variable.  If you have memory problems, you could keep a global }
162: { check variable (instead of two as we are doing), and replace the }
163: { next line with "init_form( check )."  That will be slower, but }
164: { will save 3360 (80x42) bytes. }
165:
166:     check := blank_check;                { Start a new check }
167:
168: { Read each field from the appropriate record.  Format the strings if }
169: { necessary, and insert into the blank form for printing.  Note that }
170: { printing does not occur until the entire form is ready.  This is }
171: { far easier than trying to figure out how to print each line as }
172: { you go. }
173:
174:     get_field( employee, 2, s );                 { Read employee name }
175:     reverse_name( s );                           { Put first name first }
176:     insert_string( check, s,  9, 11 );           { Pay to name }
177:     insert_string( check, s, 25, 41 );           { Check stub name }
178:
179:                     { form   file   fld row col }
180:                     {---------------------------}
181:     insert_field( check, employee,  1, 29, 59 );        { social sec no }
182:     insert_field( check, employee,  3, 10, 11 );        { address }
183:     insert_field( check, employee,  4, 11, 11 );        { city }
184:     insert_field( check, employee,  5, 12, 11 );        { state }
185:     insert_field( check, employee,  6, 12, 35 );        { zip }
186:
187:     insert_field( check, payroll, 15, 13, 62 );         { amount }
188:     insert_field( check, payroll, 15, 32, 58 );         { amount }
189:     insert_field( check, payroll,  2, 24,  2 );         { reg hrs }
190:     insert_field( check, payroll,  3, 25,  2 );         { ovrtim hrs }
191:     insert_field( check, payroll,  4, 26,  2 );         { sick hrs }
192:     insert_field( check, payroll,  5, 27,  2 );         { vacat hrs }
193:
194:     insert_field( check, employee, 12,24,  9 );         { pay rate }
195:     insert_field( check, payroll,  6, 24, 26 );         { reg pay }
196:     insert_field( check, payroll,  7, 25, 26 );         { ovrtim pay }
197:     insert_field( check, payroll,  8, 26, 26 );         { sick pay }
198:     insert_field( check, payroll,  9, 27, 26 );         { vacat pay }
199:     insert_field( check, payroll, 10, 32, 26 );         { gross pay }
200:
201:     insert_field( check, payroll, 11, 37, 12 );         { fed tax }
202:     insert_field( check, payroll, 12, 37, 22 );         { fica }
203:     insert_field( check, payroll, 13, 37, 31 );         { st tax }
204:     insert_field( check, payroll, 14, 37, 64 );         { tot deductions }
205:
206:     insert_field( check, employee, 13, 41, 11 );        { ytd wages }
207:     insert_field( check, employee, 14, 41, 26 );        { ytd fedtax }
208:     insert_field( check, employee, 15, 41, 35 );        { ytd fica }
209:     insert_field( check, employee, 16, 41, 44 );        { ytd st tax }
210:
211:     str( check_number, s );
212:     insert_string( check, s,          7, 44 );          { check no }
213:     insert_string( check, s,         29, 41 );          { check no }
214:
215:     print_form( check );
216:
217:     check_number := check_number + 1
218:
219: END; { process_one_record }
220:
221:
222: PROCEDURE initialize;
223: { Prompt operator for first check number, etc. }
224: VAR
225:     s          : string;
226: BEGIN
```

```
227:    rewrite( pf, 'PRINTER:' );
228:    IF ioresult <> 0 THEN
229:        BEGIN
230:            writeln( 'No printer' );
231:            exit( PROGRAM )
232:        END;
233:    REPEAT
234:        write( 'First check number? (<cr> to end) ' );
235:        readln( s );
236:        IF length( s ) = 0
237:            THEN exit( PROGRAM );
238:        lvalue( s, 0, check_number );        { 0 = no decimal places }
239:        writeln( 'Checks will begin with # ', check_number );
240:        writeln( 'Insert checks into printer.' )
241:    UNTIL verified( 'Are you ready to begin' );
242:    init_form( blank_check )
243: END; { initialize }
244:
245:
246: BEGIN
247:    clrscrn;
248:    writeln( chr(ret), 'Payroll Check Printer' );
249:
250:    IF executed( open_file( employee, 'EMPLOYEE.PDBF' ) ) THEN
251:    IF executed( open_file( payroll, 'PAYROLL.PDBF' ) ) THEN
252:    BEGIN
253:        initialize;                { With possible exit from program }
254:        process_all_records;
255:        writeln( 'The last check number was : ', check_number - 1 );
256:        writeln( 'The next check number is  : ', check_number )
257:    END { if }
258:
259:    { No changes made to any files.  Therefore, they do not have }
260:    { to be explicitly closed, and the program can just end. }
261:
262: END.


001: {$S+,I-}              { Compiler swapping on; I/O error checking off }
002:
003: PROGRAM paynewyear; uses pdbsunit;
004:
005: {---------------------------------------------------------------------}
006: {                                                                     }
007: {     PROGRAM          : PayNewYear -- Clears Employee YTD totals     }
008: {     LANGUAGE         : UCSD Pascal / Apple Pascal 1.1               }
009: {                                                                     }
010: {     Copyright (C) 1983 by Tom Swan. All commercial rights reserved. }
011: {                                                                     }
012: {---------------------------------------------------------------------}
013:
014: CONST
015:    decimals         = 2;         { Number decimals for all $values }
016:    digits           = 8;         { Total digits for all $values }
017:
018: VAR
019:    employee         : 0 .. max_files;      { File number }
020:
021:
022: PROCEDURE process_all_records;
023: { Set year to date totals to zero }
024: VAR
025:    ern      : integer;                { Employee record number }
026:    fld      : 0 .. max_fld;           { Employee field number }
027:    null     : string;                 { Null string }
028: BEGIN
029:    null := '';        { Zero, or null, length string }
```

```
030:     WITH fil_recs[ employee ].fil_msc DO
031:        FOR ern := 1 TO msc_lastrec DO
032:           BEGIN
033:              writeln( ern:5, ' of ', msc_lastrec:5 );   { Operator feedback }
034:              goup;
035:              IF NOT executed( seek_rec( employee, ern ) )
036:                 THEN exit( PROGRAM );
037:              FOR fld := 13 TO 20 DO
038:                 put_field( employee, fld, null )
039:           END
040: END; { process_all_records }
041:
042:
043: PROCEDURE initialize;
044: { Clear screen, welcome user and print a warning }
045: BEGIN
046:     clrscrn;
047:     writeln( chr(ret), 'Payroll Begin New Year Program', chr(ret) );
048:
049:     beep; evon;
050:     write(   ' WARNING: ' ); evoff;
051:     writeln(           ' You are about to erase all' );
052:     writeln( '          year-to-date totals in the' );
053:     writeln( '          employee file.  Press the N' );
054:     writeln( '          key now to make no changes.', chr(ret) );
055:
056:     unitclear(1);    { Prevent type-ahead accidents }
057:
058:     IF NOT verified( 'Clear all year-to-date totals' )
059:         THEN exit( PROGRAM )
060:
061: END; { initialize }
062:
063:
064: BEGIN
065:     IF executed( open_file( employee, 'EMPLOYEE.PDBF' ) ) THEN
066:     BEGIN
067:        initialize;             { with possible exit }
068:        writeln( 'Clearing totals' );
069:        process_all_records;
070:        IF ( executed( close_file( employee, update ) ) )
071:           THEN write( chr(ret), 'Year-to-date totals cleared' )
072:     END { if }
073: END.
```

Appendix A

ERROR MESSAGES

Error messages in PDBS programs are coded according to the list in Fig. A-1. These correspond in part to the same numbers reported by the UCSD Pascal *ioresult* function.

If a data file with the name ERRORS.PDBF is stored on the boot disk, then error messages will be displayed on the screen along with their numbers. If the error file is removed, then only the number will be shown.

Like all files in PDBS, the errors are stored in a data file and can be edited with the *editor* program. To make a new errors file, *create* a data file according to the *status* report in Fig. A-2. Use the *editor* to enter the error messages from Fig. A-1. The record number of each message is the same as its error code. Because the *position* of each record in ERRORS.PDBF is significant, this is an example of a file that should not be sorted or used with any program that would change the order of the error messages.

```
*ERRORS.PDBF :
       MESSAGE-------------
00001  Bad disk block
00002  Bad device number
00003  Illegal operation
00004  Hardware error
00005  Lost device
00006  Lost file
00007  Illegal file name
00008  No room on disk
00009  No device
00010  No file
00011  Duplicate file
00012  File not closed
00013  File not open
00014  Bad format
00015  Buffer overflow
00016  Write protected
00017  Too many files
00018  Disk read error
00019  Disk write error
00020  End of file
00021  Out of memory
00022  File full
00023  File empty
00024  Wrong version
00025  Interrupted by user
```

Fig. A-1. *PDBS error messages are stored in a PDBS data file.*


```
*ERRORS.PDBF
Record size ............. 21
Number of fields ........ 1
Maximum record number ... 48
Records in use .......... 25
Records not used ........ 23
Date created ............ 16-Jun-83
Date last updated ....... 20-Jun-83

#  NAME        TYPE     LEN DEC POS

1  MESSAGE     Char      20   0   1
```

Fig. A-2. *The structure of an optional file, ERRORS.PDBF, which can be stored on the boot disk. Enter the error messages from Fig. A-1 into this file using the editor program.*

Appendix B

MANAGING FREE DISK SPACE

Figure B-1 shows a typical directory of a disk with several PDBS data files. This directory was produced by the UCSD filer E(xt-dir command.

Files in UCSD and Apple Pascal 1.1 are stored in logically sequential blocks on the disk. When the end of one file butts against the beginning of the next, appending new records in the file will result in a "No room on disk" error.

When this happens, free space must be created at the end of the file. The data file will expand automatically into this space. To do this, follow the dialogue in Fig. B-2, and examine the results in Fig. B-3. All files below the one that caused the error are moved down as far as possible. After this "reverse crunch," you can continue entering records.

```
DATA:
REPORTS.PDBF       3  1-Jul-83     6   512  Datafile
PARTS.RPRT         3  1-Jul-83     9   512  Datafile
CONSOLE.SPEC       3  5-Jul-83    12   512  Datafile
CUSTOMERS.PDBF     3  4-Jul-83    15   512  Datafile
VENDORS.PDBF       3 30-Jun-83    18   512  Datafile
SOURCES.PDBF       3  1-Jul-83    21   512  Datafile
PARTS.PDBF         3 19-Jul-83    24   512  Datafile
< UNUSED >       253              27
7/7 files<listed/in-dir>, 27 blocks used, 253 unused, 253 in largest
```

Fig. B-1. Directory after receiving a "Disk full" error while adding new records to CUSTOMERS.PDBF.

```
Crunch what vol? DATA:
From end of disk, block 280 ? (Y/N) N
Starting at block # ? 18
Moving back PARTS.PDBF
Moving back SOURCES.PDBF
Moving back VENDORS.PDBF
DATA: crunched
```

Fig. B-2. *When crunching the diskette using UCSD's filer program, supply the block number (18 in the example) where you want to open up room. This number can be found in the fourth column of the extended disk directory. (See Fig. B-1.)*

```
DATA:
REPORTS.PDBF        3  1-Jul-83        6    512   Datafile
PARTS.RPRT          3  1-Jul-83        9    512   Datafile
CONSOLE.SPEC        3  5-Jul-83       12    512   Datafile
CUSTOMERS.PDBF      3  4-Jul-83       15    512   Datafile
< UNUSED >        253                 18
VENDORS.PDBF        3 30-Jun-83      271    512   Datafile
SOURCES.PDBF        3  1-Jul-83      274    512   Datafile
PARTS.PDBF          3 19-Jul-83      277    512   Datafile
7/7 files<listed/in-dir>, 27 blocks used, 253 unused, 253 in largest
```

Fig. B-3. *Crunching the disk moved three files down, leaving a large unused area just after the customer file. The file will automatically expand into this free disk space starting at block 18.*

Appendix C

PDBS ON THE IBM PC

Converting to UCSD Pascal IV.1

To use PDBS on the IBM Personal Computer and other systems using version IV.1 of UCSD Pascal, a few modifications must be made to the listings as printed in the book. All changes are documented here, using the original line numbers for reference.

The implementation of UCSD Pascal used to prepare this section was supplied by Network Consulting Inc., Discovery Park, Suite 110, 3700 Gilmore Way, Burnaby, B.C. Canada V5G 4M1. Their current phone number is 604-430-3466.

Although the modifications listed here are for the IBM PC, they should also work with any properly installed implementation of UCSD Pascal IV.1. If you are not using the IBM PC, you must write or supply a library unit containing the following routines. On the IBM, these routines, among others, are supplied in a library unit named *ibm_ special*. You may rename this unit anything you want, as long as you use the same name in the *uses* statement immediately following the identifier *implementation* in the *pdbsunit* listing (as modified in this appendix).

```
PROCEDURE highlight( onn : boolean );
{ If onn=true, switch to enhanced or highlighted video }
{ If onn=false, turn enhanced video off }

PROCEDURE video_mode( mode : integer );
{ Select or initialize the terminal according to mode }
```

273

Both of these procedures are optional. If you do not have highlighting on your terminal (or don't want to use it), you can simply construct a dummy routine that does nothing at all. If, for example, it is not necessary to initialize the *video-
_mode,* then that routine has nothing to do. Such a routine would consist of a *BE-
GIN END;* pair and nothing in between. It is probably better to leave the dummy procedures in place, rather than attempt to remove all references to them from all PDBS programs.

IBM PC, UCSD Pascal IV.1 Conversion Checklist

_____1. Make all of the modifications listed here to the program listings. All line numbers refer to the original listings as printed in the book.
_____2. Have the file SYSTEM. IV1 (supplied with your version of UCSD Pascal) and the unit IBM.SPECIAL (or your own custom unit) available for compilation. Change the *uses* statement {$U } option in *pdbsunit* to indicate to the compiler where it can find these two files.
_____3. Compile and test *pdbsunit*. Install the resulting code file in SYSTEM.LI-
BRARY, or some other library file.
_____4. Compile *evalunit, calcunit,* and *indexunit*. Install their code files in the same library file as *pdbsunit*.
_____5. Compile the rest of the PDBS program set.

General Changes—All Program Listings:

1. Use *pdbs_ string* in place of all *string* identifiers.
2. Use *pdbs_version* in place of all *version* identifiers.
3. Use *pdbs_alpha* in place of all *alpha* identifiers.
4. Use *pdbs_byte* in place of all *byte* identifiers.
5. Remove all S+ and S++ compiler swapping options.
6. Delete *crtsetup* program. Ignore instructions for creating PDBS.MISC-
INFO file, not used by this version.
7. Remove all occurrences of *applestuff* from *uses* statements.

PDBSUNIT.TEXT

1. Replace line 3 with

```
unit pdbsunit;
```

2. Replace line 36 with

```
pdbs_version = '1.0';
```

3. Replace line 47 with

```
pdbs_string =
```

4. Replace line 81 with

```
pdbs_byte =
```

5. Replace line 95 with

```
pdbs_alpha =
```

6. Insert between lines 262, 263

```
FUNCTION keypress : boolean;
```

7. Insert between lines 284, 285

```
uses {$U system.iv1}
        screenops,
        kernel( {const} maxdir,
                        vidleng,
                        tidleng,
                        fblksize,
                {type } daterec,
                        unitnum,
                        vid,
                        dirrange,
                        tid,
                        filekind,
                        direntry,
                        windowp,
                        window,
                        fib,
                {var  } thedate ),

    {$U ibm.library}
        ibm_special;
```

8. Delete lines 291 through 310.

PDBS1.TEXT

1. Delete lines 8 through 14.
2. Replace line 20 with

```
highlight( true )
```

3. Replace line 27 with

```
highlight( false )
```

4. Replace line 34 with

```
sc_right
```

5. Replace line 41 with

```
sc_up
```

6. Replace line 48 with

```
write( chr(7) )
```

7. Replace line 55 with

```
sc_erase_to_eol( sc_find_x, sc_find_y )
```

8. Replace line 62 with

```
sc_eras_eos( sc_find_x, sc_find_y )
```

9. Replace line 69 with

```
sc_clr_screen
```

PDBS2.TEXT

1. Replace line 143 with

```
IF varavail('') > min_mem + min_mem
```

PDBS5.TEXT

1. Add the following after line 216:

```
FUNCTION keypress{ : boolean };
VAR
    k : integer;
BEGIN
    unitstatus(1, k, 1 );
    keypress := ( k > 0 )
END; { keypress }
```

PDBS6.TEXT

1. Replace lines 240 through 291 with

```
PROCEDURE pdbs_init;
{ Initialize PDBS unit.  Runs once before user program begins. }
{ Local to unit }
VAR
   blankf : fib;     { as defined in Kernel }
   i : integer;
BEGIN { pdbs_init }
   sc_init;                          { From screenops unit }
   today := thedate;                 { From kernel }
   case_switch := true;              { False if not using mixed case }

{ Initialize array of files variable }

   fillchar( fil_recs, sizeof( fil_recs ), chr(0) );
   fillchar( blankf, sizeof(blankf), chr(0) );
   seminit( blankf.f_lock, 1 );
   FOR i := 1 TO max_files DO
      BEGIN   { Prepare system I/O files }
         new( fil_recs[ i ].fil_ptr );
         moveleft( blankf, fil_recs[i].fil_ptr^, sizeof(blankf) )
      END; { for }
   page_pool := NIL          { No disposed virtual pages }
END; { pdbs_init }
```

EVALUNIT.TEXT

1. Replace line 3 with

```
unit evalunit;
```

CALCUNIT.TEXT

1. Replace line 3 with

```
unit calcunit;
```

EDITOR.TEXT

1. Remove lines 15 through 28.

2. Insert the following between lines 30, 31:

```
key = ( keycopy, keydel, keydown, keyenter, keyesc,
        keyetx, keyinsert, keykill, keyleft, keyreset,
        keyright, keyup, keyzero );

keyindex = keycopy .. keyzero;
```

3. Replace line 47 with

```
exitset  : SET OF key;
```

4. Insert the following between lines 54, 55

```
prefixed : packed array[ keyindex ] of boolean;
ctrlkeys : packed array[ keyindex ] of char;
leadin   : char;
```

EDITOR1.TEXT

1. Insert the following between lines 448, 449

```
PROCEDURE read_msc;
{Read *SYSTEM.MISCINFO file for keyboard assignments}
CONST
    fnam        = '*SYSTEM.MISCINFO';           { File name }
TYPE
    buffer      = PACKED ARRAY[ 0 .. 511 ] OF char;
VAR
    faker : RECORD                    { Translates chars to bits }
                CASE boolean OF
                    true:  ( ch2: PACKED ARRAY[ 0..1 ] OF char );
                    false: ( bit: PACKED ARRAY[ 1..16 ] OF boolean )
                END; { faker }
    mscbuf : buffer;
    mscfil : file;           { Untyped file for disk block read }
BEGIN
    reset( mscfil, fnam );
    IF blockread( mscfil, mscbuf, 1 ) <> 1 THEN
        BEGIN
            writeln('Can''t read ', fnam );
            exit( PROGRAM )
        END;
    close( mscfil );

{ Assign some keys the values stored in system.miscinfo }

    leadin                  := mscbuf[ 62 ];
    ctrlkeys[ keydown   ] := mscbuf[ 79 ];
    ctrlkeys[ keyleft   ] := mscbuf[ 80 ];
    ctrlkeys[ keyright  ] := mscbuf[ 81 ];
    ctrlkeys[ keyup     ] := mscbuf[ 78 ];
    ctrlkeys[ keyesc    ] := mscbuf[ 89 ];
```

```
{ User-supplied keyboard assignments }
{ Currently set for -- IBM PC UCSD IV.1 by N.C.I. }

    ctrlkeys[ keycopy   ] := chr( 59 );    { F1 }
    ctrlkeys[ keydel    ] := chr( 60 );    { F2 }
    ctrlkeys[ keyetx    ] := chr( 61 );    { F3 }
    ctrlkeys[ keyinsert ] := chr( 62 );    { F4 }
    ctrlkeys[ keyreset  ] := chr( 63 );    { F5 }
    ctrlkeys[ keyzero   ] := chr( 64 );    { F6 }
    ctrlkeys[ keykill   ] := chr( 67 );    { F9 }
    ctrlkeys[ keyenter  ] := chr( 13 );    { return key }

    faker.ch2[0] := mscbuf[ 94 ]; faker.ch2[1] := mscbuf[ 95 ];
    prefixed[ keyright ] := faker.bit[ 1 ];
    prefixed[ keyleft  ] := faker.bit[ 2 ];
    prefixed[ keyup    ] := faker.bit[ 3 ];
    prefixed[ keydown  ] := faker.bit[ 4 ];
    prefixed[ keyesc   ] := faker.bit[ 11 ];

{ User-supplied keyboard prefixed assignments }

    prefixed[ keyreset  ] := true;
    prefixed[ keyetx    ] := true;
    prefixed[ keydel    ] := true;
    prefixed[ keycopy   ] := true;
    prefixed[ keyenter  ] := false;          { return key }
    prefixed[ keyinsert ] := true;
    prefixed[ keykill   ] := true;
    prefixed[ keyzero   ] := true

END; { read_msc }
```

2. Replace lines 458 through 464 with

```
    exitset := [ keycopy,
                 keydown,
                 keyenter,
                 keyesc,
                 keyetx,
                 keyup,
                 keykill ];
    read_msc;
```

EDITOR2.TEXT

1. Replace lines 24 through 60 with

```
PROCEDURE show_keys;
{ Display editing keys legend (optional) }
CONST
    tags =
    { F1    F2    F3    F4    F5    F6    F7    F8    F9    F10 }
    { 123456123456123456123456123456123456123456123456123456123456 }
    'Copy  Delch Accpt Insrt Reset Zero  none  none  Kill  none ';
    y        = 24;              { Y coordinate to begin.  1 line needed. }
VAR
    i : integer;
BEGIN
    IF legend THEN
```

```
    BEGIN
        gotoxy( 0, y );
        clreoln;
        for i := 1 to 10 do
            begin
                evon;
                write( i mod 10, '-' );  { 1, 2, 3, 4, 5, 6, 7, 8, 9, 0 }
                evoff;
                write( copy( tags, ((i-1)*6)+1, 6 ) )
            end { for }
    END
END; { show_keys }
```

EDITOR3.TEXT

1. Insert the following between lines 188, 189

```
FUNCTION getctrl( VAR ch : char ) : boolean;
{ Get a character, possibly a control key }
{ Return TRUE -- control char typed.  translated value in ch }
{ Return FALSE - normal char typed.  char value in ch }
{ Assumes all control keys including leadin are chr(0)..chr(31) }
VAR
    ki : keyindex;
BEGIN
    read( keyboard, ch );
    IF eoln( keyboard )
        THEN ch := chr( ret );
    IF ch >= chr(32)
      THEN
        getctrl := false                { not a control key, return ch }
      ELSE
        BEGIN
            getctrl := true;
            IF ch = leadin
              THEN
                IF keypress
                  THEN
                    BEGIN
                        read( keyboard, ch );      { 2nd of 2-char sequence }

                    { Check prefixed control keys }
                        FOR ki := keycopy TO keyzero DO
                            IF prefixed[ ki ] THEN
                                IF ch = ctrlkeys[ ki ] THEN
                                    BEGIN
                                        ch := chr( ord(ki) ); {translate}
                                        exit( getctrl )  {stop search}
                                    END { if }
                    END
                  ELSE
                    { return leadin char typed normally }
              ELSE
                FOR ki := keycopy TO keyzero DO
                    IF NOT prefixed[ ki ] THEN
                        IF ch = ctrlkeys[ ki ] THEN
                            BEGIN
                                ch := chr( ord(ki) );
                                exit( getctrl )
                            END { if }
```

```
         END { else }
END; { getctrl }

FUNCTION ch2key( ch : char ) : key;
{ Translate character into ordinate type, keys }
VAR
   x : key;
BEGIN
   moveleft( ch, x, sizeof(x) );
   ch2key := x
END; { ch2key }
```

2. Replace line 193 with

```
         CASE ch2key(ch) OF
```

3. Replace line 219 with

```
         ,done := ( ch2key(ch) IN exitset )
```

4. Replace line 278 with

```
         IF getctrl( ch )
```

5. Replace line 347 with

```
         IF last_char = chr( ord(keyup) )
```

6. Replace line 354 with

```
IF last_char IN [ chr( ord(keydown) ), chr( ord(keyenter) ) ]
```

7. Replace line 358 with

```
    ELSE last_char := chr( ord(keyetx) )
```

8. Replace line 361 with

```
      IF last_char = chr( ord(keycopy) )
```

9. Replace line 377 with

```
      IF last_char = chr( ord(keykill) )
```

10. Replace line 389 with

```
         IF last_char = chr( ord(keyesc) )
```

11. Replace line 396 with

```
UNTIL ( last_char IN [ chr( ord(keyesc) ), chr( ord(keyetx) ),
                                        chr( ord(keykill) ) ] );
```

12. Replace line 397 with

```
        edit_rec := ( last_char <> chr( ord(keyesc) ) )
```

INDEX

Program and library unit names are printed in **bold face**. The index was prepared with the PDBS programs, *create, editor, append, sort,* and *delete.* The raw data, containing the index entries and page numbers, was processed with a modified version of the *list* program, and then edited with a text editor to produce the format you see here.